Read This First

The information in this book is as up-to-date and accurate as we can make it. But it's important to realize that the law changes frequently, as do fees, forms and procedures. If you handle your own legal matters, it's up to you to be sure that all information you use—including the information in this book—is accurate. Here are some suggestions to help you:

First, make sure you've got the most recent edition of this book. To learn whether a later edition is available, check the edition number on the book's spine and then go to Nolo's online Law Store at www.nolo.com or call Nolo's Customer Service Department at 800-728-3555.

Next, even if you have a current edition, you need to be sure it's fully up-to-date. The law can change overnight. At *www.nolo.com*, we post notices of major legal and practical changes that affect the latest edition of a book. To check for updates, find your book in the Law Store on Nolo's website (you can use the "A to Z Product List" and click the book's title). If you see an "Updates" link on the left side of the page, click it. If you don't see a link, that means we haven't posted any updates. (But check back regularly.)

Finally, we believe accurate and current legal information should help you solve many of your own legal problems on a cost-efficient basis. But this text is not a substitute for personalized advice from a knowledgeable lawyer. If you want the help of a trained professional, consult an attorney licensed to practice in your state.

2nd edition

Dealing With Problem Employees

A Legal Guide

by Attorneys Amy DelPo and Lisa Guerin

edited by Janet Portman

Second Edition	JULY 2003
Editor	JANET PORTMAN
Illustrations	MARI STEIN
Cover Design	TONI IHARA
Book Design	TERRI HEARSH
Proofreading	SUSAN CARLSON GREENE
Index	SUSAN CORNELL
Printing	ARVATO SERVICES, INC.

DelPo, Amy, 1967-
    Dealing with problem employees : a legal guide / by Amy DelPo and Lisa Guerin.
      p. cm.
    Includes index.
    ISBN 0-87337-968-3
    1. Labor laws and legislation--United States--Popular works. 2. Labor discipline--Law
and legislation--United States--Popular works. 3. Problem employees--Legal status, laws,
etc.--United States--Popular works. I. Guerin, Lisa, 1964- II. Title.

KF3457.Z9D45 2003
658.3'045--dc21

                                              2003051039

For information on bulk purchases or corporate premium sales, please contact the Special Sales Department. For academic sales or textbook adoptions, ask for Academic Sales. Call 800-955-4775 or write to Nolo, 950 Parker Street, Berkeley, CA 94710.

Acknowledgements

First and foremost, we would like to express many thanks to our editor and boss, Janet Portman. Not only is her skill with a red pen unparalleled, but she is also a humane taskmaster. If all supervisors were as good humored, respectful and kind, employment lawyers throughout the country would have to find new work.

Thanks, too, to Nolo founder and man-about-town Jake Warner. His enthusiasm for this project never wavered, even when we had our doubts.

We are also grateful to Nolo's Stan Jacobson for his tireless research efforts and good cheer, and to Ella Hirst, for her meticulous work on the state-law charts that appear in our books.

We'd also like to express our gratitude to former Nolo editor, employment law doyenne and author Barbara Kate Repa, whose previous work on this topic inspired us to write a whole book about it. Some of her words live on here.

And finally to Nolo itself. This is a great company to work for—one that serves as a shining example of the wonderful things that can happen when a company treats its employees with dignity and respect.

Amy DelPo and Lisa Guerin
May, 2001

Thanks to three people who made my work on this book possible:

To my dear husband, Paul, who has given me so much, including the encouragement and freedom to jump off the gerbil wheel of litigation and work at a job that I truly love.

And to my parents, Ray and Eleanor, who gave me my education—and a solid foundation on which to build a wonderful life.

Amy DelPo
May, 2001

Thanks to my friends and former colleagues in the employment law trenches—everyone at Rudy, Exelrod and Zieff, Mike Gaitley, Deborah England and particularly John True—for your guidance and inspiration.

Thanks also to my family and friends, who support and encourage me—and keep my life interesting.

Lisa Guerin
May, 2001

Table of Contents

6 Making the Decision to Fire

7 Planning For The Aftermath

8 Severance and Releases

9 How to Fire

10 Looking Forward

11 Hiring a Lawyer

Appendix

Index

Introduction

Sooner or later, it happens even to the most conscientious employers. No matter how carefully they hire workers, how many incentives they give for strong performance or how diligently they try to create a positive and productive work environment, all employers—large and small—will one day have to deal with a problem employee.

In fact, you might have picked up this book because that day has already come for you. Perhaps an employee has allowed her performance to drop or demonstrated attitude problems that won't go away; or a worker has sexually harassed other employees, stolen from the company or threatened violence. On the other hand, you may have picked up this book because you're concerned about the bigger picture. You're frustrated with the number of employee problems that crop up year after year. Instead of simply reacting to each problem as it arises, you want to be more proactive.

Whether you're facing a specific employee problem right now or want guidance about employee problems in general, this book can help. We do not think that employee problems are inevitable, nor must they fill you with anxiety and fear. In the chapters that follow, we provide you with all of the practical and legal information you need to handle the specific employee problems you are facing right now and to create policies and procedures that will reduce the number and degree of problems you face in the future. As an added bonus, the strategies that we describe in this book will make your workplace more collaborative and employee-friendly, thereby increasing morale and fostering feelings of loyalty and mutual respect. Everyone in your company will benefit from the healthier workplace these strategies will create.

A.   The High Cost of Problem Employees

For many employers, figuring out whether and how to discipline or fire a worker is one of the most stressful parts of the job. And these concerns are well-founded—ignoring or mishandling worker problems can be very costly, indeed. Here are some reasons why.

1. Lawsuits

Lawsuits brought by former employees are increasingly common—and increasingly costly. According to a 1997 survey conducted by the Society for Human Resource Management (SHRM), almost 60% of those polled said that their business faced at least one employment-related lawsuit during the previous five years. And according to Jury Verdict Research, employers lose these lawsuits a whopping 67% of the time—and pay a median award of $218,000. These figures don't even include the cost of paying a lawyer to defend you, which can run from the tens even into the hundreds of thousands of dollars.

The New Coke: $192.5 Million Dollars Poorer

The biggest corporations often face the biggest lawsuits—and lose the largest amount of money. For example, Coca Cola recently settled a race discrimination case for a mind-boggling $192.5 million dollars. Although this was a class action case in which many workers banded together to sue the company in a single lawsuit, that settlement figure is going to show up even on Coke's bottom line.

2. Employee Turnover

If you ignore problem employees or handle employment problems in ineffective or Draconian ways, you will soon have an employee retention problem. The worker who is having trouble will receive neither the guidance nor the opportunity necessary to improve. He will likely be fired or quit. And if he doesn't, your other employees—who will have to pick up the slack for that problem worker or, even worse, have to put up with that worker's abuse and mistreatment—will soon look for greener pastures.

So you'll hire new employees, right? Well, keep in mind that the cost of replacing a worker is much higher than you might imagine. The U.S. Department of Labor estimates that it costs businesses a full third of a new hire's salary to replace an employee. And the cost of replacing management workers runs much higher. Wouldn't it be easier—and less expensive—to hang on to the good employees you already have and to help your problem employees turn their performance around?

3. Poor Morale

Problem employees can really drag down the spirit of a workplace. As coworkers watch that difficult worker get away with breaking the rules, mistreating others, failing to perform or produce at required levels or treating you insubordinately, they will feel resentful, angry and unappreciated—and perhaps even frightened if the troublemaker poses a threat to their safety or well-being.

If you don't take action to stop the downward spiral, you will face any number of associated problems, in addition to the employee turnover described above. You will have trouble recruiting new workers and difficulty getting the most out of your remaining employees. You might even find yourself with an epidemic of workers with poor attitudes on your hands. Workers who feel that they are being treated unfairly or taken advantage of are more likely to resort to small acts of revenge—including theft and fraud (which, according to the American Management Association, costs businesses somewhere between 40 to 65 billion dollars a year).

4. The Bottom Line

The bottom line is that problem employees hurt *your* bottom line. Lawsuits, employee turnover and low morale cost you money and harm the productivity of your business. All that time problem employees spend harassing coworkers, arguing with you or attending to personal matters is time spent not working. And all the time your other employees spend complaining to each other about a problem worker, doing the work that should be done by that worker and laying bets on when you will finally get up the nerve to fire him is likewise lost to your business.

B. How This Book Can Help

So what can you do about your problem employees? Plenty—and this book can help. Here, we offer you proven strategies for dealing with most common employment problems, legal information on your rights and responsibilities as an employer, practical tips that will help you get the job done and information on how to avoid hiring employees who may become problems.

The information we provide will help you:

- effectively deal with specific employment problems that come up in your workplace
- avoid hiring problem employees in the first place
- turn problem employees into productive, valuable workers
- safely and legally terminate those employees who can't or won't improve
- tap into the potential of all of your workers
- promote productivity, loyalty and camaraderie in your workforce, and
- stay out of legal trouble.

We start in Chapter 1 by examining the most common types of employee problems—and by explaining what strategies might help resolve them. In Chapter 2, we explain the law of the workplace—the basic legal rules that you must keep in mind when making employment decisions. In Chapters 3 through 5, we take an in-depth look at several management practices—performance evaluations, progressive discipline and investigations—that will prevent most problems from cropping up. For those problems that do arise, these same practices will enable you to deal with them effectively and legally. These chapters include sample policies you can use in your own workplace.

For those situations where nothing else works, we devote four full chapters to firing problem employees. These chapters include information on the following:

- how to decide whether you should fire the employee—including whether you've done all you can to protect yourself from lawsuits (Chapter 6)
- how to handle post-termination issues, such as references, unemployment compensation and continuing insurance (Chapter 7)
- how to decide whether to offer a severance package (including what to include in the package and whether to ask the employee to sign a release agreeing not to sue you) (Chapter 8), and
- how to legally and safely terminate an employee, step by step (Chapter 9).

Chapter 10 will help you develop sound hiring and personnel policies to weed out the problem employees of the future. In Chapter 11, we explain how to find and work with an employment lawyer.

C. Who Should Read This Book

This book is for anyone who oversees employees—that means private business owners, human resource professionals, supervisors and managers. If you want to learn about the law, pick up practical advice, tips, strategies and policies that will help you manage more effectively and treat your employees fairly, this book is for you. We wrote this book with the conscientious, well-intentioned employer in mind.

D. Who Should Not Read This Book

This book is not for people who work in state or federal government. Although many of the strategies that we discuss in this book could be applied to government workers, most employment laws operate slightly differently—or not at all—in the public setting. If you are a manager or supervisor of government employees, this book probably isn't for you.

This book is also not for people who are looking for ways to "get around" workplace laws. If you are looking for a guide that will show you how to skirt the boundaries of the law, this book won't help. Our goal is to help well-meaning employers deal with their employment problems legally and effectively—not to help shady operators evade their legal responsibilities.

E. Icons Used in This Book

 This icon alerts you to a practical tip or good idea.

 This is a caution to consider potential problems you may encounter.

 This icon refers to related information in this book, other Nolo books or other resources. ■

Chapter 1

What's Your Problem?

*I*n the chapters that follow, we will talk extensively about strategies for dealing with employee problems. Before we do that, however, we'd like to turn the spotlight on the problems themselves. After all, that's why you bought the book in the first place, right? You've got a problem and you want to solve it.

In this chapter, we examine specific employee problems and look at how you can address them. As part of this discussion, we will refer to the strategies and management techniques that we discuss in the rest of the book, including:

- performance evaluations (see Chapter 3)
- progressive discipline (see Chapter 4)
- effective investigations (see Chapter 5)
- suspension (see Chapter 5)
- termination (see Chapters 6 through 9), and
- hiring (Chapter 10).

The chart at the end of the chapter, "Problems and Strategies," sum-marizes your strategies to the typical problems discussed in the text.

Healthy Practices For A Healthy Workplace

If you were to take a survey of successful employers—those who attract and retain good employees, enjoy a positive reputation in the business community and stay out of legal trouble, all the while producing quality goods or services—you'd find that they share more than their success. Although these employers may differ in the types of policies they use and the way they adapt those policies to their unique workplaces, they all follow similar practical habits in dealing with their employees, practices that promote positive employee relations, reduce the number of employee problems and provide protection from lawsuits.

The following are just a sampling of employer practices that will promote a healthy work environment for you and your employees. We will discuss these and others throughout this book.

- **Communicate with your employees.** Make sure they know your expectations. Tell them when they are doing well or poorly.
- **Listen to your employees.** They have valuable insight into your workplace—and into the solutions to many employee problems.
- **Act consistently.** There's real value in applying the same standards of performance and conduct to all of your employees and avoiding favoritism. Workers quickly sour on a boss who plays favorites, bestowing plum assignments on his pets and piling thankless grunt work on those who are out of favor.
- **Follow your own policies.** After all, why should your employees follow the rules if you are willing to bend them whenever the mood strikes?
- **Treat you employees with respect.** Your workers will treat you as you treat them. And workers will literally thrive in a workplace where they feel respected and fairly treated. In addition, workers who must be disciplined, investigated or fired will take the bad news much better if they feel that you have treated them decently throughout the process.

Healthy Practices For A Healthy Workplace (continued)

- **Make job-related decisions.** You should always be guided by criteria related to the job and the worker's ability to do that job—not by an employee's characteristics (race, gender or disability, for example), personal activities and or your own whims.
- **Take action when necessary.** The sooner you deal with an employee problem, the better your chance of nipping it in the bud.
- **Keep good records.** Good employers keep regular, complete records of major employment decisions and conclusions, including performance evaluations, discipline, counseling sessions, investigations and firings. These records provide invaluable evidence that you were driven by sound business reasons, not illegal motivations. Remember, if you end up in a lawsuit, you'll not only have to explain what you did and why—you will also have to prove it.

A. Performance/Productivity Problems

For the most part, your business will only be as good as your employees. This simple fact makes performance and productivity problems a real threat to the success of your business. For this reason, resolving performance problems is one of the most important tasks of an employer or manager.

In some cases, detecting this type of problem will be as simple as observing an employee and noting the subpar nature of his work. Or you might receive weekly printouts of employee productivity and notice that an employee's numbers are low. In other cases, an employee will be able to hide his subpar performance or productivity. You will know something is wrong somewhere, but you won't be able to nail down exactly who is working below your standards.

The most effective way to deal with employee performance/productivity problems is through a performance evaluation system. As you will learn in Chapter 3, such a system will force you to track each employee, so you will always know exactly who is doing what. It will also give employees a clear understanding of your expectations so that they can tailor their work performance to meet them.

If an employee fails to live up to your expectations, a performance evaluation system will foster the communication and collaboration you need to address the problem. At review time, you'll discuss what the employee may need to turn his or her performance around. And if the employee doesn't improve, your performance evaluation system will lay the groundwork for progressive discipline (see Chapter 4) and, if necessary, termination (see Chapters 6 through 9).

When faced with a performance or productivity problem, look beyond the employee's willingness—or lack thereof—to do well. Consider the work environment and any personal issues that could have an impact on the employee's performance. For example, simply telling the employee to do better will accomplish little if the employee's supervisor is the true cause of the problem. Similarly, if the employee doesn't have the necessary skills to do the job or if his wife has just left him, you'll have to take these factors into account.

If an employee is new to the job, consider the following issues before you reach a conclusion:

- Did you give the employee adequate training? For example, did you teach the employee how to use your accounting system, or did you assume that he could figure it out on his own? If you did the latter, it may explain why the employee is taking more time than he should to do his work—perhaps he is struggling with a system he doesn't understand.
- Does the employee have the necessary skills? For example, the new artist you hired may be very talented, but if she doesn't

know how to use a computer, she won't be able to create computer graphics.

- Does the employee understand what is expected of him? For example, the salesperson you hired may not know that she is also supposed to clean the store when business is slow.
- Have you provided the employee with adequate tools and resources for doing his job? For instance, if employees must share equipment such as computers and printers, this will have an impact on productivity that really isn't the fault of individual employees.
- Are there any rules or systems that make it difficult for the employee to do his job? For instance, have you asked a supplier to deliver goods by such a late date that it makes it very difficult for your employees to work with the material and produce what's expected in time?

If the employee has been in the job for a while, think about the following possible causes for the drop in performance:

- If there have not been performance/productivity problems in the past, what has changed in the employee's personal or work situations that might explain the trouble?
- Does the employee have a new supervisor? New coworkers? New customers? If so, maybe the employee is having trouble working with the new person. Or maybe the new person—and not the employee—is the true cause of the problem.
- Is there anything happening in the employee's personal life that is now affecting his work, such as a new child or a divorce?
- Has the employee developed a substance abuse problem? (See Section E, below, for more about substance abuse.)

Of course, the best way to find the answers to all of these questions is through careful communication with the employee and thoughtful observation of the workplace.

B. Interpersonal Problems

Interpersonal problems—employees not getting along with each other, with customers and vendors or with managers and supervisors—arise in endless contexts. Sometimes, the problem is a simple workplace issue that can be solved by moving an employee's desk or changing an employee's work group. Other times, the problem is far more complex and has its roots in the employee's personal life or psyche. Still other times, the problem is really about prejudice, hate and illegal discrimination.

We explore the various contexts in the subsections below. Regardless of the sort of interpersonal problem you have on your hands, however, know this: It is perfectly legal for you to discipline employees who have negative attitudes or who fail to get along with coworkers, customers, vendors, managers and supervisors. It is also legal to fire them if they don't improve. Your performance evaluation and progressive discipline systems (Chapters 3 and 4, respectively) will be invaluable in laying the groundwork for such discipline and termination.

1. Employees With Contextual Problems

The most common type of interpersonal problem—and the one with the fewest legal entanglements—involves the employee whose problems are fairly minor and are generally contextual to the workplace. Maybe the employee doesn't get along with this particular supervisor; or perhaps this employee's workstation is so noisy that it makes him tense. Usually, employers can easily address these problems—by putting the employee in a different work group, for example, or by moving the employee's workstation to a quieter part of the office.

If the employee has never had interpersonal problems in the past, consider what has changed in the employee's work environment. If the problem is with a supervisor, for example, is this the first supervisor with whom the employee has had conflicts? If so, then perhaps the fault lies with the supervisor and not with the employee.

If the problem can't be easily solved, you should impose consequences on poor behavior or attitudes through your performance evaluation and progressive discipline systems. Otherwise, you and the rest of your workforce will suffer.

2. Employees With Personal Problems

Some employees have problems that exist independently of the workplace. These problems are usually the result of the employee's own personal issues or personality. Although these problems can be more thorny for you to deal with than the contextual problems described above, they still find their solutions in performance evaluation and progressive discipline systems.

a. Difficult Personalities

Sooner or later, every workplace will have someone who is just a bad apple, who can't get along or whom everyone dislikes—for a reason. An employee might have a hair-trigger temper, for example, or a cruel sense of humor.

This is the employee who undoubtedly has similar problems wherever he goes, with other employers, coworkers, friends and family. No matter what adjustments you might make to his schedule, environment or other working conditions, you'd still have a problem employee. Perhaps years of therapy might make a difference to this employee— but it's not your place to suggest it, let alone pay for it.

Of course, it pays to try intervention to see if it will work—after all, you won't know you have a hopeless case until you've tried. But if all signs point to the door, this is the time to terminate. If you have conscientiously used your performance evaluation and progressive discipline systems and noted how the employee's attitude has negatively affected his job performance (and possibly the performance of his coworkers), you should be on very solid legal ground when you do so.

EXAMPLE: Boris works at an accounting firm and considers himself quite the comic. He loves teasing his coworkers about everything under the sun—from the way they wear their hair to the various personality quirks that they have. As a result, no one likes to work with Boris, and each of his coworkers has complained to Ann, their supervisor. At Boris' performance evaluation, Ann gives Boris a low ranking on his ability to work with others. Boris is shocked and hurt. He tells Ann that it's part of his personality to tease people—that he can't help it. Ann tells him that he'd better help it, because if he doesn't shape up, he'll be disciplined and even terminated. Now it's up to Boris—he can either suppress his jokes and keep his job, or he can give in to his natural tendencies and find another place to work.

b. Difficult Personal Situations

It would be nice if employees could leave their personal problems at home, but they can't. A tough personal life can derail even the most conscientious employee.

For the employer, this is a particularly difficult issue: Your employee is not obligated to tell you about personal, non-work difficulties, and even if you know about the situation, you're usually in no position to dictate solutions. The most you can do is offer understanding and flexibility—which is often just what the employee wants and needs. If that fails, you should resort to your progressive discipline system. No matter how sympathetic you are to an employee's situation, you can't allow an intractable personal problem infect your workplace.

EXAMPLE: Ever since Rose's teenage son was arrested for drug use, Rose has been useless at work after 3:00. She worries about what he's doing every day after school. She spends afternoons fretting and distracted until she leaves at 5:00. Her productivity has dropped off significantly. Rose's boss, Jose, doesn't want to lose Rose, who is a good worker, but he also can't afford to have her wasting her afternoons in this way. Jose suggests a flexible work schedule to Rose. Rather than working 9:00 to 5:00, she can work from 7:00 to 3:00. That way, her work schedule will coincide with her son's, and she can be home when he gets out of school. Rose accepts the new schedule, and her productivity returns to its old level.

EXAMPLE: Marco's wife left him six months ago. Since then, he's grown cranky and withdrawn. He yells at customers and snaps at coworkers. At his performance evaluation, Marco's supervisor, Louise, tells him that if he doesn't improve his interpersonal skills, he will receive a written reprimand and, ultimately, termination. Marco says that he doesn't care. Louise asks if there is anything she can do to help, but Marco only shrugs and says no. Marco continues to be a problem—even after receiving the written reprimand. Although Louise is sympathetic to his situation, she cannot afford to lose customers and to alienate good employees. She has no choice but to terminate Marco.

3. Discrimination

Some employee interpersonal problems are actually the result of ignorance, hate and prejudice. For example, an employee might not get along with an African-American supervisor because that employee harbors racial prejudices. Or a Jewish employee might not get along with coworkers because the coworkers are anti-Semitic. If what appears at first glance to be an interpersonal problem is really a discrimination problem, you've got a serious situation on your hands—one that carries potential legal liability. (See Chapter 2, Section E for a discussion of anti-discrimination laws.) Whether the employee is the perpetrator or the victim, this sort of problem requires a swift and effective response from you.

Be on the lookout for this situation if the employee is of a different race or gender from his coworkers or possesses any other characteristic that makes him "different." Investigate the problem to see how serious it is, then discipline any coworkers or managers who have harassed or discriminated against the employee based on race, gender or any other personal characteristic that's protected by law. It's not unusual for employees who are the targets of discrimination to fight back—sometimes with combative, anti-social behavior. If you focus on the reaction instead of the cause, you'll miss the opportunity to correct the situation at its roots—and you may be inviting a lawsuit. The person who looks like a problem worker to you may look like a twice-victimized employee to a jury.

If you learn that an employee is harassing or discriminating against others, you must act against the employee, and act fast—not only is a lawsuit likely, it will be the worst kind: a discrimination lawsuit that brings on its coattails low worker morale, bad publicity and high punitive damages awards. Get to the bottom of what is happening by conducting an effective investigation. (See Chapter 5 for information about conducting thorough and effective investigations.) No matter how good a performer an employee is, be prepared to discipline and/or terminate her if you find that she has introduced illegal discrimination into your company.

If discrimination and harassment issues start occurring in your workplace with unsettling frequency, it might be time for you to be more proactive. Consider using diversity training to deal with a workplace culture that is hostile toward women or toward people of a certain race or religion.

C. Insubordination

An employee is insubordinate when he refuses to follow a direct order or a workplace rule. Don't confuse insubordination with a negative attitude or foot-dragging. Those responses reflect interpersonal problems and are not as serious as flat-out refusals.

Like the interpersonal problems discussed above in Section B, insubordination occurs in varying contexts. Refusals that are based on no good reason, legally or practically, are the easiest to deal with—discipline or terminate the employee (see Section 1, below). But if certain reasons underlie the refusal—such as a safety concern or a legality concern— watch out. You'll need to take other, more corrective measures (see Sections 2 and 3, below).

1. Unjustifiable Insubordination

Sometimes, employees don't follow rules or orders because they just don't like them—for example, the rules are too difficult or they involve too much work. When refusals are based on whim or personal reasons, you are free to respond with appropriate discipline.

Of course, the trick here is knowing whether the insubordination is truly unjustifiable. If the employee didn't know about the order or rule, or if the employee thought the rule was unreasonable or unfair, you might want to take a step back, give the employee another chance and consider whether the rule or order should be adjusted.

If you think that the refusal is unjustified, you should use your progressive discipline system (see Chapter 4). For employees who refuse to follow less important work rules and orders, you might discipline a first offense with an oral reminder, which is the first step of a progressive discipline system (see Chapter 4, Section B). For refusals involving more important issues, you could discipline a first offense with a written reprimand (see Chapter 4, Section B). For work rules that relate directly to physical safety or to serious business issues (such as keeping trade secrets secret), you can immediately suspend and terminate the employee—even for a first offense. (See Chapter 6, Section A for more about first offenses that can result in termination.)

2.   Concerns About Safety

If an employee refuses to follow a rule or order because he thinks it's unsafe, you must investigate his concerns. This is because the employee's complaint has put you on notice that something in your workplace might be dangerous or unhealthy. If you ignore the employee's concern —for example, if you think it's unfounded or if you think the employee is lying—and if your workplace is indeed unsafe, you will violate state or federal workplace safety laws. Willful violation of such laws can carry heavy penalties and fines. In addition, if one of your employees gets hurt because of the unsafe condition, that employee might be able to sue you outside of the workers compensation system because you knew about the unsafe condition and failed to fix it. This means your business could be liable for the employee's injuries and could be on the hook for a variety of damages that won't be covered by your workers compensation insurance policy, including punitive damages, emotional distress damages and lost wages.

You must also refrain from disciplining the employee. State and federal workplace safety laws give employees the right to refuse to work if they think a workplace is unsafe. And they prohibit you from penalizing an employee who refuses to work in unsafe conditions or who complains about a violation of these laws. Even though you may think that you are disciplining the employee for insubordination, not for complaining about health and safety issues, third parties—such as your state labor board or a judge and jury—might see it differently.

EXAMPLE: Lily works at an oil refinery where there has recently been a fire that killed 10 of her coworkers. Although the owner shut the plant down for several days after the fire, he is now ordering employees back to work. Lily believes that the plant is still unsafe and still poses a fire hazard, and she tells the owner this. She refuses to return to work on this basis. Not only must the owner investigate Lily's concerns, he cannot terminate her for insubordination. If he fails to investigate her concerns and if another fire kills still more workers, the families of those workers could sue him for large amounts of damages. In addition, he could go to prison for forcing people to work in deadly conditions that he was alerted to and should have investigated.

If you investigate an employee's concerns and determine that they are without merit, inform the employee of your findings. If the employee continues to refuse to follow the order or rule, you can resort to progressive discipline, secure in the knowledge that you have a documented investigation to support any decisions you make.

The federal workplace health and safety law is the Occupational Safety and Health Act, or the OSH Act (29 U.S.C. §§ 651 to 678). This law is enforced by the federal Occupational Safety and Health Administration (OSHA), in conjunction with state health and safety offices (see the Appendix for a list of state offices). You can read the federal law by looking in the federal statutes at your local law library, or you can use Nolo's Legal Research Center at www.nolo.com. To learn about the OSH Act, go to the OSHA website at www.osha.gov. Contact your state labor department for information about your state's health and safety law. (See the Appendix for contact details.) In addition, Nolo has a book with an entire chapter devoted to the OSH Act: *Federal Employment Laws*, by Amy DelPo and Lisa Guerin (Nolo).

3. Concerns about Illegality

Concerns about illegal conduct in the workplace arise in a variety of circumstances. Although the most obvious occurs when an employee is ordered to commit an actual crime—for example, to steal money from a customer or to sell pharmaceutical drugs on the black market—such events are relatively rare.

Illegality problems more commonly arise when an employer asks an employee to do something that violates a workplace law or regulation. For example, an employee might refuse to work overtime because he believes your order violates federal wage and hour laws. Similarly, an employee might refuse to send certain types of waste to a landfill because the contents exceed state regulations. Even though those types of instances don't actually result in crimes, they do result in illegal conduct—and employees are perfectly within their rights to refuse to take part.

If an employee refuses to follow a rule or order because he thinks it is illegal, you must investigate his concerns. The employee's concern is putting you on notice that illegal conduct or practices may be happening in your workplace. If you ignore the concern and a government agency later finds out about the practices, it will consider your violations of the law to be willful and knowledgeable.

In addition, you should not discipline an employee for refusing to engage in conduct that he believes to be illegal. Many states have laws explicitly prohibiting employers from penalizing employees who refuse to engage in illegal conduct. If you terminate such an employee, you might find yourself on the losing end of a wrongful termination lawsuit.

If you investigate the employee's concerns, and conclude that they are without merit, inform the employee of your findings. If the employee continues to refuse to follow the order or rule, you can resort to progressive discipline, secure in the knowledge that you have a documented investigation to support any decisions you make.

D. Excessive Absenteeism and Sick Leave Use

Even a model employee occasionally misses a day or two or is laid low with a bout of the flu or another more serious problem. This person is not a problem employee.

Some employees, however, miss so many work days that their absences become a problem. These employees might have legitimate reasons for their absences or they might not—either way, their absences cause trouble for you. The consequences for companies commonly include:

- **Increased wage costs.** If the employee called in sick, you had to pay him wages for that day. In addition, you might have had to hire temporary help or pay other employees overtime to cover the position.
- **Decreased productivity.** An employee who has a high number of absences is a less productive employee. He'll spend time catching up when he returns and may require assistance from other workers to bring him up to speed.
- **Low morale.** If other employees have to work harder to make up for the absent employee, they may feel stressed and overworked.

Sometimes employees are indeed sick when they use the leave; other times, however, they use the leave to extend their vacation, to have a mental health day or to deal with a personal problem (such as taking the car to the mechanic or caring for a child on a school holiday). As with other issues we've discussed in this chapter, such as interpersonal problems and insubordination, it's important for employers to understand the reasons behind the absenteeism before deciding on a course of action. The subsections below cover the most common situations and advise you on practical, legal responses.

1. Family Absences

Employees often need to take time off from work to care for a family member—such as a child, parent or spouse—who is sick or recuperating. Under federal law and many state laws, you may have to give employees leave from work to deal with these sorts of issues. These laws are called family and medical leave laws. If an employee's absences are the result of the employee *properly* taking leave under one of these family and medical leave laws, the employee is not a problem employee and you cannot impose discipline. (See Chapter 2, Section D for more about family and medical leave laws and your obligations under them.)

2.   Disabled Employees

If an employee is using a large amount of sick leave, she might be suffering from a medical condition that qualifies as a disability under state or federal disability laws. If that is the case, you cannot discipline the employee—and you might even have a duty to accommodate the employee's disability. (See Chapter 2, Section E for more about disability rights laws and your obligations under them.) If you can't accommodate the employee's disability, you might have to terminate the employee. Before taking this step, however, consider consulting an attorney.

3.   Using Sick Leave as a Pretense

Your employees may be using sick leave as a way to extend vacations or take a mental health day. These are not legitimate uses of sick time and—assuming there are no medical leave or disability issues in the background (see Sections 1 and 2, above)—you are legally free to re-spond with appropriate steps. Usually, employers start at the bottom of the progressive discipline ladder and give an oral reminder for the first offense (see Chapter 4, Section B). Repeated abuse of sick leave merits sterner measures.

One way to discourage this type of behavior is to require all employees who call in sick to personally speak to their supervisor rather than just leaving a message with the receptionist. The supervisor can then assess how sick the employee is and ask questions that put the employee on the spot: What symptoms do you have? What are you doing to treat yourself? Are you going to see a doctor? Employers who have used this approach have reported a drop in employee use of sick leave.

If an employee appears to be abusing the sick leave policy, some employers require that employee to provide doctor's notes verifying that the employee is sick. If you choose this approach, be sure that it is a clear part of your progressive discipline policy—that you tell employees, via your personnel handbook, that you will ask suspected abusers of sick leave to provide verification. You'll want to be sure that no employee can claim that you have singled him or her out for special, onerous treatment.

Some employers deal with the problem by not paying employees for time they miss as a result of being sick. Of course, there are a number of drawbacks to this method. For example, employees may come into work when they are sick because they don't want to lose the pay. They could infect you, the rest of your employees and customers. Also, you might have trouble recruiting people to come work for you when you tell them that you don't provide paid sick leave.

Another approach is to combine vacation leave and sick leave into one category. That way, employees know that when they call in sick, they are reducing the amount of time that they can take for vacation. On the plus side for the employees, they feel free to take time when they need it and don't have to lie to you about their reasons.

4. Employees Who Really Are Sick—A Lot

You may have an employee who is frequently and genuinely ill. Once this employee uses all of his allotted paid sick leave and any right he has to unpaid leave under family and medical leave laws, you have a tough situation on your hands.

If the employee is suffering from a medical condition that qualifies as a disability under state or federal disability laws, you might have a duty to accommodate the employee's disability. (See Chapter 2, Section E for more about disability rights laws and your obligations under them.)

If the employee is not disabled, however, you may have to put your sympathies aside and discipline—even terminate—the employee for excessive absences. After all, you can't run a business by paying employees who are at home sick a great deal of the time. You must be able to rely on your employees to show up to work with reasonable regularity.

E. Drugs and Alcohol

Employees who abuse alcohol and drugs (including illegal drugs, prescription drugs and over-the-counter drugs)—either on their own time or at work—can pose significant and wide-ranging problems for their employers, managers and coworkers. These problems can include diminished job performance, lowered productivity, absenteeism, tardiness, high turnover and increased medical and workers' compensation bills. These employees can also make your workplace more volatile and more dangerous, and they can make you vulnerable to legal liability.

1.   Alcohol Use at Work

Your employee handbook (or your verbally announced workplace policies) should make it clear to employees that drinking on the job is not allowed. If you catch an employee actually using alcohol at work, you can deal with it through your standard progressive discipline procedures. Depending on the circumstances, you can do anything from giving the employee an oral reminder to immediately suspending and terminating the employee.

The consequences should depend in part on whether the employee has endangered the health and safety of others. For example, if the employee drinks a beer while operating a forklift, that conduct might deserve more severe discipline than a secretary who drinks a glass of wine at her desk.

If you serve alcohol at social gatherings during working hours, you're treading in dangerous waters. If you serve wine at a company lunch, for example, you are taking the risk that some employees will drink a little too much and therefore return to their workstations intoxicated. Similarly, employees might bring some of the alcohol back to their workstations and continue drinking even after the gathering has ended. Obviously, either situation is bad for business—and can pose a safety risk depending on the employee's job. The best course of action is to not serve alcohol at gatherings that take place during working hours. If you feel you must, however, make it clear to your employees that they are not to drink to the point of intoxication and that they cannot bring alcohol back to their workstations. If you have employees who perform dangerous jobs—such as a welder or a truck driver—you should not allow them to partake in the alcohol served at the event.

2. Off-Hours, Off-Site Use of Alcohol

Many people use alcohol when not at work. Most employers aren't concerned about an employee's light or moderate alcohol consumption—as long as it has no effect on the employee's work performance. But when off-site, off-hours drinking begins to take its toll on the worker's ability to do his or her job, you have reason to take action.

Alcoholics are protected by the federal Americans with Disabilities Act. This means that you cannot make an employment decision based solely on the fact that a person abuses alcohol. You can, however, make a decision—including a decision to discipline or terminate—

based on the employee's inability to meet the same performance and productivity standards that you set for all of your employees.

Understand that you will be responding to the *results* of the employee's drinking—not the drinking itself. Maintaining this distinction is important because it will help avoid any claims by employees that you are discriminating against them based on a disability—alcoholism—or that you are inappropriately intruding into their private lives. Put another way, your concern is not with the fact that the employee drinks after hours or even that the employee has a drinking problem. It is perfectly legal, however, to be concerned with the employee's poor work performance that results from his drinking.

> **EXAMPLE:** Stephanie runs a coffee shop in the business district of her city. Her business brings in the most money between 6:00 a.m. and 9:00 a.m. when customers come rushing in to grab a cup of coffee on their way to work. Lately, she has been having trouble with one of her counter workers. Bob arrives to work tired and distracted and has been mixing up customers' orders. Bob has a reputation for being quite a drinker, and he stays up to all hours of the night drinking with his friends. Sometimes, he doesn't even go home before he shows up to work at 5:30. Stephanie doesn't care that Bob drinks, but she does care that he makes customers irate when he mixes up their orders. She disciplines him for his inattention—first giving him an oral warning, next giving him a written reprimand. When he doesn't improve after these measures, she fires him.
>
> A few months after she fires Bob, Stephanie hires another counter worker named Irene. Soon, Stephanie realizes she has another problem on her hands. Irene has a nervous personality and has trouble handling the hectic and fast-paced atmosphere of the coffee shop. She can't handle more than one order at a time and she often mixes up orders when there are a lot of customers in the shop. Although Irene doesn't drink, she poses essentially the same problem for Stephanie that Bob did—she makes customers angry

with her mistakes. Stephanie takes the same disciplinary measures against Irene that she took against Bob, giving her an oral warning and a written reprimand. When Irene doesn't improve, Stephanie fires her, too.

3. Drug Use and Possession

The law makes big distinctions between the legal and illegal use of drugs. You need to pay strict attention to these distinctions when dealing with your employees.

As we explain more fully below, your ability to govern legal drug use by your employees may be limited by disability laws. The legal use of drugs includes the proper use of prescription and over-the-counter drugs. By contrast, the law gives you a great deal of leeway in combating the illegal use of drugs in your workplace. The illegal use of drugs includes the use of illegal drugs and the misuse or abuse of legal drugs, such as prescription or over-the-counter drugs.

a. Legal Drug Use

Many employees properly use prescribed or over-the-counter drugs. Most employers sensibly believe that it's none of their business, as long as the employee's job performance is not impaired.

Things get trickier, however, if legitimate drug use affects the way an employee does her job. For example, medications that make a person drowsy might make it downright dangerous for a worker to do a job that requires him to be attentive and alert. Medication may also impair a person's judgment and abilities.

If an employee's performance is affected by an employee's proper use of prescription or over-the-counter drugs, your response options may be limited by state and federal disability laws. Depending on the way that the drug use affects the employee, and depending on whether the employee suffers from a disability within the meaning of these laws, you may have to accommodate the employee's use of the drugs.

(Chapter 2, Section E covers disability laws and their impact on workplace drug issues.)

b.   Illegal Drug Use and Possession

If an employee appears at work under the influence of illegal drug use, you are not limited by disability rights laws. Deal with that employee through your standard progressive discipline procedures (see Chapter 4). If the employee has not created a safety threat or is not in a highly sensitive position in your company, a written reprimand is probably appropriate for a first offense.

However, if the employee has endangered the physical safety of others—for example, if he drove the company van after smoking marijuana—something more drastic is called for. If the employee has a drug problem, one option is to suspend him until he successfully completes a treatment program. Some employers, however, choose a no tolerance policy under these circumstances and immediately suspend and terminate the employee.

Because the use or sale or possession of illegal drugs is a crime, most employers immediately suspend and then terminate employees who engage in this type of behavior at work.

Develop a Substance Use Policy

Employers who want to take the initiative in addressing substance use can do so by developing formal substance abuse policies. By educating managers and workers about substance abuse, you can avoid some problems before they begin. And providing rehabilitation services to employees who abuse substances gives these employees a chance to reform.

Any policy you create should begin with a firm statement describing why the policy is necessary. Explain how substance abuse affects your business, using concrete examples of the impact of substance abuse. Include a description of how substance abuse affects employees as individuals—their health, their families and their chances for job advancement. Stress that one purpose of the policy is to help employees overcome their problem.

Your policy should also describe how you plan to detect substance abuse. You have three options:

- The least intrusive and least expensive way is to simply rely on managers and supervisors to observe their workers.
- A more intrusive and more legally complicated method is to search employees and their property at the company.
- The most intrusive, most expensive and most legally complicated method is to drug test employees. (See Chapter 5, Section F for information on drug testing.)

Whatever detection method or methods you choose, your policy should explain them in detail. The policy should also explain what role, if any, managers and supervisors have in enforcing the policy. Your policy should also explain how you plan to respond to proof of substance abuse. It should clearly set forth the disciplinary or rehabilitative actions you will take.

To find out more about creating your own substance abuse policy and education program, contact the National Clearinghouse for Alcohol and Drug Information. The NCADI is the information service of the Substance Abuse and Mental Health Services Administration and the U.S. Department of Health and Human Services. You can contact the NCADI by mail at 11426-28 Rockville Pike, Suite 200, Rockville, MD 20852; by phone at 800-729-6686 or on the Internet at www.health.org.

4.   Investigating Substance Use

If you suspect an employee is under the influence of illegal drug use or alcohol at work, your most difficult task may be finding proof of your suspicions. Circumstantial evidence can be important. If the employee slurs his speech, has bloodshot eyes and can't walk a straight line, be sure to note these things and write them down.

Never reach a conclusion without talking to the employee. There might be a reasonable explanation for the behavior that will influence how—or even whether—you discipline the employee. For example, the employee may tell you that he just started taking a prescription allergy medicine that has affected him more substantially than he thought it would. As noted above in subsection 3a, if problems arise because an employee is properly using prescription drugs, your options may be limited by disability laws.

If there are no acceptable reasons for the employee's condition, you might be ready to impose discipline. Some employers choose to test employees for alcohol and drugs before lowering the boom, especially if they plan to terminate. Before taking this step, be sure you are familiar with the legal limitations on your rights to test. (See Chapter 5, Section E for a discussion of investigating drug use.)

Don't give them something to talk about. Although you should always keep employee problems as confidential as possible, it's particularly important when dealing with suspected drug and alcohol abuse. If you publicly accuse an employee of drug or alcohol abuse or allow your suspicions to become known, you leave yourself vulnerable to a defamation lawsuit from the employee.

Special Rules for Federal Contractors and Grantees

The Federal Drug-Free Workplace Act of 1988 (41 U.S.C. §§ 701-707) requires private companies that contract with the federal government for $100,000 or more to certify that they maintain a drug-free workplace. The law also applies to all companies that receive grants from the Federal government, regardless of the dollar amount.

As part of this certification process, the contractor must:

- post a statement notifying employees that the contractor prohibits the possession and use of drugs in the workplace
- post a statement that informs employees what the sanctions will be for violating the policy
- distribute the policy statement to all employees who will be working on the government project
- inform all employees who will be working on the government project that they must abide by the policy statement
- establish a drug-free awareness program that includes information about the dangers of drug use and any available drug counseling programs
- require employees to notify the contractor of any criminal drug conviction for a violation occurring in the workplace no later than five days after the conviction
- inform the federal agency with whom it is working about the conviction
- sanction the employee for the violation, and
- strive in good faith to maintain a drug-free workplace.

The Act neither authorizes nor prohibits drug testing in the workplace.

In the wake of this federal law, many states passed their own drug-free workplace laws. To find out if your state has such a law, contact your state labor department. (See the Appendix for contact details.)

F.   Theft and Dishonesty

Theft can cost your business money—and imperil its very existence. The American Management Association attributes 20 percent of all business failures to employee theft. That's not surprising, given that businesses lose approximately $40 to $65 billion dollars a year from internal theft and fraud.

Of course, not all thefts and lies are fatal—or even serious. An employee who takes a pen for personal use is quite different from an employee who steals money from your office safe. Similarly, an employee who lies so that he can leave early to watch a football game is different from an employee who lies to make it appear that he is being productive when he isn't.

For minor transgressions—such as using a stamp on a personal letter or using the photocopier to make personal copies—you can start the employee on the lowest rung of the progressive discipline ladder with an oral reminder (see Chapter 4, Section 1). Before disciplining an employee for theft, however, make sure that the company has not implicitly condoned the practice. Do you use the photocopier to make personal copies? If so, your employees may have inferred—even if incorrectly—that they were allowed to do so as well.

If you are faced with significant losses—such as the theft of trade secrets from your safe or money from a coworker—dispense with progressive discipline and suspend/terminate immediately. (See Chapter 6, Section A for a discussion of problems that justify immediate termination.) In some cases, you might even consider calling the authorities.

G. Violence

Violence in the workplace comes in many forms. It might be something as questionable as horseplay among coworkers or as frightening as an employee who brings a gun into the building. Your response to violence from an employee will depend in large part on how serious the violence is. Regardless of the level of violence, however, you must respond.

Your employee handbook or your announced oral policies should include firm and explicit policies against horseplay, threats, fighting and weapons in the workplace. Using your progressive discipline ladder, allocate appropriate responses for employees who engage in such behavior. It's common for employers to give written reprimands for first offenses of horseplay and fighting and to suspend and terminate immediately someone who attacks a coworker, makes a serious threat of physical harm or brings a weapon to work.

It's very important to thoroughly investigate instances of fighting. You'll need to know whether the incident was really a fight between two equals or an attack by one employee on another. Clearly, if it's a one-sided attack, you'll respond differently to the victim than to the attacker. (See Chapter 5 for more about conducting investigations of workplace misconduct.)

If you do not respond firmly and swiftly to violent behavior, you leave yourself vulnerable to a lawsuit if the violent employee physically harms a coworker, vendor or customer. The argument against you is that by not removing the violent employee from your workplace, you allowed a potentially violent situation to develop.

H. Morality Issues

Some employers are concerned with their employees' moral conduct. For example, living together without being married, unmarried pregnancy, illegitimate children, abortions, sexual relationships between coworkers and homosexuality can spell "problem employee" to many employers— even if the employee is otherwise exemplary.

In the discussion below, we describe the legal restrictions on morality requirements. These legal restrictions, however, don't tell the whole story. Any employer who looks beyond business-related issues to an employee's personal life is asking for trouble—both with the law and with the employees themselves. Generally speaking, it just isn't good business sense—or employer sense—to dally in the morals of one's employees. Only in the rarest circumstances where morality truly is part of your business purpose—in a church, for example, or in a non-profit devoted to a moral point of view—should you consider imposing any of the requirements described below.

1.   Living Together, Illegitimate Children and Abortions

These sorts of morality requirements exist in rather murky legal waters.

Generally, the federal law allows private employers to impose restrictions against cohabitation, illegitimate children and abortions so long as the restriction doesn't violate anti-discrimination laws.

However, as you will learn in Chapter 2, federal anti-discrimination laws prohibit you from discriminating against anyone based on that person's race, religion, sex, national origin, age or disability. They also prohibit you from discriminating against someone based on her preg-

nancy or on medical conditions related to the pregnancy. In legal jargon, the groups protected by anti-discrimination laws are known as "protected classes." Where, you might ask, do unmarried couples, unwed mothers and women having abortions fit into these categories?

The answer is that if your policy primarily affects members of a protected class, your policy may be illegal—even though you never intended to discriminate. And the reality is that requirements against co-habitation, unwed mothers and abortions do tend to affect one protected group more than employees at large, which means it's hard to impose such requirements without discriminating.

For example, the federal Equal Employment Opportunity Commission (EEOC), the agency that enforces federal anti-discrimination laws, has argued that workplace prohibitions against illegitimate births and abortions do affect one protected class—African Americans—more than workers in general. The agency has also stated that prohibitions against unmarried pregnancy and illegitimate children disproportionately affect women more than men, because men can more easily hide these characteristics than can women. In legal terms, these groups (African-Americans and women) are "adversely affected" by the policies.

Courts respond inconsistently to these theories, which makes it difficult to draw firm conclusions about the legality of such restrictions.

State law adds another twist. Many states have laws explicitly prohibiting discrimination based on marital status. This would mean that any restriction you have against unmarried couples living together would be illegal in your state. In addition, many states have laws and constitutional provisions that guarantee to state citizens the right of privacy—even from their employers. The morality provisions that we discuss in this section would tend to violate employees' privacy rights.

To find out whether your state prohibits discrimination based on marital status, refer to the "State Laws Prohibiting Discrimination in Employment" chart in the Appendix. To find out about other state law restrictions, contact your state labor department or your state fair employment office. (See the Appendix for contact information.)

Given the complicated nature of both state and federal law in this area, consult an attorney if you feel it is important to impose requirements based on cohabitation, illegitimate children and abortions.

2.   Sexual Relationships Among Employees

You may want to regulate your employees' romantic relationships with each other—either on moral grounds or because you fear that the relationship will eventually affect your business. On the latter score, at least, your fear is not unfounded. Office romances can have a negative impact on the morale of coworkers, and they leave you vulnerable to a sexual harassment lawsuit if the relationship ends. In addition, they often reduce the level of productivity of the people involved. A soured relationship can make the two unhappy participants less effective workers.

If you would like to discourage office romance, you are legally free to do so as long as you don't allow your policy to focus on one particular group. For example, it would be discriminatory to punish only women for engaging in office romance, or only people of a certain religious background. (See the Appendix for charts describing federal and state anti-discrimination laws.)

The best option is to take a moderate approach and only deal with the effects of the romance. For example, if someone's productivity drops because he is involved in an office romance, deal with him through your performance evaluation system in the same way you would deal with any employee who had low productivity. If someone is absent a lot because of an office romance, respond to her as to any employee who has an absenteeism problem.

If the romance is between an employee and a supervisor or manager, take a more aggressive approach and make sure that the relationship is truly consensual. Discuss the sexual harassment laws and tell the employee what he should do if he ever feels that the romance has turned involuntary. Make sure the employee knows about and understands your policies against sexual harassment, discrimination and retaliation. Document everything you tell the employee about this issue and everything the employee tells you.

If an employee who is involved in an office romance ever implies or states explicitly that the romance is not consensual, you must act immediately to investigate and address the situation. Otherwise, you leave yourself vulnerable to a sexual harassment lawsuit.

3. Homosexuality

Some employers do not want gays or lesbians working for them because they believe that homosexuality is immoral or is an undesirable quality in an employee.

There is no federal law prohibiting private employers from discriminating against an employee because of that employee's homosexuality. However, a number of state laws and local ordinances do prohibit discrimination on the basis of sexual orientation. To find out if your state has such a law, refer to the "State Laws Prohibiting Discrimination in Employment" chart in the Appendix to this book. To find out if your city or county has an ordinance prohibiting discrimination on the basis on sexual orientation, contact your city or county clerk's office or consult with your local library.

Summary of Problems and Strategies

The chart that follows lists a number of common employment problems—and strategies you can use to handle them. Each of these strategies is described in more detail in later chapters.

Problem	Main Strategies	Issues to Consider
Poor performance/ productivity (new hire)	• Performance evaluation. • If that doesn't work, progressive discipline. • If that doesn't work, termination.	• Does the employee know what is expected of him? • Does the employee need more training? • Does the employee have the proper skills? • Does the employee feel free to ask for assistance? • Is the employee a slow starter? • Does the employee need additional resources? • Are you providing incentives for the employee to do well? • Is anything happening in the employee's personal life that is distracting him? • Is anything happening in the employee's work environment that is preventing him from performing well?

Summary of Problems and Strategies (continued)

Problem	Main Strategies	Issues to Consider
Sudden drop in performance/productivity	• Performance evaluation. • If that doesn't work, progressive discipline. • If that doesn't work, termination.	• What has changed in the employee's work environment? • Has the employee been put in a new work group? • Has the employee been assigned to a new manager or supervisor? • Does the employee know what is expected of him? • Does the employee need more training? • What has changed in the employee's personal environment? • Is the employee having troubles at home? • Is the employee developing a substance abuse problem?

Summary of Problems and Strategies (continued)

Problem	Main Strategies	Issues to Consider
Coworkers dislike employee	• First, find out why co-workers dislike the employee through a formal or informal investigation. • If it's a simple personality conflict, can you change the employee's shift or department? • Consider raising the issue in a performance evaluation. • If the employee is at fault, consider progressive discipline. • If coworkers are at fault, consider progressive discipline for them.	• Why don't they like the employee? • Does he do inappropriate things? • Is racism behind the co-workers' feelings? Sexism? Another form of discrimination? If so, do not transfer the employee or change his shift. Take care of the employee and stop any harassment and intimidation that might be taking place. • Do they dislike the employee because he is racist, sexist or otherwise discriminatory? If so, investigate immediately and use progressive discipline to make the employee stop the offensive behavior.
Coworker complains that the employee has made sexually inappropriate comments and gestures	• Investigate to see if the employee really did engage in this conduct. • If the employee did engage in the conduct, use progressive discipline in minor cases, termination in egregious cases.	• Is the employee guilty of the conduct? • How many times has the employee done this? • Has the employee done this to anyone else?

Summary of Problems and Strategies (continued)

Problem	Main Strategies	Issues to Consider
Coworker complains that the employee has made racially inappropriate comments	• Investigate to see if the employee really did engage in this conduct. • If the employee did engage in the conduct, use progressive discipline in minor cases, termination in egregious cases.	• Is the employee guilty of the conduct? • How many times has the employee done this? • Has the employee done this to anyone else?
Employee refuses to follow a direct order	• Find out why the employee refused to follow the order. • If the employee does not have a legitimate reason, use progressive discipline. • If the employee refused based on safety concerns, do not discipline the employee. Investigate the concerns. • If the employee refused based on legality concerns, do not discipline the employee. Investigate the concerns.	• Why did the employee refuse to follow the order? • Did the employee understand the order? • Was the order reasonable? • Did the employee have legitimate concerns about the order? • Is something happening in the employee's personal environment? • Is something happening in the employee's work environment?

Summary of Problems and Strategies (continued)

Problem	Main Strategies	Issues to Consider
Employee refuses to follow a work rule	• Find out why the employee refused to follow the rule. • If the employee does not have a legitimate reason, use progressive discipline. • If the employee refused based on safety concerns, do not discipline the employee. Investigate the concerns. • If the employee refused based on legality concerns, do not discipline the employee. Investigate the concerns.	• Why did the employee refuse to follow the rule? • Did the employee know about the rule? • Did the employee understand the rule? • Is the rule reasonable? • Did the employee have legitimate concerns about the rule? • Is something happening in the employee's personal environment? • Is something happening in the employee's work environment?
Employee refuses to follow a rule/order because of concerns about safety	• Investigate the employee's concerns. Do not discipline the employee.	• Employees have the right to refuse to work if they think it is unsafe.
Employee refuses to follow a rule/order because of concerns about legality	• Investigate the employee's concerns. Do not discipline the employee.	• Employees have the right to refuse to engage in illegal conduct.

Summary of Problems and Strategies (continued)

Problem	Main Strategies	Issues to Consider
Employee fails to show up for work and fails to notify you	• Use progressive discipline.	• What is happening in the employee's work environment? • Is it safe and comfortable? • What is happening in the employee's personal environment? • Is the employee developing a substance abuse problem?
Employee uses excessive sick leave	• Communicate with the employee to determine whether his use of the leave is legitimate. • Consider whether the employee has a right to use leave under state or federal family and medical leave laws. • Consider whether the employee needs for you to accommodate a disability under state or federal disability rights laws. • If the employee's use of the leave is not legitimate, use progressive discipline. • If that doesn't work, consider terminating the employee.	• What is happening in the employee's work environment? • Is it safe and comfortable? • What is happening in the employee's personal environment? • Is the employee developing a substance abuse problem? • Are you covered under state or federal family and medical leave laws? • Are you subject under state or federal disability rights laws?

Summary of Problems and Strategies (continued)

Problem	Main Strategies	Issues to Consider
Employee wants to take unpaid leave for a family problem	• Consider the employee's request. Do not discipline the employee.	• Are you subject to federal or state leave laws? • Is the employee eligible for unpaid leave under state and family leave laws? • Is the employee's family problem something that qualifies for leave?
Employee wants to take unpaid leave for a medical condition	• Consider the employee's request. Do not discipline the employee.	• Are you subject to federal or state leave laws? • Is the employee eligible for unpaid leave under state and family leave laws? • Is the employee's medical condition something that qualifies for leave?
Employee is at work under the influence of illegal drug use or alcohol	• Investigate. Make sure the employee is actually guilty of the conduct. • Progressive discipline or termination, depending on the circumstances.	• Has the employee threatened the health and safety of coworkers, customers or the public? • What is happening in the employee's personal environment? • Does the employee have a substance abuse problem? • Would a treatment program help the employee?

Summary of Problems and Strategies (continued)

Problem	Main Strategies	Issues to Consider
Employee uses alcohol at work	• Investigate. Make sure the employee is actually guilty of the conduct. • Progressive discipline or termination, depending on the circumstances.	• Have you implicitly condoned the use? • Has the employee threatened the health and safety of coworkers, customers or the public? • What is happening in the employee's personal environment? • Does the employee have a substance abuse problem? • Would a treatment program help the employee?
Employee sells or possesses illegal drugs at work	• Investigate. Make sure the employee is in fact guilty of the conduct. • Termination. In some circumstances, call the authorities.	
Illegal drug use or alcohol affects employee's performance	• Performance evaluations. • Progressive discipline.	• What is happening in the employee's personal environment? • Does the employee have a substance abuse problem? • Would a treatment program help the employee?

Summary of Problems and Strategies (continued)

Problem	Main Strategies	Issues to Consider
Employee's legal drug use is affecting his performance	• Performance evaluation.	• The employee may be protected by the federal Americans with Disabilities Act or by a state disability rights law. • You may have to reasonably accommodate the employee.
Employee steals from you	• Investigation. Did the employee really do what he is accused of doing? • In minor cases, progressive discipline. • In egregious cases, termination. • When circumstances warrant, contact the authorities.	• Did the employee think it was OK to take the property? • Did you implicitly approve the employee's use of the property?

Chapter 2

Employment Law Basics

*N*o matter what type of employment problem you're facing—from how to investigate a complaint to whether to discipline or even fire a worker—you must start with a working knowledge of the law. Employment law provides the basic framework for many decisions you will make as an employer. It dictates what you can and cannot do and how you must treat your workforce.

If you don't know the law, you can't follow it. And failing to follow workplace laws can be very costly. If you act illegally, you might face employee lawsuits or investigations by government agencies. You will certainly see a decline in productivity, morale and team spirit in your workforce. You may even see your reputation in the business community suffer.

The first step to avoiding these problems is to learn your basic legal rights and obligations as an employer. Here we explain these legal rules. Throughout the rest of the book, we will show you how to implement policies and make employment decisions that will pass legal muster— often referring back to the basic legal information presented here. Along the way, we will explain not only what the law requires, but also what practical steps you can take to reduce your chances of ending up in court.

This chapter explains employment law as it relates to the issues most likely to come up with problem employees: firing and discipline. But your legal obligations as an employer don't end there, of course. For detailed information on your other responsibilities towards your employees— on everything from wage and hour issues and benefits to workplace safety and paperwork requirements—see *Everyday Employment Law: The Basics,* by Lisa Guerin & Amy DelPo (Nolo) or *The Employer's Legal Handbook,* by Fred Steingold (Nolo).

A. Employment at Will

As a private employer in the United States, you start off with the law on your side when dealing with your employees. Although workers have specified rights in some situations, employers generally have plenty of latitude to make the employment decisions they feel are right for their businesses. This latitude is protected by an age-old legal doctrine called "employment at will."

Unlike many legal terms, employment at will means just about what it sounds like: at-will employees are free to quit at any time and for any reason, and you are free to fire them at any time and for any reason—unless your reason for firing is illegal. We cover these illegal reasons to fire, including discrimination, bad faith and public policy violations, in Sections C through E, below.

Different rules apply in Big Sky Country. The state of Montana does not recognize the doctrine of at-will employment. In Montana, an employee who is fired without good cause after completing the employer's probationary period (or after six months of work, if the employer has no probationary period) has been wrongfully discharged. This means the employee can sue for lost wages and benefits and for punitive damages (damages intended to punish the employer), if the firing was fraudulent or malicious. If you do business in Montana, make sure you always have good cause (as described in this chapter) to fire your workers.

Generally, you may fire an at-will employee for even the most whimsical or idiosyncratic reasons—because you don't like his style of dress or the sound of her voice, or simply because you want to hire someone else as a replacement. You are also free to change the terms of employment—job duties, compensation or hours, for example—for any reason that isn't illegal. Your workers can agree to these changes and continue working or reject the changes and quit. In other words, the employment relationship is voluntary. You cannot force your employees to stay forever, and they cannot require you to employ them indefinitely.

Employment at will (and your corollary right to fire at will) must be understood in light of its opposite, which is acting "for cause" (sometimes called "good cause" or "just cause"). An employment decision made for cause has a sound business reason behind it. For example, a demotion based on late work would be "for cause," but a demotion based on an annoying personal characteristic (such as the way a worker eats his lunch in the company lunchroom) would not. Decisions that are made "for cause" are always legal.

Layoffs and Downsizing

Because this book covers only those management challenges presented by problem employees, we don't get into all of the reasons why you might need to demote or fire workers who pose no problems in the work-place. However, good cause to fire encompasses more than an individual worker's poor performance or misconduct. Any legitimate, business-related reason for firing—including business troubles and financial downturns—qualifies. If you are forced to downsize, cut back, close a facility or shut down some of your operations, for example, you will almost certainly have to lay off workers—and you will have good cause to do so.

You may be wondering how one management approach—using your at-will powers—and its opposite—acting for cause—can both be legal. The answer has more to do with the legal system than with logic. Employment law develops as courts decide individual lawsuits and as legislatures pass laws to deal with particular issues of public concern. Sometimes, a court or legislature decides that a certain employment practice or decision is so unfair or unacceptable that it should be illegal, despite the general rule of employment at will. These decisions have curtailed, but not killed, the at-will doctrine.

1.   Legal Limitations on Employment at Will

The employment-at-will doctrine gives you broad legal protection when making employment decisions. But this protection is limited in two ways:

- **Employment contract.** First, the doctrine doesn't apply to employees who have an employment contract, whether written, oral or implied, that puts some limits on the employer's right to fire. For these employees, the language or nature of the contract usually spells out the terms of employment, including when and for what reasons the employees can be fired. Employment contracts are discussed in Section B, below.
- **State or federal laws.** Second, Congress, state legislatures and judges have carved out several exceptions to the doctrine of employment at will. Generally, these exceptions prevent you from taking any negative action against an employee (including disciplining, demoting or firing) in bad faith (Section C), in violation of public policy (Section D) or for a discriminatory or retaliatory reason (Section E).

2. Practical Limitations on Employment at Will

A further limitation on your ability to fire at will has less to do with the law than with human nature. Although the law gives you the right to fire or to change the job of an at-will employee for any reason, no matter how frivolous, in reality, employers who lack a sensible basis for their employment decisions run risks both legal and practical. These risks include:

- **Productivity and morale problems.** If you fire or discipline a worker without a good reason, the rest of your workforce will be confused and uneasy. Other workers will fear that their jobs may also be at risk. Employees who believe they might be fired or demoted even if they are doing a good job have less incentive to follow performance standards and other rules of the workplace. Conversely, if you set clear rules for performance and follow them consistently, your employees will know what is expected of them and will be encouraged to excel in order to keep their jobs and be rewarded.

- **Recruiting and hiring difficulties.** Once word gets out that an employer fires or disciplines employees without good reason, new employees will be harder to come by. After all, why should an employee take a job that can be lost at any time if another employer will offer a measure of job security or at least a fair shake? On the other hand, an employer who has a reputation for fairness and good employee relations has the upper hand in hiring and recruiting.
- **Lawsuits.** An employee who has been treated unfairly is an employee motivated to sue. And despite the doctrine of employment at will, jurors sometimes find ways to punish an employer they perceive to be unfair, arbitrary or callous. Even if the employee ultimately loses the lawsuit, the employer will spend precious time and money fighting it out in court.

3. The Real Value of Employment at Will

As you can see, despite the theoretical protection extended by the employment-at-will doctrine, there are both legal and practical limitations on what used to be an employer's unfettered power to make decisions concerning his employees. And you may well ask yourself: In view of these limitations, what is the at-will doctrine really worth? If you can be sued for ignoring the legal rules and will suffer a demoralized workforce for disregarding the practical realities, why would you ever want to fire (or demote or discipline) at will?

The candid answer is that, most of the time, you wouldn't. The best way to maintain a good relationship with your employees and promote efficient operations is to make sure that you have a solid business reason—in other words, good cause—for every employment decision you make. And really, why would you want to run your business any other way? Making decisions based on arbitrary or personal motives rather than objective business-related reasons can only hurt your company's bottom line in the long run.

The real value of employment at will comes not in the workplace, but in the lawyer's office—and the courtroom. Lawyers, judges and juries can always quibble with your reasons for firing—did you give the employee enough warnings? Was the employee's behavior really so bad that firing was warranted? Were other employees who committed similar types of misconduct treated in exactly the same way? Once you have to prove that you really did have good cause to fire, anything can happen. But, you won't have to defend your decision as long as you reserve your right to fire at will. Faced with strong at-will provisions *and* cause for termination, very few lawyers will be willing to represent any employees you have to fire. And if you somehow end up in a lawsuit, chances are good that the judge will agree to throw out any contract claims against you, based solely on the employment at-will doctrine.

B. Employment Contracts

People sign contracts in order to make their dealings more predictable by binding each other to certain obligations. For example, a manufacturing company can look for a buyer every time it has goods ready to sell, and it can charge whatever price the market will bear. Or it can enter into a contract that obliges a particular buyer to purchase a certain amount of goods at a set price on a regular basis (and obliges the manufacturer to produce those goods and sell them to the buyer for the agreed-upon price).

As you can see from this example, a contract offers the benefit of predictability at the expense of flexibility. If the manufacturing company discovers a new buyer who would pay much more for its goods, it cannot just back out of its contract with the first buyer. So it is with an employment contract—the parties are required to fulfill their contractual obligations to each other, even if they might later want to change or abandon their agreement.

Employees who have employment contracts are often not subject to the at-will doctrine. If, as one of its contractual obligations, the employer has limited its right to fire at will or promised the employee a job for a set period of time, that contract trumps the at-will rules discussed in Section A, above. These employment contracts often spell out the length and terms of the worker's employment and specify how and when the employment can end. Sometimes, these contracts require good cause for termination, or they might spell out in detail the types of employee misconduct or business troubles that would allow either party to end the contract.

Not all employment contracts limit an employer's right to fire at will, however. Some contracts expressly reserve this right to the employer, while setting forth other agreed-upon terms of the employment relationship (pay, position, job duties and hours, for example). We explain how and when you might use either a contract limiting your right to fire or a contract preserving your at-will rights in the sections that follow.

There are three types of contracts that might be used—or might crop up—in an employment relationship:

- **A written contract:** Here, you and the employee sit down and negotiate (or at least review) a document that you both intend will become an employment contract. For example, you and your employee might sign a document outlining the details of the work to be performed and how much the employee will be paid. This type of contract is explained below in subsection 1.

- **An oral contract:** An oral contract has the same features as a written one—except there's no paper and no signatures. For example, if you make certain promises or statements to your employee about the employment relationship and your employee agrees to accept the job on those terms, the two of you might have made an oral contract. These are explained in subsection 2.

- **An implied contract:** These are contracts that you may never have intended to make—but a judge or jury, considering all that was said and done, has concluded that a contract was all but articulated or signed. For example, if you convey to your employee, through some combination of oral statements, written policies and conduct, that the employee will be fired only for cause, the employee may be able to convince a judge or jury that you should be held to your words and actions. Implied contracts are explained in subsection 3.

1. Written Contracts

A written employment contract typically details the terms of the employment relationship. There are no laws specifying what information must go into an employment contract—that's up to you and your employee. Typical contract provisions include information on the start date and length of employment, a description of job duties, details about compensation, bonuses and benefits, clauses protecting trade secrets and confidential information and termination provisions.

Written employment contracts can serve two very different purposes. Some employers enter into written contracts with their employees in order to preserve their at-will rights. Once an employee has agreed, in writing, that the job is at will, that employee will find it very difficult (usually impossible) to later make any kind of claim to the contrary against the employer. Most courts will not allow an employee to claim that she had an oral or implied contract limiting the employer's right to fire in the face of a written at-will agreement. These contracts (explained in subsection a, below), simply offer a little extra at-will insurance for employers.

On the other hand, if an employer wishes to attract or retain a particularly stellar employee, the employer might offer a written contract that binds the employee to work for a set period of time and promises that the employment will last until that term is up—unless the employee commits some sort of misconduct. This prevents the employer from firing at will, instead binding the employer to whatever the contract requires. It also prevents the employee from quitting during the life of the contract, except for reasons set out in the agreement. In these contracts (discussed in subsection b, below), both employer and employee give up their at-will rights: The employer can no longer fire at will, just as the employee can no longer quit at will. If either breaks the contract, the other can sue for damages.

EXAMPLE: James was hired by Funco.com to work in its online commerce division. After he interviewed for the position, Funco sent him an offer letter detailing his start date, job responsibilities and salary. The letter stated that James would be employed at will. Funco asked James to sign the offer letter to seal the deal, which James did. Because the letter does not limit Funco's right to fire him or change the terms of his employment at any time, for any reason, James is an at-will employee.

EXAMPLE: Funco hired Carlos as its Chief Financial Officer. Because Carlos had a number of job offers from other Internet startups, Funco worried that he might be wooed away shortly after starting work. Carlos was also concerned that Funco might decide to change its executive team if its profits did not meet expectations. To allay these fears, Funco and Carlos entered into a one-year employment contract. Both agreed that Carlos would work as Funco's CFO for one year at a specified salary; during that time, he could be fired only for good cause. Carlos is not an at-will employee. If Funco fires or demotes him without good cause or reduces his compensation, Carlos can bring a lawsuit for breach of contract.

a.   Written Contracts That Preserve Your Right to Fire At Will

To write an employment contract that preserves your right to fire at will, you must:

- include explicit language stating that employment is at will
- exclude any restrictions, however indirect, on your right to fire, and
- get your employee to sign the agreement (and sign it yourself).

Let's look at these requirements in more detail.

Explicit language. Any document that you and the employee sign, or any letter you send to the employee (such as a letter offering a job), must include a clear and explicit statement that the employment is at will.

Restrictions. If the contract or letter contains any restrictions on your right to fire, you may lose your ability to terminate at will. Examples of contract language that could limit your right to fire include:

- **Statements about how long the employment relationship or contract will last.** If the contract says that the employment will continue for a measurable period of time (a year, for example, or the duration of a particular project), the employee generally cannot be fired during that period without good cause.
- **Guarantees of continued employment.** If the employee is promised a job, the employer is legally obligated to provide it unless the employee breaches the contract in some way.
- **Promises of progressive discipline.** If the contract requires the employer to follow certain disciplinary steps before firing an employee, the employee is entitled to those protections.
- **Provisions limiting the employer's right to terminate.** Many written employment contracts detail exactly how and when the employment relationship can end. In some contracts, either the employer or the employee has the right to end the relationship as long as she provides a certain amount of notice (90 days, for example). Other contracts provide that the employee can be fired only for good cause or for reasons specifically detailed in the contract. Some of the more common contractual grounds for termination include commission of a crime, gross incompetence and financial wrongdoing.

Signatures. Many employers include a statement in their handbook or employee manual that employment is at will—and courts will consider this language in the employer's favor when faced with an employee's contract claim. However, the best way to protect your at-will rights is to get the employee's signature on a clear at-will agreement. This prevents the employee from later arguing (as some do about language in a handbook) that he didn't know about or read the statement.

If you decide to use a written contract or signed offer letter, give the employee two copies signed on behalf of the company and ask her to sign and return one of them. When you receive the signed copy of the letter or contract, put it into the employee's personnel file. Of course,

Offer Letter Preserving At-Will Employment

May 5, 20XX

Cameron Norman
3333 Nolo Drive
Berkeley, CA 12345

Dear Cameron,

I am pleased to offer you the position of Customer Service Representative for Sportgirl, Inc. We will give you a copy of our Employee Handbook on your first day of work, September 1, 200x, which explains our personnel policies. The purpose of this letter is to set forth the terms of your employment.

You will work in the Customer Service department at our main office in Menlo Park. You will receive an annual salary of $38,000, plus the benefits described in our Handbook. You have chosen to work the opening shift, from 6 a.m. through 2 p.m., Tuesday through Saturday.

I look forward to working with you, as does the Customer Service team. We sincerely hope that you are happy as an employee at Sportgirl, Inc. We value teamwork and strive to make work fun for our employees. However, we cannot make any guarantees about your continued employment here. Sportgirl, Inc. is an at-will employer. While we hope things work out, you are free to quit at any time, for

Offer Letter Preserving At-Will Employment (continued)

any reason, just as Sportgirl, Inc. is free to terminate your employment at any time, for any reason.

Please sign and return the enclosed copy of this letter, acknowledging your acceptance of employment with Sportgirl, Inc. under the terms set forth in this letter. Welcome aboard!

Marion Hopkins
Marion Hopkins
Human Resources Manager

My signature reflects that I have read and understood this letter. I understand that my employment is at will. No other representations regarding the terms and conditions of my employment have been made to me other than those recited in this letter.

_____
Cameron Norman

_____
Date

you shouldn't take any subsequent actions—such as promising job security or saying you will fire employees only for certain offenses—that will undermine the at-will message of your letter. If you have to fire the employee and he claims that you breached an employment contract, you'll have the signed agreement on file to support your position that the employment has always been at will. The sample letter above, "Offer Letter Preserving At-Will Employment," shows how one employer wrote her offer letter.

b.   Written Contracts Requiring Good Cause to Fire

Because of the substantial benefits of the at-will doctrine, many employers refuse to enter into any employment contract that limits their right to fire. However, if you really need to retain a particular employee or you want to sweeten your offer to that perfect applicant, you might consider giving up your at-will rights. A written contact requiring cause to fire might make sense when dealing with these employees:

- **Highly marketable employees.** If you are recruiting an employee with valuable skills or credentials, a written employment contract promising some job security might be enough to woo her to your company. And if the contract obligates her to work for you for a set period of time, she is less likely to be recruited away by another suitor.

- **Employees who are key to your company's success.** It's a lesson from Business 101: Keep those employees on whom your business depends. If the employee you are hiring is that important to your company, consider using a written employment contract to hang on to him.

- **Employees who will have access to your trade secrets.** If your trade secrets are vital to your company's success, you might consider entering a written contract with those employees who will have regular access to them. A guarantee of job security may also help convince these employees to sign a noncompete or nondisclosure agreement. (See Chapter 8, Section F for more information on these agreements.) And they may feel more loyal to the company—and less likely to go work for a competitor—if you make a commitment to keep them on board.

- **Employees who will have to make a sacrifice to work for you.** At some point, you may want to hire an employee who will have to give something up to take the job. You might want to hire an employee away from a secure position at another company, for example, or hire someone who will have to move to accept the position. Or you may want someone to come work for you even though it would mean taking a pay cut. In these situations, a written employment contract promising some job security might convince an employee to come work for you despite the hardships.

Remember that any time you enter into this type of employment contract, you are limiting your right to fire the employee. Even if circumstances warrant offering a contract, do so only if you have good reason to believe that the worker will fit in with your business. If you are unsure, consider using a probationary period, during which you and the worker can decide whether the employment relationship will work, before limiting your right to fire in an employment contract. (For detailed information on hiring, see Chapter 10.)

2. Oral Contracts

Many times there won't be a document memorializing the start of an employment relationship. The employer simply offers the employee a job to perform particular duties for a specified salary, and the employee agrees and shows up for work. Although these informal arrangements are rudimentary contracts, they are not the types of agreements that restrict an employer's right to fire.

There's nothing to stop an employer and employee from discussing other employment issues like wages, hours and responsibilities. But if you announce limits on your right to terminate, such as a promise that the employee will be fired only for good cause or financial reasons, you've probably destroyed the at-will freedom that you would otherwise have. If an employee can prove that you violated an oral agreement by terminating him without a good reason or by changing other agreed-upon terms of his employment, he can sue you for breach of contract.

Here are some examples of the kinds of statements that might create an oral contract restricting an employer's right to fire at will:

- **Promises of job security.** Few employers would promise lifelong employment. However, if you tell prospective or current employees that they will have a job as long as they perform well or that the company does not fire employees without good cause, you will have to live up to these promises or risk a lawsuit.
- **Assurances of raises, promotions or bonuses.** If you promise rewards to employees who perform well, a court might interpret that as a guarantee that employees will receive the benefits you promise and will not be fired as long as their performance is up to snuff.
- **Statements about termination.** Of course, if you explicitly promise an employee that she will not be fired except for certain reasons, you have restricted your right to terminate.

EXAMPLE: Jun interviews for a position as a bookstore clerk. At the close of the interview, the manager offers him a job working 40 hours a week at $7 per hour. Jun agrees to take the job and shows up for work as promised the following week. Because the bookstore has not made any promises to Jun about the length of his employment or the security of his job, Jun is an at-will employee. The bookstore can fire him, demote him or change the terms of his employment.

EXAMPLE: Julia is recruited to manage a chain of grocery stores in California. Although she is interested in the job, she has heard rumors that the company might merge with a national grocery chain and is worried that her job might not survive the merger. When she raises this concern during her interviews, the CEO assures her that she is part of the company's long-term plans and that she will keep her position even if the merger goes through. These statements are probably enough to create an oral employment contract limiting the company's right to fire Julia.

Detailed oral contracts are rare, in the employment field and elsewhere. An agreement that is not reduced to writing is more likely to be forgotten, misconstrued or disputed later. Usually, both sides will want the agreement written down to avoid confusion in the future.

⚠ Oral contracts provide fertile ground for legal battles. It can be very difficult to prove the existence or terms of an oral contract, especially if each participant remembers the conversation differently. If this happens, a jury will have to decide who is telling the truth. You can avoid these problems by simply writing down any employment agreement you make with your employees.

3. Implied Contracts

An implied employment contract is a legal hybrid. It is an enforceable agreement that has not been reduced to a formal contract or explicitly stated orally, but instead is implied from a combination of oral statements, written statements and conduct.

To prove an implied contract, an employee will have to show that you led him to believe he would not be fired without a good reason. The employee doesn't have to prove that you wrote or said those words, however. Instead, the employee must show that your statements, personnel policies and actions towards the employee all led him to the reasonable belief that his job was secure.

a.   Creating an Implied Contract

Implied contracts are usually created over time, out of language in personnel manuals, performance evaluations, conversations with your employees and the way you treat your workers. When determining whether an implied employment contract exists between you and a former employee, a judge will consider a number of factors, including whether you:

- gave the employee regular promotions, raises and positive performance reviews
- assured the worker that her employment was secure or would continue as long as she performed well
- promised, explicitly or implicitly, that the employee's position would be permanent
- employed the worker for a lengthy period before firing her, or
- adopted policies that place some limits on your right to fire workers at will. Examples of such policies include mandatory progressive discipline policies (policies that—unlike the sample policy we provide in Chapter 4—don't give the employer leeway to depart from the stated procedure or fire for any reason), policies providing that new employees will become permanent after serving a probationary period and policies promising regular promotions and raises if performance meets a certain standard.

Need help writing policies that won't create an implied contract? See *Create Your Own Employee Handbook,* by Lisa Guerin & Amy DelPo (Nolo). Packed with sample policies, this book comes with a CD-ROM you can use to put your handbook together.

EXAMPLE: In 1979, Marguerite took a job as an accountant with EZ Ink Printing. EZ Ink's employee manual stated that employees were not considered permanent until they completed a 90-day probationary period. The manual also contained an exhaustive list of offenses for which employees could be terminated and stated that other types of misconduct would be handled through its progressive discipline policy.

For more than 20 years, Marguerite built her life around EZ Ink—assuming that she would be able to keep her job there until she reached retirement age. Marguerite received regular raises and promotions, and her supervisor often spoke of her bright future at the company. In 2000, however, EZ Ink fired Marguerite. EZ Ink had no beef with Marguerite's job performance; instead, the head of the company wanted to offer the position to a friend.

Marguerite would likely be able to win a lawsuit against EZ Ink based on breach of an implied contract. By its conduct, the company led Marguerite to believe that she would not be fired once she became a permanent employee unless she did something truly awful. When the company fired Marguerite without good cause, it exposed itself to legal trouble.

⚠ **Each state has its own rules about what an employee must show to prove an implied contract.** Some states don't consider all of the factors listed above. If you have serious concerns about creating an implied contract, you may want to talk to an attorney.

b.   The Risk of Creating Implied Contracts

Employers generally try to avoid creating implied employment contracts. And for good reason: These contracts limit your right to fire workers without giving you anything in return. Unlike a written or oral contract, which can bind employer and employee equally, an implied contract generally works only one way—against the employer.

There are certain steps you can take to make it harder for an employee to fit together bits and pieces of your conversations and policies into the mosaic of an implied contract. You can:

- **State that employment is at will.** In your written employment policies, including your employee handbook or personnel manual, state clearly that employment at your company is at will and explain what this means. (See Chapter 10 for information on at-will provisions and other workplace policies.)

- **Ask employees to sign an at-will agreement.** Most courts agree that an employee who signs an agreement stating that her employment is at will cannot later claim that she had an implied employment contract limiting the employer's right to fire her. Consider asking your employees to sign a simple form acknowledging that their employment is at will. (If you used a written contract or offer letter as explained in subsection 1a, you've already done this).

- **Don't make promises of continued employment.** If you tell your employees that their jobs are secure, that they will not be fired without good cause or even that the company has never had to fire a worker, you risk creating an expectation that they will not be fired. Avoid these types of comments, particularly common while interviewing potential employees and giving performance reviews.

- **Train your managers.** With few exceptions, your managers' actions and statements will be legally attributable to your company— just as if you had said or done them. Managers must understand your policies and procedures, especially regarding discipline, performance reviews and employment at will. If your managers make any statements or take any actions contrary to these policies —like promising a worker that he won't be fired—you may be facing an implied contract claim.

- **Keep your disciplinary options open.** If you adopt a progressive discipline policy, make sure to include clear language preserving your right to fire employees at will—as does the sample policy we provide in Chapter 4. If you list offenses for which firing is appropriate, state that the list is not exhaustive and that you reserve the right to fire for any reason.

- **Don't refer to employees as "permanent."** Many employers have an initial probationary or temporary period for new employees, during which the company is free to fire the worker. If the worker survives this period, the company calls her a permanent employee entitled to benefits and so forth. To some courts, this language implies that once an employee becomes permanent, she can be fired only for good cause. If you choose to use a probationary period, be clear that you retain the right to fire at will once that period is over.

C. Breaches of Good Faith and Fair Dealing

Employers have a duty to treat their employees fairly and in good faith. What this duty amounts to, as a practical matter, varies from state to state. Simply firing or disciplining a worker is not enough to breach this duty—an employer who treats employees honestly and with respect, even those employees who must be disciplined or fired, runs no risk. However, an employer who treats an employee in a particularly callous way or fires an employee for a malevolent reason—particularly if the firing was intended to deprive the employee of benefits to which she would otherwise be entitled, such as retirement benefits—may be successfully sued for violating this basic principle.

Courts have held that employers breached the duty of good faith and fair dealing by:

- firing or transferring employees to prevent them from collecting sales commissions or vesting retirement benefits
- intentionally misleading employees about their chances for future promotions and raises
- soft-pedaling the bad aspects of a particular job, such as the need to travel through dangerous neighborhoods late at night, and
- transferring an employee to remote, dangerous or otherwise undesirable assignments to coerce her into quitting without collecting the severance pay and other benefits that she would otherwise receive.

⚠ **Not every state allows employees to sue an employer for violating the duty of good faith and fair dealing.** And some states allow only employees who have an employment contract to bring these claims. Because of this variation in state law, you may want to consult with a lawyer if you are concerned about good faith and fair dealing claims—the duty might not even apply to you.

D. Violations of Public Policy

An employer violates public policy when it fires or disciplines an employee for reasons most people would find morally or ethically wrong. If an employer takes any negative action against an employee that a judge or jury would find contrary to public policy, that employee may end up winning a lawsuit in which the employer is ordered to reinstate the employee, rescind the discipline or pay money damages. Earl Warren, the late Supreme Court Justice, summed it up best: "You just can't do that!"

Although it's hard to pin down the precise meaning of public policy, in the employment law field there's a wealth of cases that illustrate the concept. You could be violating public policy if you take negative action against an employee for:

- exercising a legal right, such as voting, joining a union, filing a worker's compensation claim (see subsection a), taking family medical leave (subsection b) or refusing to take a lie detector test
- refusing to do something illegal, such as submit false tax returns, defraud customers or service providers, sell faulty equipment or lie on government reports, or
- reporting illegal conduct or wrongdoing, by filing a complaint with a government agency (whistleblowing) or, in some states, reporting misconduct of public concern to higher management within the company. This might include complaints that employees are lying to government officials or endangering the public by selling products that don't meet safety standards.

States have different rules about what constitutes a public policy. The federal government and some states have laws explicitly prohibiting employers from firing or punishing employees for doing certain things, like reporting a health and safety violation or taking family medical leave—some of these laws are discussed below. Some states allow employees to file public policy lawsuits even when no statute spells out exactly what the employer can and cannot do. The best rule for employers is to consult an attorney whenever you are considering taking action against an employee who has recently exercised a civic right, refused to engage in questionable activity or blown the whistle on workplace problems.

1. Workers' Compensation Claims

Workers' compensation laws provide replacement income and payment for medical expenses to workers who are injured on the job or become ill because of their work. These laws are a mandatory alternative to the legal system—if an employee suffers an injury that falls within the ambit of these laws, that employee may not file a lawsuit against the employer. Instead, he must go through the workers' compensation system to get compensated for his injuries. In exchange for this protection from lawsuits, the employer must pay—generally by purchasing workers' compensation insurance through the state or a private insurer. Insurance rates are typically based on the size of your payroll and the hazards of your industry. However, the number and size of the claims against you might also be a factor in determining your premiums.

In most states, a worker can file a lawsuit against an employer who fires or punishes him for bringing a workers' compensation claim. Contact your state workers' compensation office for information on the workers' compensation system, your state's coverage and insurance requirements and state retaliation laws.

Workers' Compensation Offices

The following is a list of workers' compensation offices where you can find more information about your state's law. This list was last reviewed in April 2003.

Alabama
Workers' Compensation Division
Department of Industrial Relations
Montgomery, AL
334-242-2868
http://dir.state.al.us/wc

Alaska
Workers' Compensation Division
Department of Labor
Juneau, AK
907-465-2970
www.labor.state.ak.us/wc/wc.htm

Arizona
Industrial Commission
Phoenix, AZ
602-542-4661
www.ica.state.az.us

Arkansas
Workers' Compensation Commission
Little Rock, AR
501-682-3930
www.awcc.state.ar.us

California
Division of Workers' Compensation
Sacramento, CA
800-736-7401
www.dir.ca.gov/dwc/
    dwc_home_page.htm

Colorado
Division of Workers' Compensation
Denver, CO
800-390-7936 or 303-318-8700
www.coworkforce.com/DWC

Connecticut
Workers' Compensation Commission
Hartford, CT
860-493-1500
www.ctdol.state.ct.us/

Delaware
Division of Industrial Affairs
Office of Workers' Compensation
Wilmington, DE
302-761-8200
www.delawareworks.com/divisions/
    industaffairs/workers.comp.htm

District of Columbia
Department of Employment Services
Labor Standards Bureau
Office of Workers' Compensation
Washington, DC
202-671-1000
http://does.dc.gov/services/
    wkr_comp.shtm

Florida
Department of Financial Services
Division of Workers' Compensation
Tallahassee, FL
800-342-1741
www.fldfs.com/wc/

Workers' Compensation Offices (continued)

Georgia
Board of Workers' Compensation
Atlanta, GA
404-656-3875
www.state.ga.us/sbwc/

Hawaii
Disability Compensation Division
Department of Labor and Industrial
   Relations
Honolulu, HI
808-586-9174
http://dlir.state.hi.us/

Idaho
Industrial Commission
Boise, ID
208-334-6000 or 800-950-2110
www2.state.id.us/iic/

Illinois
Industrial Commission
Chicago, IL
312-814-6611
www.state.il.us/agency/iic/

Indiana
Workers' Compensation Board
Indianapolis, IN
1-800-824-COMP or 317-232-3809
www.in.gov/workcomp/

Iowa
Division of Workers' Compensation
Des Moines, IA
515-281-5387 or 800-562-4692
www.iowaworkforce.org/wc

Kansas
Division of Workers' Compensation
Department of Human Resources
Topeka, KS
785-296-3441
www.hr.state.ks.us/wc/html/wc.html

Kentucky
Department of Workers' Claims
Frankfort, KY
502-564-5550
http://labor.ky.gov/dwc

Louisiana
Office of Workers' Compensation
   Administration
Baton Rouge, LA
800-201-2499 or 225-342-7555
www.laworks.net

Maine
Workers' Compensation Board
Augusta, ME
207-287-3751 or 888-801-9087
www.state.me.us/wcb

Maryland
Workers' Compensation Commission
Baltimore, MD
800-492-0479 or 410-864-5100
www.wcc.state.md.us

Massachusetts
Department of Industrial Accidents
Boston, MA
800-323-3249 or 617-727-4900
www.state.ma.us/dia

Workers' Compensation Offices (continued)

Michigan
Bureau of Workers' and Unemployment Compensation
Lansing, MI
517-322-1296 or 888-396-5041
www.michigan.gov/bwuc

Minnesota
Workers' Compensation Division
Department of Labor and Industry
St. Paul, MN
800-342-5354 or 651-284-5032
www.doli.state.mn.us/
workcomp.html

Mississippi
Workers' Compensation Commission
Jackson, MS
601-987-4200
www.mwcc.state.ms.us/

Missouri
Division of Workers' Compensation
Department of Labor and Industrial
Relations
Jefferson City, MO
573-751-4231
www.dolir.state.mo.us/wc/index.htm

Montana
Department of Labor and Industry
Helena, MT
406-444-6543
http://dli.state.mt.us/

Nebraska
Workers' Compensation Court
Lincoln, NE
402-471-6468 or 800-599-5155
www.state.ne.us/home/WC/

Nevada
Division of Industrial Relations
Carson City, NV
775-684-7260
http://dirweb.state.nv.us

New Hampshire
Workers' Compensation Division
Department of Labor
Concord, NH
800-272-4353 or 603-271-3176
www.labor.state.nh.us/
workers_compensation.asp

New Jersey
Department of Labor
Division of Workers' Compensation
Trenton, NJ
609-292-2515
www.state.nj.us/labor/wc/
wcindex.html

New Mexico
Workers' Compensation
Administration
Albuquerque, NM
505-841-6000
www.state.nm.us/wca

Workers' Compensation Offices (continued)

New York
Workers' Compensation Board
Albany, NY
518-474-6674
www.wcb.state.ny.us/index.html

North Carolina
Industrial Commission
Raleigh, NC
800-688-8349
www.compstate.nc.us

North Dakota
Workers' Compensation Bureau
Bismarck, ND
800-777-5033 or 701-328-3800
www.ndworkerscomp.com

Ohio
Bureau of Workers' Compensation
Columbus, OH
800-644-6292
www.state.oh.us/odjfs/ouc/index.stm

Oklahoma
Workers' Compensation Court
Oklahoma City, OK
800-522-8210 or 405-522-8600
www.owcc.state.ok.us

Oregon
Workers' Compensation Division
Salem, OR
503-947-7810 or 800-452-0288
www.cbs.state.or.us/external/wcd/

Pennsylvania
Bureau of Workers' Compensation
Harrisburg, PA
717-787-5279
www.dli.state.pa.us/

Rhode Island
Department of Labor and Training
Division of Workers' Compensation
Cranston, RI
401-462-8100
www.dlt.state.ri.us/webdev/wc/
default.htm

South Carolina
Workers' Compensation Commission
Columbia, SC
803-737-5700
www.wcc.state.sc.us

South Dakota
Division of Labor and Management
Department of Labor
Pierre, SD
605-773-3681
www.state.sd.us/dol/dlm/dlm-
home.htm

Tennessee
Workers' Compensation Division
Labor and Workforce Development
Nashville, TN
615-532-2731
www.state.tn.us/labor-wfd/
wcomp.html

Workers' Compensation Offices (continued)

Texas
Workers' Compensation Commission
Austin, TX
513-933-1899
www.twc.state.tx.us

Utah
Industrial Accident Division
Salt Lake City, UT
801-530-6800
www.ind-com.state.ut.us/indacc/
indacc.htm

Vermont
Department of Labor and Industry
Workers' Compensation Division
Montpelier, VT
802-828-2286
www.state.vt.us/labind/wcindex.htm

Virginia
Workers' Compensation Commission
Richmond, VA
804-367-8600 or 877-664-2566
www.vwc.state.va.us/

Washington
Department of Labor and Industries
Olympia, WA
360-902-5999
www.lni.wa.gov/

West Virginia
Workers' Compensation Division
Charleston, WV
304-926-5000
www.state.wv.us/scripts/bep/wc/

Wisconsin
Workers' Compensation Division
Madison, WI
608-266-1340
www.dwd.state.wi.us/wc/default.htm

Wyoming
Workers' Safety and Compensation
Division
Cheyenne, WY
307-777-6763
http://wydoe.state.wy.us/
doe.asp?ID=9

2. Family and Medical Leave

The federal Family and Medical Leave Act, or FMLA (29 U.S.C. §2601 and following) and some state laws require employers to let their employees take time off work to deal with certain family and medical problems. Employers may not fire or discipline a worker for taking leave covered by these laws.

The FMLA will apply if three conditions are met:

- you have 50 or more employees who work within a 75-mile radius (all employees on your payroll—including those who work part time and those on leave—must be included in this total)
- the employee seeking leave has worked for you for at least 12 months, and
- the employee has worked at least 1,250 hours for you (about 25 hours a week) during the 12 months immediately preceding the leave.

An eligible employee may take leave to care for a newborn or newly adopted child, to care for a seriously ill spouse, child or parent

or to recuperate from his own serious health condition. Employees are entitled to take up to 12 weeks of unpaid leave per 12-month period for these purposes. When the employee's leave is over, you must reinstate the employee to the same position he held prior to taking leave. If you fire or discipline a worker for taking family or medical leave, the worker can sue you.

Almost half of the states have laws that are, in some respect, more protective than the FMLA—some provide for longer periods of leave, some cover smaller businesses, some allow employees to take leave for a larger variety of family issues (including attending children's school conferences and dealing with domestic violence) and some allow employees to take leave to care for a wider circle of family members (such as grandparents, in-laws and life companions). You can find a state-by-state list of laws immediately below. You will have to follow whichever law gives your workers more protection in any given situation, the FMLA or your state's law.

For more information about the FMLA, contact the U.S. Department of Labor's Wage and Hour Division. To find out about your state's family and medical leave laws, contact your state department of labor. (See the Appendix for all contact details.) You can also find information on the FMLA and state leave laws at the website of the National Partnership for Women & Families, www.nationalpartnership.org, 1875 Connecticut Avenue, NW, Suite 710, Washington, DC, 20009, (202) 986-2600. You can also find a comprehensive discussion of the FMLA and other federal employment laws in *Federal Employment Laws: A Desk Reference* by attorneys Amy DelPo & Lisa Guerin (Nolo).

State Family and Medical Leave Laws

This chart covers some basic aspects of state family and medical leave laws. The federal FMLA applies to all covered employers in every state. However, an employer must follow those portions of the state or federal law that provide the most protection for employees.

We don't address every aspect of these laws (such as notice requirements, medical certifications or reinstatement rules). For more information, contact your state's department of labor and be sure to check its website, where most states have posted their family leave rules. (See Appendix for contact details.)

States that are not listed below do not have laws that apply to private employers or have laws that offer less protection than the FMLA.

California

Cal. Gov't. Code § 12945; Cal. Lab. Code §§ 230 and following

Employers Covered: Employers with 5 or more employees must offer pregnancy leave; with 25 or more employees must offer leave for victims of domestic violence or sexual assault and school activity leave.

Eligible Employees: All employees.

Pregnancy/Maternity: Up to 4 months' for disability related to pregnancy.

Family Member's or Employee's Serious Health Condition: Family member includes registered domestic partner.

School Activities: 40 hours' per year.

Other: Reasonable time for issues dealing with domestic violence or sexual assault, including health, counselling and safety measures.

Colorado

Colo. Rev. Stat. § 19-5-211

Employers Covered: All employers who offer leave for birth of a child.

Eligible Employees: All employees.

Adoption: Employee must be given same leave for adoption as allowed for childbirth.

Connecticut

Conn. Gen. Stat. Ann. §§ 31-51kk to -51qq; 46a-51(10); 46a-60(7)

Employers Covered: Employers with 75 employees must offer childbirth, adoption and serious health condition leave; with 3 employees, must offer maternity disability.

Eligible Employees: Any employee with one year and at least 1,000 hours of service in last 12 months.

Childbirth: 16 weeks' per any 24-month period.

Adoption: 16 weeks' per any 24-month period.

Pregnancy/Maternity: "Reasonable" amount of maternity disability leave.

Family Member's or Employee's Serious Health Condition: Family member includes parents-in-law. 16 weeks' per any 24-month period.

State Family and Medical Leave Laws (continued)

District of Columbia

D.C. Code Ann. §§ 32-501 and following; 32-1202

Employers Covered: Employers with at least 20 employees.

Eligible Employees: Employees who have worked at company for at least one year and at least 1,000 hours during the previous 12 months.

Childbirth: 16 weeks' per any 24-month period.

Adoption: 16 weeks' per any 24-month period.

Pregnancy/Maternity: 16 weeks' per any 24-month period.

Family Member's or Employee's Serious Health Condition: 16 weeks' per any 24-month period. Family member includes persons sharing employee's residence and with whom employee has a committed relationship.

School Activities: Up to 24 hours of leave per year.

Hawaii

Haw. Rev. Stat. §§ 398-1 to 398-11; 378-1

Employers Covered: Employers with at least 100 employees must offer childbirth, adoption and serious health condition leave; all employers must offer pregnancy leave.

Eligible Employees: Employees with 6 months of service are eligible for childbirth, adoption and serious health con-

dition benefits; all employees are eligible for pregnancy and maternity leave.

Childbirth: 4 weeks' per calendar year.

Adoption: 4 weeks' per calendar year.

Pregnancy/Maternity: "Reasonable period" required by discrimination statute and case law.

Family Member's or Employee's Serious Health Condition: 4 weeks' per calendar year. Family member includes parents-in-law, grandparents, grandparents-in-law, stepparents. Hawaii's leave law does not include employee's own serious health condition.

Illinois

820 Ill. Comp. Stat. §§ 147/1 and following

Employers Covered: All.

Eligible Employees: Employees who have worked at least half-time for 6 months.

School Activities: 8 hours' per year, but no more than 4 hours' per day.

Iowa

Iowa Code § 216.6

Employers Covered: Employers with 4 or more employees.

Eligible Employees: All.

Pregnancy/Maternity: Up to 8 weeks' for disability due to pregnancy, childbirth or legal abortion.

State Family and Medical Leave Laws (continued)

Kentucky

Ky. Rev. Stat. Ann. § 337.015

Employers Covered: All.

Eligible Employees: All.

Adoption: Up to 6 weeks' for adoption of a child under 7 years old.

Louisiana

La. Rev. Stat. Ann. §§ 23:341 to :342; 23:1015 and following; 40:1299.124

Employers Covered: Employers with at least 25 employees must offer pregnancy/maternity leave; with at least 20 employees must comply with bone marrow donation provisions; all employers must offer leave for school activities.

Eligible Employees: All employees are eligible for pregnancy/maternity or school activities leave; employees who work 20 or more hours per week are eligible for leave to donate bone marrow.

Pregnancy/Maternity: "Reasonable period of time" not to exceed four months, if necessary for pregnancy or related medical condition.

School Activities: 16 hours' per year.

Other: Bone marrow donation, up to 40 hours paid leave per year.

Maine

Me. Rev. Stat. Ann. tit. 26, §§ 843 and following

Employers Covered: Employers with 15 or more employees at one Maine location.

Eligible Employees: Employees with at least one year of service.

Childbirth: 10 weeks' in any two-year period.

Adoption: 10 weeks' in any two-year period (for child age 16 or younger).

Family Member's or Employee's Serious Health Condition: 10 weeks' in any two-year period.

Maryland

Md. Code Ann., [Lab. & Empl.] § 3-802

Employers Covered: Employers that allow workers to take leave for the birth of a child.

Eligible Employees: All employees.

Adoption: Employee must be given same leave for adoption as allowed for childbirth.

Massachusetts

Mass. Gen. Laws ch. 149, §§ 52D, 105D; ch. 151B, § 1(5)

Employers Covered: Employers with 6 or more employees must provide maternity and adoption leave; all employers must offer leave for school activities.

Eligible Employees: Full-time female employees who have completed probationary period, or 3 months of service if no set probationary period, are eligible for maternity and adoption leave. Employees who are eligible under FMLA are eligible for all other leave.

State Family and Medical Leave Laws (continued)

Childbirth/Maternity: 8 weeks'.

Adoption: 8 weeks' for child under 18, or under 23 if disabled.

School Activities: 24 hours' per year total (combined with medical care under "other").

Other: 24 hours' per year for events directly related to medical or dental care of a minor child or elderly relative age 60 or over. (24 hours' total when combined with school activities.)

Minnesota

Minn. Stat. Ann. §§ 181.940 and following

Employers Covered: Employers with at least 21 employees at one site must provide maternity leave; with at least 20 employees must allow leave to donate bone marrow; all employers must provide leave for school activities.

Eligible Employees: Employees who have worked at least half-time for one year are eligible for maternity leave; at least 20 hours per week are eligible for leave to donate bone marrow; at least one year are eligible for school activities.

Childbirth/Maternity: 6 weeks'.

Adoption: 6 weeks'.

Family Member's or Employee's Serious Health Condition: Can use accrued sick leave to care for sick or injured child.

School Activities: 16 hours' in 12-month period. Includes activities related to childcare, preschool or special education.

Other: Bone marrow donation, up to 40 hours paid leave per year.

Montana

Mont. Code Ann. §§ 49-2-310, 49-2-311

Employers Covered: All.

Eligible Employees: All.

Childbirth: "Reasonable leave of absence."

Pregnancy/Maternity: "Reasonable leave of absence."

Nebraska

Neb. Rev. Stat. § 48-234

Employers Covered: Employers that allow workers to take leave for the birth of a child.

Eligible Employees: All employees.

Adoption: Employee must be given same leave as allowed for childbirth to adopt a child under 9 years old or a special needs child under 19. Does not apply to stepparent or foster parent adoptions.

Nevada

Nev. Rev. Stat. Ann. §§ 392.490, 613.335

Employers Covered: All.

Eligible Employees: Parent, guardian or custodian of a child.

Childbirth: Same sick or disability leave policies that apply to other medical conditions must be extended to childbirth.

State Family and Medical Leave Laws (continued)

Pregnancy/Maternity: Same sick or disability leave policies that apply to other medical conditions must be extended to pregnancy or miscarriage.

School Activities: Employers may not fire or threaten to fire a parent, guardian or custodian for attending a school conference or responding to a child's emergency.

New Hampshire

N.H. Rev. Stat. Ann. § 354-A:7(VI)

Employers Covered: Employers with at least 6 employees.

Eligible Employees: All.

Childbirth: Temporary disability leave for childbirth or related medical condition.

Pregnancy/Maternity: Temporary disability leave for childbirth or related medical condition.

New Jersey

N.J. Stat. Ann. §§ 34:11B-1 to 34B:16

Employers Covered: Employers with at least 50 employees.

Eligible Employees: Employees who have worked for at least one year and at least 1,000 hours in previous 12 months.

Childbirth: 12 weeks' (or 24 weeks' reduced leave schedule) in any 24-month period.

Adoption: 12 weeks' (or 24 weeks' reduced leave schedule) in any 24-month period.

Pregnancy/Maternity: 12 weeks' (or 24 weeks' reduced leave schedule) in any 24-month period.

Family Member's or Employee's Serious Health Condition: Family member includes parents-in-law. Child includes legal ward. Parent includes someone with visitation rights.

New York

N.Y. Lab. Law §§ 201-c; 202-a

Employers Covered: Employers that allow workers to take leave for the birth of a child must allow adoption leave; employers with at least 20 employees at one site must allow leave to donate bone marrow.

Eligible Employees: All employees are eligible for adoption leave; employees who work at least 20 hours per week are eligible for leave to donate bone marrow.

Adoption: Employees must be given same leave as allowed for childbirth to adopt a child of preschool age or younger, or no older than 18 if disabled.

Other: Bone marrow donation, up to 24 hours of leave.

North Carolina

N.C. Gen. Stat. § 95-28.3

Employers Covered: All employers.

Eligible Employees: All employees.

School Activities: Parents and guardians of school-aged children must be given up to 4 hours of leave per year.

State Family and Medical Leave Laws (continued)

Oregon

Or. Rev. Stat. §§ 659A.150 and following; 659A.312; Or. Admin. R. §§ 839-009-0200 and following

Employers Covered: Employers of 25 or more employees (for at least 20 weeks for the year before or for the same year that leave is taken) must provide childbirth, adoption and serious health condition leave; all employers must allow leave to donate bone marrow.

Eligible Employees: Employees who have worked 25 or more hours per week for at least 180 days are eligible for childbirth, adoption and serious health condition leave; employees who work an average of 20 or more hours per week are eligible for leave to donate bone marrow.

Childbirth: 12 weeks' per year.

Adoption: 12 weeks' per year.

Pregnancy/Maternity: 12 weeks' per year.

Family Member's or Employee's Serious Health Condition: 12 weeks' per year. Family member includes parents-in-law, same-sex domestic partner and domestic partner's parent or child.

Other: In addition to 12 weeks' for sickness of family member or own serious health condition, employee may take 12 weeks' for illness, injury or condition related to pregnancy or childbirth. Parents who have taken 12 weeks maternity or adoption leave may take an additional 12 weeks' to care for sick child.

Bone marrow donation, up to 40 hours' or amount of accrued paid leave (whichever is less).

Pennsylvania

18 Pa. Cons. Stat. Ann. § 4957

Employers Covered: All.

Eligible Employees: All.

Other: Victims or witnesses of crimes, or family member of victim or witness, must be allowed time off and may not be penalized or threatened for attending court.

Rhode Island

R.I. Gen. Laws §§ 28-48-1 and following

Employers Covered: Employers with 50 or more employees.

Eligible Employees: Employees who have worked an average of 30 or more hours a week for at least 12 consecutive months.

Childbirth: Up to 13 weeks' in any two calendar years.

Adoption: For adoption of child up to 16 years old, up to 13 weeks' in any two calendar years.

Family Member's or Employee's Serious Health Condition: Up to 13 weeks' in any two calendar years. Family member includes parents-in-law.

State Family and Medical Leave Laws (continued)

South Carolina

S.C. Code Ann. § 44-43-80

Employers Covered: Employers with 20 or more workers at one site in South Carolina.

Eligible Employees: Employees who work an average of at least 20 hours per week.

Other: Bone marrow donation, up to 40 hours' paid leave per year.

Tennessee

Tenn. Code Ann. § 4-21-408

Employers Covered: Employers with at least 100 employees.

Eligible Employees: All female employees who have worked 12 consecutive months.

Childbirth: Up to four months of unpaid leave (includes nursing).

Pregnancy/Maternity: Up to four months of unpaid leave (includes nursing). Employee must give 3 months' notice unless a medical emergency requires the leave to begin sooner.

Other: Provisions must be included in employee handbook.

Vermont

Vt. Stat. Ann. tit. 21, §§ 471 and following

Employers Covered: Employers with at least 10 employees must provide parental leave for childbirth and adoption; with at least 15 employees must provide family medical leave to care for a seriously ill family member or to take a family member to medical appointments.

Eligible Employees: Employees who have worked an average of 30 or more hours per week for at least one year.

Childbirth: 12 weeks' per year.

Adoption: 12 weeks' per year to adopt a child age 16 or younger.

Family Member's or Employee's Serious Health Condition: 12 weeks' per year. Family member includes parents-in-law. Serious illness is one that poses imminent danger of death and requires inpatient care in a hospital or extended home care under the direction of a physician.

School Activities: Up to 4 hours of unpaid leave in a 30-day period (but not more than 24 hours' per year) to participate in child's school activities.

Other: Combined with school activities leave, up to 4 hours of unpaid leave in a 30-day period (but not more than 24 hours' per year) to take a family member to a medical, dental or professional well-care appointment or to respond to a family member's medical emergency.

Washington

Wash. Rev. Code Ann. §§ 49.78.010 and following; 49.12.265 and following; 49.12.350 to .370; Wash. Admin. Code 296-130-010 and following; 162-30-020

Employers Covered: All employers must provide family care leave. Em-

State Family and Medical Leave Laws (continued)

ployers with 8 or more employees must provide pregnancy and post partum disability leave. Employers with 100 or more employees must provide parental leave.

Eligible Employees: All employees are eligible for family care leave. Employees who have worked at least 35 hours per week for the previous year are eligible for parental leave.

Childbirth: Family care leave—employee may use any paid leave to care for spouse or child before, during and after childbirth. Pregnancy/post partum disability leave—employee entitled to same leave as for sickness or other temporary disability, in addition to 12 weeks' allowed under FMLA. Parental leave—12 weeks' during any 24-month period to care for a newborn or an adopted child under 6.

Adoption: Employers that allow workers to take leave for the birth of a child must provide the same leave to adoptive parents of children under the age of six.

Pregnancy/Maternity: Family care leave—employee may use any paid leave to care for spouse or child before, during and after childbirth. Pregnancy/post partum disability leave—same amount as for sickness or other temporary disability, in addition to 12 weeks' allowed under FMLA.

Family Member's or Employee's Serious Health Condition: Family member includes parents-in-law, grandparents and stepparents. 12 weeks' during any 24-month period to care for a terminally ill child under 18. All employees can use any paid leave to care for sick family member.

Wisconsin

Wis. Stat. Ann. § 103.10

Employers Covered: Employers of 50 or more employees in at least six of the preceding 12 months.

Eligible Employees: Employees who have worked at least one year and 1,000 hours in the preceding 12 months.

Childbirth: 6 weeks' per 12-month period.

Adoption: 6 weeks' per 12-month period.

Pregnancy/Maternity: 6 weeks' per 12-month period.

Family Member's or Employee's Serious Health Condition: 2 weeks' per 12-month period. (8 weeks' total leave per year when combined with maternity or adoption leave.)

Other: Employee may substitute accrued paid or unpaid leave.

Current as of February 2003

3.   Health and Safety Complaints

Federal law and the laws of most states prohibit employers from firing or disciplining a worker for complaining about violations of health and safety laws. The main federal law covering threats to workplace safety is the Occupational Safety and Health Act, or OSHA (29 U.S.C. §§651 to 678). OSHA broadly requires employers to provide a safe workplace—one that is free of dangers that could physically harm those who work there. The law also prevents employers from firing or disciplining a worker for filing an OSHA complaint. Many states also have their own OSHA laws and most protect workers who complain about health and safety violations.

These laws give workers the right to refuse to follow a workplace rule or order that causes a safety hazard and to refuse to work at all if the workplace is unsafe. Employers faced with these types of complaints should promptly investigate the allegedly unsafe condition (following the guidelines in Chapter 5) and take action to remedy the danger.

For more about the Occupational Safety and Health Act. You can find a comprehensive discussion of OSHA and other federal employment laws in *Federal Employment Laws: A Desk Reference* by attorneys Amy DelPo & Lisa Guerin (Nolo).

E.   Discrimination and Retaliation

Perhaps the most common complaint employees take to court is the claim that they were fired or disciplined for discriminatory reasons. These claims can be tough to combat. They are intensely personal and upsetting for all involved, which increases the danger that emotions rather than reason will hold sway. And there are strong legal prohibitions against discriminating in the workplace. Even when you are sure that you fired or disciplined a worker for a valid, non-discriminatory reason, there is always the chance that an administrative agency, judge or jury will disagree. Your first line of defense is to familiarize yourself with the laws that might be invoked against you so you can stay out of trouble in the first place.

State laws may be broader. Although the discussion below focuses on federal law, each state also has a set of laws governing employment discrimination. These laws are often broader than their federal counterparts, which means that you might be covered by your state's law even if you aren't covered by the corresponding federal law. It also means that your state's law might cover more classes of people than federal law. State laws regarding discrimination in employment are listed in the Appendix, along with the state agencies that enforce those laws.

1. Title VII

Since 1964, the federal Civil Rights Act (also known as Title VII, 42 U.S.C. §2000 and following) has prohibited discrimination in the workplace. Title VII is enforced by the federal Equal Employment Opportunity Commission (EEOC) and applies to all companies and labor unions with 15 or more employees. It also governs employment agencies, state and local governments and apprenticeship programs. Title VII does not apply to federal government employees or independent contractors.

Under Title VII, employers may not intentionally use race, skin color, gender, religion or national origin as the basis for workplace decisions, including promotion, pay, discipline and termination. Title VII covers every aspect of the employment relationship, from pre-hiring ads to working conditions, performance reviews, firing and post-employment references.

Anyone Can Be Discriminated Against

Some employers mistakenly believe that only minority or female workers can claim discrimination in the workplace. Quite the contrary, even white men can make a successful discrimination charge if they can prove that they were treated differently because of their race or gender. If you decide to terminate a few white men so you can hire more women and workers of color to make your workforce more diverse, you could end up facing a lawsuit for discrimination. Whenever you make an employment decision based on the skin color or gender of the worker, you risk a discrimination charge.

If a court finds that you have discriminated against an employee in violation of Title VII, it can order you to do any or all of the following:

- rehire, promote or reassign the employee to whatever job was lost because of discrimination
- pay any salary and benefits the employee lost as a result of being fired, demoted or forced to quit because of discrimination. This might include lost wages, pension contributions, medical benefits, overtime pay, bonuses, shift differential pay, vacation pay and/or participation in a company profit-sharing plan.
- pay damages to compensate for personal injuries caused by the discrimination, including medical expenses (these damages may also include damages for emotional distress and punitive damages, but the amount of these damages is limited to between $50,000 and $300,000, depending on how many employees you have)
- change your policies to stop the discrimination and prevent similar incidents in the future, and
- pay attorney's fees to an employee who proves that you discriminated.

For more about Title VII. You can find a comprehensive discussion of Title VII and other federal employment laws in *Federal Employment Laws: A Desk Reference* by attorneys Amy DelPo & Lisa Guerin (Nolo).

Guarding Against Discrimination Claims

Unfortunately, there is no sure fire way to guarantee that you will never face a claim of discrimination. However, there are some steps you can take to protect yourself from legal liability, including:

- **Keep careful records.** If you can prove that you fired a worker for legitimate business reasons, you will defeat a discrimination claim. This makes documentation very important. Keep written records of discipline, performance problems, counseling sessions or misconduct by the employee as they occur. If you are later faced with a charge of discrimination, you will be able to show that you had a sound basis for your decision.
- **Be fair and consistent.** If you can show that you treated the fired worker the same as your other employees, a discrimination claim will falter. Conversely, if a jury is convinced that you are harder on workers of a certain race or gender, you will be in trouble.
- **Examine your workplace demographics.** If the complaining worker is a distinct minority in your business, a lawsuit is more likely. For example, if firing a female employee will leave you with no women in a particular department or job category, the worker may argue that you fired her because you do not want women in that position. If you are in this situation, your reason for taking action must be especially strong. We suggest consulting a lawyer before taking any significant disciplinary measures.
- **Don't make biased comments.** It should go without saying that any statement you or your managers make about an employee will come back to haunt you if that employee is later fired or demoted. Even if you had a valid reason for your decision, any prejudicial statements that you made will make a jury believe that you were motivated by prejudice, not sound judgment.
- **Let the person who hired do the firing.** Recent court decisions demonstrate that an employer is less likely to be found guilty of discrimination if the same person hired and fired the worker. After all, it doesn't make sense that a manager who willingly hired a

Guarding Against Discrimination Claims (continued)

worker of a particular race or gender would later develop prejudice towards that group so strong that he is driven to fire the worker.

- **Examine your motives.** Unfortunately, some employers are driven by discriminatory motives but don't realize it. Perhaps you do hold certain workers to a higher standard or are more likely to suspect certain workers of misconduct. Do you act on the basis of personal beliefs about, for example, whether mothers should work or older workers are capable of learning new skills? Guard against letting these beliefs influence your employment decisions by applying your policies consistently to all workers, judging all workers according to objective, performance-based goals and having another person review your employment decisions.

Every state and many cities and counties also have laws prohibiting discrimination in employment. These prohibitions often echo federal laws in that they outlaw discrimination based on race, color, gender, age, national origin and religion. But some state and local laws go into more detail, sometimes creating distinct categories of protected workers that are not covered by federal law. In Louisiana, for example, it is illegal to discriminate on the basis of a worker's sickle cell trait. In Minnesota, it is illegal to discriminate against people who are collecting public assistance. And in Michigan, employees cannot be discriminated against on the basis of height or weight. Also, some state laws cover employers with fewer than 15 employees.

State laws prohibiting discrimination in employment, along with the agencies responsible for enforcing anti-discrimination laws in each state, are listed in the Appendix. You can read these state laws by using Nolo's Legal Research Center at www.nolo.com. You can research municipal anti-discrimination laws at the headquarters of your community's government, such as your local city hall or county courthouse.

Policies That Discriminate

The discrimination claims we discuss in this subsection all require that an employer *intend* to discriminate—that is, an employee can win a lawsuit by proving that the employer took a negative action because of the employee's race, sex or other protected characteristic.

However, there is another type of discrimination claim that does not require this intent. In these lawsuits, the worker does not claim that the employer intentionally discriminated. Instead, the worker argues that the employer had a workplace rule or job requirement that had the effect of screening out large numbers of employees of a particular race, sex or other protected characteristic. For example, a rule that required workers to be a certain height might result in excluding a disproportionate number of women. Or, an employer who required management employees to have a college degree might exclude more employees of certain races than other races. Discrimination claims that are based on the effect of an employer's actions are known as "disparate impact" claims.

The employer can defend against these claims by showing that the particular rule or requirement was job related and necessary to the business. For example, a strength requirement would certainly be allowed if the job required heavy lifting. The fact that more women than men would be ineligible for the job would not make the employer guilty of discrimination.

We do not cover these claims in detail because they rarely come up in the context of firing or disciplining a single employee—instead, these claims are often made about the hiring process, and they are usually brought on behalf of the entire excluded group. For a "problem employee" to make a disparate impact claim, she would have to argue that the rule the employer relied upon to fire or discipline her has a disproportionately negative impact on certain employees. These claims are sometimes made but they are rare.

2. Sexual Harassment

The same statutes that ban sex discrimination, discussed above, also prohibit sexual harassment. These laws are enforced by the EEOC at the federal level and by the agencies listed in the Appendix at the state level.

Sexual harassment is any unwelcome sexual advance or conduct on the job that creates an intimidating, hostile or offensive work environment. More simply put, sexual harassment is any offensive conduct related to an employee's gender that a reasonable woman or man should not have to endure at work.

Sexual harassment can take a wide variety of forms. An employee who has been led to believe he or she must sleep with the boss to keep a job has been sexually harassed, as has one whose coworkers regularly tell offensive, sex-related jokes. An employee who is pinched or fondled against his or her will by a coworker has been sexually harassed, as has one whose colleagues leer nonstop. An employee who is constantly belittled and referred to by sexist or demeaning names has been sexually harassed, as has one who is subject to repeated lewd or pornographic remarks.

An employer has a duty to take reasonable steps to stop harassment. The U.S. Supreme Court has recently clarified that an employer who has a strong written anti-harassment policy and a procedure for investigating harassment complaints can use these policies as a defense in a harassment lawsuit. If the employee fails to take advantage of these policies and does not report harassment, her claim is much weaker. However, if an employer only pays lip service to preventing harassment—by failing to distribute its policies or failing to investigate complaints, for example—the employee has a stronger claim. See Chapter 5, Section A for more details.

You can find valuable free information on harassment at the EEOC's website at http://www.eeoc.gov. In addition, lots of free information about sexual harassment is available in the Employment Section of Nolo's website at http://www.nolo.com.

3. Disability Discrimination

The Americans with Disabilities Act or ADA (42 U.S. Code § 12102 and following) is a federal law that prohibits discrimination against people with physical or mental disabilities. The ADA covers companies with 15 or more employees and applies broadly to private employers, employment agencies and labor organizations. Although state governments must follow the ADA, state employees cannot sue if their ADA rights are violated.

The ADA bans various practices throughout the employment process, such as asking applicants questions about their medical conditions or requiring pre-employment medical examinations. In the firing context, the ADA prohibits employers from terminating a worker because of his disability or because the worker is unable to perform her job without a reasonable accommodation.

a. What is a Disability?

The ADA protects only "qualified workers with disabilities." A qualified worker is a worker who can perform the essential functions of the job, with or without some form of accommodation (see below). For an impairment to be considered disabling, it must be long term. Temporary impairments, such as pregnancy or broken bones, are not covered.

A worker is legally disabled if he falls into one of these three categories:

- The worker has a physical or mental impairment that substantially limits a major life activity (such as the ability to walk, talk, see, hear, breathe, reason, work or take care of oneself), even when he is taking medications or using other measures (such as a prosthetic limb or hearing aid) to remedy the effects of the condition. Courts tend not to categorically characterize certain conditions as disabilities. Instead, they consider the effect of the particular condition on the particular employee.

> **EXAMPLE:** Ronelle has multiple sclerosis (MS), a disorder that can restrict several major life activities, including walking, seeing, concentrating and performing manual tasks. However, Ronelle's condition is currently relatively mild. Although she has to make sure to get enough rest and exercise, she has no difficulty doing daily tasks. Ronelle is not disabled under the ADA, although she may become disabled if her condition progresses.

> **EXAMPLE:** Brian has bipolar disorder, a mental condition associated most commonly with wide swings in mood, from euphoric highs to depressive lows. Although many people with bipolar disorder can control their illness through medications and careful monitoring, Brian's condition has proved resistant to treatment—he has required hospitalization on several occasions, when he was unable to care for himself, reason or sleep. Brian is disabled under the ADA.

- He has a record or history of such an impairment. In other words, you may not make employment decisions on the basis of your employee's past disability.

> **EXAMPLE:** Dan had a heart attack and bypass surgery. Since then, he has worked hard to improve his diet, get more exercise and lower his blood pressure. Although Dan had a few medical restrictions following his surgery, his doctor quickly released him from these restrictions and pronounced him fit to work. If his employer fires Dan, fearing that he may have

another heart attack and become unable to work, that
employer has discriminated against Dan based on his record
of disability.

- He is regarded by the employer—even incorrectly—as having
  such an impairment. You can't treat workers less favorably
  because you believe them to be disabled. An employee who
  brings a "regarded as" lawsuit does not claim to be disabled.
  Instead, he argues that the employer treated him as if he were
  disabled and thereby unable to do his job, when in fact he was
  perfectly capable of performing. These claims generally come
  up when the employee has some kind of impairment that doesn't
  rise to the level of a legal disability or when the employer acts
  on the basis of stereotypes about certain impairments rather
  than on the actual abilities of the employee.

  EXAMPLE: Diego walks with a slight limp from a childhood
  accident. Although his gait is slightly impaired and he is unable to run quickly, Diego is able to walk and stand for long
  periods of time. Diego was not promoted to the position of
  plant foreman because his employer believed he would be
  unable, because of his limp, to walk the plant floor and keep
  an eye on his workers. Diego has been discriminated against
  because he was regarded as disabled, even though his limp is
  not a disability under the ADA. Although he was capable of
  doing the job, his employer treated him as if he were unable to
  walk.

  EXAMPLE: Mihran became depressed when his marriage ended.
  He sought assistance from a therapist, who counseled him and
  referred him to a doctor for anti-depressant medication. Although
  Mihran has been down, his depression is relatively mild; he
  has not missed any work or suffered any work-related problems
  because of it. Mihran's boss fired Mihran upon learning of his

condition, believing that a person with a mental illness was more likely to miss work, act irrationally or even become violent in the workplace. Mihran's employer acted on the basis of stereotypes about mental illness rather than on Mihran's abilities and job performance. Mihran could sue his employer for regarding him as disabled.

b. Reasonable Accommodation

Accommodating a disabled worker means providing assistance or making changes in the job or workplace that will enable the worker to do her job. For example, an employer might lower the height of a desktop to accommodate a worker in a wheelchair, provide TDD telephone equipment for a worker whose hearing is impaired or provide a quiet, distraction-free workspace for a worker with Attention Deficit Disorder.

It is your employee's responsibility to inform you of her disability and request a reasonable accommodation—you are not legally required to guess at what might help the employee do her job. However, once an employee tells you that she is disabled, you must engage in what the law calls a "flexible interactive process"—essentially, a brainstorming dialogue with your worker to figure out what kinds of accommodations might be effective and practical. You are not required to give your worker the precise accommodation she requests, but you must work with your worker to come up with a reasonable solution.

However, an employer is not required to provide an accommodation if doing so would cause the business "undue hardship." When considering whether a requested accommodation involves undue hardship, courts will look at the cost of the accommodation, the size and financial resources of your business, the structure of your business and the effect the accommodation would have on your business.

> **EXAMPLE:** Doris has a spinal cord injury. She suffers from some paralysis and uses a wheelchair. Doris applies for a position as a secretary in a new accounting firm. Because she is physically

unable to type, Doris asks her employer to accommodate her disability by hiring another employee to act as her typist— Doris would dictate, and the typist would type. Because the company is new and is running on a tight budget, it cannot afford to hire two workers to do one job. The company proposes, instead, that Doris use voice recognition software, to which Doris agrees.

EXAMPLE: Erik has Attention Deficit Disorder. He is easily distracted and unable to concentrate on a project if there is any background noise or activity. Erik has worked in the financing department of a car dealership for a year; his employer accommodated his disability by allowing him to have his own office, with a door that closes, in the back of the dealership. Erik would like to become a salesman. He proposes that the dealership change its busy showroom floor to accommodate his disability by dimming the lights, disconnecting the public address and intercom systems and limiting the number of customers who may shop at any given time. This accommodation is unreasonable—the dealership will suffer significant losses in business and efficiency by making these changes.

c. Alcohol and Drugs

Alcohol and drug use pose special problems under the ADA. Employees who use (or have used) alcohol or drugs may be considered disabled under the law. However, an employer can require these employees to meet the same work standards—including not drinking or using drugs on the job—as non-disabled employees. Here are some guidelines to follow when dealing with these tricky issues:

- **Alcohol.** Alcoholism is a disability covered by the ADA. This means that an employer cannot fire or discipline a worker simply because he is an alcoholic. However, an employer can fire or discipline an alcoholic worker for failing to meet work-related performance and behavior standards imposed on all employees—even if the worker fails to meet these standards because of his drinking.

    EXAMPLE: Mark has worked as a secretary in Laura's law firm for five years. He has always received glowing performance evaluations, and he is well liked by the entire firm. One day, Laura discovers that Mark attends Alcoholics Anonymous meetings every Saturday night. She fires Mark because she does not want people with alcohol problems working for her. Her actions violate the ADA because she based her decision solely on Mark's status as an alcoholic and not on any job-related reason.

    EXAMPLE: Maria runs a small hometown newspaper. John, her city council reporter, periodically misses the city council meetings or shows up late. Maria has noticed that this happens when the meetings are held on Friday mornings. John's poker night is Thursday night, and he tends to drink to excess. Maria has used progressive discipline with John, giving him a verbal reminder and a written reprimand. She has even offered to give John time off to enter an alcohol treatment program. He refused the offer. Maria has told John that the next time he misses a city council meeting, she will terminate him. She will not be violating the ADA because she is firing him for failing to meet the same performance standards that she expects of all of her reporters and not because he has an alcohol problem.

- **Illegal Drug Use.** The ADA does not protect employees who currently use illegal drugs. These workers are not considered "disabled" within the meaning of the law and therefore don't have the right to be free from discrimination or to receive a reasonable accommodation. However, the ADA does cover workers who are no longer using drugs and have successfully completed (or are currently participating in) a supervised drug rehabilitation program.

- **Use of Legal Drugs:** If an employee is taking prescription medication or over-the-counter drugs to treat a disability, you may have a responsibility to accommodate that employee's use of drugs and the side effects that the drugs have on the employee. However, you do not have to accommodate legal drug use if you cannot find a reasonable accommodation.

> **EXAMPLE:** Elaine works as a seamstress at a textile plant. The plant operates on three shifts. Elaine must take a medication to treat depression. The medication makes her lethargic for a few hours after she wakes up in the morning. To accommodate the effects that the medication has on Elaine, the textile plant allows Elaine to work a mid-shift—from 11:00 in the morning to 7:00 at night.

> **EXAMPLE:** Myrtle drives a school bus for the Unified School District. She is diagnosed with depression and given medication for her condition. The medication makes her drowsy, and her doctor has told her that she cannot drive while taking the medication. Because driving is an essential function of Myrtle's job, the Unified School District has no choice but to terminate her.

Avoiding Disability Discrimination Claims

The ADA can be confusing to employers. It is a relatively new law, and courts are constantly redefining its terms and scope. As a result, even employers who want to comply are sometimes left unsure of precisely what the law requires. Because of this uncertainty, employers would be well-advised to consult a lawyer before firing or disciplining a person with a disability.

Here are a few general guidelines to help you avoid problems:

- **Talk to your disabled workers.** Once a worker tells you of her disability and need for an accommodation, ask what changes would help the worker do her job. If the worker proposes an unreasonable change, suggest some alternatives that might be effective. Have a discussion periodically to make sure things are going smoothly.

- **Respect your disabled workers' privacy.** The ADA requires you to keep certain medical information confidential. It is good policy to treat *all* medical information about workers on a "need to know" basis. A supervisor may need to know about the limitations a particular worker has, but coworkers might not. Similarly, you need to know how your worker's disability affects her job performance, but you do not need to know what impact it has had on her sex life or relationship with her family. Too much discussion of a disability can lead the disabled worker to feel stigmatized and resentful—a potent recipe for a lawsuit.

- **Make objective evaluations of performance.** Apply the same performance standards to all of your employees. This will help ensure that you do not let unconscious negative attitudes about disabled workers color your employment decisions.

- **Take steps to include disabled workers in all company activities.** Often, physically disabled employees are unintentionally left out of company activities—particularly those held offsite—because of accessibility problems. If you are planning a company picnic, holiday party, training session or team-building activity, make sure your disabled employees can attend and participate fully.

For additional information on the ADA, contact the following resources.

The U.S. Equal Employment Opportunity Commission ADA Helpline at 800-669-4000, or the U.S. Department of Justice ADA Information Line at 800-514-0301.

The U.S. government's website on disabilities at http://www.disability.gov.

Job Accommodation Network (JAN), 918 Chestnut Ridge Road, Suite 1, West Virginia University, P. O. Box 6080, Morgantown, WV 26506-6080; 800-232-9675 or 800-526-7234; Computer Bulletin Board: 800-342-5526.

You can also find a comprehensive discussion of the ADA and other federal employment laws in *Federal Employment Laws: A Desk Reference* by attorneys Amy DelPo & Lisa Guerin (Nolo).

4. Pregnancy Discrimination

The Pregnancy Discrimination Act or PDA (42 U.S.C. §2076) amended Title VII to prohibit employers from discriminating against an employee because of her pregnancy, childbirth or related medical condition. This means you must treat pregnant workers the same as your other workers, and you may not fire or demote an employee because she is pregnant. However, you do not have to treat pregnant workers any better than your other employees.

> **EXAMPLE:** Donna's doctor has told her that she must stay in bed during the last four months of her pregnancy. Donna has already used up most of her FMLA leave for the year (see Section D). If Donna's employer has a policy or practice of offering extended periods of leave to workers who are temporarily disabled, he must make the same opportunity available to Donna. However, if the employer does not allow any workers to take leave beyond what the FMLA requires, he does not have to give Donna the leave she requests—and he can fire her for missing four months of work, if he chooses.

Employers get into legal trouble under the PDA when they make unwarranted assumptions about pregnant employees' desire and ability to work. For example, some employers assume that pregnant women will not be able to work, and the employers fire them, force them to take leave or transfer them to lesser duties. This is illegal. It is also illegal to fire a pregnant woman when an employer assumes that she will not want to work once she has a child.

> **EXAMPLE:** Hermione works for a shipping company. She used to work in the office, doing administrative work and keeping track of orders. For the last year, she has worked loading packages into the company's trucks, a job with better pay and benefits. Hermione is pregnant. If her employer transfers her back to her office job because he assumes she will be unable to load packages, that could be an act of discrimination if Hermione is still able to do her job. However, if Hermione's doctor restricts her from all lifting during her pregnancy and Hermione requests the transfer, the same job move would be perfectly legal.

For more about the Pregnancy Discrimination Act. You can find a comprehensive discussion of the Pregnancy Discrimination Act, Title VII and other federal employment laws in *Federal Employment Laws: A Desk Reference* by attorneys Amy DelPo & Lisa Guerin (Nolo).

5.   Age Discrimination

The Age Discrimination in Employment Act or ADEA (29 U.S. Code §§621-34) makes it illegal for employers to discriminate against workers on the basis of age. However, the ADEA protects only those workers aged 40 or older. Younger workers are not covered by the law. The ADEA applies to private employers with more than 20 employees, employment agencies and labor organizations. Many states also prohibit age discrimination; some of these laws protect younger workers as well or offer wider protections. See the Appendix for more details on state anti-discrimination laws.

The ADEA has been amended several times since it was passed in 1967. Initially, the law protected only those workers between the ages of 40 and 70, leaving workers older than 70 to be fired or forced into mandatory retirement. Since 1986, the ADEA has protected all employees aged 40 or older, with a couple of exceptions:

- **Police officers and fire fighters:** The ADEA lets local governments establish a retirement age of 55 or older for these employees, as long as the employer provides a valid alternative test that employees can take to prove that they remain physically fit after reaching the retirement age.
- **High-level executives:** The ADEA allows private employers to force an employee into retirement if (1) the employee is 65 or older, (2) the employee has worked for at least the previous two years as a high-level executive or policy maker and (3) the employee is entitled to retirement pay of at least $44,000 per year from the employer. The employee must be eligible to start receiving this pay within 60 days of retirement, and the pay

cannot be "forfeitable"—if the retirement plan allows the company to stop payments or reduce the amount of pay to an amount below $44,000 per year because of the employee's actions (if the employee sues the company or goes to work for a competitor, for example), that pay is forfeitable and the exception doesn't apply.

Age-Related Comments Cause Problems for Employers—Including the EEOC

Most people are mindful that disparaging comments about race, gender or religion are strictly forbidden in the workplace. For some reason, however, managers seem to be less inhibited about making age-related remarks. Court decisions about age discrimination are replete with employer comments about old folks, old timers, gray hairs, senior moments and old dogs who cannot learn new tricks. While these statements alone may not be enough to prove discrimination, they will certainly upset older workers—not to mention a jury.

Apparently, even the EEOC—the federal government agency that enforces the Age Discrimination in Employment Act—is not immune. The EEOC has been sued for age discrimination by two senior trial attorneys who used to work in its Atlanta office. These lawyers claim that they were forced into early retirement after a top agency official insisted they be fired. That official allegedly said that older people lack motivation, and that the office would become more productive and efficient if younger workers replaced older workers.

For more about the Age Discrimination in Employment Act. You can find a comprehensive discussion of the ADEA and other federal employment laws in *Federal Employment Laws: A Desk Reference,* by attorneys Amy DelPo & Lisa Guerin (Nolo).

6.   Retaliation

All of the anti-discrimination laws discussed in this section prohibit employers from retaliating against employees for either filing a complaint of discrimination or cooperating in an investigation of a discrimination complaint. Many state laws contain a similar ban. These claims are especially dangerous to employers because juries seem particularly offended by retaliation and routinely deliver the highest damages awards for these claims.

To prove retaliation, an employee must show that she was punished because she made a good faith complaint or cooperated in an investigation. As a practical matter, an employee's retaliation claim will fail unless she can show that the person who punished her knew about the complaint. The greater the time interval between the complaint and the negative action, the more likely it is that a jury will conclude that the complaint and the discipline were not related.

The best way to avoid a retaliation claim is not to fire or discipline employees who have complained unless the reasons for your decision are well documented, persuasive and sound. If you are able to show that the reason for your action—be it performance problems, insubordination or misconduct—pre-dated the employee's complaint, your defense will be stronger. Avoid any reference to the employee's complaint in the disciplinary or termination process and related documents. If you refer to the employee as a "troublemaker," "squeaky wheel" or "complainer," a jury may decide that you punished the employee because of her complaints. ■

Chapter 3

Performance Evaluations

*A*s the saying goes, "An ounce of prevention is worth a pound of cure." In the workplace, the high cost of problem employees—in terms of money, time and lost productivity—means that the most effective management tactic of all is preventing the problems from happening in the first place. That's where performance evaluations fit into an overall strategy for dealing with problem employees. If you institute a sound performance evaluation process and use it consistently with all employees (not just the ones giving you trouble), you will prevent a lot of problems from ever cropping up.

Of course, no system is foolproof. Sooner or later—despite your best efforts—you are bound to have difficulties with an employee or two. When this happens, your performance evaluation system will be there as your first line of defense. Not only will it help you identify and deal with most problems before they rage out of control, it will also lay the groundwork for discipline and, if necessary, legally defensible termination in cases where the problems just won't go away. We'll explain more about the benefits of the system in Section A, below. Section B alerts you to the risks.

Structured communication between you and your employees is at the heart of a good evaluation system. We do not use the word "structured" lightly. For your evaluation system to be effective—both practically and legally—you must do much more than have freewheeling heart-to-heart chats with your employees. You must do each of the following:

- Work with employees to set job-related goals and standards for their performance. We'll show you how in Section C.
- Regularly observe and document their performance in relation to those goals and standards. Section D gives you more information.
- Meet with them periodically to discuss their performance and to redefine their goals, if necessary. Section E explains this process.
- Conduct a formal performance appraisal at the end of each year. Section F shows you how to conduct one.

⚠ Do not make the mistake of equating an evaluation system with feedback. Some employers think that as long as they periodically let employees know how they're doing—a pat on the back here, a shake of the finger there—they've got the evaluation angle covered. Far from it. Although casual feedback is part of an overall evaluation system, you must supplement it with thorough, planned and well-documented reviews.

A. The Benefits of an Evaluation System

Most successful employers share common goals and challenges. If you're like them, you'll want to tap into the potential of every employee. You know that your business will benefit if employees feel like part of a team and feel loyal to you, your business and their coworkers. You've learned that it's sound policy both to reward good employees and encourage them to strive for more and to help wayward employees get back on track. Now and then, you need to reduce the dead weight of problem employees who, despite all efforts, can't or won't do their jobs to your satisfaction.

An effective evaluation system will help you achieve these ends and more. Indeed, a performance evaluation system provides a solid foundation for all aspects of the employer/employee relationship, helping you to:

- examine each employee as an individual and evaluate that employee's strengths and weaknesses
- identify and reward good employees, thereby fostering loyalty and providing motivation to those employees to continue to work hard and to achieve
- stay on top of the needs of your workforce, which ensures employee retention and increases productivity and innovation, and
- identify and deal with problem employees, sometimes providing you with the opportunity to turn those employees into valuable,

productive workers, other times laying the groundwork for discipline and, if necessary, termination.

Your evaluation system has benefits that reach beyond the relationship between you and your employees. The system will help you avoid lawsuits (or cut them short) because it forces you to keep documents that will support sound employment decisions and defeat employee claims of illegal treatment. For example, faced with your file that contains written proof of your repeated attempts to correct a seriously wayward employee, a lawyer may think twice before agreeing to represent that employee in a wrongful termination lawsuit against you. Consistent evaluation also provides an objective framework by which you evaluate all of your employees, which lessens the ability of one employee to claim that you singled her out and discriminated against her.

B. The Risks of the System

One unhappy truth of employment law is that instituting a sound and effective performance evaluation system is a bit like tying your own hands. The more consistently you apply the system, the more likely a court is to find that you have limited your ability to terminate your employees at will. (See Chapter 2, Sections A and B for a thorough discussion of the employment-at-will doctrine.)

This concept is counter-intuitive and a bit nonsensical. After all, the law should *reward* employers who treat their employees fairly, give them the benefit of feedback and counseling and provide them with opportunities for growth and improvement, right? Well, we think so, but "the law"—that hodge-podge of rules created by lawmakers and judges—doesn't. The truth is that the more protections you give your employees and the better you treat them, the more likely it is that you are creating an implied contract with them—a contract that may interfere with your ability to terminate them at will. (See Chapter 2, Section B for a discussion of implied contracts.)

All of this being said, we believe that the benefits of a performance evaluation system far outweigh the risks. Indeed, the rewards you reap in terms of improved performance and productivity and morale will make you less likely to cling to that at-will power anyway. After all, you always have the right to fire an employee for just cause—and a sound performance evaluation system strengthens, rather than destroys, that right. (See Chapter 2, Section A for an explanation of termination for just cause.) Furthermore, firing based on just cause is always a safer bet legally than firing at will.

In addition, you can lessen the risks by following the guidelines in Chapter 2, Section B. Require your employees to sign a hiring letter that states that their employment is at will. Insert at-will clauses into your employee handbook, if you have one. Never make promises to your employees about the permanency of their employment. If you make it clear to your employees that you are an at-will employer—through your actions and through writings signed by the employees—a court is very unlikely to find that you have created an implied contract simply by instituting a performance evaluation system like the one suggested in this book.

C. Step 1: Create Job-Related Standards and Goals

Before you can accurately measure an employee's performance, you must identify what you'll measure that performance against. Evaluating without engaging in such a process is a bit trying to measure a room without a ruler. You can eyeball the space and make a guess—and you might come pretty close. But you won't know exactly how much space you've got until you take out your ruler, measuring tape or yardstick. So it goes with performance evaluations.

In this section, we offer a method that forces you and the employee to be very concrete and specific about what constitutes a job well done. We suggest using two measuring sticks:

- standards, which reflect how you want all employees in a specific job to perform, and
- goals, which reflect the ways in which both you and the employee would like to see the employee grow and improve over a specified time.

Standards and goals give you more than just a system by which you can measure performance. They also give employees a way to measure their own progress. As the year proceeds, employees can constantly refine and adjust their work to make sure they are on track. You may even find that employees will exceed your (and their) expectations.

An added side benefit of standards and goals is improved employee morale. Nobody likes to work in the dark, not knowing from day to day whether they are excelling or failing. Demystifying your expectations can improve morale by making employees feel happier and more secure.

1. What Are Job Standards?

Standards are simply a description of what you want an employee in a particular job to accomplish and how you want the work of a particular job to be performed. Every employee who holds a job should meet the same standards for that job. In other words, the standards reflect the features of the job, irrespective of the abilities or skills of the particular employee who fills it.

There are two kinds of standards: result standards and behavior standards.

- A result standard is a concrete description of a result that you expect from any employee who holds a particular job. For example, a result standard for newspaper reporters might be to write three stories a week; for proof readers, to miss no more than one error per story; for a salesperson, to make $10,000 in sales each quarter.

- A behavior standard is a description of how you want employees in a particular job to behave while getting the job done. Often, behavior standards reflect your values. For example, your company might place a high value on customer service. A behavior standard based on that value might be that a salesperson must answer all customer questions cheerfully and respectfully, even if it requires the patience of Job.

2.   Identifying Job Standards

To identify the standards you'd like to apply to a job, look at how the job fits within your business. What are the essential elements of the job? What is the purpose of the job? You might find some good answers in the job description you wrote when filling the position. (See Chapter 10 for more about hiring and job descriptions.) Historically, what have employees in that job been able to accomplish?

Employees themselves can be a valuable resource for pinning down standards for the jobs they hold. Consider talking to them first. Don't forget to talk to others in your business who interact with and depend upon the person who fills a particular job. For example, when defining a vehicle dispatcher's job, you might learn from the drivers that a key factor in making their jobs go smoothly is the dispatcher's ability to give clear and concise directions. The dispatcher himself might not have thought of that.

Only choose standards that are truly business related. This is important for both practical and legal reasons. It doesn't do you or the employee any good to force the employee to live up to a standard that doesn't help your business. For example, requiring chefs to be friendly to customers is a bit nonsensical if they don't have any contact with customers. Furthermore, the law will not look too kindly on you if you punish an employee for not living up to a standard that isn't business related. Remember the discussion of just cause from Chapter 2? Disciplining, demoting or terminating an employee for failing to meet a standard that is not business related does not constitute just cause.

Take particular care when identifying behavior standards. Employers often make the mistake of using vague language when describing them. For example, an employer might say it wants employees to "take initiative" or "self start." But what do these things really mean? To be useful, the standard should give the employee some insight into what you really expect. If you and the employee could disagree on what's expected, it will be difficult to decide whether the employee has fulfilled the standard.

To guard against vagueness, focus on what you want the employee to *do*, not on who you want the employee to *be*. For example, how would an employee act, or what would he do, if he were to "take initiative"? Would he create his own product ideas? Would he develop his own sales contacts? Would he implement his own ways of attracting business? As you can see, focusing on actions gives the employee insight into what you expect, while also giving you a concrete way to measure the employee's performance.

3. Communicating Job Standards

Tell an employee the standards of the job he holds as soon as you hire him. If the standards change—for example, you downsize your business and need to redistribute responsibilities—tell the employee about the requirements of his new position as soon as you can.

4.   What Are Job Goals?

Personal, developmental goals comprise the second measure by which you will evaluate your employees. These goals are ones that you tailor to each employee as an individual, depending on the employee's strengths and weaknesses. Goals are different from standards in that they will not be the same for all employees in the same job category.

5.   Choosing Job Goals

Together, you and the employee will choose personal goals based on:
- weak spots you see in the employee's overall performance that you'd like the employee to improve upon
- strengths and abilities that you'd like the employee to nurture and develop, and
- skills that the employee can learn that will help him improve his job performance.

For example, a store manager might do a great job overseeing the day-to-day operations of the store, but have weak writing skills that make her reports impossible to understand. A personal goal for her would be to take a writing course at a local community college. Or your best salesperson might decide that learning Spanish would help him serve your Spanish-speaking customers better. A personal goal for him would be to complete a conversational Spanish course by the end of the year.

Collaboration is the key to successful goal setting. If the employee helps to create the goals, chances are that he will genuinely want to meet them. Asking an employee to join you in setting personal goals has an added bonus: Many times, employees know their strengths and weaknesses better than you do—and they may even understand their job in ways that you haven't considered. You might be pleasantly surprised to hear their ideas on how they can do their jobs better.

When you and your employees discuss goals, be sure that, however laudable, the goal is firmly related to the employee's job. Otherwise, at best you'll be wasting time and energy—and spending company money on skills or interests that don't really help your company. At worst, you'll be courting legal trouble. To be legally safe in basing an employment decision on an employee's ability or inability to meet a goal, that goal must be job-related.

At some point, you should formally meet with each employee to discuss goals. For a new employee, schedule a goal-setting meeting in the first few months of her employment. That way, the employee will have goals to work toward during her first year with you. Also at that meeting, apprise the employee of the standards that you expect her meet (as explained in subsection 2, above) and give her some informal feedback on any work that she has already done for you. For current employees, the goal-setting meeting and the end-of-the-year evaluation are the same. (See Section F, below, for a discussion of the end-of-year evaluation.)

Before your meeting, encourage the employee to prepare for it by thinking about how he can improve his current abilities and whether there are skills he would like to acquire. Explain that you want to identify goals for him to strive for—both for the benefit of the company and for the employee's own career development. At the meeting, you and the employee will choose the employee's goals for the next year.

After you have identified the goals, find out what, if anything, the employee needs from you to meet the goals. For example, in order to teach more advanced classes, an instructor may need to attend a continuing education course, which you will need to pay for. Or if you expect a chef to handle a more complicated menu, you may need to provide more helpers in the kitchen.

Agree on a timeframe and set deadlines that *both* of you will meet.

6. Writing Standards and Goals

For standards and goals to be useful to you and the employee, you must write them down in a formal document. In the year-long process of evaluating and coaching, you and the employee will refer to this document to assess the employee's performance and keep the employee on track. At the end of the year, your evaluation of the employee will revolve around this document, for the essential question answered by your evaluation will be: Did the employee's performance live up to these standards and goals?

How you write these standards and goals will also be important should a judge or jury ever second-guess either your evaluation of the employee or any personnel decisions that you base on the evaluation. You should therefore write the standards and goals in such a way that anyone reading them would know what they mean.

Here are some tips for writing standards and goals:

- Be specific and avoid generalities. For example, don't say things such as "work harder" or "improve quality." Rather, say things such as "increase sales by 20 percent over last year."
- Focus on what you want the employee to do, not on who you want the employee to be. For instance, don't say "be a friendlier person." Instead, say "reduce customer and coworker complaints."
- Use concrete details, such as names, numbers and dates.
- Use active verbs, not passive verbs. This will underscore your expectation that the *employee,* not some disembodied force, is the one whom you expect to perform. For example, don't say "deadlines will be met." Rather, say "John will meet 75% of his deadlines this quarter."
- If it is a goal that you are writing, state the date by which you want the employee to achieve the goal.
- Be realistic—you don't want to ask so much of the employee that you doom him to failure or wear him out. On the other hand, you don't want to make things too simple. If you don't encourage him to reach beyond his current level, you and the employee might never tap into his potential.
- Unless it is obvious, describe how the standard or goal relates to the job.

Once you have written down standards for a job and goals for an employee, rank the entries within each category from most important to least important. This way, the employee will know how to allocate her time and energy. If the employee isn't able to make it through the entire list by the time the next review rolls around, at least the most important standards and goals will have been addressed.

EXAMPLES OF HOW TO PHRASE JOB STANDARDS:

Bad: Answer more customer service hotline calls.

Good: Answer a weekly average of 10 customer service hotline calls per shift to improve the productivity of the hotline desk.

Bad: Edit faster.

Good: Edit a weekly average of 120 inches of copy per shift.

Bad: Be self motivated.

Good: Generate and develop your own customer base. At least half of the new accounts in your area should be ones that you have developed yourself.

EXAMPLES OF HOW TO PHRASE PERSONAL GOALS:

Bad: Make budget meetings shorter.

Good: Jason will investigate ways to shorten budget meetings from the current average of one hour to an average of 30 minutes. Jason will accomplish this 30-minute reduction by June.

Bad: Andy will improve his plant transplant technique.

Good: Andy will observe senior nursery personnel when they perform difficult transplants. He will study *Western Gardening's* chapter on transplants and will take responsibility for at least ten transplants per week by April, 200X. By September, 200X, he will perform at least 15 transplants per week, of which at least 12 are successful.

D. Step 2: Observe and Document Employee Performance

An effective evaluation system requires ongoing observation and documentation of employee performance. This means that you must be mindful of your employees and their performance throughout the year and not just in the days preceding an evaluation meeting. When you observe something—either good or bad—record your observation in one form or another.

Most of your recordkeeping can be informal and brief—it doesn't have to eat up too much of your time. To the extent that it does take up time, however, the time will be well spent. When you formally evaluate an employee, you will have already done most of the work, having amassed a detailed record of the employee's performance for the entire year (or whatever time period it is that you are reviewing). Instead of racking your memory or spending time reconstructing events, you can simply review your notes.

Documenting employee performance as it happens also increases the fairness of your year-end summation. Indeed, having a year's worth of documentation ensures that your year-end evaluation will be based on the employee's entire performance, not just the most recent events or the ones that happen to stick out in your memory. And if you ever have to justify to a judge or jury any negative actions you have taken against an employee, you'll be more successful if you can point to a careful and complete paper trail.

Finally, your commitment to a regular documentation program can save you from unfair charges of retaliation. Suppose you begin documenting an employee's performance—but only after that employee files a discrimination complaint against you or complains about unsafe working conditions. Even if the employee's dismal performance would justify whatever negative action you might take, it will look like you are retaliating against the employee on account of the complaint. Retaliation is illegal—and it is rich fodder for a lawsuit. By contrast, if you had documented proof that the performance problems began well before the employee filed his complaint, you are in a good position to refute a retaliation claim. (See Chapter 2, Section E for more about retaliation.)

In this section, we describe a three-pronged approach to documenting employee performance. We suggest using:

- a performance log, which is your own record of what an employee has done—or not done—throughout the year
- kudos, which are notes that you give to an employee to recognize exceptional performance, and
- ticklers, which are notes that you give to an employee to alert him that he has veered off track.

Don't document after the fact. Employers who fail to regularly document their workers' performance may be tempted to do so later, when they are sued by a disciplined or terminated employee. It's perfectly OK to write down your impressions of how an employee performed, even when some time has passed since the incidents you're describing—but it's dishonest to attempt to pass off these writings as having been made earlier. If a judge learns of your attempts, your "documentation" will be disregarded and your credibility as a witness will drop.

1. Maintain a Performance Log

The best way to document an employee's performance is to keep a list of incidents involving the employee. We suggest that you keep a log— in a paper file, a computer file or a notebook—on each employee whom you supervise. When the employee does something noteworthy— either good or bad—take a moment to jot it down in the log.

Noteworthy actions are those that concern the way the employee performs his job or behaves in your company. Although the vast majority of entries will relate to the goals and standards that you and the employee have set, there may be times when the employee does something that is outside the context of those standards and goals. Those incidents can go into the log as well. Include comments, compliments or complaints that you receive about an employee—but ignore rumors and gossip.

Of course, you won't need to make entries for every day that the employee shows up for work. Only include those incidents that are out of the ordinary or contrary to your company rules or procedures. For example, you might note when a worker shows up late, makes an extra effort to meet a deadline or performs exceptionally well on a project.

⚠ Once you begin keeping track of negative incidents, you must be consistent. If there is no entry for a date that the employee worked, a judge or jury will assume that the employee performed at an acceptable level for that day—no better, no worse. If you add details to the log while testifying in court, you'll have a tough time explaining why you didn't follow your own system—and why your current rendition of events should be believed over the empty spot in your log.

Your log will serve as your memory when you sit down to formally evaluate the employee. Because it's a tool for you to use, the log is not part of the personnel file. You don't need to worry about the quality of your writing or the beauty of the presentation. You can even hand write it if you like.

Despite the informal nature of the log, however, there may come a time when other people will see it. If the employee sues your company, the log will be an important piece of evidence that the employee's lawyer will inspect. For this reason, don't put anything in the log that you would not want aired in a courtroom. Here are some guidelines to follow when writing log entries:

- Include concrete and specific details—dates, times, places, names, numbers and so on.
- Be accurate. Don't exaggerate.
- Don't use slurs or other inappropriate or derogatory terms.
- Don't use language that could be construed as discriminatory or illegally biased.
- Avoid personal attacks. Instead, concentrate on behavior, performance, conduct and productivity.
- Make each entry complete, so that anyone reading it could understand what happened.
- Stick to job-related incidents. Don't include entries about the employee's personal life or aspects of the employee that have nothing to do with the job.

If you decide to give an employee a kudos, ticker or some sort of progressive discipline (see Chapter 4), you should note that in your log as well. Don't bother including all of the details in the log, however; you will have already documented them in the kudos, etc.

Sample Confidential Performance Log

Employee Name: Paul Nolo

Employee Title: Copy editor

Date:	Incident:	Kudos/ Tickler/ Oral Reminder/ Written Warning?
1/2/20XX	Paul arrived 15 minutes late for work —did not call me to tell me that he would be late. His only excuse was that he overslept.	N/A
2/3/20XX	Paul worked all weekend to ensure that he met his deadline for the Single Mothers series. *[Note: Details saved for kudos.]*	Kudos given to Paul and placed in personnel file.
3/1/20XX	Paul was 45 minutes late for his shift. *[Note: Details saved for memo.]*	Informal verbal reminder given. See memo in personnel file.
4/4/20XX	Eleanor Lathom is a reporter who worked with Paul on the Single Mother series. She mentioned to me today that she thought Paul was really easy to work with and that she thought he really helped her to improve her writing. *[Note: Details saved for kudos.]*	Kudos given to Paul and placed in personnel file.
6/2/20XX	Today I noticed that Paul was having trouble editing a story on a jury verdict in a case that took place in Alameda County Superior Court. *[Note: Details saved for tickler.]*	Tickler given to Paul and placed in personnel file.

2. Give Real-Time Feedback

In addition to keeping a running log, periodically give the employee real-time feedback concerning his performance. Whenever an employee does something of note—either good or bad—you don't have to wait until an appraisal meeting or written performance evaluation to let him know about it. Indeed, you shouldn't wait. After all, one of the features of an effective performance evaluation system is ongoing feedback.

a. Give Kudos When Employees Do Well

When you can praise an employee for a job well done, you should do it. Not only will this raise employee morale and give employees incentive to do better, it will improve your overall relationship with your workforce. People are more likely to accept and act on criticism when you give it in the context of a fair and positive employment relationship.

We suggest giving employees notes called "kudos" to commend them when they do something especially good. Kudos do not have to be elaborate. They are simply small notes that you give to the employee (and copy to the employee's personnel file) that let the employee know that you notice and appreciate his efforts. You don't have to spend a lot of time writing them, but you should observe the same rules that we listed for writing log entries in Section D1, above.

Reserve kudos for noteworthy times. If you start to give kudos for every little thing that an employee does satisfactorily, you will undermine their value. When an employee does the job you hired him to do, his paycheck will be reward enough.

⚠️ **Never make promises in kudos, such as "you have bright future at this company" or "you're going to go far here."** If you do, a court might hold you to them. Simply thank the employee for doing well and leave it at that.

Sample Kudos

To: Paul Nolo

From: Amy Means

Date: 2/3/20XX

Thanks for working all weekend so that you could meet your deadline for getting the Single Mothers series to production. I know that the stories were longer than we thought they would be, so they required more editing time than we had anticipated.

You chose to work through the weekend without my asking you to. You did so with good cheer and with team spirit.

One of your goals for this year is to decrease the number of deadlines that you miss. Your efforts this weekend were a step on the path to achieving that goal.

The fact that you made your deadline means that workers in production will not have to work over-time to get the series into the paper. I want you to know that we really appreciate your effort.

b. Give Ticklers When Employees Veer Off Track

If an employee's performance begins to slip, there's no reason to wait until the formal evaluation meeting to let the employee know that you've noticed and are concerned. You can send a note—like a tip or a reminder —to inform the employee that he needs to adjust his performance. We suggest giving employees notes called "ticklers" for this purpose.

Use a tickler to coach and counsel an employee. If you want, you can even give advice in the tickler. Or you can simply remind an employee of a standard or a goal that he won't meet unless he changes his behavior. But don't overdo it—these are meant to be friendly reminders from a caring boss, not a constant barrage from someone who is watching like a hawk.

Ticklers are not the same as written reprimands, which you use for more serious performance and disciplinary problems. (See Chapter 4, Section B for more about written reprimands.) If the employee has done something seriously wrong, discipline is called for, not a tickler. (See Chapter 4 for more about progressive discipline.)

As is the case with kudos, ticklers do not need to be elaborate. You do not have to spend a lot of time writing them, but you should observe the same rules that we listed for writing log entries in subsection 1, above.

Sample Tickler

To: Paul Nolo

From: Amy Means

Date: 6/2/20XX

This afternoon, you edited a story by Joey James on a jury verdict in the McClandish case. You had some trouble editing the story because you lack knowledge of the court system. For example, you inserted an error in Joey's story by saying jury verdicts have to be unanimous. (FYI: A jury only needs a simple majority to reach a verdict in a civil case.)

You also had to take time to call Joey so that you could add a sentence explaining what a superior court is. This is something you should have been able to write on your own.

One of your personal goals for this year is to educate yourself on the court system so that you can edit legal stories more quickly and effectively. As you know, your next performance review is in October, so you only have four more months to achieve that goal.

If you are having trouble identifying a way to educate yourself about the court system, come see me and we will come up with something together. Otherwise, I will expect you to achieve this goal by the date of your performance review.

E. Step 3: Conduct Interim Meetings to Discuss Progress and Problems

After several months of observing the employee in relation to the standards and goals that you've set, you will be ready to discuss her progress and to make any necessary adjustments. We recommend you do this in a meeting six months after the employee's last formal evaluation, which takes place at the end of the employee's work year. (See Section E, below, for a discussion of formal evaluations.) In the case of a new employee, you would schedule this meeting six months after the employee started working for you. You can hold more than one interim meeting during the employee's work year if you like.

1. Preparing for the Interim Meeting

Prepare for the meeting by reviewing your documentation (logs, kudos and ticklers) and organizing your thoughts. Be ready to give the employee specific advice and feedback—not merely vague impressions. Take a few minutes to review the standards and goals that the two of you set for the year. Decide whether they were realistic—if they weren't, think about how to modify them.

You both will get more out of the meeting if the employee prepares for it, too. Give the employee a few days' notice of the date and explain what you want to discuss (the discussion topics are covered below). Ask the employee to spend some time thinking about how the past six months on the job have been—what's been good and what could be changed or improved.

2. Holding the Meeting

Begin your meeting by giving the employee your overall impressions of her performance over the past six months. Note what has been done well—and poorly. Share any compliments or complaints you've received from coworkers.

Next, review the standards and goals that the employee has for the year. If the standards and goals still seem realistic to you, discuss whether the employee is on track for meeting them. If not, why not and what can be done about it? If—after six months of working with them—the standards and goals now seem unrealistic, discuss how they should be modified.

Be sure that you give the employee an opportunity to present her thoughts about her performance. What does she think she has accomplished over the past six months? Does she need any help to perform better? Does she need assistance or advice from you? Has she encountered any obstacles that make it difficult for her to perform her job?

If the employee has done anything that might lead to disciplinary action, discuss that conduct now. Depending on the nature of the conduct and the progressive discipline system that you have in place, this meeting may also serve as an oral reminder to the employee. (See Chapter 4, Section B for more about oral reminders and progressive discipline.)

Your demeanor and attitude will make the difference between a meeting that is productive and one that is not. Always treat the employee with understanding and respect. Resist any temptation to become angry or emotional. Never engage in personal attacks.

3. After the Meeting

While the details of the conversation are still fresh in your mind, write a memo to the employee's personnel file with a summary of what you and the employee said. Include your views on the employee's performance at this interim point and describe what plans, if any, the two of you agreed to for the next work period—the time between this meeting and the next review.

F.   Step 4: Conduct an End-of-Year Evaluation

At the end of every year that an employee works in your company, you should formally evaluate the employee by writing a performance appraisal and meeting with the employee. You should also establish new goals for the employee for the coming year. Many employers choose the end of-the-year evaluation as a time for rewarding a good employee with a salary increase, promotion, bonus or the like.

1.   Draw Conclusions

The end-of-the year evaluation is the time for you to take a long hard look at the past year and consider the employee's performance, productivity and behavior. Gather and review all of the relevant documents and records. If you've followed the documentation advice in Section C, above, you've already done a lot of the work.

In addition to your own documentation, you should use other company records that reflect on the employee's performance and productivity. These records include objective data such as:

- sales records
- daily or weekly call records
- deadline reports
- output reports
- budget reports
- stock reports, and
- time records.

After you have gathered all of the relevant documents and records, review them as a whole.

2.   Write the Appraisal

When you have drawn your conclusions about the employee's performance, it's time to write the appraisal. Our performance evaluation, shown below, is one way to design an appraisal form. You can copy that form or create your own.

Our form is a series of sections—one for each standard and goal. We suggest that you address the standards first, in order of their importance; then turn to the goals, again in order of priority (you ranked both when setting them with the employee, as explained above in Section C). For each standard and goal, there are numbered sections for you to:

1. Give the priority of the standard or goal.
2. State the standard or goal.
3. Write your conclusion as to whether the employee met the standard or goal.
4. Give reasons that support your conclusion in Section 3.
5. Record the employee's comments.
6. Jot down notes of the meeting.
7. Rate the employee's performance on a numerical scale.

At the end of the form, there's a place for you to note any disciplinary problems that have arisen during the year.

Performance Evaluation

Employee: _____

Job Title: _____

Appraiser: _____

Job Title: _____

Appraisal Period: _____

Rating Scale:

   5 = The employee performed exceptionally well and exceeded the standard/goal.

   4 = The employee exceeded the standard/goal.

   3 = The employee met the standard/goal.

   2 = The employee did not meet the standard/goal but did make some progress toward it

   1 = The employee performed poorly and failed to meet the standard/goal by a significant margin.

N/A = For reasons beyond the employee's control, the standard/goal could not be met. (Explain the reasons.)

Standards (Ranked in order from most important to least important):

Standard Number _____:

State the Standard: _____

_____

Did the employee meet the standard? _____

_____

Appraiser's Comments: _____

_____

Employee's Comments: _____

_____

Performance Evaluation (continued)

Appraisal Meeting Notes: _____

_____

Rating: _____

Standard Number _____:

State the Standard: _____

_____

Did the employee meet the standard? _____

_____

Appraiser's Comments: _____

_____

Employee's Comments: _____

_____

Appraisal Meeting Notes: _____

_____

Rating: _____

Standard Number _____:

State the Standard: _____

_____

Did the employee meet the standard? _____

_____

Appraiser's Comments: _____

_____

Employee's Comments: _____

_____

Appraisal Meeting Notes: _____

_____

Rating: _____

Performance Evaluation (continued)

Goals (Ranked in order from most important to least important):

Goal Number _____:

State the Standard: _____

_____

Did the employee meet the standard? _____

_____

Appraiser's Comments: _____

_____

Employee's Comments: _____

_____

Appraisal Meeting Notes: _____

_____

Rating: _____

Goal Number _____:

State the Standard: _____

_____

Did the employee meet the standard? _____

_____

Appraiser's Comments: _____

_____

Employee's Comments: _____

_____

Appraisal Meeting Notes: _____

_____

Rating: _____

Summary of Any Disciplinary Problems: _____

_____

a.   The Narrative Evaluations

You'll give your narrative evaluation of the employee in Sections 3 and 4 on our form. In Section 3, state your conclusion as to how successfully the employee met the standard or goal you are writing about. Then, in Section 4, explain the basis for your conclusion, using specific details and examples. If there are disciplinary issues to address, you'll explain them at the end of the form.

Follow these guidelines when writing the narrative portions of the appraisal:

- Use concrete and specific details—dates, times, places, names and numbers. When you can, refer to specific documents.
- Use active voice, not passive voice. For example, avoid "Research has been consistently late" in favor of "Mary has been consistently late when turning in her research."

- Use a tone that is respectful toward the employee.
- Never use slurs, other inappropriate or derogatory terms or language that could be construed as discriminatory or illegally biased.
- Be accurate. Don't exaggerate or embellish.
- Make sure each entry is complete, so that anyone reading it could understand your conclusions and the basis for each.

b.   The Rating Portion

In addition to writing a narrative description of the employee's performance, you should rate the employee on an established scale—one that you use for all employees. On our form, the rating portion is Section 7.

Most employers use a five-point scale that rates an employee based on how well—or how poorly—the employee met the standard or goal being rated. It goes something like this:

5 = The employee performed exceptionally well and exceeded the standard/goal.

4 = The employee exceeded the standard/goal.

3 = The employee met the standard/goal.

2 = The employee did not meet the standard/goal but did make some progress toward it.

1 = The employee performed poorly and failed to meet the standard/goal by a significant margin.

N/A = For reasons beyond the employee's control, the standard/goal could not be met. (Explain the reasons.)

If you rate the employee anything other than a "3," take extra care to ensure that your narrative supports your rating.

Sample Performance Appraisal

Employee: Paul Nolo
Job Title: Copy editor

Appraiser: Amy Means
Job Title: Copy desk chief

Appraisal Period: 1/11/20XX through 1/11/20XX

Goal Number 1:

State the goal: Paul was to reduce the number of missed deadlines. We set a target for him of an average of one missed deadline or fewer per month during the appraisal period.

Did the employee meet the goal? Yes. As the attached Deadline Report shows, Paul missed an average of .078 deadlines per month during the appraisal period.

Appraiser's comments: Throughout this year, I personally observed Paul making a concerted effort to achieve this goal. He received no ticklers this year reminding him to talk less while at work (he received five last year), and he took fewer personal phone calls. As the attached Time Report shows, he reduced his editing average time per column inch from two minutes last year to one and a half minutes this year. One incident in particular illustrates Paul's desire to meet this goal. We assigned Paul to edit the Single Mother series, and we gave him 40 work hours to do it in. When Paul received the stories, however, he saw that they were much longer than we had budgeted for. Instead of using the length of the stories as an excuse for missing the deadline (which would have increased the company's production costs on the series), Paul—on his own initiative—

Sample Performance Appraisal (continued)

worked through the weekend to meet his deadline. I gave Paul a kudo for this effort. It is attached to this appraisal.

Employee's comments:

_____

_____

_____

_____

_____

_____

_____

Appraisal Meeting Notes:

_____

_____

_____

_____

_____

Rating: 5

3.   Schedule the Meeting and Give the Employee Time to Prepare

You and the employee will benefit more from the meeting if both of you are prepared. When you schedule the meeting, ask the employee to reflect on the past year before coming to the meeting. Suggest that she review her standards and goals and come to her own conclusions about whether she met them. Ask her to think about the areas in which she felt she excelled over the past year and the areas in which she needs improvement. Tell her that you and she will be setting her goals for the coming year, so she should come prepared with ideas of her own about what she wants to accomplish.

4.   Conduct the Evaluation Meeting

Once you have assessed the employee and written your performance appraisal, you are ready to actually meet with the employee and discuss your thoughts and conclusions.

Most likely, this meeting will be the most significant and important interaction that you have with the employee all year. Not only will you assess performance for the entire year, you'll give advice, offer coaching on ways to improve and set new goals for the coming year. In sum, you can think of this meeting as an interim meeting *plus*. (Interim meetings are explained above in Section E.)

In addition, this is your chance to get feedback from the employee. What does she think of her job? Of the workplace? Of your business as a whole? Has she encountered any obstacles within the workplace that make it difficult for her to do her job well? Does she see areas in which you or your managers could help employees improve their performance and productivity? Are there resources that employees need that you aren't giving them?

Some experts suggest meeting with the employee before writing the performance appraisal. They argue that you don't really have all the information you need for your review until you have spoken to the employee and heard what she has to say. We recommend instead that you write the appraisal first and then meet with the employee. The very act of writing the appraisal forces you to organize your thoughts and conclusions, which will make your meeting more meaningful than it would be if you rely on your memory and impressions. On our appraisal form, we leave room for both employee comments and meeting notes. If you learn something during the meeting that truly alters your conclusions, you can re-write the appraisal.

a.   The Time and Place for Your Review

Given the importance of the meeting, be sure to set aside sufficient time —at least an hour. Nothing feels more insulting to an employee than an appraisal given in a distracted rush. Similarly, pick the appropriate place for the meeting. If you can, avoid your office, which is your home turf. A conference room—neutral ground—is ideal. You can spread out your records and documents and sit next to each other—a subtle but important affirmation that the evaluation is meant to be a discussion, not a dressing-down.

b.   Conducting the Review

Using your written evaluation as a guide, discuss each standard and goal separately. Explain your conclusions about progress on every standard and goal. If you noticed ways in which the employee could have done something differently, tell her. Ask for her opinions and thoughts. Does she think she met the standard or goal? If she didn't, why not? Did she encounter any obstacles? Could she have used some assistance from you?

Be very sure that you give the employee time to talk and explain her point of view. If you don't listen to your employees, you undermine the evaluation process, which is meant to be collaborative, not a time to issue pronouncements. And you'll miss out on an opportunity to learn about your company from the people on the front lines, too.

Before the end of the meeting, ask the employee to write her comments on the form (Section 5 on our form). Discuss each comment with her as she works her way through each standard and goal. Alternatively, you can give the employee a blank copy of the evaluation form and have her complete the "employee comments" sections prior to the meeting. If you solicit employee comments this way, be sure that you fully discuss every comment written on the form. You'll need to staple the employee's evaluation form to the one you prepared, so that together the two documents make one completed form.

Evaluate an employee's performance, not his personality. It is a very rare employee who will change his personality for you, but he might change his actions and performance if you give him advice and coaching. Focusing on personality will make the evaluation process more tense and bitter than it should be—and increase the risk that an unhappy employee will take his displeasure to court.

Watch Out for Hidden Biases

Even the most well-intentioned employers sometimes fall prey to hidden biases. Ask yourself whether you:
- judge more favorably people who are similar to you or whom you like
- judge less favorably people who are different from you or whom you dislike
- can be overly influenced by a single positive or negative personality trait
- engage in stereotyping, or
- refuse to change your first impressions despite evidence to the contrary.

5. Establish New Goals

End the appraisal meeting by establishing new goals for the coming year. Save this task for the end of the meeting, after you have completely finished discussing the employee's performance over the past year. Although you will have come to the meeting prepared with ideas for goals, keep your mind open during the meeting. You may learn something from the employee during the meeting that will help you create better goals.

After you and the employee have discussed ideas for goals, craft them according to the guidelines in subsections B4 and B5, above.

When the meeting is over, write a memo to the employee's personnel file summarizing the meeting. ■

Chapter 4

Progressive Discipline

*M*otivating employees to improve behavior and productivity is every employer's goal. Managing employees with a system of progressive discipline is how to achieve it. The system uses a range of disciplinary measures, from mild to severe, to give problem employees the opportunity to improve. In cases where employees do not improve, the system sets the stage for fair, lawsuit-resistant discipline and termination.

The essence of progressive discipline is not threats or punishment—practices no one enjoys—but collaboration and fairness. As you hand out discipline, you communicate with your employees, listen to their views and invite them to participate in finding a resolution to the problem. By including employees in the process, progressive discipline invests employees in whatever strategy you two decide upon—thereby increasing the chances that the employees will actually follow the game plan and improve their behavior. In addition, by treating employees fairly and with respect, progressive discipline fosters feelings of loyalty among your workforce.

In this chapter, we examine progressive discipline with an eye toward the system's usefulness in managing problem employees and in protecting you from lawsuits. We also give you practical and concrete advice on how to create a progressive discipline policy in your business. Specifically, we examine:

- the ways in which progressive discipline can improve an employee's behavior (Section A)
- when and how to implement each step of the progressive discipline system (Section B)
- strategies for handing down effective discipline (Section C)
- how you can implement a progressive discipline system while still preserving the at-will status of your employees (Section D), and
- how to design a system for your workplace (including a sample written progressive discipline policy) (Section E).

⚠️ **If your employees are unionized, your progressive discipline policy may be limited—or superceded—by the terms of the collective bargaining agreement.** Read your collective bargaining agreement before implementing a progressive discipline policy. If you have doubts about whether your policy will conflict with its provisions, consult a labor attorney. (See Chapter 10 for information on hiring an attorney.)

A. Getting Results With Progressive Discipline

If you've had your share of problem employees—particularly those whom you've had to terminate—chances are you can say about some of them, "I saw it coming." But was the end really inevitable? For some, yes; but for others, you probably wish you could have corrected the problem and retained the employee. If you discipline your employees progressively, you'll intervene early on, giving everyone involved a chance to improve the situation before it's too late.

1. Match the Discipline to the Problem

In a progressive discipline system, employers use a range of disciplinary actions and counseling sessions to motivate employees to improve the problem they are having, whether an attitude problem, a performance problem, a productivity problem or something else. (See Chapter 1 for a discussion of common types of employee problems.)

The disciplinary measures range from mild to severe depending on the nature and frequency of the employee's misconduct. In other words, the system allows you to fit the discipline to the problem in the following way:

- you give informal oral reminders to employees who violate a minor rule for the first time
- you give written reprimands and counseling sessions to employees who violate a major rule for the first time or who fail to improve

after receiving one or more informal oral reminders or a previous written reprimand

- you suspend employees who commit a severe and egregious act of misconduct for the first time or who fail to improve after receiving one or more written reprimands, and

- you terminate employees when all of the above fails or when the behavior is extreme.

The best way to understand how progressive discipline works is to envision a ladder. The employee who commits a very minor offense—such as coming to work late one day—steps onto the first rung of the ladder. There, he receives merely a friendly reminder from you that you expect him to be on time and that his tardiness creates problems for his coworkers. If he continues to come to work late, he will gradually climb the ladder, receiving progressively more intense discipline and counseling from you. If his tardiness persists despite the discipline and counseling you give him, he will eventually reach the top of the ladder, where he will face termination.

Employees who commit more serious offenses step onto the disciplinary ladder at a higher point. For example, an employee who yells at a customer, even if it's the first time he's done such a thing, needs more than a friendly reminder from you. You might give him a formal written reprimand. From that point on, when it comes to how he treats customers, he will either climb the ladder, receiving progressively more serious treatment from you, or step down from the ladder and improve.

At some point, offenses will become so old that it's unfair to move the employee up to the next step. For example, if an employee was late for work once five years ago and received an oral reminder at that time, it probably isn't fair to give him a written reprimand for the next offense. After all, he's gone at least five years without being late—that's pretty good. The next time he's late, give him another oral reminder.

How About Good Old-Fashioned Punishment?

If all of this talk of respect and understanding sounds a bit much to you, you're not alone. Many an employer pursues a strictly punitive, no-tolerance policy with employees.

This approach does have some advantages. Punishment tends to result in a rapid change in employee behavior, and it's relatively cheap and easy. It doesn't require much thought or time on the part of the employer, managers or supervisors.

Punishment's disadvantages, however, far outweigh its advantages:

- Punishment creates feelings of fear and resentment in a workforce. These feelings erode employee loyalty and result in high turnover. Punishment encourages employees to get back at their employer through sabotage or theft.
- Punishment often gives employees the feeling that they are just cogs in the machinery. As a result, they stop taking pride in their jobs, don't take initiative and approach their jobs without enthusiasm.
- Punished employees become unwilling to talk frankly with employers about problems in the workplace. They'd rather hide mistakes and problems than deal with them.
- Punished employees often direct their energy at not being caught breaking rules rather than at improving their behavior.
- Punishment does not give employees the tools they need to improve their conduct. Employers end up losing employees who might have turned into good, productive workers if only they'd been given the chance.
- Often, punishment does not give employers the chance to create the paper trail they will need if a punished or terminated employee decides to sue.
- Punishment does not concern itself with fairness in the way that progressive discipline does. Most jurors are employees, not employers, and they do not look too kindly on employers who punish without giving employees a fair chance.

2.   Counsel, Listen and Plan

Although the term implies punishment, progressive discipline is really about communication and collaboration between employers and employees. On each rung of the progressive discipline ladder, you

- tell the employee what the problem is and what the consequences will be if he proceeds to the next rung
- give him a deadline by which he must show some improvement
- explain how the problem affects you, his coworkers and the business as a whole
- listen to the employee and consider what he has to say about why the problem is happening, and
- strategize with the employee to find a solution—which might include help from you or other members of management.

3.   Transform Problem Employees

A progressive discipline system can be particularly effective with employees who could be productive—and even exceptional—with just a little assistance from you. Think of these people as diamonds in the rough: They're not the best now, but with a little polishing they can become valuable assets to your business. You may have employees who fit the following descriptions.

a.   The Oblivious Employee

Some employees have no idea that they aren't measuring up. For them, the first rung of the progressive discipline ladder—a gentle reminder— is often all it takes to solve the problem.

> **EXAMPLE:** Eleanor works as a clerk in a hardware store, where she is supposed to be at work at 9:00 every morning. She began taking a dance class on Thursday nights and coming late to work on Fridays because she was tired from the night before. After three late Fridays

in a row, Eleanor's boss, Luke, stopped her as she arrived at 9:45. He gently reminded her that she is supposed to be at work at 9:00 every day. He explained that the mornings are quite busy, when contractors and workers pick up supplies for their day's work, and that it's important to assist them and get them checked-out as quickly as possible. If service is slow, these customers will go elsewhere. Eleanor felt terrible that she may have jeopardized the store's reputation for efficiency. She told Luke that she had no idea her tardiness was affecting the business and she thanked him for letting her know. She promised to be on time from now on.

b.   The Employee Who Needs a Little Help

Some employees could perform well if only one or two small things changed in their work environment. Often, the change is something as simple as physically moving an employee's work area, changing a work assignment or placing the employee under a different supervisor. Of course, the only way you can know how to deal with these problems is to talk to the employee. In a progressive discipline system, you ask for feedback from employees as to why the problems are occurring. And you strategize with them to find solutions.

> **EXAMPLE:** Diane has been a hard-working clerk in Paul's accounting office for more than ten years. Six months ago, Paul hired a new clerk named Betsy and put her desk right next to Diane's. Recently, Paul noticed that Diane's productivity has dropped. Paul used the first rung of the progressive discipline ladder and gently told Diane that she has not been doing as much work as he would like. During the counseling session, Diane confided in Paul that she and Betsy have become good friends and that they tend to talk a lot during work. She suggested that moving her desk away from Betsy's might help her resist talking so much during work hours. Paul agreed and Diane's productivity returned to its former high level.

c.   The Employee Who Needs a Little Push

Some employees intentionally break rules or perform below their abilities for as long as they can get away with it. Often, this type of employee will shape up as soon as he knows you are on to him—and as soon as he realizes that he could lose his job if he continues to misbehave or perform poorly. In a progressive discipline system, you give this employee the push he needs and inform him of the consequences of his actions. You also give him deadlines for improvement.

> **EXAMPLE:** Raymond works weekends at the local animal hospital, cleaning out the cages and exercising the animals. He decided to skip Saturdays because he assumed the vet, who works weekdays, would never know. One weekend, however, the vet came in on a Saturday and discovered that Raymond hadn't cleaned the cages. The vet called Raymond and reminded him that the cages must be cleaned both days. The next Saturday, the vet came in again and found uncleaned cages. This time, he gave Raymond a written reprimand, telling him that if he failed to clean the cages again, he would lose his job. Raymond realized that the vet was serious and decided that his job was more important than goofing off on Saturdays. The vet never had trouble with Raymond again.

4.   Reduce the Risk of Lawsuits

A good progressive discipline policy can protect you from lawsuits in more ways than one. As an initial matter, the system is fair to employees —and employees who have been treated fairly are less likely to sue.

For those employees who still might want to sue, however, your use of progressive discipline will be invaluable. That's because your file will include documentation of the employee's misconduct and your responses to it. As you will see below in Section B, every rung you climb on the progressive discipline ladder will be reflected in the employee's personnel file. The file will contain memos of the dates and circumstances of all instances of misconduct and every warning you or a manager or a supervisor gave to the employee, plus copies of all written warnings. If the employee claims that you acted unfairly or had an illegal motive for your employment decisions, all you have to do is point to the file. These layers of warnings, reprimands, chances and second chances often make it very difficult for a disgruntled employee to find a lawyer willing to take the case—because it's a sure loser.

B. Using Progressive Discipline in Your Workplace

As a problem employee's misconduct increases or becomes more severe, he climbs up the ladder, receiving more intense discipline from you as he progresses, eventually facing termination if he's unable to reform. "The Progressive Discipline Ladder," below, shows the various stages in detail.

In this section, we discuss each step of the progressive discipline ladder, including the types of misbehavior that warrant each step and how to deliver the discipline. Keep in mind that you will have to tailor our suggestions to fit your business. For example, only you can decide:

- How many oral warnings to give an employee before progressing to a written warning. For example, a business that will suffer significantly if employees are late, such as a chauffeur service, might want to allow only one oral reprimand before moving to a written reprimand for the second incident of tardiness.
- Which offenses are minor and which ones are major. For instance, an off-color joke in a children's ballet school has more serious repercussions than on a construction site.
- How many written reprimands to give an employee before resorting to suspension and termination.

All employees—whether unionized or not—are legally entitled to have a coworker with them at workplace meetings that might result in disciplinary action. If an employee asks to have someone with him during a disciplinary meeting, ask for the request in writing, so that he cannot later claim that you violated his privacy by allowing someone else to be present.

1. Step One: An Informal, Oral Notice

Telling your employee that you're displeased with his performance is usually the first step in a progressive discipline system. Your tone in giving this notice is up to you. It can be either gentle or sharp—but it must always be respectful.

Regardless of what tone you choose, never lose sight of the fact that this is an official conversation between you and the employee. Don't joke around when delivering the news and don't try to soften it. Make it clear that this is a disciplinary measure. Explain the consequences if the problem continues.

a. When Is This Step Appropriate?

An oral reprimand is appropriate for employees who have violated a minor work rule for the first time. Minor work rules commonly include prohibitions against tardiness, foul language and smoking.

This step is also appropriate when you are letting an employee know for the first time that you are displeased with his performance or productivity. If you have a performance evaluation system in your workplace, this step might take the form of a tickler. (See Chapter 3, Section C for a discussion of performance evaluations and ticklers.)

b. How to Deliver the Discipline

Talk to the employee in private, as soon as possible after the misconduct. In your conversation, be sure to cover:

- your expectations of the employee

- how the employee has failed to meet your expectations—usually either by breaking a work rule or by performing below your standards
- how this failure affects you, his coworkers and the company, and
- the consequences he will face if he breaks the rule again or continues to perform below expectations. (Usually, the consequences will be a written reprimand and counseling session as described in Step 2, below.)

Make it clear to the employee that you want to hear his side of the story, too. Some employees won't hesitate to give it to you; others will be reticent. You can draw the employee out by asking:

- why he broke the rule or is failing to perform up to your standards
- if and how he thinks that he can improve, and
- if he needs any assistance from you to improve.

During the meeting, you and the employee should develop a strategy and target date for improvement. If the employee needs assistance from you or additional training to improve, set deadlines for those things to happen.

⚠ **Don't give false praise in order to soften the blow or make yourself feel better about delivering discipline.** Insincere praise could come back to haunt you during a wrongful termination suit, when the employee's lawyer will ask you why, if the employee was so praiseworthy, you decided to terminate her (the implication will be that you really had an illegal motive for the firing, such as discrimination or retaliation). Say only what you mean and believe.

Document the misconduct and the oral notice. (See the sample "Memo Documenting Misconduct and Oral Notice," below.) There are several reasons for documenting an event. Memories fade, and your documentation will memorialize facts and impressions that you would otherwise forget as time passes. You might refer to this documentation in the future when you are making decisions about additional discipline,

The Progressive Discipline Ladder

Misconduct	Discipline
Step 1	
• Performing and/or producing below expectations, or • Violating a minor work rule.	• Informal oral notice.
Step 2	
• Continuing to perform and/or produce below expectations, despite one or two (or whichever number you deem appropriate) oral notices, or • Violating a minor work rule, second or third offense (or whichever number you deem appropriate), or • Violating a major work rule, first offense.	• First written reprimand, and • First counseling session between you and the employee.
Step 3	
• Continuing to perform and/or produce below expectations despite written reprimand(s), or • Continuing to violate a minor work rule or a major work rule despite written reprimand(s), or • First offense of serious and egregious misconduct.	• Suspension.
Step 4	
See Chapter 6	• Termination.

performance evaluations, raises, demotions or promotions. Also, your documentation might someday serve as evidence that the event actually took place and that it happened in the way that you say it happened.

The following are some guidelines for you to follow when documenting:

- Document the event as close to the time it happened as possible. When you write the documentation, you want your memory to be fresh. The more time that passes, the less reliable the document will be.
- Don't put anything in the document that you wouldn't want aired in a courtroom. This means no racial slurs, no comments about a person's age or gender or religion, no foul language (unless you are quoting the employee) and no jokes.
- Be detailed in describing what happened. Include dates, times, places and witness names.
- Be objective and not subjective. Don't insert opinions into your document. Stick to the facts. Use your senses: I saw, I heard, I smelled.
- Include a summary of everything the employee did and everything the employee said.
- Include a summary of everything that you did and everything that you said.
- Include a summary of witness names, including what they saw or did or told you.

Place a copy of the documentation in the employee's personnel file. Do not give a copy to the employee. After all, this is not a written reprimand.

Sample Memo Documenting Misconduct and Oral Notice

TO: Michael Smith's Personnel File

FROM: Dean Jordan, Shift Supervisor

DATE: March 10, 20XX

CC: Layne Wilson, Human Resources Manager
        John March, Plant Manager

This morning at 9:14 I saw Michael Smith enter the plant. He is supposed to be here at 9:00. As he walked past my office, I asked him to step inside, which he did.

I informed him that all day-shift workers are required to be at their posts by 9:00 every morning unless they call in with an excuse. I asked him if he was aware of that rule, and he said yes. I asked him if there was a reason that he was late this morning, and he told me: "No, I just overslept."

I told him that he should call in the next time he oversleeps, and he agreed to do so.

I reminded him that he is a valuable part of our operation and that his tardiness delays the work of everyone on the crew. I warned him that the next time he was tardy for work without calling in, he would receive a written reprimand that could affect his chances for advancement here. I told him I'd hate to see that happen because I think he is a skilled electrician.

Sample Memo (continued)

Attached is a copy of Mr. Smith's time card, showing that he punched in at 9:14 this morning.

Members of Mr. Smith's crew this morning could also verify his tardiness. Their names are Michael Wallace, Cherry Marks and Linus Jones.

Dean Jordan
Dean Jordan

Delivering Discipline You Don't Agree With

Unless you run the company, sooner or later you'll find yourself in the position of being told to impose discipline that you don't agree with. Or, if you're a supervisor, you may have to ask a manager to deliver discipline that you know she wouldn't impose if the decision were up to her.

Dissention within the ranks of management is a real problem that you should avoid at all costs. When employees realize that management is not united, some will take advantage by playing to the more lenient among you. Productivity and efficiency will usually suffer.

In addition, a reluctant disciplinarian might intentionally or unintentionally let on to the employee that she does not think the discipline is warranted or fair. At best, this will make the discipline less effective; at worst, it will encourage the employee to file a lawsuit.

There is no easy, comfortable solution to this predicament. If you're a reluctant manager, you can voice your concerns to your manager or supervisor, but not to the employee or his coworkers. If, after hearing your concerns, the company still wants you to issue the discipline, you must deliver it as if you agree with it. If you can't, you might give some thought about whether you should continue to work in a company that places you in positions you find untenable.

If you're a supervisor, listen to your manager's concerns and consider whether the disciplinary decision is still sound in light of them. If it is, explain to your manager why you think the discipline is merited—then tell her to impose it straightforwardly, without apologies.

2.   Step Two: Written Reprimand and Counseling Session

The second step of the progressive discipline ladder consists of two parts: a formal written reprimand that you give to the employee and place in the employee's file and a counseling session between you and the employee.

a.   When Is This Step Appropriate?

Employees reach this rung of the progressive discipline ladder when they:

- continue to violate a minor work rule after receiving one or more informal oral warnings
- fail to improve after receiving one or more oral warnings regarding poor performance or productivity, or
- break a major work rule for the first time.

Only you can decide what constitutes a major work rule. It must be something so important that it justifies skipping the oral notice and immediately giving the employee a written reprimand. Major work rules often involve safety on the job, building or plant security and confidentiality of trade secrets or other closely guarded information. Some employers also include unauthorized absences from work, falling asleep on the job and careless or unauthorized use of company property.

b.   How to Deliver the Reprimand

Giving a written reprimand to an employee is a serious step. The reprimand tells the employee that he needs to improve or he will be suspended or fired. It also allows you to record your view of what happened and why. This document will become an important piece of evidence if the employee sues you for wrongful termination.

As you can see, you have two very different audiences for the reprimand. One is the employee, who will already be familiar with you, your company and the specifics of what happened. The other potential audience is lawyers, judges and jurors—people who don't know you or the employee, the details of your workplace or the specifics of what happened. When writing the reprimand, try to keep both audiences in mind. In addition to the tips for documenting an oral notice for the file, explained in Section B, above, keep in mind the following points:

- Include the date, your name and the employee's name. List everyone to whom you plan to give a copy of the reprimand.
- Make it detailed enough so that the potential second audience—the one who doesn't know you, your workplace or the employee—can understand what the employee did and why he is being reprimanded.
- Use facts when describing the employee's misconduct. Answer the basic questions: who, what, when, where, why and how.
- Summarize any other disciplinary actions that have been taken against the employee for the same or similar misconduct.
- State specifically how you want the employee to improve and what consequences the employee will face if he doesn't improve.
- Attach any relevant documents.

Write the reprimand before meeting with the employee, but don't give it to him until you meet.

Sample Written Reprimand

TO: Michael Smith

FROM: Dean Jordan, Shift Supervisor

DATE: December 12, 20XX

RE: Formal Reprimand

This constitutes a formal written reprimand to you regarding your tardiness. You have the right to write a response to this reprimand. If you choose to do so, your response will be attached to this reprimand and placed in your personnel file.

Misconduct:

You arrived at work at 9:20 on December 11, 20XX. You did not call me, your shift supervisor, to say that you were going to be late.

Work Rule Violated:

Any day-shift worker who is going to be late must call his or her shift supervisor with an excuse prior to the beginning of the shift. This rule is listed in your employee handbook on page 21.

Summary of Past Misconduct:

You have been late without an excuse on two previous occasions—March 10, 20XX and June 13, 20XX. On each of those occasions I gave you oral warnings telling you that you must call your shift supervisor if you are going to be late. I explained to you that you hamper the work of your entire crew when you are late without calling in. In addition, when there is no phone call,

Sample Written Reprimand (continued)

I must assume that you won't show up at all and I must call a substitute. This costs the company money.

Also in those oral warnings, I told you that you would receive a written reprimand if you continued to come to work late without calling first with an excuse.

I have attached to this reprimand memos documenting those oral warnings.

Expected Improvement:

You are to always phone your shift supervisor if you are going to be late for work.

Consequences if You Fail To Improve:

If you are late to work again without phoning in, you will be suspended immediately. If, after your suspension, you are late to work again without phoning in, you will be terminated.

Dean Jordan

Dean Jordan, Shift Supervisor

cc: Layne Wilson, Human Resources Manager
    John March, Plant Supervisor

My signature below indicates that I have read this reprimand and that I have had the opportunity to review it with my supervisor. My signature does not indicate whether or not I agree with the contents of the reprimand.

_____   _____
Michael Smith   Date

Meet with the employee as soon after the misconduct as possible. Ask the employee to read the reprimand in your presence. Discuss each section of the memo, give the employee the chance to ask you any questions and remind him that he may write a response to the reprimand if he wants. If he chooses to write a response, give him a set amount of time to do it—a day or two is usually sufficient. (After all, you don't want this to drag on indefinitely.)

Don't forget that all employees—whether they are in a union or not —have the right to have a coworker present with them at meetings that might result in disciplinary action. If an employee asks to have some-one with him during a disciplinary meeting, ask for the request in writing, so that he cannot later claim that you violated his privacy by allowing some-one else to be present. Although the law is not clear on whether you must inform an employee of this right, your collective bargaining agreement might be. If you are disciplining a unionized employee, be sure to consult your agreement on this issue.

During the counseling session, try to formulate a strategy for im-provement. Set a deadline and ask if you can provide any assistance, such as added training or equipment. Remember, you're sending two messages here: that you want the employee to improve, but that you will suspend him—and even fire him—if he continues to engage in misconduct.

At the end of your meeting, ask the employee to sign the reprimand. Occasionally, an employee will refuse, even after you've pointed out that the signature only reflects the fact that the employee has read—and not necessarily agreed with—the reprimand. Such refusals are often grounded in a naïve belief that an unsigned reprimand is less damaging or the facts recited in it less true. Ask the employee why he won't sign and be sure to include his reasons in the memo of the meeting, which you'll write up for the file.

If, after talking about his reasons, the employee still refuses to sign, don't force him. Instead, ask him if he will write a sentence on the back of the memo stating that he refuses to sign it. If he won't do this, send a copy of the memo to his residence, return receipt requested. This way, the employee cannot claim later that he didn't receive the reprimand.

Document the meeting as soon as it is over. Place the documentation in the employee's personnel file.

3. Step Three: Suspension

Suspension—being sent off the job for period of time—is the third step of the progressive discipline process. It's a very serious measure with significant consequences for the employee.

a. When Is This Step Appropriate?

In most businesses, employees face suspension when they:

- continue to violate the same minor work rule or major work rule after one or more written reprimands
- fail to improve after one or more written reprimands regarding poor performance or productivity, or
- commit a serious and egregious act while at work.

An egregious act is behavior on the job that a reasonable employer would find highly dangerous or counterproductive. Egregious acts are often illegal—but not all illegal acts are egregious (for example, you wouldn't normally suspend an employee who gets a parking ticket while driving the company van). And some egregious acts are perfectly legal—such as leaving work for the entire day—yet deserving of suspension. All of the following are egregious acts that warrant immediate suspension:

- brandishing a weapon at work
- threatening the physical safety of a coworker, customer or manager
- using illegal drugs at work
- stealing from work

- sexually harassing a coworker, customer or manager, or
- harassing or taunting someone based on that person's race or religion or some other characteristic that is protected by law.

Often, behavior that warrants suspension can also support outright termination (see Chapter 6 for a discussion of how to determine when termination is the appropriate choice). If you aren't sure whether to suspend or terminate, you may want to suspend the employee while you think about it.

In some cases, you may not know for certain whether the employee actually engaged in the conduct. When this happens, you can suspend the employee while you conduct an investigation and discover the truth. (See Chapter 5 for a discussion of investigations.)

> **EXAMPLE:** Paul manages a sporting goods store where Jim and David work as clerks. One day, Jim tells him that David brought a gun into the store and threatened him with it. Jim tells Paul that David put the gun into his locker.
>
> Paul opens David's locker but doesn't find a gun. He confronts David, who tells him that it was Jim who had made threats with a gun. Paul doesn't know whom to believe, but he is certain that something serious happened. Paul suspends both Jim and David, tells them to go home immediately and not to return to work until notified—after he completes his investigation.

b.   Suspending With Pay or Without?

You can suspend hourly, non-exempt employees with or without pay. In most cases, you cannot suspend salaried, exempt employees without pay. From both a practical and legal standpoint, suspensions with pay are less risky and less inconvenient for employers—less risky because a paid employee is not as likely to sue as is one who isn't being paid, and less inconvenient because you don't have to interrupt your payroll system. Whatever system you choose, however, you must be consistent across classes of employees and across types of offenses. For example, if you suspend a rank-and-file worker without pay for sleeping on the job, then all suspensions of rank-and-file workers for sleeping on the job should be without pay. (See Chapter 5, Section C3 for more about suspension pending investigation.)

Some employers, who are willing to offer a second suspension before termination, will pay the employee for the first suspension but not for the second. Only you can decide if such a system will work for you and for your payroll or accounting department.

⚠️ **If you suspend an employee pending an investigation, we advise that you do so with pay.** If you decide to suspend without pay, however, and discover that the employee is innocent, pay him retroactively. To do otherwise is grossly unfair and only adds insult to injury—a lethal combination that often pushes an employee right to the courthouse steps.

c. Choosing the Length of the Suspension

The suspension should be long enough to have an impact on the employee. After all, the idea is to send a message—not to give your employee a vacation from work. When deciding the length of a suspension, follow these guidelines:

- If the absence of the suspended employee hinders your operations or makes remaining employees work harder or longer, consider a shorter rather than a longer suspension.
- If the suspension is without pay, it shouldn't be so long that it becomes overly burdensome for the suspended employee. Most employees cannot afford to go too many days without being paid.
- If you are suspending pending investigation of possible egregious conduct, the suspension may have to be open-ended. Suspend the employee until the investigation is completed.

d.   How to Suspend an Employee

Do not inform an employee of a suspension through an email or through a letter. Schedule a meeting with the employee and inform him there. What you say to the employee during the meeting depends on the reasons for the suspension, as explained below.

Follow the suggestions in subsections 1b and 2b, above, for conducting your suspension meeting. Because suspension is such a serious step, be extra careful that you are clear, respectful and open to hearing the employee's version of what happened. Remember that suspension has a greater impact on an employee's psyche and pocketbook than do oral warnings or written reprimands.

Before conducting the suspension meeting, think about what you will do if the employee fails to improve after returning from the suspension. Will you terminate the employee or suspend him a second time? If you won't offer a second suspension, be sure that you communicate this—and then stick to it. If you would consider a second suspension, don't box yourself into the possibility of a second chance by announcing it. Tell the employee that the consequences are another suspension *or* termination. As soon after the meeting as possible, document what was said.

Suspending an employee who has not improved after receiving one or more written reprimands. Begin by telling the employee that you are suspending him, why and for how long, and whether it's with or without pay. Refer to the oral notice (if there was one) and the written reprimand and counseling session. At this point, reiterate what was said and written at those earlier times—your expectations and the impact of the employee's misconduct on coworkers and the company. Tell the employee the ways in which he has failed to improve. If the employee failed to follow a plan for improvement, review that plan and ask why he hasn't followed it (or, if he has tried to follow it, why the strategy didn't work).

If you think the employee might still have a chance at turning himself around, strategize with the employee again about ways for him to improve. Be sure to ask the employee whether he needs any assistance from you to improve.

Finally, make it very clear to the employee what consequences he will face if he fails to improve after the suspension.

Suspending an employee while you investigate allegations against him and/or to determine whether you are going to terminate him. Begin by telling the employee that you're suspending him, why and for how long and whether it's with pay or without. If you are going to conduct an investigation, explain this to the employee. If you're not going to conduct an investigation but will use the time to determine whether you should terminate the employee, explain this while taking care not to raise false hopes about what will happen after the suspension.

Suspending an employee who has committed an egregious act of misconduct. Begin by telling the employee why you are suspending him and for how long. Tell the employee whether the suspension will be with or without pay. Explain to the employee why you consider his misconduct to be so egregious that it warrants a suspension. Explain to him how the misconduct affects his coworkers and the company. Make it very clear to the employee what consequences he will face if he commits the misconduct again. Most of the time, committing the same misconduct after a suspension results in termination.

e.   While an Employee is on Suspension

When you suspend an employee, do so completely. Don't call the employee on work-related matters or ask the employee to do any work at home. If the employee's absence creates a hardship for your business or other employees, make the length of the suspension as short as possible.

Other employees will need to know why their coworker is absent. We advise telling them that the employee is on suspension, but not disclosing the reason for the suspension. To do so might violate the employee's privacy and could leave you vulnerable to a defamation lawsuit.

Employers are sometimes tempted to tell remaining workers not to contact the suspended employee. Although you may order coworkers to not contact the employee about work-related matters, don't order them to refrain from personal contact with the suspended employee. Many coworkers are friends and have social contact outside of work. You would be treading on dangerous ground if you tried to control the off-work relationships among your employees.

While the employee is on suspension, turn off his email account and block his access to the company computer system. During the suspension meeting, get his keys to the building and his company credit card, which you'll keep until the suspension is over.

4.   Step Four: Termination

Although termination is generally viewed as the last step of the progressive discipline ladder, it is more than mere discipline. More often than not, termination occurs after all else has failed—coaching, counseling, training, discipline and even suspension have not turned this problem employee into a valuable and productive part of your team.

Sometimes, you will choose to terminate the employee after having spent months working with him, trying to get him to improve. Other times, you will choose to terminate the employee immediately after he commits an egregious act—such as physically assaulting someone at work. Regardless of the reason, the decision to terminate an employee is often the most difficult one an employer will make. There are numerous issues and pitfalls to consider. We guide you through this decision in Chapter 6.

C. Guidelines for Effective Discipline

No matter where your employees are on the progressive discipline ladder, how you hand down the discipline is as important as the discipline itself. Always follow these guidelines when administering progressive discipline.

1. Be Consistent

Discipline all offenses in the same manner. Always give the same discipline for a particular offense. Treat all employees the same. Absolutely do not play favorites.

Keep track of the discipline that you hand out—know what you have done from day to day, week to week and year to year. For example, if an offense deserved a written warning last year, than it deserves a written warning this year unless your workplace rules have changed.

There are important legal and practical reasons behind the need for consistency. From a legal standpoint, consistency helps to insulate you from lawsuits. If you treat some employees differently from others, you leave yourself vulnerable to accusations that you are discriminating or retaliating against those employees. On the other hand, if you hand down the same discipline to every employee who commits a particular offense, it will be difficult for an employee to argue that the real reason behind the discipline was his race or religion or some other protected characteristic. (See Chapter 2, Section E for a discussion of protected characteristics and discrimination in the workplace.)

From a practical standpoint, treating all employees the same will reinforce your image as a fair employer and increase employee loyalty. In addition, you can use consistent discipline to indirectly communicate your expectations to your employees. For example, if everyone who is ten minutes late for work gets a written reprimand, then you've made it clear to the entire workforce that you expect employees to be on time— that being on time is an important aspect of their jobs. It will also communicate to them that the consequence of tardiness is a written reprimand in their personnel files.

2. Think Before You Act

Only discipline when you are sure of the facts. Be sure the employee actually did something wrong before you discipline him. Don't rely on rumors or assumptions. Sometimes, you will need to conduct a thorough investigation before you act. (See Chapter 5 for more about investigations.) When you talk to the employee, listen to his side of the story and consider the possibility that he is telling the truth.

The damage to your workplace when you wrongly discipline an employee can be quite severe. An employee who feels that you are disciplining him for something he did not do will be resentful and angry. This will undermine the value of the progressive discipline system and will destroy your standing as a fair employer—in the mind of this particular employee and in the minds of his coworkers.

Worse yet, wrongly disciplining an employee leaves you vulnerable to a lawsuit. And if the employee gets his day in court, you won't look terribly sympathetic to the jury.

3. Be Reasonable

Before disciplining an employee for breaking a rule, make sure that the employee knew or should have known about the rule and the consequences for breaking it. Employees can find out about rules and consequences in a myriad of ways—for example, the employee handbook might list the rule and its consequences or you might have explained them to the employee through an informal reminder.

Similarly, before disciplining an employee for poor performance or poor productivity, make sure that the employee knew he was failing to meet your expectations and that he had the chance to improve but didn't. The best way to keep employees informed of your expectations of them

—and of whether they are exceeding those expectations or failing to meet them—is through regular performance evaluations. (See Chapter 3 for more about performance evaluations.)

4.   Communicate and Discipline Promptly

If weeks or months pass before you communicate your displeasure, you increase the chances that the employee will feel you are being arbitrary or unfair. If other employees have observed the misconduct and your lack of response, they'll conclude that you don't care or that the misbehavior carries no consequences.

Delay also leaves you vulnerable to claims of discrimination and retaliation. If you wait months before disciplining an employee, the employee may connect the discipline to something other than his misconduct. For example, if the employee requests that you accommodate a disability *after* his unrelated misbehavior but *before* you get around to disciplining him, he may claim that the discipline is really retaliation for his request for accommodation. If he takes his grievance to a lawyer, you may find yourself at the other end of a lawsuit.

> **EXAMPLE:** Marcie works as a secretary at a large law firm. For several months, Marcie's boss, Ed, noticed numerous errors in her work. He wanted to fire her but was in the middle of a big trial and decided to wait until it was over before dealing with the issue. Ed never told Marcie that he was unhappy with her work, and he didn't save any examples of her poor performance.
>
> In the meantime, Marcie complained to Ed that another attorney in the firm was sexually harassing her. At this point, Ed realized he had a big problem. He still wanted to terminate Marcie because of her poor work, but he realized that doing so now would leave him open to a charge of retaliation—Marcie might claim that the termination resulted from the harassment complaint, not the substandard work. Ed would have a hard time refuting her claim because he

hadn't documented her errors or given her any oral or written warnings that she was not meeting his expectations. Ed decided he couldn't risk a lawsuit and unhappily continued to put up with Marcie's poor work.

5.   Discipline in Private

Some employers think that disciplining employees in front of coworkers sends a message to the entire workforce or that disciplining employees in front of customers increases customer loyalty by making them feel that the employer cares about them. These theories are quite misguided —there are no circumstances in which it's appropriate to publicly reprimand or discipline an employee. Not only will the disciplined employee feel that you have poured salt on the wound, his coworkers will as well. Instead of being seen as a fair employer, you'll look like a bully.

Public discipline is also unwise from a legal standpoint. If the employee ever sues you, this public humiliation could become part of an emotional distress or defamation claim.

6.   Keep It Confidential

Your dealings with a disciplined employee should not go beyond the two of you if possible. Most of the time, there will be no reason for you to talk to others about the employee's misconduct or the discipline you have chosen. Tell the employee that you will operate this way.

However, you may learn about problems that you'll need to take up with others, particularly if the employee's misconduct involves additional employees. For example, if someone's physical safety is in danger or there's something illegal going on, you may need to reveal your source (or it may become obvious when you take action). If you're in this situation, make it clear to the employee that you will have to use the information he has given you, but will do so in as discreet a manner as possible.

Depending on how large your organization is, you may have to tell others in the company, such as human resources staff, the employee's supervisor and the office manager, about the employee's misconduct and what was said and done at a disciplinary meeting. When you speak to the employee, inform him that you will only tell people on a need-to-know basis.

Confidentiality is important for two main reasons. First, it will help foster trust between you and your employees. If they know they can trust you, they will be frank with you about their situation and about issues in your business. This frankness is essential if you are to turn a problem employee into a valuable employee. It is also necessary if you are to learn about problems among your workers and in your business. Your employees can be the most effective quality control tools you have—if they trust you and if you trust them.

Second, confidentiality is an important safeguard against lawsuits. If you reveal too much about an employee's troubles, you risk adding fuel to any legal fire the employee might have against you. This fuel can come in the form of an emotional distress or defamation claim.

7. Discipline Actions, Not Personalities

Your goal in disciplining employees should be to improve their conduct, not to tear down their character. If you focus on an employee's person-ality, you may cause the employee to become defensive or angry or hurt—or all three. An employee in that state of mind will fight you and rationalize his actions rather than improve his conduct. If, on the other hand, you focus on the misconduct and on a strategy for improvement, you preserve the employee's dignity in the face of your displeasure, and you might even empower the employee by allowing him to develop with you a strategy for improvement. In this way, you promote in the employee feelings of trust in you and feelings of worth within himself.

8.   Follow Your Policies

If you have a written progressive discipline policy, you must follow it—even when you don't want to. From an employee relations standpoint, your failure to follow your own policies will only make you look arbitrary and unfair. In addition, you might have trouble convincing employees to follow rules when you fail to do so. Set an example. Show your employees that you have as much respect for rules as you want them to have.

From a legal standpoint, failing to follow your own progressive discipline policy leaves you vulnerable to lawsuits. Even if you have a good reason for firing someone, you'll have trouble proving it if you didn't follow your own policy. In addition, some courts might view a written policy as a type of contract between you and your employees. If you fail to follow the policy, you could be liable to the employee for breach of contract.

9.   Do Not Discriminate

The law absolutely prohibits you from being harder on some employees than others because of race, religion, national origin and gender, among other things. (See Chapter 2, Section E for a discussion of protected classes and discrimination.) Treat all employees the same. Don't let prejudices enter into your decisions.

10. Document Everything

Many of the legal advantages of a progressive discipline system will be lost if you don't document the employee's misconduct and your responses to it. If the employee ever sues you, your ability to prove the employee's misconduct and your attempts to correct it will be necessary for you to prevail in the lawsuit.

D. Preserve the At-Will Status of Your Employees

Practicing progressive discipline in your workplace carries with it one very significant risk: It may actually limit your ability to terminate your employees at will. (See Chapter 2 for a discussion of the doctrine of employment at will.)

You may recall this issue from the discussion of performance evaluations in Chapter 3. It works the same way here. The more protections you give your employees and the better you treat them, the more likely it is that you are creating an implied contract with them—a contract that may interfere with your ability to terminate them at will. (See Chapter 2, Section B for a discussion of implied contracts.)

All of this being said, we believe that the benefits of a progressive discipline system far outweigh this risk. Indeed, the rewards you reap in terms of turning problem employees around or laying the groundwork to discipline and terminate employees who don't improve will make you less likely to cling to that at-will power anyway. After all, you always have the right to fire an employee for just cause—and a sound progressive discipline system strengthens, rather than destroys, that right. And firing based on just cause is always a safer bet legally than firing based on at-will status. (See Chapter 2 for an explanation of termination for just cause.)

In addition, you can reduce this risk by following the guidelines in Chapter 2, Section B. Require your employees to sign a hiring letter that indicates their employment is at will. Insert at-will clauses into your employee handbook, if you have one. Never make promises to your employees about the permanency of their employment, and use a written progressive discipline policy that contains at-will language. (See Section E, below.)

E.　A Sample Written Progressive Discipline Policy

In this section, we provide you with a sample written progressive discipline policy that you can distribute to your employees or place in your employee handbook. You may have to tailor it to meet your needs and those of your business and employees. Although this policy should minimize any risks involved in publishing a progressive discipline policy, we can't give you a 100 percent guarantee. (See Section D, above, for more about the risks of having a progressive discipline policy.)

If you choose to draft your own progressive discipline policy for publication, keep these guidelines in mind:

- When listing types of conduct that might result in disciplinary action, include a statement at the end that the list is not exhaustive and that the listed items are merely illustrations. This will give you the latitude you need to respond to problems that aren't on the list, and it will help prevent a claim that the policy constitutes a contract between you and the employees.
- Avoid tables that match disciplinary actions with types of misconduct.
- Eliminate any terms that might be misconstrued to guarantee continued employment to the employee. For example, avoid references to "permanent employment," "employment for life," "employee rights," "guarantees," "due process," the company "family," and "grounds" or "causes" for termination.
- Make it clear that you can deviate from the progressive discipline policy if you feel it is appropriate to do so.
- State that the policy does not change that fact that both you and the employee can terminate the employment relationship at any time, with or without cause, and with or without notice. In other words, reserve your right to terminate the employee at will.

Sample Progressive Discipline Policy

Any employee conduct that, in the opinion of the Company, interferes with or adversely affects our business is sufficient grounds for disciplinary action.

Disciplinary action can range from oral warnings to immediate discharge. Our general policy is to take disciplinary steps in the following order:

- oral warning(s)
- written reprimand(s)
- suspension, and
- termination.

However, we reserve the right to alter the order described above, to skip disciplinary steps, to eliminate disciplinary steps or to create new and/or additional disciplinary steps.

In choosing the appropriate disciplinary action, we may consider any number of the following things:

- the seriousness of your conduct
- your history of misconduct
- your employment record
- your length of employment with this company
- the strength of the evidence against you
- your ability to correct the conduct
- your attitude about the conduct
- actions we have taken for similar conduct by other employees
- how your conduct affects this company, its customers and your coworkers, and
- any other circumstances related to the nature of the misconduct, to your employment with this company and to the affect of the misconduct on the business of this company.

We will give those considerations whatever weight we deem appropriate. Depending on the circumstances, we may give some considerations more weight than other considerations—or no weight at all.

Sample Progressive Discipline Policy (continued)

Some conduct may result in immediate termination. Here are some examples:

- theft of company property
- excessive tardiness or absenteeism
- arguing or fighting with customers, coworkers, managers or supervisors
- brandishing a weapon at work
- threatening the physical safety of customers, coworkers, managers or supervisors
- physically or verbally assaulting someone at work
- any illegal conduct at work
- using or possessing alcohol or illegal drugs at work
- working under the influence of alcohol or illegal drugs
- failing to carry out reasonable job assignments
- insubordination
- making false statements on a job application
- violating company rules and regulations, and
- unlawful discrimination and harassment.

Of course, it is impossible to compile an exhaustive list of the types of conduct that will result in immediate termination. The ones listed above are merely illustrations.

You should remember that your employment is at the mutual consent of you and this company. This policy does not change this fact. This means that you or this company can terminate our employment relationship at will, at any time, with or without cause, and with or without advance notice.

As a result, this company reserves its right to terminate your employment at any time, for any lawful reason, including reasons not listed above. You also have the right to end your employment at any time.

Chapter 5

Complaints and Investigations

*E*mployers may learn of problems at work—and problem employees—in several ways. Customers, vendors or other third parties might complain of an employee's conduct, or a manager or supervisor might observe the behavior personally. Sometimes, you'll discover evidence of misconduct by an unknown employee—such as graffiti, vandalism, theft or anonymous harassing notes. However, the most common way employers find out about misconduct is through employee complaints.

When faced with the possibility of an incident of workplace wrong-doing, even one that you've witnessed firsthand, your first step must be to figure out what really happened. Did you see or hear all that was relevant? If your information comes via a complaint, is the complaint accurate? No matter what the source, how serious is the misconduct? How many employees are involved? Has poor management contributed to the problem? And, perhaps most important, what should the company do to remedy the situation?

A complete, impartial and timely investigation can answer all these questions. Indeed, a proper investigation is one of the most important tools an employer has for dealing with problem employees. An investigation will help an employer manage misconduct and assure workers that their complaints and concerns are taken seriously. The very existence of an investigation procedure will underline the importance of following workplace rules and even provides a valuable defense to a harassment, discrimination or wrongful termination lawsuit.

To get these benefits, however, an employer must investigate every incident and complaint of serious misconduct quickly and carefully. This chapter will explain how to do just that. Here we explain:

- when an investigation is necessary (Section A)
- how to create a complaint policy and procedure that will encourage employees to come forward with their concerns (Section B)
- how to plan the investigation (Section C)
- techniques for interviewing and gathering evidence (Sections D and E)

- how to investigate without invading your workers' privacy (Section F), and
- how to reach a decision and take action, if necessary (Section G).

⚠ If your workers are unionized, they may be entitled to special rights and procedures during the investigation. All of your workers have certain rights—the right to privacy (covered in Section F) and the right to bring a representative to investigatory interviews that might lead to discipline, for example. However, unions often negotiate additional rights for their members. If your workplace is unionized, check the collective bargaining agreement to find out if there are special procedures you must follow in your investigation.

A. When Is Investigation Necessary?

Not every infraction of workplace rules demands a full-scale investigation. Clearly, no investigation is necessary if everyone agrees on what happened, for example. If the person accused of misconduct admits the facts of the allegation, you can move on to deciding an appropriate way to resolve the problem.

1. Minor Problems

Sometimes, misconduct comes to your attention that simply doesn't warrant spending the time and energy a detailed investigation would require. If the problem is relatively minor, you might consider a scaled-down investigation. For example, if an employee is accused of misconduct that wouldn't merit a written warning or other serious disciplinary measure, such as being tardy a single time, playing a radio too loudly or keeping an untidy desk, you can probably dispense with the detective work. Simply speak to the person who complained and the accused employee, warn that the behavior needs to stop and document your conversations.

When deciding whether an investigation is warranted, think about how similar incidents or complaints have been handled in the past. If you have generally investigated similar problems, you should consider doing so now. If legal trouble later develops, you want to be able to show that you were fair and consistent with your employees and that you treated their complaints with equal concern.

2.   Incidents that Require More Attention

Often, however, there will be some dispute over the basic facts of an allegation of significant wrongdoing. The employee accused of wrong-doing may deny having said or done anything wrong, argue that the complaining employee misunderstood what was said, done or intended or even claim that the complaining employee is lying. Witnesses—if there are any—might lend support to the complaining employee, back up the accused employee or tell a different story altogether. Documents relating to the incident may be inconclusive or non-existent. In these situations, an investigation is necessary to get to the bottom of things.

3.   Allegations of Harassment

While every complaint of serious workplace misconduct should be investigated, complaints of harassment merit special attention. Having an investigation policy that you promptly implement when learning of a complaint can help you avoid liability in certain cases—even if the employee proves that she was harassed. Here are the rules.

When harassment has serious, job-related consequences for the employee—such as getting fired, demoted or reassigned—you will always be legally responsible for your managers' or supervisors' harassment, even if the employee never complained and you had no idea what was going on. You will also be responsible for harassment by a supervisor or manager that you know about, even if it doesn't result in a job-related action against the employee (for example, when a manager tells sexual jokes or repeatedly asks an employee out on dates in front of you). However, if a manager or supervisor is subjecting employees to this second type of harassment (harassment that doesn't result in a negative job action against the worker) and you *don't* know about it, you may be able to avoid liability by showing that

- you had a non-harassment policy
- you regularly conducted prompt, complete and impartial investigations of harassment complaints, and
- the harassed worker delayed in making a complaint or failed to complain at all.

The policy behind this defense is pretty simple: If an employer has an investigation policy that it follows faithfully, the employee has to use it if she wants the problem to stop. If an employee fails to make a complaint, you will have no notice of the problem and, therefore, no reason to investigate or take action. But in order to take advantage of this protection, you must make it clear to your employees that you will investigate their complaints fully and fairly. The only way to drive this point home is to investigate every harassment complaint and let everyone know that this is your policy. This way, no employee can argue that she failed to report harassment because she didn't think you would do anything about it. Remember that once you learn of a manager's or supervisor's harassment of this second type—through a complaint or in any other way—you are responsible for any harassment that continues after you find out. This gives you an incentive to investigate and take action quickly.

> **EXAMPLE:** Sheila's boss, Roger, has asked her out several times. She has turned him down each time, explaining that she has no romantic interest in him and would prefer to keep their relationship professional. Roger refuses to approve Sheila's scheduled raise because she will not go out with him. Roger's employer will be legally responsible for Roger's harassment, even if Sheila never complains about it, because she has been subjected to a negative job action.

EXAMPLE: Katherine works on the production line in an auto manufacturing plant. Her coworkers and supervisor, mostly men, constantly tell sexual jokes and refer to women in crude terms. The top executives in the company visit the plant. Although the men are on their best behavior during the official tour, several executives remain in the building after the tour to review paperwork and overhear the men's crude remarks. The company will be liable for any harassment Katherine suffers following the visit. Although she has not made a complaint, the company now knows about the problem and has a duty to take action.

EXAMPLE: Same as the second example, above, except the executives never visit the plant. If Katherine wants to hold the company responsible for her harassment, she will have to make a complaint to put the company on notice of the problem. If Katherine fails to make a complaint, she can hold the company responsible only if she can show that (1) the company had no policy against harassment, or (2) the company did not take complaints seriously, failed to investigate or failed to act on reported problems. For example, if Katherine can show that several women from her plant had complained in the last year and nothing had been done about the problem, the employer will be liable despite her failure to complain.

⚠️ **You can learn more about your liability for your managers' or supervisors' acts from the EEOC (the Equal Employment Opportunity Commission), the government agency responsible for enforcing laws against discrimination and harassment in the workplace.** Read their guidelines, entitled "EEOC Enforcement Guidance: Vicarious Employer Liability for Unlawful Harassment by Supervisors" (June 1999), available from the EEOC's website at www.eeoc.gov/docs/harassment.html.

⚠️ **Although many states have adopted the rules explained in this section (which come from federal law) and most others are likely to adopt them, there may be a few states that buck the trend.** States that have stronger anti-harassment laws might not follow the Supreme Court's lead. An employment lawyer can help you figure out if you need to take additional steps to protect yourself.

B. Complaint Policies and Procedures

If your company has an employee handbook, policies manual or any form of written guidelines for employees, you should have a written complaint and investigation policy. A written procedure for handling employee complaints will encourage employees to bring problems to your attention, giving you an opportunity to find out about—and resolve—workplace difficulties right away. Your managers and supervisors will know what their responsibilities are if they observe misconduct or receive a complaint. And, if you are later sued, you will be able to show the judge or jury that you took workplace complaints seriously.

Some employers feel intimidated at the thought of writing their own personnel policies. But a complaint policy needn't be filled with legalisms or technical language—indeed, the best policies aren't. The primary goal of having a policy is to encourage your employees to come forward with complaints. A short statement, written in simple, direct language, is the best way to accomplish this.

1. What Your Complaint Policy Should Include

Your policy should describe the conduct about which employees can complain, how to make a complaint and what will happen once a complaint is filed.

a. Prohibited Conduct

A complaint policy should spell out, in simple terms, what conduct will be investigated. If you already have a progressive discipline policy (see Chapter 4), sexual harassment policy or other written guidelines describing unacceptable workplace behavior, you can use those policies for guidance.

List the types of misconduct that you would like your employees to report (for example, harassment, discriminatory conduct or comments, violent behavior or threats of violence, safety violations and theft and/or misuse of company property). You can also include a catchall category at the end of your list, allowing employees to raise concerns about any type of behavior that makes them feel uncomfortable, upset or unsafe. Even if these other complaints do not rise to the level of serious workplace issues, your employees will feel that you are interested in their well-being—and you will be able to nip developing problems in the bud.

b. How to Make Complaints

Next, tell your workers how to make a formal complaint if they are victims of, or witnesses to, any of these prohibited behaviors. Encourage your employees to come forward by making the process as clear and easy to follow as possible.

You must first decide who will be responsible for taking complaints. Many employers ask workers to complain to their direct supervisor or manager. If you choose this option, make sure that employees can also complain to someone outside of their chain of command, such as a human resources manager, another supervisor or even the head of the company. If an employee is being harassed or mistreated by his or her own supervisor, this allows the worker to bypass that person and complain to someone else. Also, workers may simply feel more comfortable talking to someone who won't be responsible for evaluating their performance and making decisions on promotions, raises and assignments.

Make sure that the people whom you designate to take complaints are accessible to employees. For example, if your human resources department is located in a distant office or your local human resources manager works a part-time schedule, choose alternate complaint-takers who are local and available.

c.   Investigation

While you need not describe your investigative procedures in detail, your policy should assure your employees that serious complaints will be investigated quickly, completely and fairly.

d.   Retaliation

It is illegal to punish or otherwise take any negative action against an employee who comes forward with a good-faith complaint of harassment, discrimination, illegal conduct or health and safety violations. An employee complains in good faith if he honestly and reasonably believes the complaint to be true. Even if an investigation proves the employee wrong, you cannot take action against the complaining employee unless he acted maliciously or carelessly. For example, you could discipline an employee who falsely accused a coworker of wrongdoing out of spite.

The most obvious forms of retaliation are termination, discipline, demotion, pay cuts or threats of any of these actions. More subtle forms of retaliation may include changing the shift hours or work area of the accuser, changing the accuser's job responsibilities or reporting relationships and isolating the accuser by leaving her out of meetings and other office functions. Employers can get in trouble here. Although it often makes sense to change the work environment so that the accuser doesn't have to report to or work with the accused, those changes cannot come at the accuser's expense.

Your complaint policy should assure employees that no action will be taken against them for complaining in good faith. Promise to take all necessary steps to prevent and discourage retaliation. Assure employees that you will act quickly to prevent any further harassment or mistreatment while the investigation is pending. (Retaliation is covered in more detail in Chapter 2, Section E.)

e.   Managers' Responsibilities

Your managers and supervisors can help you ferret out serious workplace misconduct. Your policy should state that managers and supervisors are responsible for reporting violations of company rules and for taking and acting on complaints from your employees.

f.   Confidentiality

Your policy should make clear to your employees that you will keep the complaint confidential *to the extent possible*. You cannot reasonably promise not to tell anyone about the complaint because, after all, you may have to tell the alleged wrongdoer about the complaining employee's statements and perhaps interview witnesses about the incident. However, you should disclose information about a complaint strictly on a need-to-know basis. Employees will be more likely to come forward if you assure them that you will handle complaints as confidentially as you can.

g.   Corrective action

Your policy should state that you will conduct a prompt and thorough investigation after receiving a complaint. Make it clear that you will take immediate disciplinary action in the event that you decide that the accused employee violated company policy.

2.   A Sample Complaint Policy

Good complaint policies are remarkably consistent. Although they may differ on the details, all cover the same major points in straightforward, easy-to-understand language. Below you'll find a sample complaint policy that you can add to your employee handbook, distribute to your employees and/or post in your employee lounge or break room.

Our policy assumes that you have other written personnel policies spelling out standards of workplace behavior, including policies regarding workplace discrimination and harassment. If you have no such written policies, you will have to explicitly describe the types of conduct that are prohibited. The policy also assumes that you have a human resources department. For smaller employers, you can delete these references and replace them with the names of your designated complaint-takers.

Remember that the policy shown below is only a sample. You may have to adapt it to meet the needs of your employees and workplace and to conform to your other written policies. (For more information on workplace policies—including a list of topics you might want to cover in an employee handbook—see Chapter 10.)

Sample Company Complaint Policy

The Company is committed to providing a productive work environment free of threats to the health, safety and well-being of our workers, including but not limited to illegal harassment, discrimination, violations of health and safety rules and violence. The Company also has an open-door policy, by which employees are encouraged to report problems in the workplace to any management employee or member of the human resources staff for resolution.

Any employee who witnesses or is subjected to inappropriate conduct in the workplace may make a complaint to his or her supervisor, any other manager in the company or any member of the Human Resources Department. Any manager who receives a complaint, hears about or witnesses any inappropriate conduct is required to immediately notify the Human Resources manager. Inappropriate conduct includes any conduct prohibited by our company policies about harassment, discrimination, workplace violence, health and safety, drug and alcohol use and progressive discipline. In addition, we encourage employees to come forward with any workplace complaint, even if the subject of the complaint is not explicitly covered by our written policies.

Once a complaint has been made, the Human Resources Department will determine how to resolve the problem. For serious complaints alleging harassment, discrimination and other illegal conduct, the Human Resources Department will immediately conduct a complete and impartial investigation. All complaints shall be handled as confidentially as is possible. When the investigation is complete, the company will take corrective action, if appropriate.

The company will not engage in or allow retaliation against any employee who makes a good faith complaint. If you believe that you are being subjected to negative treatment because you made a complaint, report the conduct immediately to any member of the Human Resources Department.

C. Preparing to Investigate

Once you receive a complaint or otherwise learn of potential misconduct, it's time to plan your investigation. After you figure out who will investigate, the investigator will decide whom to interview and what documents to review. And you may have to take some immediate action, before the investigation is complete, to prevent further misconduct.

1. Choose the Investigator

Who investigates a complaint will depend on the size of your company, the identity of the complaining employee and accused employee and the severity of the charges. Regardless of workplace size or type of complaint, however, your investigator must meet two essential job requirements: experience and impartiality.

a. Experience

An experienced investigator who knows what to look for, how to find it and how to evaluate what she finds will likely do a better job for you than someone who hasn't tackled a job like this before. Your investigator should have some experience in investigating complaints or at least some education and training on the subject. For larger companies, someone from the human resources department is usually the best bet. Human resources personnel can get training and educational materials on investigation techniques through professional associations. Smaller companies that don't have a human resources staff may use other managerial employees to conduct the investigation, as long as they have experience in personnel matters.

There's another reason to choose experience over inexperience: If you're sued by the employee who complained or the employee who was disciplined, the investigation will become crucial evidence. You will rely on it to show that you reacted reasonably to the complaint, and the employee will argue that your investigation, or the conclusion you reached, was faulty. If the employee can show that your investigator had no experience or training in conducting investigations, a jury is more likely to second-guess the investigator's decisions, question the quality of the investigation and disregard the investigator's findings.

This doesn't mean that even the smallest company must have an experienced investigator on staff, however. You can supplement your designated investigators' lack of practical experience by giving them educational materials and sending them to seminars and trainings on investigative techniques. When faced with serious complaints, you might consider bringing in an outside investigator (see subsection c, below).

b.   Impartiality

The person who investigates must be perceived within the workplace—and particularly by the employees involved in the complaint—as fair and objective. Someone who supervises, or is supervised by, either the complaining employee or the accused employee should not perform the investigation. Similarly, you shouldn't choose an investigator who has known difficulties with any of the main players. Once you have come up with a potential investigator, ask the complaining employee if she believes that person can be fair and impartial. If she does not and her concerns seem reasonable, you would do best to choose someone else.

Of course, if you run a small business, you might not have a wide range of potential investigators to choose from. In that case, just make sure that whoever does the job doesn't have an axe to grind with either the complaining or the accused employee.

c.   Outside Investigators

In some situations, it makes good sense to ask for outside, professional help to investigate a complaint of workplace wrongdoing. Many law firms and private consulting agencies will investigate workplace complaints for a fee. You might consider bringing in outside help if:

- you receive more than one complaint about the same problem (for example, several women complain that a particular manager has harassed them)
- the accused is a high-ranking official in the business (such as the president or CEO)
- the complaining employee has publicized the complaint in the workplace or in the media
- the complaining employee has hired a lawyer, filed a lawsuit or filed charges with a government agency, such as the Equal Employment Opportunity Commission, the Occupational Safety and Health Administration, the Wage and Hour Division or a similar state agency
- the accusations are extreme (allegations of rape, assault or significant theft, for example), or
- for any reason, no one is available to investigate the complaint fairly and objectively.

You can get referrals for professional investigators through management newsletters, trade associations, other business contacts and even through listings in the yellow pages. For complaints of discrimination and harassment, your state's fair employment practices agency may be able to provide referrals. These agencies are listed in the Appendix.

Even if you hire an outside investigator, you are responsible for any actions you take based on the investigator's findings. Hiring an outside investigator doesn't insulate you from liability for the investigation or the decisions you make based on that investigation. You are ultimately responsible to your employees, even if you hire a professional to do some of the work for you. For this reason, work closely with the outside investigator to make sure that the investigator receives all relevant information, conducts a thorough and fair investigation and documents the findings. And although a professional investigator can certainly give you advice about what action to take when the investigation is through, you should always make the final decision.

Hiring an outsider instead of using your own staff may have one significant drawback (besides the expense). According to an opinion issued by the Federal Trade Commission (FTC), people who are in the business of investigating complaints and writing reports on their findings for others—the professional consultants and possibly even a law firm whom you might call in to conduct your investigation—must follow the technical requirements of the Fair Credit Reporting Act or FCRA (15 U.S.C. §1681) when investigating complaints of workplace misconduct. If the FCRA applies, employers who use an outside investigator must:

- tell the accused employee that an investigation will be conducted and a report made
- advise the employee of his right to be told the proposed scope of the investigation
- get the employee's written consent before obtaining the report, and
- give a copy of the report to the accused employee before taking any adverse action against the employee based on its contents, then wait "a reasonable period" before taking action.

These requirements raise a great many thorny questions for conscientious employers. For example, what should an employer do if the accused employee won't consent to the investigation? Will witnesses tell the whole truth if they know the accused employee will receive a copy of the report? What if the employer needs to take immediate action, rather than waiting a reasonable period after the report is prepared?

To date, every court to consider the issue has decided that employers do not have to comply with the FCRA. And, Congress is considering amending the law to make clear that it doesn't apply to workplace investigations. However, until the law is changed, there are no guarantees—if you're concerned about this issue, consider consulting a lawyer before hiring an outside investigator.

For more about the Fair Credit Reporting Act. You can find a comprehensive discussion of the FCRA and other federal employment laws in *Federal Employment Laws: A Desk Reference* by attorneys Amy DelPo & Lisa Guerin (Nolo).

d.   Specialized Investigators

Sometimes, the nature of the complaint should affect your choice of investigators. For example, some women might feel more comfortable discussing a sexual harassment complaint with a female investigator. Some larger companies try to make an investigator of each gender available for just this reason. Or, if the investigation involves technical issues (figuring out whether an employee sabotaged a computer program or violated safety rules in a production line, for example), you should try to choose an investigator—or make someone available to assist the investigator—who has enough background to understand the details.

2.   Starting the Investigation

Once you have chosen an investigator, that person can begin the investigation. For the balance of this discussion, we'll assume that you are the one doing the investigating, though of course it might just as well be your HR staff, another appropriate manager or an outside consultant. Start by reviewing relevant policies, gathering background information and possible evidence and planning whom to interview.

a.   Review Relevant Policies

You'll need to determine which company policies and guidelines might apply to the situation, such as a sexual harassment policy, workplace violence policy or noncompetition agreement. Even if you're familiar with your company rules and procedures, it's a good idea to review these policies before proceeding. If you're using an outside investigator, you must give her everything she needs to become familiar with your workplace and its standards and procedures.

b. Review and Gather Background Information and Evidence

The next steps involve reviewing background information and gathering evidence. You should:

- read the complaint and gather and read any relevant paperwork, such as personnel files, attendance records, emails, performance reviews or documentation of previous misconduct, and
- collect and review any physical evidence, such as a weapon, illegal drugs, graphic images or work materials.

These documents and items should be placed in a locked file cabinet or other safe place.

c. Plan the Interviews

At this point, you should have a fairly good idea of whom to talk to. In some cases, only the complaining employee and the accused employee should be interviewed—if the complaint is about an incident that no one else witnessed, heard or was told about later, for example. In other situations, there may be many potential witnesses. If the incident underlying the complaint occurred during a staff meeting or company social event, there may be dozens of potential witnesses. In these cases, the investigator should ask both the complaining and the accused employee which workers were most likely to have seen or heard the disputed event.

Regardless of the number of people who are eventually interviewed, the complaining employee should be interviewed first, followed generally by the accused employee and the witnesses. This order can be changed to accommodate employees' schedules, in the interests of moving as quickly as possible.

It's a good idea to have some idea of what questions to ask (interviewing is covered in more detail in Section D, below). The investigator need not script every interview question in advance. However, the interviewer should take a few notes on topics to cover in each interview.

As each witness is interviewed, the investigator can review and add to these notes.

3. Take Immediate Action if Necessary

Sometimes, an employer learns of possible misconduct so egregious that immediate steps must be taken, even before the investigation is complete. For example, if an employee complains that her supervisor has fondled her repeatedly, an employee threatens to bring a gun to work or a worker appears to be stealing company trade secrets to give to a competitor, you don't have the luxury of waiting until your investigation is complete. Some action must be taken at once to protect your employees and prevent further harm.

If the misconduct is between two employees (sexual harassment, insubordination or fighting, for example), an employer might choose to separate the employees until the investigation is finished. By assigning one or both to different shifts, or switching managers or job responsibilities temporarily, an employer can alleviate the immediate problem and investigate more thoroughly. Be careful not to take any action against the complaining employee that could be construed as retaliation, however. If one employee must move to a less desirable position temporarily, your best bet is to move the accused employee.

If one employee is accused of (or has been reported for) extreme misconduct, consider suspending that employee, with pay, while you investigate the situation. When you suspend the employee, explain the complaint or behavior at issue and ask to hear the accused employee's side of the story. Assure the employee that you will investigate the incident and reach a decision as quickly as possible.

4. Get Started Right Away

Once you have prepared to investigate, it's time to get started. Your first priority: Don't delay. Ideally, you should begin investigating within a day or two of receiving the complaint—and complete the investigation within a week or two, depending on how complicated the allegations are. Of course, there will be times when outside circumstances and conflicting schedules make immediate investigation tough. These brief, unavoidable delays can't be helped. However, if you drag your feet unnecessarily, you will send the message that you don't take the complaint seriously. And if the misconduct continues in the meantime, a court might find you responsible for failing to investigate and take care of the problem right away.

D. Conducting Interviews

Most investigations consist primarily of interviews with the employees involved, including the employee who complained, the employee accused of wrongdoing and any witnesses to the incident. More often than not, at the end of the investigation employers have to rely solely on statements from the main players and witnesses to get to the truth— and these statements may contradict each other. If the main participants in the incident flatly deny each other's claims, you will have to sort out who is telling the truth. How can you decide whose story is more credible in these "he said, she said" situations? The first step is to conduct interviews designed to elicit as much information as possible. The more facts an interviewer can draw out of each witness, the easier it will be to figure out what happened and why.

1. Tips on Conducting an Effective Interview

The general interviewing tips that follow will help you elicit information from any witness. (In this discussion, we'll assume that you are the one doing the interviewing, but these tips apply equally to an investigator from your HR department or any other person in management.) Following these tips, we'll suggest specific approaches and questions for interviewing the person who complained, the person accused and witnesses to the wrongdoing.

a.   Keep an Open Mind

Some employers who don't want to believe that misconduct or harassment is taking place right under their noses tend to make light of complaints of wrongdoing. Other employers jump to the opposite conclusion, assuming that an employee would not complain without good cause. Neither approach is sound. If you start your investigation believing you already know what happened, you will inevitably miss some important details. By contrast, if you keep an open mind until your investigation is complete, you will conduct more thorough interviews—and receive more candid answers to your questions.

> **EXAMPLES:**
> **Don't Ask:** Why did you pressure Maria to falsify her time card?
> **Ask:** Did you and Maria discuss her time card? What did each of you say?
>
> **Don't Ask:** What were you thinking, bringing a knife to work?
> **Ask:** Did you bring a knife to work last Thursday? Why?

b.   Ask Open-Ended Questions

Your goal when conducting an interview is to get your witness to talk about what happened as much as possible. The best way to accomplish this is to pose open-ended questions that ask the witness to describe what he or she heard, said or did and why. By contrast, if you ask questions that suggest the answer you want to hear or use questions that call only for a yes or no answer, you will be the one doing all the talking.

> **EXAMPLES:**
> **Don't Ask:** Did you arrive at three o'clock?

Ask: What time did you arrive?

Don't Ask: Did you hear John tell Ping that she would not be paid for her overtime work unless she agreed to have lunch with him?

Ask: Did you hear John and Ping talking last week? Tell me what you heard.

c.   Keep Your Opinions to Yourself

As your investigation progresses, you will inevitably start to develop some opinions about what really happened. Don't share these opinions with your witnesses. If your statements or the tone of your questions suggest that you have already reached a decision, witnesses will be less likely to speak freely with you. Some witnesses might be afraid of contradicting your version of events; others might feel there is no point in explaining what really happened if you have already made up your mind. In the worst case scenario, a witness might believe you are conducting an unfair or biased investigation—and challenge the outcome in court. Avoid these problems by keeping your conclusions to yourself until the investigation is complete.

EXAMPLES:

Don't Ask: I have already heard from several people that Sameh was absent from last week's mandatory meeting. Is that what you remember?

Ask: Was Sameh at last week's mandatory meeting?

Don't Ask: Can you confirm that LeShawn punched Darrell on the loading dock?

Ask: Did you see an incident between LeShawn and Darrell on the loading dock? Tell me what happened.

d.   Focus on What the Witness Knows

Many people have a difficult time distinguishing fact from opinion
when describing what they have seen or heard. For example, a witness
who tells you why another person did something is really giving you
her opinion of why that person acted as he did. By convincing your
witnesses to focus on the facts, you can prevent speculation and rumor
from affecting your decisions.

> **EXAMPLES:**
> **If you're told:** Lawrence has been out to get Graciela since the day
> he started working here. But I'm not surprised; he doesn't like
> reporting to a woman.
> **You might ask:** What have you seen or heard that leads you to
> believe Lawrence is out to get Graciela? Have you heard him
> raise his voice or treat her disrespectfully? Have you ever heard
> Lawrence say anything about reporting to a woman or make
> any disparaging comments about women in general?
>
> **If you're told:** Everyone knew that Evelyn was going to lose her
> temper and get violent. It was just a matter of time.
> **You might ask:** What do you mean by get violent? What did you see
> or hear Evelyn do? Why did you believe Evelyn was going to
> lose her temper? What did she say or do to make you think she
> was on edge? When you say everyone knew, do you mean that
> you discussed this with others? Who did you talk to about it,
> and what did they say?

e.   Find Out About Other Witnesses or Evidence

In order to conduct a complete investigation, you should ask every
person you interview whether they know of other witnesses or physical
evidence relating to the incident. If the witness is the accused or
complaining employee, ask if anyone else saw or heard the incidents in
question and whether they told anyone about the incident when it

happened. Find out if either took any notes about the problem or if any workplace documents—e-mails, memoranda or evaluations, for example—relate to the incident.

EXAMPLES:

If you're told: Robert and I had a loud argument by the elevators. He told me I wouldn't get my raise unless I agreed to withdraw my complaint that he had harassed me. Afterwards, I was so upset that I ran back to my office in tears.

You might ask: Was anyone else near the elevator when the argument took place? Did anyone hear what Robert said to you? Did you see anyone on your way back to your office? Did you talk to anyone about what happened?

If you're told: Julie sent me an e-mail apologizing for giving me a bad review. She said her manager made her change my performance appraisal after I filed a workers' compensation claim.

You might ask: Do you have a copy of Julie's e-mail to you? Did she copy anyone on the e-mail? Did you see the performance appraisal before it was changed? Do you have a copy?

f. Ask About Contradictions

Sometimes, one witness contradicts what another has said. The accused and complaining employees are perhaps most likely to contradict each other, but even uninvolved witnesses might give conflicting stories. The best way to get to the bottom of these disputes is to ask about them directly. Once you get down to specifics, you may find that everyone agrees on what happened, but not on whether it was appropriate.

If the witnesses continue to contradict each other even after you have pointed out the conflicts in their stories—if the accused flatly denies the complaining employee's statements, for example—ask each witness why the other might disagree.

EXAMPLES:

If you're told: I never sexually harassed anyone. I treat the women who work for me with respect.

You might ask: Tanya says that you touched her waist and hips several times while she was distributing paperwork to clients and says that you made a joke about her spending the night at her boyfriend's house. Did this happen? Could Tanya have misinterpreted something you said? Do you think Tanya might have made up these allegations? Why?

If you're told: Darnell told us at last week's morning meeting that anyone who complained about safety problems in the warehouse would get in trouble. He basically threatened to fire anyone who reported an accident.

You might ask: Two other people in your work group said that Darnell told all of you he had reported two safety violations to his manager. They said he encouraged you to bring any safety concerns to him, and he would bring them to the company's attention. Did this happen? Did you have a different conversation with Darnell? Why do you think these people remembered the meeting differently?

g. Keep It Confidential

Complaints can polarize a workplace. If workers side with either the complaining employee or the accused employee, the rumor mill will start working overtime. Worse, if too many details about the complaint get out, you may be accused of damaging the reputation of the alleged victim or alleged wrongdoer—and get slapped with a defamation lawsuit.

Avoid these problems by insisting on confidentiality and practicing it in your investigation. Tell each witness only those facts necessary to conduct a thorough interview. The accused employee deserves to hear the allegations against him or her, but peripheral witnesses don't need to know every detail. Caution each witness that the investigation is confidential and should not be discussed with coworkerss or friends. And set a good example by being discreet. Hold interviews in a private place where you won't be overheard (or off-site, if the workplace doesn't allow for privacy). Don't discuss the investigation at staff meetings or in the lunchroom and avoid gossip at all costs.

> **EXAMPLES:**
>
> **Don't Ask:** Sylvia says that Roger asked her out several times and tried to bring her back to his room after the holiday party. She also says that Roger made a lot of x-rated jokes in front of clients, and that you might have heard some of these jokes during the meeting with Pets-R-Us. Did you hear any of these jokes?
>
> **Ask:** Did you attend the pitch meeting with Pets-R-Us? Who else was there? Did Roger make any jokes during this meeting? Tell me what he said.
>
> **Don't Ask:** Fernando has complained that Martin gave him a bad performance evaluation, and he thinks it's because Martin dislikes Latinos. Fernando believes that he has made more successful cold calls than anyone else on his shift. He thought you might be able to confirm this, since you compile the monthly productivity reports. Is this true?
>
> **Ask:** Do you compile monthly productivity reports? Do these reports contain the cold call success rate for each salesperson? Do you recall who had the highest success rate for the afternoon shift? May I see a copy of these reports for the last year?

h.   Don't Retaliate

It is against the law to punish someone for making a complaint of harassment, discrimination, illegal conduct or unsafe working conditions. As explained above in Section B1, your commitment to following this law should be clearly reflected in your complaint policy—and this is the time to honor it. Assure every person you interview that you are eager to hear their side of the story and that they will not be retaliated against for coming forward.

EXAMPLES:

If you're told: I'm having some problems working with Maurice, but I don't want to cause trouble.

You might ask: I'm glad you brought this issue to my attention. Coming forward with a problem does not cause trouble. We would really be in trouble if you kept this information to yourself, and your team's work suffered as a result. No one in the company will retaliate against you or take any action against you for coming forward. Now, what has been happening with Maurice?

If you're told: I've seen some pretty heated conversations between Maria and Simone, but it's really none of my business. I don't want Simone to think that I'm not a team player.

You might ask: I need to find out what's been going on between Maria and Simone, and anything you can tell me about those conversations will help me get to the bottom of this. If there are problems in your work group, everyone's work suffers and everyone feels uncomfortable. No one will be allowed to retaliate against you or treat you poorly because you spoke to me. Both Maria and Simone have been told that these issues would be investigated. I've warned both of them not to retaliate, and I'll make sure that they don't. What have your heard Maria and Simone say to each other?

i.   Respect Your Workers' Privacy

Keep your questions focused on work-related issues, not on your workers' private lives. Although the law differs from state to state, employers are generally on shaky legal ground if they ask about—or make employment decisions based on—a worker's conduct off the job. Instead, limit your questions to the worker's performance or conduct on the job. Even if a worker's problems on the job are related to personal concerns, you are free to discipline or counsel the worker as you see fit as long as you stick to job-related criteria.

Sometimes, a worker will volunteer personal information during an interview. For example, a worker might tell you that particular problems in his private life are affecting his work demeanor and performance. If this happens, you can feel free to offer a sympathetic ear as long as the worker feels comfortable confiding in you—and try to come up with workplace solutions that might help. However, you should not ask probing questions about an employee's life outside the workplace, even if the employee raises the issue. The deeper you delve into personal issues, the greater your risk of invading the worker's privacy. (For more information on your workers' privacy rights, see Section F.)

> **EXAMPLE:** Although Jack has always been a considerate and competent employee, he has been acting erratically at work for a couple of months. He has seemed tired and short-tempered, and his attention to detail has really suffered. Last week, Janice complained that Jack had neglected to follow safety procedures while loading packages and that his carelessness caused her a minor injury. When Janice spoke to Jack about it, he cursed at her and stormed away. The drastic change in Jack's behavior leads his employer to believe that something in Jack's private life might be affecting his work.
>
> **Don't Ask:** Is everything OK between you and your boyfriend?
> **Ask:** Your coworkers and I have all noticed that you just haven't seemed yourself lately. You've been short-tempered and careless, and your performance has really suffered. Why has this happened?
>
> After the employer asks why Jack is having work problems, Jack says that he is having a rough time in his personal life right now and would prefer not to talk about it.

Don't Ask: But if your personal life is affecting your work, I need to know what is going on. Did you and your boyfriend break up? Are you having health problems?

Ask: I understand that you want to keep your personal life private, and I respect that. If there is anything that I can do to help, please let me know. But we do need to talk about your work performance. Let's talk about how you can get yourself back on track here.

j. Ask to be Contacted With New or Additional Information

Close every interview by thanking the witness and asking her to contact you if anything else comes to mind. You'll be surprised by how frequently a witness will return with follow-up information. For example, a witness might see or hear pertinent new information or remember a significant detail only after mulling over the interview later. And some witnesses might hold back important information during the interview, trying to decide whether to come clean. If you offer every witness an opportunity to continue the conversation, you are more likely to get the full story. And should your investigation be challenged in court, you will be able to prove that you made every effort to gather all the facts.

Of course, you also need to conclude your investigation as quickly as possible. To insure that the process can be wrapped up, remind witnesses that they should come to you as soon as they can, so you can consider their information in reaching your decision.

EXAMPLE:

Don't Say: Have you told me everything you remember about these incidents? Because you won't be able to change your statement once I start talking to other witnesses.

Say: Please remember that my door is always open, if you remember anything later or there is something you need to add to your statement. Also, if you learn of any new information that relates to the complaint, please bring it to my attention right away.

It's Never Too Late

What should you do if a worker comes to you with new information only after you've reached a decision—and acted on it? The answer depends on whether the new information, if accurate, would change your conclusions. If not, you can simply make a note of the new information and stick with your earlier decision.

If the new information might change your mind, you will have to look into it. If, after investigating, you are satisfied that the information is accurate, you should make any necessary adjustments to your conclusions and actions. For example, if you receive new information showing that the misconduct was worse than it seemed, you might have to impose more severe discipline. If the additional details show that another employee was actually responsible for the problem, you might have to rescind your discipline of one employee and impose discipline on the other.

One thing you can't do: ignore the new evidence. Although it might be tempting to simply stick with your original conclusions and disregard the new information as "too late," this will get you into trouble. If that new information shows that you have disciplined a worker unjustly or failed to discipline a worker who engaged in serious wrongdoing, you have to take action to undo your mistake. Once you learn that you were wrong—even through no fault of your own—you are responsible for correcting the situation.

k. Write it All Down

Take notes during every interview. Before starting the interview, note the date, time and place, the name of the witness and whether anyone else was present. Write down all the important facts that the witness relates or denies, and if the witness offers opinions, be sure that you identify them as such. Before the interview is over, go back through your notes with the witness to make sure you got it right. These notes will help you remember what each witness said later, when you are making your decision.

Although it may sound like overkill, you might also consider asking each witness to sign and date a written statement of what was said during the interview. A signed statement will help you defend yourself in court if the investigation is challenged as biased or incomplete—and will discourage people from changing their stories on the witness stand.

EXAMPLE:

Don't Write: I spoke to Joan today. She said that Richard has been acting strange lately, but she hasn't really seen any fights between Sam and Richard. She thinks Richard might act out violently sometime soon.

Write: I interviewed Joan Suzuki today, June 14, 200X, regarding Sam Levine's complaint (see Complaint Form in file). We met in my office at 3 p.m. I asked Joan whether she had seen any incidents between Richard Hart and Sam in the last two weeks. Joan said that she thought Richard has been acting very strange lately. When I asked her to explain, she said that Richard seemed distracted and angry and that he had been complaining to others in the work group about his ex-wife's petition for an increase in child support. Richard told her that Sam had denied his request for a raise and that Sam was responsible for all of his problems. Joan also said that Richard had made several jokes during shift meetings about "going postal" and that he told Sam "you will be the first to go." This is the only incident she has seen between Sam and Richard. Joan said that she was frightened by Richard's change in behavior.

Joan confirmed that Jose, Jocelyn and Cherise heard Richard's jokes at the meetings. I thanked her for her information, and encouraged her to come forward with any additional information immediately. I asked her to treat the investigation confidentially. I assured her that Richard has been suspended pending the outcome of the investigation and that the company would act swiftly to deal with the situation as soon as the investigation was complete.

2.   Interviewing the Complaining Employee

Often you'll become aware of a problem employee by way of a complaining coworker. Your interview with the coworker may be straightforward and low-key, or it may be laden with emotion and tension—or somewhere in between. No matter what the atmosphere, you'll need to elicit basic information that will help you learn what has happened and where you should direct additional investigation. This section gives you additional tips on interviewing questions, suggestions for handling a difficult interview and pointers on how to end the interview session.

a.   Questioning the Complaining Employee

Start your investigation by getting the details from the complaining employee. Remember to use the tips explained in subsection 1, above. Here are some sample questions to consider:

- What happened? If the complaint involves several incidents or a pattern of misconduct over a period of time, start with the most recent problem and work backwards.
- Who was involved? What did that person say or do?
- What was your response or reaction, if any?
- When and where did the incident(s) take place?
- Did anyone witness the incident(s)?
- Did you tell anyone about the incident(s)?
- Do you know of anyone who might have information about these incidents?
- Have you been affected by the incident(s)? How?
- Do you know of any similar incidents involving other people?
- Do you know of any evidence—documents or otherwise—relating to your complaint?

b.   Difficult Interviews

Employees often find it extremely difficult to come forward with a complaint, especially a complaint about discrimination or harassment. Many employees complain only as a last resort, after trying informally to stop the misconduct. An employee who complains may be wrestling with difficult feelings of embarrassment, anger, sadness and fear.

When an employee finally does decide to complain, these emotions may spill out during the interview. The worker may cry, become angry or even change his mind halfway through the process. Your best response is to listen and be understanding. Assure the employee that you know this is difficult and emotional, and that you want to get to the bottom of things. If the complaining worker tries to "take back" the complaint, say that you will have to investigate anyway and would like the worker's cooperation. If the employee is afraid of the accused employee, think about what immediate steps you can take to calm these fears, such as separating the workers. However, don't try so hard to sympathize that you lose your objectivity in the investigation. Remember, your job is to find out all the facts before making a decision.

> **EXAMPLE:**
>
> **If you're told:** If Thomas finds out I complained about him asking me out, he'll never promote me to the team leader position. I've worked so hard for that promotion; maybe it isn't worth filing a complaint.
>
> **Don't say:** I can't believe Thomas was so disrespectful to you! By the time I'm through with him, he won't be in a position to be deciding on any promotions. He'll be lucky to have a job!
>
> **Don't say:** If you aren't willing to make a formal complaint, there is nothing I can do to help you. You will just have to decide whether this is important enough to warrant a full-fledged investigation.

Say: I am going to look into what happened, talk to Thomas and any witnesses, then decide what the company will do. I understand that you are worried about your promotion. But I won't allow anyone, including Thomas, to retaliate against you for coming forward. And once I know about potential harassment, as I do now, I have a legal responsibility to investigate and figure out what to do.

If the complaining employee requests it, you might let her bring a friend to the interview. You are not legally required to allow this, and there are pros and cons to having another person present. If the employee is very emotional, having a support person might help her feel more comfortable and tell her story more completely. And if your investigation is challenged later, the support person will be one more witness to your conscientious efforts. However, having a third party present might make it more difficult for you to establish a rapport with the complaining witness. And it will add one more person to the list of those who know about the complaint and investigation, which makes confidentiality more difficult.

c. Concluding the Interview

Once you have finished your questions, conclude the interview by giving the employee some idea about what to expect. Tell the employee you plan to interview the accused worker and any other witnesses, review any additional evidence and complete the investigation as soon as possible. Ask the employee not to tell anyone at work about the complaint or the investigation. Emphasize that you will keep things confidential to the extent possible, but might have to reveal some information to conduct a thorough investigation.

Thank the employee for bringing the complaint to your attention. Assure the worker that he or she will not be retaliated against for coming forward, and ask that you be told of any retaliatory conduct, whether by the accused employee or anyone else. Finally, because complaining employees often can't remember all the details during the initial interview, stress that your door is always open if he has more to say or additional facts come to light.

3.   Interviewing the Accused Employee

Your goal when interviewing the accused employee is to get his or her side of the story. The best way to do this is to be forthright, by explaining that a complaint was made (or potential misconduct was noted by management), describing the conduct in question and asking the employee to respond. Be clear that you have not yet reached any conclusions and that you will listen carefully to everyone involved before taking any action.

a.   The Accused's Right to Bring a Coworker

Since 1975, union members have had the right to bring a union representative to any investigative interview that could result in disciplinary action against the employee. Recently, the NLRB (National Labor Relations Board), the federal government agency that oversees issues of union-management relations, decided that non-unionized employees also have the right to a representative. (*Epilepsy Foundation of Northeast Ohio*, 331 NLRB No. 92 (July 10, 2000), available on the NLRB's website at www.nlrb.gov.)

This decision is legally binding on private employers. As a result, any employee can insist, as a condition of participating in an interview, on bringing a representative along. This right applies only to investigative interviews that the employee reasonably believes will result in disciplinary action—a definition that likely includes any investigation of serious workplace misconduct.

Although the employer has no obligation to inform the employee of this right, the employer must allow a representative if requested by the accused employee or forego the interview altogether. In most cases, it will make sense to include the representative in the interview. The representative can ask crucial questions, make sure the accused employee doesn't leave out any important facts and help present his or her side of the story. Also, the accused employee is more likely to feel fairly treated if you allow a representative. And you will have another witness to your careful handling of the interview, should the investigation be challenged later. However, if the representative is unnecessarily disruptive, if he won't let the accused employee get a word in edgewise or is overtly hostile to you, for example, you can ask to hear only from the accused employee.

If the worker brings a representative, you should document the representative's statements as well as the statements of the accused employee. If the accused employee challenges the investigation or your decision later, you can be sure that the representative will show up as a witness on his behalf. In that case, you will want some written documentation of what the representative said, so you can let the jury know if he changes his story.

b.   Questioning the Accused Employee

It can be very difficult to interview someone accused of wrongdoing. The accused worker may be angry, frightened and upset about the accusations and will certainly see you as the enemy. After all, if the worker actually committed the misconduct in question, he will be worried about his job. If he didn't, he will be upset about being accused. Either way, these can be very uncomfortable situations for the employee—and for the investigator.

When you interview the accused, give her every opportunity to offer her side of the story. Be very clear with the employee that you have not yet made up your mind and that you will evaluate all of the evidence, including statements by witnesses suggested by the accused employee, before you reach a conclusion.

Here are some sample questions to consider:

- What is your response to the complaint or allegations?
- Why might the complaining employee lie? (If the accused employee says the allegations are false.) Could the complaining employee have misunderstood your actions or statements? Have

you and the complaining employee had problems working together?

- What happened? When and where? (If the accused employee does not completely deny the allegations.)
- Did anyone witness the incident(s)?
- Did you tell anyone about the incident(s)?
- Do you know of anyone who might have information about these incidents?
- Do you know of any evidence—documents or otherwise—relating to these allegations?

c.   Concluding the Interview

Close the interview by telling the accused employee what will happen next. Explain that you will interview witnesses and review other evidence before reaching a final conclusion. Ask the employee to keep the investigation confidential and give assurances that you will do the same, to the extent possible. Stress that retaliation against the complaining employee is strictly prohibited. Finally, ask the employee to bring any new or additional information to your attention at once.

4.   Interviewing Witnesses

There are many kinds of witnesses—some have seen or heard, first-hand, the misconduct at issue, while others have only heard rumors. Some will be privy to an entire dispute, while others have only a bit of information to share. And some may have an axe to grind (or favor to curry) with either the complaining or accused employee.

Your goal in interviewing witnesses is to find out what they know without unnecessarily revealing information. While the accused employee has the right to know what allegations have been made against him or her, third party witnesses have no such right—and you have good reasons to maintain confidentiality. If the allegations turn out to be false, the accused employee can sue you for defamation if you publicized them recklessly. Even if no lawsuit is in the offing, you can cut down on gossip and rumor in the workplace by keeping a tight lid on the investigation.

When deciding what to ask a witness, think about who suggested the witness and why. Did the complaining employee tell you that the witness saw the misconduct? Did the accused employee tell you that he or she confided in the witness after an incident? Sticking to the facts the witness is supposed to have will help you keep things confidential.

Here are some questions to consider for third-party witnesses:

- What did you see or hear?
- When and where did this take place?
- Did you tell anyone about the incident?
- Did the complaining employee tell you anything about the incident?
- Did the accused employee tell you anything about the incident?
- Have you personally witnessed any other incidents between the complaining employee and the accused employee?
- Have you heard these issues discussed in the workplace? When, where and by whom?
- Have you ever had any problems working with the complaining employee? The accused employee?

When your questions have been answered, thank the witness for participating. Stress that the interview and the investigation must remain confidential; tell the witness not to discuss either with coworkers.

E. Written and Physical Evidence

In many cases, there will be no evidence of wrongdoing other than witness statements. Much office misconduct is interpersonal—conducted face to face, rather than in writing. If the alleged misconduct consists of verbal or physical harassment, threats or violence, there may be no documents or other tangible pieces of evidence related to the incident.

Sometimes, however, documents play an important role in the investigation. For example, if an employee complains that his supervisor has discriminated against him, you might review the employee's personnel file to see how the supervisor has documented their exchanges. Similarly, if an employee claims that her coworkers sexually harassed her by sending her obscene messages and images over the office email system, you can review those materials directly.

Documents might also help you pin down crucial details. For example, if an employee claims that he was out of the office on a day when he was accused of workplace misconduct, you can check attendance records to find out the truth. Or, if an employee accuses her supervisor of giving her a poor performance review after she complained of harassment, you can look at the complaint and review to find out when the complaint was made, when the performance review was drafted and whether the review was changed at any time.

Finally, consider whether any physical evidence other than documents might be relevant. If the company confiscated a weapon or illegal drugs that the employee is accused of bringing to work, for example, those should be part of the investigation. In cases of theft, you may have fingerprinted the offices of those employees who reported missing items. If the company's trade secrets have been stolen, you might need to examine your computer system and access codes. However, don't be so zealous in your evidence gathering that you invade the privacy of your workers, as discussed in Section F, below.

F.   Employees' Rights to Privacy

As you decide how to question witnesses and what documents and other physical evidence to review (and how to collect it), you must be mindful of your employees' privacy rights. Depending on your state's laws and your own policies, you might be on shaky ground if you rummage through your workers' lockers, desks or email messages. More stringent rules apply to more intrusive searches, like drug tests and lie detector tests. (For information on interviewing employees without violating their privacy rights, see Section D1, above).

1. The Right to Privacy in the Workplace

The law protects a worker's right to privacy, but this right is limited. After all, the workplace is less private than the bedroom or the doctor's office. The workplace belongs to your company, and you are entitled to take some steps to make sure your workers are performing their jobs safely and appropriately. However, if you intrude unnecessarily into your employees' private concerns or property, you can get into legal trouble.

How can you tell whether you have crossed this line? Unfortunately, there are few hard and fast rules. The best you can do is to look at the question the way a judge would if faced with the facts in your workplace incident. A judge will evaluate the strength of two needs—the worker's reasonable expectations of privacy and your justification for performing the search—and determine which need is stronger. Your search will be considered legitimate and legal if your justifications outweigh the worker's reasonable expectations of privacy. Below, we explain how to measure these competing needs.

a. Employees' Reasonable Expectations of Privacy

The key to understanding whether your employees have a reasonable expectation of privacy is to focus on the word *reasonable*. From a legal standpoint, a reasonable expectation is one that a reasonable person would have in the same or similar circumstances. In other words, the expectation of the employee is measured against a standard. Just because a person expects to have privacy in a certain situation doesn't mean that the law will recognize that expectation—it must be one that most reasonable people would share.

When trying to figure out whether your workers have a reasonable expectation of privacy in a given situation, you need to consider:

- your policies, and
- your common sense.

Your policies. Your workers do not have a legitimate expectation of privacy if you have warned them that their communications or workspaces are not private. Many companies limit their workers' privacy expectations by adopting policies that explicitly allow searches of work areas, email monitoring and so on. If you have a policy stating, for example, that lockers are subject to search or that all email messages may be read, your workers won't be able to argue that they nonetheless expected that their lockers or email would be private. If you have this type of policy, you are free to conduct a search as long as you have a valid, work-related justification.

Common sense. Another way to measure a person's expectation of privacy is to simply subject it to the test of common sense. Think about whether your average reasonable worker would consider a particular space private. For example, if your employees routinely use each other's desks, a worker probably has no reasonable expectation that his desk will remain private. However, if your workers keep personal items in their desks and take care to lock their desk drawers, they might reasonably expect more privacy. If your workers wear uniforms that are laundered on the premises, they probably have no expectation of privacy if they leave something incriminating in a pocket. However, many workers would feel violated if you searched the pockets of the clothes they were wearing.

Common sense also tells us that a worker's expectation of privacy in his private belongings or his body is very strong, indeed. If you are considering a more intrusive search of a worker's own property—of purses and backpacks, for example—you must have a very compelling justification. And physical searches of an employee's body are always a bad idea. Talk to a lawyer before wading into these dangerous legal waters.

If your policies do not warn your employees that you might search and monitor the workplace, consider talking to a lawyer before you conduct a search. The law in this area is changing rapidly, as new technologies make it easier than ever to monitor your workers. Every year, state legislatures and Congress consider a number of proposed laws to protect workers' privacy rights. If you misjudge the situation, the searched worker can sue you for invasion of privacy.

b.   Your Need to Investigate

A judge will balance your employees' reasonable expectations of privacy against your need to intrude. Only if your need is legitimate *and* overriding will your search pass legal muster. For example, if an employee complains that she has received harassing email, you have a strong justification to find out who sent them. (If you don't—as you know from reading this book—you could face serious legal liability.) If you have been told that an employee has a weapon in her desk, you have legitimate reasons for a search. And if you have had persistent theft problems during one shift, a locker search limited to employees on that shift will probably withstand legal scrutiny.

In considering your justification for searching, a judge might also consider the way in which you conduct the search. If your search methods are particularly intrusive, you could get into trouble—even if you have a legitimate purpose in conducting the search. For example, let's say you are searching a locker to investigate the theft of a fairly large item. Although you have a strong justification to search, you have no reason to read the worker's diary, rifle through the worker's wallet or examine prescription drug bottles—even though all of these items might be in the locker that you are entitled to search.

2. Lie Detector Tests

If a worker denies accusations of wrongdoing, you might be tempted to use a lie detector test (or polygraph) to get to the truth. You should think twice, however. These tests have been virtually outlawed by the federal Employee Polygraph Protection Act (29 U.S.C. §2001), which generally prohibits private employers from requiring their workers to submit to a lie detector test, or for disciplining a worker who refuses to take such a test. This law makes an exception for workers who are accused of theft or embezzlement that causes your company to lose money. Even in these circumstances, however, strict rules apply to how the test is conducted. To find out more about the Act, contact the Department of Labor or check out their website at http://www.dol.gov.

For more about the Employee Polygraph Protection Act. You can find a comprehensive discussion of the EPPA and other federal employment laws in *Federal Employment Laws: A Desk Reference,* by attorneys Amy DelPo & Lisa Guerin (Nolo).

3.   Drug Tests

Drug testing is a dicey legal issue for employers—and one you should approach with extreme caution. Drug tests are highly intrusive, yet they can also be invaluable tools for preventing drug-related accidents and safety problems. Although you are not legally prohibited from performing drug tests, you must have a strong, legitimate reason for doing so.

The law of drug testing is changing rapidly as more employees file lawsuits claiming that a particular drug test violated their rights to privacy. Because drug testing is so intrusive, a worker who convinces a jury that he was tested illegally could cost you a lot of money—and ruin your reputation as a fair employer. Before you perform any drug test or adopt a drug test policy, we strongly advise that you get some legal advice. In the event that you proceed with legal assistance, here are some guidelines to consider.

a.   Whom to Test

Avoid a policy of testing every employee for drugs or random drug testing. Unless all of your workers perform dangerous jobs, random tests cast too wide a net. If you test all of your workers across the board, you are, by definition, not acting on a reasonable suspicion about a particular worker. A drug test is most likely to withstand legal scrutiny if you have a particular reason to suspect an employee of illegal drug use, or if the employee's job causes a high risk of injury.

b.   When to Test

Your drug testing will be on the safest legal ground if your primary motive is to ensure the safety of workers, customers and members of the general public. You're most likely to withstand a legal challenge if you limit testing to:

- employees whose jobs carry a high risk of injury to themselves or others (such as a forklift operator or pilot) or involve security (a security guard who carries a gun, for example)

- workers who have been involved in accidents—for instance, testing a delivery driver who inexplicably ran a red light and hit a pedestrian
- employees who are currently in or have completed a rehabilitation program, and
- workers whom a manager or supervisor reasonably suspects are illegally using drugs. For example, if a manager notices signs of impairment (slurred speech or glassy eyes), sees the worker using an illegal drug, finds illegal drugs in the worker's possession or observes a pattern of abnormal or bizarre behavior by the employee, a drug test is probably justifiable.

c.   How to Test

Even if you have the strongest reasons for testing, you can still get into legal trouble over the way that you test. To be safe, make sure that you:

- Use a test lab that is certified by the U.S. Department of Health and Human Services or accredited by the College of American Pathologists.
- Consult with a lawyer in developing your testing policy and procedures.
- Use a testing format that respects the privacy and dignity of each employee, to the extent possible. If the drug test you use requires a urine sample, allow workers to give the sample privately or provide a monitor of the same sex, for example.
- Have a written policy in place about drug use in the workplace (including a discussion of the disciplinary steps you will take and under what circumstances) and your testing procedures (including when the test will be given, how the test will be administered and what substances—at what levels—the test will detect).
- Require employees to read your drug and alcohol policy and testing policy nd sign an acknowledgment that they have done so.

- Document why you felt it was necessary and how the test was performed each time you administer a drug test.
- Keep the test results confidential.
- Be consistent in how you deal with workers who test positive.

You cannot force a worker to take a drug test against his will. However, you can fire an employee who refuses to take a drug test, as long as you had sound reasons for testing.

G. Making the Decision

Now comes the hardest part. Once you have interviewed all the witnesses and gathered relevant evidence, you have to decide what really happened. If the complaining employee and the accused employee have offered conflicting stories—as often happens—you will have to figure out who is telling the truth. After you have made your assessments, you must decide what action to take (if any) and document your decisions.

1. Interview the Main Players Again

Before making your decision, consider setting up another interview with the accused employee. Have you heard any major new allegations or information since you last interviewed the accused worker? If witnesses have added significant details or documents supporting the complaining employee have surfaced, it is probably a good idea to get the accused employee's response to these additional facts. Courts are more likely to find an investigation was fair and thorough—and its outcome reliable— if the accused employee is given the opportunity to respond to all the evidence before the employer makes a final decision.

You should also consider another interview with the complaining employee. If the accused employee or witnesses have denied the complaining employee's allegations or offered reasons why the complaining employee might not be telling the truth, let the complaining employee respond.

2.   Evaluate the Evidence

If there is no dispute about what actually happened, you can skip right to subsection 3, below. However, if there are important disagreements between the witnesses—and particularly if the accused worker denies the facts of the complaint—you will have to figure out where the truth lies.

To begin, review the evidence you have gathered and your notes from interviews. Are there any facts to which everyone agrees? What are the major points of contention? As to each of these disputes, what did the witnesses say? Are there any documents supporting one version or the other?

Now you have to assess the credibility of each version of the facts. Although figuring out who's telling the truth can be difficult, your common sense will help you sort things out. As you're sifting the evidence, consider:

- **Plausibility.** Whose story makes the most sense? Does one person's version of events defy logic or common sense?
- **Source of information.** Did the witness see or hear the event directly? Did the witness report his or her firsthand knowledge, or rely on statements from other employees or rumors?
- **Corroboration and conflicting testimony.** Are there witnesses or documents that support one side of the story? Does the evidence contradict one person's statements? Do the witnesses support the person who suggested you interview them?
- **Contradictions.** Did any of the witnesses contradict themselves during your interview?
- **Demeanor.** How did the witnesses act during the interview? Did they appear to be telling the truth or lying? Did the accused employee have a strong reaction to the complaint or no reaction at all? Did the complaining employee seem genuinely upset?
- **Omissions.** Did anyone leave out important information during the interview? Is there a sensible explanation for the omission?
- **Prior incidents.** Does the accused employee have a documented history of this type of misconduct?

- **Motive.** Does either the complaining worker or the accused worker have a motive to lie about, or exaggerate, the incident? Is there any history between these employees that affects their credibility?

Once you've considered these factors, you will often find that one version of events is really implausible, or at least that it makes a lot less sense than the other. In investigations as in science, the adage holds true: The most obvious explanation is usually correct. However, if the web is still hopelessly tangled even after you've scrutinized every detail, you might have to end the investigation by admitting that you cannot figure out what really happened. If there is evidence on both sides and it could have happened either way, this is your best option. We explain how to do this in subsection 3b, below.

> **EXAMPLE:** Stuart complained that Darcy had threatened to fire him for reporting to jury duty. Stuart said that Darcy made this threat in the lunch room on April 28, 200x. Darcy seemed very surprised by this allegation; he agreed that he spoke to Stuart in the lunch room about his jury summons but that he said only that he hoped Stuart didn't get picked to sit on a jury because jury duty can be so boring. Darcy suggested that the investigator speak to several witnesses, all of whom confirmed his side of events. Darcy also said that Stuart had seemed upset since his last performance review, when Darcy noted that Stuart hadn't met several of his performance goals for the year. When the investigator interviewed Stuart a second time to get his reaction to this, Stuart admitted that the witnesses were there but insisted that they must have heard Darcy incorrectly. He also admitted his bad feelings about the performance review.
>
> In this case, the investigator can conclude that there was no wrongdoing. All of the witnesses support Darcy's version of events. Stuart cannot explain this discrepancy. Darcy has also offered a reason for Stuart's complaint, which Stuart has not denied.

EXAMPLE: Same as above, but one witness (a friend of Darcy's) confirms Darcy's version of the conversation and one witness (a coworker with whom Stuart often has lunch) confirms Stuart's version. Although Stuart admits his bad feelings about the performance review, he points out that he went to Darcy's manager shortly after his evaluation to talk about the review. The manager confirmed Darcy's opinion of Stuart's performance and explained how Stuart could improve. Stuart says that he felt more comfortable about the evaluation after this conversation, although Darcy was upset that Stuart went over his head and complained. Darcy denies being upset about this.

Without more evidence, the investigator cannot reach a conclusion. There is a witness on each side. Both Stuart and Darcy claim that the other has a motive to lie, and both claim to be telling the truth. Darcy's manager can confirm his conversation with Stuart, but does not know if Darcy was upset about the conversation or if Stuart remained upset about the evaluation. In short, this one could go either way.

3.   Decide What to Do

Once you have evaluated the evidence, you must decide whether company policies were violated or misconduct occurred. This decision will dictate what further actions you should take and what you should tell the employees involved.

a.   No Misconduct

There are several situations in which you might find that no misconduct occurred. If something happened between the complaining and accused employee but nothing illegal or prohibited by your company policies occurred, you might find that there was no misconduct. In these situations, you should consider whether the accused employee's behavior (and/or the complaining worker's conduct) warrants counseling or warning.

In rare cases, you might conclude that the complaint was false. If the complaining employee acted in good faith (for example, if he or she misunderstood an incident or was confused about the accused employee's actions), no further action will generally be necessary. If the complaining employee acted maliciously, however, discipline against the complaining worker is in order. Consider the employee's motives, how serious the allegations were and the disruptions to your workplace to determine an appropriate response. In the most egregious cases, termination might be warranted.

b.   Inconclusive Results

In some cases, you may be unable to figure out what happened. If the results of your investigation are inconclusive, you should tell both the complaining and accused employee why you reached this conclusion. You might also remind the accused worker of the rule he or she allegedly violated, to make sure everyone understands your expectations. If your investigation uncovered confusion about a particular policy (such as what constitutes sexual harassment or what is required under a safety rule), consider providing some workplace training for all of your employees.

c.   Misconduct

If you find that the accused employee has engaged in serious misconduct, you must take immediate corrective action against the wrongdoer. In deciding on an appropriate disciplinary action, use your progressive discipline policy as a guide. When you make your decision, consider the strength of the evidence. Remember, you may have to defend whatever action you take in court. Do you have strong, firsthand, corroborated evidence of wrongdoing? If you are going to take harsh disciplinary measures, consider whether the evidence you gathered will support your decision.

Once you have decided how to discipline the wrongdoer, take care of it immediately. Meet with the employee to inform him or her of the results of the investigation and the discipline you will impose.

You must also meet with the complaining employee. Explain what you discovered in your investigation, that the accused employee has been disciplined, and any future steps you will take to prevent further problems. Assure the employee that he or she can come to you with any concerns about the situation.

The Role of the Complaining Employee

Even if you take immediate and effective action against the wrongdoer, the complaining employee may be upset. Perhaps the complaining employee believes a harsher punishment should have been imposed, feels that his or her job performance or reputation has suffered because of the complaint or does not believe the wrongdoer will shape up.

You are under no obligation to impose the punishment your complaining employee favors. After all, you are the boss; you have an obligation to the accused employee and the rest of your workforce to be fair and reasonable. However, you should listen carefully to the complaining employee's concerns. Perhaps the employee who claims that the wrongdoer will never change is worried about retaliation or further misconduct. If so, you can assure the complaining employee that you will deal swiftly with any such behavior. An employee who believes she has suffered unfairly because of the misconduct may have a point: If he or she was unfairly denied a promotion, raise or leave, for example, you should consider conferring these benefits retroactively.

Although complaining employees may well have their own axes to grind, they can also help you figure out whether you have chosen an effective remedy. If the resolution you've chosen isn't going to work, better to hear about it now when you can fix the problem than later from a jury.

If you decide that misconduct occurred, consider whether your workplace needs some training. If your investigation turned up significant confusion about company rules or appropriate workplace behavior, prevent further problems by training your employees on what you and the law require.

4. Document Your Decision

If you've taken our advice, you've already documented every step of your investigation. At this point, you should have a written complaint (or your notes from meeting with the complaining employee), notes from your other interviews (or written statements from the witnesses) and copies of any relevant documents or policies. You should also make a note of any proposed witness who was not interviewed and the reasons why no interview was conducted.

Some investigators, particularly consultants who specialize in conducting investigations, prepare investigation reports. Although the contents of these reports vary, most contain a summary of the complaint, a list of witnesses contacted, a summary of each witness' statement, a list of documents or policies consulted, the investigator's conclusions and recommendations and the reasons for those conclusions.

You need not go to the trouble of preparing an exhaustive report. However, you should preserve your notes from the investigation and write down your conclusions. Remember, you might have to prove to a jury that you acted reasonably and your conclusions were sound. If you have documented the reasons for your decision, you will have an easier time remembering the details—and convincing the jury that you considered all the angles before taking action.

If the results of your investigation were inconclusive, document the reasons why you were unable to sort things out. Note the conflicting evidence carefully. This documentation will be invaluable if similar allegations are later made against the accused employee. You will have a record of previous problems to support any discipline you might impose.

Attention to Detail

Figuring out how much detail to include in an investigation report or other documentation of an investigation can be very tricky. If your investigation doesn't end the matter and you are later sued by the complaining employee (for failing to take effective action) or the accused employee (for acting precipitously), chances are good that you will have to hand over this document to your opponent—and the jury.

Your documentation doesn't have to memorialize every thought that crossed your mind during the investigation—nor should it. If you include a lot of extraneous detail, a jury might have trouble following your decision-making process. But make sure to write down all of the major decisions you made and why. For example, if you did not believe a witness' statement, make a note of that and the reasons for your skepticism. Similarly, if you concluded that no misconduct occurred, write down all of the reasons for your decision. If you write extensive notes but later claim to have left out an important detail, the jury may well believe that you are trying to build a case after the fact.

Your documents should include a notation of any discipline you imposed on the wrongdoer. If your meeting with either the wrongdoer or the complaining employee was eventful, you might want to include some notes from that meeting as well.

Once you've written down your conclusions, place them—along with all other documents relating to the investigation—in a special file devoted to the investigation. Do not place any documents relating to the investigation in any employee's personnel file. Although you may need to include some information in an employee's records (for example, the discipline imposed on a wrongdoer or the fact that an employee made a complaint that you found to be false), you should keep your notes and report in a separate investigation file. Keep the file with your other confidential employment records (such as employee medical records). This will help you avoid claims that you spread private or damaging information about your workers.

Sample Written Investigation Report

FROM: Myrtle Means
TO: File
RE: Investigation of Cynthia Smith Complaint
DATE: September 03, 200X

I completed my investigation of Cynthia Smith's complaint against Jackie Starr on August 27, 200X. Cynthia complained that Jackie had harassed her about her disability. Cynthia said that Jackie had made jokes about her wheelchair and had complained about having to make the restroom wheelchair-accessible (see notes from my interview with Cynthia on August 19, 200X).

I spoke to Jackie on August 20, 200X. Notes from this interview are in the file. Jackie denied treating Cynthia any differently from her other direct reports. However, Jackie admitted that she had joked about Cynthia's wheelchair when her team was planning the company picnic; Jackie said she made these jokes because she felt bad that Cynthia would not be able to participate in some of the activities. She said Cynthia laughed, and she was surprised to hear that Cynthia was upset. Jackie also said that she made jokes about having to wait in line to use the women's restroom, because a stall had to be removed to make the room accessible to Cynthia.

Sample Written Investigation Report (continued)

Three witnesses heard Jackie's comments about the picnic, Tom Jones, Kathleen McDermott and Diego Cameron. Tom and Diego both felt uncomfortable about Jackie singling out Cynthia; Kathleen didn't think Cynthia minded the jokes. All three confirmed that Jackie made jokes about Cynthia participating in the three-legged race and the volleyball game. See my notes from these interviews.

Martina Kowalsky heard Jackie complain about the restroom. Martina said that Jackie complained that 20 women were inconvenienced just so Cynthia would be more comfortable. My notes from my interview with Martina are in the file.

I concluded that Jackie had acted inappropriately towards Cynthia. All of the witnesses confirmed the details of Cynthia's complaint. Jackie also confirmed the facts of the allegations, although she denied that she mistreated Cynthia. I gave Jackie a written warning on August 28, 200X. I explained to her that she had violated the company policy against disability harassment, had treated her employee disrespectfully and had used poor judgment. I warned her that she would be fired if her behavior did not improve imme- diately. I arranged for her to attend a diversity management seminar next month.

I informed Cynthia of the results of my investiga- tion on August 28, 200X. I also told her that I had given Jackie a written warning and required her to

Sample Written Investigation Report (continued)

attend training on diversity in the workplace. I asked Cynthia if she felt comfortable continuing to report to Jackie. Cynthia said that she did. She said that Jackie treated her fairly in work assignments and evaluations. Cynthia said that she hoped the training would help Jackie understand workers with disabilities. I told Cynthia that the company was very sorry for what happened to her and that she should feel free to come to me with any concerns about her working relationship with Jackie in the future. I also told Cynthia that the company planned to move the company picnic to a location with paved walkways and ramps and to hold events and games in which every worker could participate.

Chapter 6

Making the Decision to Fire

*N*o matter how good your employee relations, discipline policy and intentions, one day you'll be faced with one of the toughest decisions employers have to make: whether to fire an employee. Perhaps you've tried counseling, written warnings and improvement plans, but nothing has helped your worker's performance problems or spotty attendance. Or maybe an employee has committed a single act of blatant misconduct—threatened a coworker, stolen from the company or showed up for work obviously drunk and ready to cause trouble. Whether the problem is long simmering or new, it's time to decide whether termination is the right response.

This chapter will take some of the guesswork and anxiety out of that decision. First, we discuss the types of misconduct, performance issues and attitude problems that should prompt you to think about letting a worker go. Then we explain, step by step, what to consider when you're making the decision. These guidelines will help you figure out if you have a valid, legal reason to fire, when you should consider salvaging the employment relationship and whether you've done all you can to protect yourself from a wrongful termination lawsuit.

A.   Is It Time to Consider Firing?

Most employers start thinking about terminating an employee in one of two situations. In the first, a worker commits a single act of serious misconduct that's dangerous or potentially harmful to the business. Employers usually learn about these problems immediately, through reports from coworkers or customers or from first-hand experience with the employee. These problems must be handled quickly and carefully.

In the second common scenario, an employee has performance or conduct problems that have persisted, despite the employer's efforts to counsel and correct. Although these problems are not immediately threatening to the company, they will eventually erode the morale and discipline of other workers and the productivity of the business. Once the worker has demonstrated that he cannot (or will not) improve, wise employers consider termination.

1. Once Might Be Enough: Dangerous, Illegal or Deceptive Conduct

If an employee commits any of the following types of misconduct, even a single time, you should immediately investigate and consider firing. These are all serious offenses that may endanger the worker, other employees and/or your business:

- **Violence.** This includes fighting with coworkers; pushing and shoving; throwing books, furniture or office items; vandalizing company property or any other physical acts against people or property.

- **Threats of violence.** Statements from a worker that he will harm, "get" or kill anyone (including him- or herself) or will bring a weapon to work merit immediate attention.

- **Stalking.** This comes up most often in cases of sexual harassment or workplace romance gone astray, but can also arise out of pure hostility—an employee may stalk a supervisor or manager in order to intimidate that person, for example.

- **Possession of an unauthorized weapon.** Your workplace policies should clearly spell out that weapons are not allowed in the workplace unless authorized and necessary to perform work duties.

- **Theft or other criminal behavior directed towards the company.** These acts include embezzling, defrauding the company or illegally using the company's intellectual property.

- **Dishonesty about important business issues.** The occasional fudge about progress on a project or reasons for time off is probably not a firing offense, but an employee who lies about whether orders have been filled, customers have been served or important business goals have been met must be dealt with.

- **Use of illegal drugs or alcohol at work.** Using drugs or alcohol at work (other than drinking at company events where alcohol is served, such as office parties or happy hours), or showing up at work obviously impaired, is cause for concern.

- **Harassing or discriminatory conduct.** If an employee is accused of serious harassment—including touching another employee sexually or insisting on sexual favors—you must look into it immediately. Investigation is also warranted if an employee has been accused of discriminatory conduct—for example, using homophobic slurs, treating men and women differently or refusing to use vendors or contractors of a particular race.
- **Endangering health and safety in the workplace.** An employee who fails to follow important safety rules, uses machinery in a dangerous way or exposes coworkers to injury—whether intentionally or through inattention or lack of care—could be a huge liability for you.
- **Assisting a competing business.** Revealing your trade secrets to a competitor or using your intellectual property to work for or start a competing company is extremely serious.

As soon as you learn about these types of misconduct, suspend the worker immediately (with pay) and investigate the incident using the techniques in Chapter 5. Getting the employee out of the workplace will protect the safety of other workers and prevent further dangerous behavior. But don't immediately fire the worker. Instead, take the time to figure out—by talking to the worker and others, by examining company records and by checking other evidence—what really happened. Even if things are as they appear to be, investigating before you fire will let the worker and other employees know that you are acting fairly and giving the worker the benefit of the doubt. If the employee challenges your termination decision in a lawsuit, the fact that you acted with deliberation and an excess of fairness will sit well with the judge or jury.

Once you are confident that you have all the facts, you will generally be legally justified in firing a worker who commits these types of misconduct.

Dealing with Dangerous Employees

Taking any negative employment action against a worker who has threatened or committed violence can be scary. However, it may help to know that experts believe employment policies which encourage open communication, mutual respect and an opportunity to air grievances—like the policies we have described in earlier chapters—go a long way towards diminishing the potential for violence.

If you are faced with suspending a worker for violence, threats or carrying a weapon, make sure to communicate the reason for your decision calmly and respectfully, giving the employee an opportunity to respond. Assure the worker that you want to hear his side of the story, that you will investigate the situation quickly and that you will not make any final decisions until you have talked to everyone involved. Don't lose your temper or speak with sarcasm or humor.

If you believe that the employee may become violent, have security personnel stand by to assist you. Hold your suspension meeting at the end of the last day of the work week, when fewer workers will be on site. You should also consider getting advice from a workplace violence consultant. For more tips on avoiding and handling workplace violence, contact the Workplace Violence Research Institute, 1281 Gene Autry Trail, Suite K, Palm Springs, CA 92262; 760-416-1476; www.nonworkviolence.com.

Lawsuits for Failure to Fire

Yes, it's true—in many states, you can actually be sued for not firing a worker (or in legal parlance, "negligent retention.") If you knew—or should have known—that your employee posed a risk of danger to other employees or the public, and if that employee harms others while working for you, you can be sued for failing to fire that worker.

For example, if you discover that one of your employees has threatened to harm a coworker and you fail to take the threat seriously, the coworker might be able to sue you if the threat is carried out. Similarly, if you suspect that your delivery worker is driving under the influence but you fail to take steps to investigate or put a stop to the situation, you may be liable to a pedestrian whom the worker hits while driving drunk.

To avoid these problems, investigate complaints or incidents of misconduct quickly and carefully. Don't think that a "What I don't know won't hurt me" approach can shield you from legal liability. Judges have ruled that even employers who don't know of an employee's dangerous conduct may be held responsible if a reasonable employer (one who keeps his eyes and ears open) would have known. Once you have investigated, immediately discipline or terminate the worker, as appropriate.

2. Persistent Issues: Performance, Attendance and Attitude Problems

Some workers are just unable or unwilling to improve, no matter how many times they are counseled, warned or disciplined. At some point, you will have to decide whether these employees have reached the last rung of your progressive discipline policy's ladder. (See Chapter 4 for more about progressive discipline.) If an employee fails to improve after a couple of written warnings or a suspension for misconduct, you will certainly have good cause for termination. Consider termination for persistent problems like these:

- **Poor performance.** Workers who cannot measure up to your reasonable expectations are expensive to carry and will cause morale problems among the employees who must pick up the slack.

- **Violations of minor safety and health rules.** An employee who violates a major rule falls in the "one time only" category, described above in subsection 1. However, if an employee repeatedly fails to follow even minor health and safety requirements—like a ban on smoking or a requirement to use equipment in a particular way—is either extremely careless or has a bad attitude. Either way, it's a problem you must address.

- **Insubordination or attitude problems.** Smart employers don't want a workplace full of sycophants, but a worker who always bucks authority, refuses to take orders or questions your every request will quickly compromise your leadership and ability to get things done.

- **Sleeping on the job.** Probably most of your workers have the occasional low-energy day after a late night. But an employee who regularly uses the workday to catch up on sleep undoubtedly has a serious productivity problem.

- **Abuse of leave (taking unauthorized or unearned leave or using leave for improper purposes).** Employees who take unfair advantage of your leave policies not only hurt your company's productivity but also encourage other workers to break the rules.
- **Excessive absences or tardiness.** It's a simple fact: an employee cannot do his job if he is rarely at work. At some point, a worker's repeated absence or lateness will affect your bottom line—and the morale of your workers who show up faithfully, on time.

Don't Be Afraid to Fire Non-Performers

If you are like most employers, firing a worker may be cause for great anxiety and perhaps even a little guilt. It's a big decision, and one that may have far-reaching effects on the life of the fired worker and your company. But don't let these concerns stop you from firing a truly incompetent worker. Retaining these problem employees will put a damper on workplace morale, reduce your company's productivity, encourage other workers to behave badly and cause you no end of frustration. Even given the risk of litigation that comes with any firing, your business will ultimately be better off if you get rid of these employees.

When you consider whether to fire someone for persistent misconduct, look at the history of prior warnings or counseling sessions. For example, a worker who has been late several times in the last few months presents a larger problem than one who has been late several times in the last few years. If the misconduct is spread over a long period of time, consider giving the worker another chance, even if you have reached the end of your progressive discipline policy. Juries tend to be a bit skeptical about employers who rely on stale infractions as a reason to fire.

B. Making the Decision to Fire: An Employer's Checklist

Each employee—even each problem employee—is different. Although workplace difficulties can be broadly grouped into types—performance problems, poor attendance or violence, for example—every worker's situation is unique. This can make it tough for employers to be sure that their management decisions are consistent and fair.

It can also be difficult for employers to sort out their own feelings about a worker who may have to be fired. After all, we spend many of our waking hours at work, developing relationships that are not only professional, but social and personal as well. When an employer is trying to figure out whether to fire a worker, these personal feelings inevitably come into play. This isn't necessarily a bad thing—your intuition about people, your sense of whether they will be able to improve and turn things around and your knowledge of how their personal situations might be affecting their workplace conduct can all help you make smart management decisions. But employers have to be careful not to let personal feelings dictate their firing decisions. Any appearance of favoritism can lead to bad feelings, anger and lawsuits.

You can minimize these problems by following the same basic decision-making process every time you need to decide whether firing is warranted. This will help ensure that your decisions are consistent and professional—and will hold up in court if you're sued. Follow the ten steps explained below to assure yourself that you've considered every angle before getting rid of that problem employee.

Take Away the Element of Surprise

When you consider whether to fire a worker, picture yourself breaking the news to the employee. What reaction do you imagine the worker will have? If your answer includes the word "surprised," proceed with caution —chances are that you have not done everything you should to protect yourself from a lawsuit.

A worker will not be surprised by the possibility of termination if you widely publicize your workplace policies (so your workers know what is expected of them), give fair, accurate and regular performance evaluations and follow your progressive discipline policy consistently. A worker who is genuinely surprised by a firing discussion is one who was not aware of company policy, did not understand that his behavior was falling short of your expectations or did not think the company would enforce its own rules. A worker should know there is a problem well before receiving a pink slip.

An employee who knows her behavior or conduct is inappropriate and has been given an opportunity to improve is more likely to accept termination graciously. After all, she has been on notice of the problems in the relationship and may even have taken steps to find another job. In contrast, an employee who is surprised to be terminated is more likely to harbor anger and vengeful feelings towards the employer—which in turn make lawsuits and even workplace violence a possibility.

1.   Step 1: Investigate the Conduct or Incident

If you have already investigated the incident or if the accused worker admits that he committed the misconduct in question, move on to Step 2. If there's some question as to what has happened, however, your first step is to investigate and come to a conclusion. No matter how serious the offense, you must take the time to investigate—even when you catch the employee apparently "in the act." There is always the possibility, no matter how slim, that things are not what they appear to be. And the worker might have an explanation or reason for the misconduct that is not immediately apparent.

For serious offenses, like those listed above in Section A1, suspend the worker temporarily (with pay) to remove her from the workplace while you investigate. Talk to the suspended worker to get her side of the story. Then follow the guidelines in Chapter 5 to get to the bottom of things.

As part of your investigation, consider whether the worker's supervisor has had similar problems with other employees—which would raise the possibility that you're dealing with management problems, not isolated worker problems. If the supervisor has trouble coaching or managing workers to help them improve, complains of other employees being insubordinate or has more trouble managing employees of a particular race, gender or age, you may want to transfer the employee to a different supervisor and offer another chance to improve. You should also take immediate steps to deal with your rogue supervisor.

> **EXAMPLE:** Roy's supervisor, Phyllis, reports that Roy yelled at her during a staff meeting, saying that she was a dreadful manager and was destroying the team's morale. Phyllis demands that Roy be fired. After an investigation, the head of HR concludes that Roy did make these comments. However, the investigation also uncovers that Phyllis has been requiring her entire team to work overtime without pay for the past month to meet a deadline; Phyllis also threatened to discipline anyone who complained. One team member has quit, and others have gotten sick because of stress and over-work. Roy explained that he simply reached the end of his rope when Phyllis complained, during the staff meeting, about the quality of the team's work. In this case, although Roy was insubordinate, Phyllis is the real problem employee.

2.   Step 2: Check the Worker's Personnel File

Never proceed without reading the personnel file—even if you think you know its contents. What you find—and what you *don't* find—can have important legal repercussions.

a.   Persistent Problems

If you are dealing with persistent problems in performance, attendance or attitude, and you have followed the tips in Chapters 3 and 4, you should find documentation of these issues in the file. Unless the problem came on suddenly, the worker's performance evaluations should note these deficiencies and suggest goals for improvement. There should also be notes from verbal warnings and counseling sessions, written warnings and possibly a written notice of suspension. If you have proper documentation of the worker's problems, move ahead to Step 3.

If you do not find sufficient documentation of the problem and your efforts to help the employee improve, you should seriously consider giving the employee another chance. This time, make sure to follow your discipline policy to the letter and document each step.

> **EXAMPLE:** Ramon's employer is considering firing him for poor performance. When she reviews Ramon's personnel file, she finds that he received a written warning from his new supervisor three months ago for failing to meet his sales quota. The employer knows that Ramon has had performance problems for more than a year. However, Ramon's previous manager failed to keep track of these problems, choosing instead to speak informally to Ramon without documenting the conversations. In this case, Ramon should probably be disciplined instead of fired. If he fails to improve after the company has properly implemented its discipline policy—with documentation—firing can be considered.

Does the File Contain Evidence of Good Performance?

When you review your employee's personnel file, pretend you're a lawyer representing your employee. Are there documents you could use to show that the worker should not have been fired? If your answer is yes, think twice before firing—or the next time you see those documents might be in a courtroom, in support of your former employee's wrongful termination lawsuit.

Favorite exhibits of the employee's lawyer include glowing performance appraisals, merit raises, commendations and promotions—particularly if they appear to contradict your reasons for firing. Of course, even the worst employee may have some good qualities, which you've duly recorded in evaluations. But if you are firing a worker for poor performance despite positive reviews and merit increases, you are asking for trouble.

This advice goes for almost any persistent offense. An employee who gets fired for attitude problems and insubordination should not be able to point to a performance review praising her teamwork, people skills and willingness to go the extra mile. When you review the file, make sure that what you see is consistent with your reason for firing. If it isn't, your employee should probably be given more time to improve. Or you should consult with an attorney.

b.   A Single Offense

If your worker has committed one of the "once is enough" offenses, there may be no previous signs of trouble in the personnel file—and that's nothing to worry about. The severity of the offense gives you good cause to fire, even if the employee was previously a shining star. Sometimes, however, the employee will have a history of misconduct. You may have decided to give the worker another chance, or perhaps the previous incident was not so serious that termination was your only option. In these cases, the file should document all prior incidents, your discussions with the worker about them and the discipline imposed.

EXAMPLE: Carrie shows up at work with a handgun in her purse. When her supervisor talks to her about it, Carrie claims that she did not know she was prohibited from bringing her gun into the workplace. Although she knows of the company's "no weapons" policy, she says that she believed the policy did not apply if the weapon was properly licensed. Carrie's explanation, though thin, might have been enough to give her another chance; however, in her personnel file is a previous written warning from her supervisor at a different branch of the company. That supervisor documented that Carrie had brought her gun to work there as well, used the same explanation and was told that the policy applied to licensed weapons, including her gun. Carrie is out of excuses and out of a job.

c.   Evidence of an Employment Contract

As you read through the file, be on the lookout for evidence of an employment contract limiting your right to fire at will. As explained in Chapter 2, employees with these written contracts can still be fired for cause—that is, a good business reason—but the existence of the contract makes it especially important that you have documented reasons for the termination.

You can create a contractual relationship with an employee even if the two of you haven't signed a document clearly labeled as an employment contract. (Creating an implied contract is explained in Chapter 2, Section B.) For example, check to see whether you made any oral agreements with your employee about his job that are memorialized in the file. (Also think back on your conversations with the employee, as discussed in Step 4.) If there are promises of continued employment or if your performance evaluations and disciplinary documents contain language contradicting the at-will relationship, you may have created an implied contract, especially if the employee has not signed an at-will statement.

An employment contract doesn't make a worker fire-proof, but it may limit your options. Remember that the language of the contract governs when you can fire an employee. For most contracts, this means you need only have a good business reason to end the employment relationship. However, if you agreed to different restrictions (for example, that the worker could only be fired for committing a criminal act or for defrauding the company), you must decide whether your intended course of action fits within the contract.

> **EXAMPLE:** Leif is considering firing his company's CFO, Oz, for poor performance. Oz has a written employment contract, guaranteeing him the position for two years unless the company is sold, Oz commits a criminal act or Oz commits misconduct that causes "severe financial harm" to the company. The company hasn't been sold, and Oz has committed no crime. However, he is not the world's greatest CFO: His filings are always late, his sloppy practices have resulted in a bank audit and the Board of Directors has complained about his sparse financial reports. Although these are serious problems that would give Leif good cause to fire Oz in general, they have not resulted in severe financial harm—and therefore do not fall within the contract's provisions. If Leif fires Oz, he could lose a lawsuit for breach of contract, despite Oz's undisputedly poor performance.

3. Step 3: Examine Your Written Policies

Next, gather together your employee handbook, personnel manual and any other written policies that have been in effect during the worker's tenure. Review these materials and make sure the worker had sufficient notice that his conduct could result in getting fired. An employee will be on notice in one (or more) of the following ways:

- **Clear written policies.** Your written policies, in a handbook or other material, may address the issues that you're dealing with now. For example, many companies have written policies prohibiting (and defining) sexual harassment, setting forth safety rules and explaining the company leave policy.

- **Other written communications.** You may have given the worker notice in some other way—through performance evaluations or written warnings—that his conduct could lead to termination. Hopefully, you've already found evidence of these warnings or evaluations in the personnel file.
- **Obvious misconduct.** Some behavior, like threatening violence or selling secrets to a competitor, is so outrageous that explicit notice is unnecessary—you can be sure that the worker knows his conduct is completely unacceptable.

Check to make sure you have followed your progressive discipline policy. If you're dealing with a one-time serious offense, does your policy give you the right to fire immediately for this type of conduct? Or does your policy reserve your right to fire for any reason? If you are facing an employee with persistent problems, have you done everything promised in your discipline policy? Have you gone through each progressive step and documented your efforts?

As you did when reviewing the personnel file, read through your policies to see whether you've placed any limitations on your right to fire workers. If there are written statements that could be construed as creating an implied contract, make sure the worker's misconduct gives you good cause to fire—it probably will.

EXAMPLE: Marisa has had persistent performance and attitude problems since she came to work for Lorenzo, all of which Lorenzo has faithfully documented. After her last written warning, Marisa was told that she would be fired upon her next offense. Lorenzo came upon Marisa using the office copier to run off invitations to a friend's wedding shower. Lorenzo decided this was the last straw—until Marisa explained that she did not know employees were prohibited from using the copier to make personal copies. Marisa pointed out that Lorenzo and several managers had all used the copier for personal copies in the last few weeks. Because no written policy prohibited personal use of the copier, and because the issue was, understandably, unclear to Marisa, Lorenzo decided not to fire her over this.

4.   Step 4: Review Statements Made to the Employee

What you say to a worker can be just as important as your written communications and policies. Take a moment to think back on conversations or statements that aren't memorialized in the employee's personnel file or the personnel handbook.

a.   Oral Statements That Contradict Written Statements or Policies

Consider whether you have said anything to the worker that is contrary to your written policies and the documents in the personnel file. For example, have you led the worker to believe she would not be fired despite her performance or other problems? Have you promised to retain the worker for a set period of time or until he is able to improve? Have you made statements indicating that you did not view the problems as serious? Think about whether you have made any comments that might lead the worker to believe he would not be fired for the conduct at issue.

If you can remember conversations or statements that contradict written evidence, you can be sure that your employee will, too. If you made general statements that might be construed as creating an implied contract not to fire without good cause (such as "you won't be fired as long as you do a good job"), then you can still fire the worker, as long as you have a legitimate business reason for doing so. However, if you made more specific promises to the employee, you should talk to a lawyer before proceeding.

b. Oral Statements That Cast You in a Bad Light

Because firing an employee always carries with it the chance that you'll be sued, you must think not only about whether you can show a judge or jury a documented, believable picture of your problem employee, but about how *you* will look, too. A clever lawyer will do her best to deflect attention from her client, whom you've rightfully terminated, by focusing on your every flaw.

When you reflect on your conversations, consider first whether you have said anything that could be construed as discriminatory or harassing. Have you made any comments about the worker's race, national origin, gender, age, religion or disability? Have you made any more general remarks on these subjects that could be considered derogatory? Have other workers complained about your comments? If there's enough evidence to pin one of these transgressions on you, you may find yourself answering harassment or discrimination charges as well as defending your decision to terminate.

> **EXAMPLE:** Reginald, who is 70 years old, has worked for Tim, who is 35, for the last ten years. They have become friends outside of work and often engage in friendly joking and teasing in the workplace. Reginald often calls Tim "pipsqueak" or "the kid," while Tim calls Reginald "old-timer" or "gramps." Neither minds these jokes. However, when Tim fires Giselle, who is 68 years old, for documented performance problems, Giselle files a lawsuit complaining that Tim discriminated against her because of her age—using his pet names for Reginald as one piece of evidence. Although those statements are probably not enough, by themselves, to win the case for Giselle, they will not help Tim in front of a jury.

Consider also whether your worker might have legitimate cause to feel sexually harassed. If you, other managers or coworkers have asked the worker out, made comments about the worker's sex life or commented excessively on the worker's appearance, you could be headed for big trouble. An employer with *any* concerns about discrimination or harassment should put the firing decision on hold and speak to a lawyer.

5.   Step 5: Examine Your Treatment of Other Workers

A fired employee's most effective argument to a jury is that you've acted unfairly, by treating the employee differently from others who have been in the same position. An employee who makes this argument can even risk admitting that he's guilty of the transgressions or poor performance you've charged him with. His complaint is not necessarily that he's an angel, but that you've singled him out for harsher consequences than the other troublemakers.

To counter this all-too-common argument, make sure that you have been consistent in your handling of similar offenses or misconduct by other workers. Have you always fired for this type of behavior? Or have you given other employees another chance or helped them try to improve?

If you have treated other employees differently, there may be a good reason for the difference. Perhaps one worker's conduct was worse, more intractable, lasted longer or caused the company more trouble. Make sure that your choice to fire this worker, while allowing others to remain, will make sense to a jury as a valid business decision.

> **EXAMPLE:** Vanessa is considering firing Jodi for repeated tardiness. Jodi has been warned and counseled half a dozen times, but has continued to arrive for work fifteen to twenty minutes late at least once a week. Jodi is a shift supervisor for a delivery company. The drivers cannot leave the company's warehouse until Jodi hands out their route assignments, so the company's entire fleet of trucks sits idle when Jodi is late. Vanessa has retained Morris, although he has also been late many times. However, Morris has not been late as often as Jodi. Also, because Morris works as a janitor, his tardiness does not affect anyone else. Because Jodi's lateness posed much

larger problems for the company, Vanessa will have no trouble justifying her decision.

If you have been inconsistent with your employees and there is no valid reason for the difference, you risk a claim of unfair treatment. In the worst case scenario, the fired worker may be able to fit himself into one of the "protected classes" (such as race, religion and age) and argue that you discriminated. Carefully review the demographics of the workers who have committed similar offenses. If the fired worker can show that you fired only non-White workers, for example, or that you were more lenient towards women or quick to get rid of the disabled, you're at risk for a lawsuit. Talk to a lawyer before you make a decision. Your inconsistencies may mask a deeper problem in fairly applying your policies to your entire workforce—one that you should deal with immediately to avoid legal trouble.

6. Step 6: Consider the Possibility of a Lawsuit

When suggesting that you review relevant documents, conversations and treatment of comparative employees, we highlighted situations where the specter of a lawsuit should make you think twice about firing right away. Now it's time to think about whether other circumstances, or the employee's personality, make it more likely that a particular worker will sue—and win.

If your situation fits into one of the following scenarios, it certainly doesn't mean that you can't fire the employee. It just means that you should make extra sure that your reasons are well-documented and business-related before you take action. And, in more questionable cases, it means you should consider consulting with an attorney.

a. The Context of the Termination

Your decision to terminate an employee doesn't arise in a vacuum. Surrounding events and circumstances—even if completely unrelated—

can be used by an employee's lawyer in a way that makes you look biased, unfair or just plain mean. Here are the issues to watch out for.

- **Timing.** If the worker recently complained of illegal activity in the workplace, such as discrimination or harassment, firing that worker may lead to a retaliation claim. Similarly, a worker who is fired shortly after exercising a legal right or complaining of improper or illegal activity might bring a public policy claim. And a worker who gets fired shortly after telling you she is pregnant, suffering from a disability that requires accommodation or announcing certain religious beliefs could decide the firing and the earlier event are linked. If her argument is plausible, she may find a lawyer willing to handle her case. Sections D and E of Chapter 2 have more information on discrimination, retaliation and public policy claims.

- **Race, gender and other protected characteristics.** If firing this employee will significantly change the demographics of your workforce, it may look like a discriminatory firing to a judge or jury. Are you firing the only disabled worker or vocal born-again Christian on your payroll? If so, consider whether the employee has any grounds to file a discrimination lawsuit.

- **Other terminations.** Consider any other employees you have fired. Do you see a pattern that could be used against you? Have you only fired women? Have you fired workers who have raised complaints about health and safety issues? Have you fired several workers on the verge of collecting their pensions? The fired employee might be able to use these similarities to prove that your motives are suspect. This kind of evidence is especially powerful in discrimination lawsuits.

EXAMPLE: Curtis is considering firing Magda for poor performance. Magda has failed to meet her sales targets for the past two quarters and does not appear to be showing much improvement. Magda filed a sexual harassment complaint one month ago, complaining that her supervisor had repeatedly asked her out and made her uncomfortable. After investigating the complaint, Curtis concluded that Magda's supervisor had acted inappropriately and issued him a written warning. If Curtis fires Magda now, she might conclude that she got fired because of her sexual harassment complaint—and the short period of time between the firing and the complaint will only help her claim. Also, it's possible that Magda's work has been suffering because of her concerns about the supervisor's behavior. In this case, Curtis should probably give Magda time to improve, as well as offering her any assistance she might need to get back on track.

b.   The Employee's Personality

You should also consider whether the worker seems like the type of person who is likely to file a lawsuit. Of course, this is not something you can predict with certainty. Any time you try to figure out what someone is likely to do based on personality traits and behavior, you run the risk that your assumptions could be wrong. However, it is still a good idea to think about whether this particular worker seems to be a litigious sort. Your conclusions will help you decide whether to offer a severance package or some other incentive in exchange for the worker's agreement not to sue, and whether to consult with a lawyer before the actual termination. (See Chapter 8 for more information on severance pay and releases, which are agreements not to sue.)

Factors you might consider in deciding whether a fired worker is likely to sue include:

- **Threats to sue.** A worker who has already said or hinted that he is considering a lawsuit, hired a lawyer, filed lawsuits against other employers or assisted someone else (a spouse or coworkers, for example) in bringing a lawsuit should be considered a risk.
- **Financial problems.** An employee who will have trouble finding another job or whose family depends on her paycheck for day-to-day expenses may have a strong incentive to file a lawsuit.

- **Psychological issues.** A worker who has already displayed a tendency to see himself as a victim or to blame others for his problems may resort to a lawsuit to correct this perceived injustice. Similarly, an employee who has a very rigid belief in right and wrong may be more likely to sue if she perceives that these rules have been violated.
- **Fairness.** We have said it many times before, but it bears repeating: A worker who feels that he has been treated unfairly is more likely to file a lawsuit. Consider whether the employee will think you have acted reasonably.

7.   Step 7: Consider the Alternatives

If you've followed the tips in earlier chapters, chances are good that you've already thought about whether some disciplinary measure short of termination might be effective. However, now is a good time to quickly revisit the issue. Do you think it's likely that the employee will be able and willing to improve? If so, a lesser punishment could work well for both of you. However, make sure that you aren't playing favorites or bending your rules without a good reason. If you have consistently fired other workers for the same behavior, you will have to consider whether making an exception in this case will be perceived as unfair.

You might want to consider an alternative to termination if the worker's problems are due to difficulties outside of work, increased responsibilities that the employee can't handle or trouble working with a particular supervisor—or if you have made some managerial missteps in your dealings with the worker.

8.   Step 8: Get a Second Opinion

If possible, have a second person from within your company review the decision to terminate. The purpose of this review is to make sure that your decision is legitimate, reasonable and well supported. The reviewer should consider how the termination would look to someone outside the company. The reviewer should also make sure that the decision is based on objective, work-related concerns and has not been influenced by favoritism, discrimination or other subjective factors.

Ideally, the person who does this review will be removed from the situation and have no stake in the outcome, such as a supervisor from a different department or a manager at another store location. The less contact the reviewer has had with the people involved, the more likely her decision will be objective. Make sure the reviewer knows that you want her honest opinion and not simply a rubber stamp approval of your decision.

The reviewer should look at the worker's personnel file, the written personnel policies and any report or notes from an investigation. Although the reviewer needn't go through the entire process we outline here, she should consider all documents relating to the firing, as well as how other employees have been treated.

Take the reviewer's comments seriously. If the reviewer finds that your decision could be challenged, find out the basis for the problem. Is there insufficient documentation in the file? Have other employees committing similar misconduct been retained? Was your decision colored by your dislike of the worker or—worse—by prejudice? Use the reviewer's comments to figure out how you can either salvage the employment relationship or properly document and support your decision.

> **EXAMPLE:** Maurice plans to fire Geri and has asked Antoinette to review his decision. Geri works as a cashier in a supermarket Maurice manages; Antoinette manages a different supermarket in the same chain. Antoinette notices that Maurice has fired two other cashiers in the past year; when she reviews their files, she sees that each of them received two written warnings for major cash shortages (over $50) from their register drawers before being fired for a third shortfall. Geri's drawer has been short only once and for a much lesser amount. When Antoinette asks Maurice about this apparent

inconsistency, Maurice says that Geri seems distracted at work since having her baby, and he is convinced that she will have further cash shortages if he keeps her on.

Antoinette tells Maurice to put the firing plans on hold. Although he may have legitimate concerns about Geri's attentiveness, his comments sound perilously close to admitting that he is treating Geri differently—more harshly than the other cashiers whose drawers were short—because she is a new mother. He seems to be making an assumption based on the fact that she's a mother rather than on her performance. Better for Maurice to wait and see whether Geri's performance actually improves or founders.

9. Step 9: Consult a Lawyer, If Necessary

If you are faced with a close call of any kind—or if you are unsure that your decision will hold up in court—consider talking to a lawyer before you take action. Except in very complex cases, an experienced employment lawyer generally should be able to review the facts and give you some legal advice in a few hours. Chapter 11 provides more information on finding and working with employment lawyers.

You would be wise to run your decision by a lawyer in these situations:

- The employee recently filed a complaint of discrimination or harassment. A lawyer can help you determine whether you will be vulnerable to a retaliation claim.
- The employee recently exercised a legal right, filed a complaint or complained to you of illegal or unethical activity. In this situation, you might risk a claim of wrongful termination in violation of public policy.
- The employee recently revealed that she is in a "protected class." If you want to fire a worker who just told you she is pregnant or suffers from a disability, for example, you should have your decision vetted by a lawyer.
- Firing the employee would change your workplace demographics. Before you fire the only woman in the accounting department or the last Latino engineer, talk to a lawyer.
- The worker is due to vest benefits shortly. If firing an employee will prevent him from vesting stock options, retirement money or other benefits, you may be hit with a bad faith claim.
- The employee has an employment contract (whether written, oral or implied) limiting your right to terminate and you are concerned that you don't have good cause to fire.
- The employee denies the acts for which you are firing him. If an employee has been accused of misconduct and denies the allegations, or if an employee disputes performance or attendance problems, consider asking a lawyer to double-check your decision. A lawyer can help you make sure that you investigated and documented your conclusions properly.

10. Step 10: Document the Reasons for Firing

Once you've considered all the angles, the only thing left to do is document your decision in an internal memorandum to the worker's file.

Your written documentation should be short and to the point. Completely and accurately describe the reason(s) why you decided to fire the worker. If the worker committed a one-time serious offense, write down what happened and why it is cause for termination. Whenever possible, specify the policy the worker violated. If the worker engaged in persistent misconduct over a period of time, specify not only the misconduct but also your efforts to remedy the problem. Write down the dates of disciplinary meetings and warnings.

> **EXAMPLE:** On June 13, 200X, Brian Thomas brought a gun to the office, in violation of the company's anti-violence policy. Brian showed the gun to several coworkers, who felt threatened by his actions. When we investigated the incident, Brian stated that he intended to use the gun to intimidate his supervisor. Brian was terminated on June 19, 200X.

> **EXAMPLE:** During a performance evaluation on March 24, 200X, I informed Katie St. John that her monthly reports had been consistently late. Katie apologized and told me she would work on timeliness. In June of 200X, I counseled Katie again on this issue. I explained that her lateness was affecting the entire department and could even delay our tax and corporate filings. In September of 200X, I gave Katie a written warning that she would face termination if she continued filing her reports late. On December 15, 200X, after Katie could provide no reasonable explanation for her continued late filings, I terminated her employment.

If you have followed the advice in this book, you should already have a lot of documentation about the worker's problem and your response. As a result, this memo can be fairly short and to the point—as long as it is also accurate and complete.

Firing Checklist

Don't proceed with a decision to terminate a problem employee until you have covered the steps listed below.

- Perform investigation, if necessary
- Check that personnel file
  - contains documentation of persistent problems
  - contains no evidence contradicting reasons for firing
  - contains documentation of prior incidents
  - contains no employment contract (or good cause to fire, if there is a contract)
- Examine written policies
  - worker had notice that conduct might result in firing
  - company has followed progressive discipline policy
  - no employment contract (or good cause to fire, if there is a contract)
- Review statements to the worker
  - no discriminatory comments
  - no harassing comments
  - no statements contrary to company policy
- Compare treatment of other workers
  - similar offenses handled consistently
  - no discrimination
- Consider possible lawsuits
  - no timing problems
  - firing won't change workplace demographics
  - no pattern in recent firings
- Consider alternatives to firing
- Get a second opinion
- Consult a lawyer if necessary
- Document the reasons for firing

Chapter 7

Planning For The Aftermath

*H*aving finally—after much agonizing—made the decision to termi-nate a problem employee, you are presumably anxious to get it over with. Your instinct may be to rush out and tell the employee immediately, while you still have the nerve and before any new problems or issues crop up.

You cannot, however, proceed with the actual firing before you think about what will happen after the termination takes place. If this seems a bit like putting the cart before the horse, it is—but it's a necessary process. Now is the time to decide certain key issues about the after-math of the termination—issues such as what you will tell coworkers and reference seekers, whether you will offer the employee continued health insurance and whether you will challenge any attempts by the fired employee to receive unemployment benefits.

You may be wondering why you must think about these issues at this stage of the process, before the employee even knows that you've decided to fire him. As you will see in Chapter 9, part of your termina-tion meeting with the employee will consist of explaining to him how you will handle these issues. And the only way you can give an effective and complete explanation is if you have thought about the issues before-hand.

A. Legal Constraints On What You Say

Throughout this book, we've advised you to choose your words care-fully—when speaking with an employee whom you're reviewing, commending or disciplining; and when speaking with others about the employee's work.

After you've terminated a worker, it's doubly important to speak cautiously, whether to the rest of your company, to prospective employers or to the world at large. If you don't watch what you say, you can get into legal hot water. Thus, before you can decide how you will handle such post-termination issues as what to tell coworkers and reference seekers, you must understand the laws that could trip you up if you aren't careful—the laws concerning defamation and blacklisting. In subsections 1 and 2, below, we'll explain these laws, then proceed to advise you how to avoid their clutches.

1. Defamation Laws

Terminated employees who think that you have wrongly maligned them to others can sue you for defamation. This means that they can sue you for what you tell prospective employers who seek a reference, and they can sue you for what you tell their former coworkers about the termination.

Before you bury your head in the sand and decide you'll zipper your mouth shut rather than talk about the termination, understand that if you tell the truth, defamation generally won't be an issue for you. To win a defamation case against you, the former employee will have to prove both of the following:

- you said things about him that weren't true, and
- the untrue statements damaged him in some way—for example, the untrue statements convinced a prospective employer not to hire the employee.

Defamation is called "slander" if your words are spoken and "libel" if your words are written down and distributed to others.

Although employers tend to fear these types of cases, the reality is that they are very difficult for the employee to win. In all states, you will prevail if you can prove that the statements you made were true. In addition, in many states you'll prevail even if the statements are not true if:

- you reasonably believed the statements were true, and
- you made them to a prospective employer who asked for a reference.

So, when deciding what you will say about the termination, feel secure in the knowledge that telling the truth will keep you clear of defamation law. Of course, there's the truth, and then there's what you can prove. Unfortunately, the latter is what really matters in the world of law. To be on the safe side, then, don't exaggerate when talking about the termination and don't air your opinions and impressions about why the worker failed. Only give information that you can prove—for example, information that you documented through your progressive discipline and performance evaluation systems.

2.   Blacklisting Laws

To safeguard a worker's ability to hunt for a job, some states have passed "blacklisting" laws that allow former employees to take legal action—criminal, civil or both—against those who try to sabotage their efforts to secure new employment.

Truthful, well-meaning comments by you to prospective employers or to your workforce probably won't get you into trouble with this type of law. This is because the employee must prove that you actively attempted to prevent him from getting a job—which means that he must prove that you did something more than simply answer questions from prospective employers or coworkers. Indeed, many blacklisting laws specifically protect employers who make their statements about an employee to someone seeking a reference. These laws state that only unsolicited comments can be the stuff of blacklisting.

The typical blacklisting case occurs when an employer makes unsolicited calls or sends unsolicited letters to companies where a terminated employee is likely to seek employment. The goal of these calls and letters is to prevent the employee from getting work anywhere.

You might think it strange that we're bringing these laws to your attention now, since a concerted effort on your part to prevent future employment for your former employee is probably the farthest thing from your mind. It helps to realize that the majority of these laws were passed during the early, tumultuous days of the labor movement, when pro-union organizers were routinely fired and powerful employers banded together to try to neutralize employees' power by making it impossible for them to secure new jobs. Although we trust that you hardly fit the picture of such an employer, you must realize that blacklisting laws can be used against you if you stray too near their prohibitions. This means that you shouldn't make well-meaning phone calls to competitors to warn them off of an employee whom you just terminated. Wait until they call you.

The chart below contains a synopsis of state laws prohibiting blacklisting. Note that many of them specifically reaffirm an employer's legal right to give accurate and honest assessments of former employees.

State Blacklisting Laws	
State and Statute	**Employer actions prohibited (if intended to prevent a former employee from obtaining other employment)**
Alabama Ala. Code § 13-A-11-123	Maintaining a blacklist. Notifying others that an employee has been blacklisted. Using any other similar means to prevent a person from obtaining employment.
Arizona Ariz. Rev. Stat. Ann. § 23-1361(A)	Having an understanding or agreement which communicates a name, or list of names or descriptions between two or more employers, supervisors or managers in order to prevent an employee from engaging in a useful occupation.
Arkansas Ark. Code Ann. § 11-3-202	Writing, printing, publishing or circulating false statements in order to get someone fired or prevent someone from obtaining employment.
California Cal. Lab. Code § 1050	Misrepresenting facts about a former employee. In a statement about why an employee was discharged or left employment, implying something other than what is explicitly said, or providing information that was not legitimately requested.
Colorado Colo. Rev. Stat. §§ 8-2-110 to 8-2-114	Maintaining a blacklist. Telling another employer that a former employee has been blacklisted. Recklessly disclosing false information about a former employee.
Connecticut Conn. Gen. Stat. Ann. § 31-51	Publishing employee's name or writing letters in order to prevent employee from obtaining employment.
Florida Fla. Stat. Ann. § 448.045	Agreeing or conspiring with another person[s] or making threatening verbal or printed communications in order to get a person fired or prevent them from obtaining employment.

State Blacklisting Laws (continued)

State and Statute	Employer actions prohibited (if intended to prevent a former employee from obtaining other employment)
Hawaii Haw. Rev. Stat. § 377-6(11)	Making, circulating or causing a blacklist to be circulated.
Idaho Idaho Code § 44-201	Maintaining a blacklist. Notifying another employer that a current or former employee has been blacklisted.
Indiana Ind. Code Ann. §§ 22-5-3-1(1.(a)) to 22-5-3-2	For an individual: Using any means to prevent a discharged employee from obtaining employment. For a company: Authorizing or allowing its agents to blacklist a discharged employee; verbally, in writing or by any other means preventing or attempting to prevent a former employee from obtaining employment.
Iowa Iowa Code §§ 730.1 to 730.3	Preventing or trying to prevent, either verbally or in writing, a discharged employee from obtaining other employment. Authorizing or permitting blacklisting. Using any written or verbal means to make false statements about an employee's honesty.
Kansas Kan. Stat. Ann. §§ 44-117 to 44-119	Using any written or verbal means to prevent a discharged employee from obtaining other employment.
Kentucky Ky. Rev. Stat. Ann. §§ 352.550	Blacklisting miner who doesn't buy from the company store.

State Blacklisting Laws (continued)

State and Statute	Employer actions prohibited (if intended to prevent a former employee from obtaining other employment)
Maine Me. Rev. Stat. Ann. title 17, § 401	Threatening injury. Using intimidation or force. Maintaining or being party to a blacklist. Preventing an employee from leaving or remaining in employment. Preventing or attempting to prevent anyone from obtaining employment.
Massachusetts Mass. Gen. Laws ch. 149 § 19	Using intimidation or force to prevent or attempt to prevent someone from obtaining or continuing in employment.
Minnesota Minn. Stat. Ann. § 179.60	Two or more businesses or employers joining together in order to interfere with or prevent a person from obtaining employment. Using threats, promises, blacklists or any other means to get someone fired. Blacklisting any discharged employee. Verbally or in writing attempting to prevent a former employee from obtaining employment elsewhere.
Montana Mont. Code Ann. §§ 39-2-801 to 39-2-804	Informing any person of the reasons for an employee's discharge without first giving the employee a written statement of the reasons. Blacklisting in any form; authorizing or allowing a company's agents to blacklist. Using words or writing of any kind; attempting verbally, in writing or by any other means, to prevent a discharged or former employee from obtaining employment elsewhere.

State Blacklisting Laws (continued)

State and Statute	Employer actions prohibited (if intended to prevent a former employee from obtaining other employment)
Nevada Nev. Rev. Stat. Ann. § 613.210	For an employer or employer's representative: Blacklisting or causing any employee to be blacklisted; publishing any employee's name or causing it. Conspiring or scheming, by correspondence or by any other means, to prevent a current or discharged employee from engaging in or obtaining other employment.
New Mexico N.M. Stat. Ann. § 30-13-3	For an employer or employer's agent: Preventing or attempting to prevent a former employee from obtaining other employment.
New York N.Y. Labor Law § 704	Making, maintaining, distributing or circulating a blacklist to prevent an employee from obtaining or continuing employment because employee exercised rights to organize, unionize or bargain collectively.
North Carolina C. Gen. Stat. § 14-355	For a person, agent, company or corporation: Preventing or attempting to prevent, by word or writing of any kind, a discharged employee from obtaining other employment.
North Dakota N.D. Cent. Code § 34-01-06	Maliciously interfering, or in any way hindering a person from obtaining or continuing other employment.
Oklahoma Okla. Stat. Ann. tit. 40 §§ 172, 173	Blacklisting or causing an employee to be blacklisted. Publishing or causing employee's name to be published. Requiring employee to write a letter of resignation.

State Blacklisting Laws (continued)	
State and Statute	**Employer actions prohibited (if intended to prevent a former employee from obtaining other employment)**
Oregon Or. Rev. Stat. § 659.805	Blacklisting or causing any discharged employee to be blacklisted; publishing or causing the name of any discharged employee to be published. For a corporation agent, administrator or any other person: Conspiring or scheming by correspondence, or by any other means, to prevent a discharged employee from obtaining employment.
Rhode Island R.I. Gen. Laws § 28-7-13(2)	Making, maintaining, distributing or circulating a blacklist to prevent an employee from obtaining or continuing in employment because employee exercised rights to organize, unionize or bargain collectively.
Texas Tex. Civ. Stat. Ann. Art. 5196(1)(4) Tex. Lab. Code Ann. § 52.031	Blacklisting or causing to be blacklisted. Publishing or placing the name of a former employee on a book or list. Conspiring or scheming by correspondence or any other means. Communicating verbally, in writing, by a sign, list or any other means, directly or indirectly. Corporation, or its agent or officer, who receives a communication preventing, or calculated to prevent, the employment of a person seeking employment, must give that person, within 10 days of a written request, a true copy, if the communication was in writing, or a true statement and interpretation of its meaning, if it was not in writing, along with the names and addresses of whoever sent it.

State Blacklisting Laws (continued)

State and Statute	Employer actions prohibited (if intended to prevent a former employee from obtaining other employment)
Utah Utah Code Ann. §§ 34-24-1 to 34-24-2 Utah Const. Art. 12, § 19; Art. 16, § 4	Blacklisting or causing any former employee to be blacklisted; publishing or causing the name of any former employee to be published. Exchange of blacklists by individuals, businesses or associations. For any individuals, corporations, or their agents or employees: Maliciously interfering with any person's obtaining or continuing in employment with another employer.
Virginia Va. Code Ann. § 40.1-27	For any person doing business in Virginia, or the agent or attorney of such a person: Willfully and maliciously preventing or attempting to prevent, verbally or in writing, directly or indirectly, a former employee from obtaining other employment.
Washington Wash. Rev. Code Ann. § 49.44.010	Willfully and maliciously sending, delivering, making or causing to be made, any paper, letter or writing, signed, unsigned or signed with a fictitious name, mark or other sign; publishing or causing to be published any statement, in order to prevent someone from obtaining employment in Washington or elsewhere. Willfully and maliciously blacklisting or causing a person to be blacklisted, by writing, printing or publishing their name, or mark or sign representing their name, in a paper, pamphlet, circular or book, along with a statement about that person. Willfully and maliciously publishing or causing to be published that a person is a member of a secret organization in order to prevent them from obtaining employment.

State Blacklisting Laws (continued)	
State and Statute	**Employer actions prohibited (if intended to prevent a former employee from obtaining other employment)**
Washington (continued)	Willfully and maliciously making or issuing any statement or paper in order to influence or prejudice the mind of an employer against a person seeking employment, or to cause someone to be discharged.
Wisconsin Wis. Stat. Ann. § 134.02	Any two or more employers joining together to: Prevent any person seeking employment from obtaining employment; Cause the discharge of an employee by threats, promises, circulating blacklists or causing blacklists to be circulated; Prevent or attempt to prevent, by blacklist or any other means, a former employee from obtaining other employment; or Authorize or allow any of their agents to blacklist a former employee.

Current as of June, 2003

B. What to Tell Coworkers

If you think the termination is going to be traumatic for you, imagine how your other employees will feel when they learn that a coworker—perhaps a friend—has been forced out of their midst. Not only will the rest of your employees want to know why you decided to take action, they may also start to fear for their own jobs. Rumors may circulate. Morale may drop. If you're terminating a popular employee, you may be nervous.

The terminated employee will no doubt be nervous as well. After all, a termination is a humiliating event, and the employee will no doubt want to know exactly how public the humiliation will be. You need to think about this issue now, prior to the termination, so that you can give the terminated employee concrete information about what you will tell his coworkers.

So what course of action should you take? Given the difficulty of the situation, you may be tempted to simply avoid the issue altogether and say nothing to your workforce about the termination. Although this instinct is understandable, it will probably only create trouble with your other employees. They are not going to simply ignore and forget about the termination—no matter how difficult the terminated employee was. Termination is the secret fear of every employee, and it is unsettling at best when it happens to a coworker.

To acknowledge the event and to encourage the rest of your employees to move past it, consider calling a meeting to announce the fact of the termination. Tell your workforce who has been terminated and as of what date. Do not give your reasons. Do not express anger or relief. Be professional and neutral. Tell your workforce that you can't go into details because you must respect the fired employee's privacy.

When you tell your workforce about the termination, you may be tempted to explain and justify your actions—both to reassure other employees that they won't be getting the axe and to restate your image as a fair and friendly employer. In most cases, however, you should resist this temptation. If you say too much in your own defense, you will necessarily be saying negative things about the terminated employee. It can only make your remaining employees uncomfortable to hear you trashing their coworker—even if the trashing is deserved. Many may fear that they are one step away from the same shoddy treatment.

In addition, the terminated employee will likely hear about everything you say to the general workforce about his termination. After all—not matter how bad an employee he was—he is likely to have a friend or two left at the company. You can bet that those friends will report your comments to him. If you allow yourself to talk at length about the termination, you risk saying things that aren't absolutely provable—and risk a defamation lawsuit in the process. Even if you do stick to absolutely provable facts, you risk humiliating the terminated employee by airing all of his problems and failings to the workforce. As we explain more fully in Chapter 9, humiliation often leads employees to a lawyer's doorstep.

Of course, this doesn't mean you can never discuss your reasons with anyone. If you have a compelling business need to tell an employee your reasons for the termination, then do so one on one in a private and confidential setting. Instruct the employee that he is not to reveal anything of what you tell him to anyone else in the organization. When you talk to the employee, remain mindful of the defamation and blacklisting laws that we described in Section A, above.

C. What to Tell Reference Seekers

When you tell the problem employee that she's fired, she will likely ask you if you'll provide a reference for her. After all, she has to find another job somehow, and she may be concerned about how to deal with questions from prospective employers. To ensure that the termination goes smoothly, you should plan before the termination meeting how you are going to handle references for this employee.

Unfortunately, the issue of giving references for terminated employees is a complicated one, and you will find yourself feeling tugged in a number of directions, some of them diametrically opposed to each other. Maybe one of the following common sentiments applies to you:

- "I want to tell the truth about the former worker, even though it's negative, but I worry that telling the truth will prevent the worker from finding another job."
- "I want to warn prospective employers against hiring this worker, but I don't want to risk a defamation suit or blacklisting suit from the former employee."

- "I want to appease an angry worker by finding him another job, but I don't want to risk a lawsuit from the new employer, who might claim that it is stuck with a dangerous employee because I wasn't completely forthcoming."

1. Decide How Much Information You Will Give

Given all of the pitfalls that we described in Section A, above, you might be inclined to give as little information as possible when prospective employers call. In fact, many employers have gone this route, choosing to simply verify dates of employment and leave it at that. This is a reasonable and perfectly legal option for you to choose.

There are, however, reasons to be more forthcoming with prospective employers. A recent study reveals that as many as 90 percent of employers ask for and check an applicant's references. Given this state of affairs, you could severely hamper an employee's job search by refusing to give information, especially if that employee has some decent qualities that might make her a good employee somewhere, though not at your business.

In addition, think for a moment about the plight of other employers. Like you, they rely on references to help them determine if someone will be a good fit for a job. If you refuse to give reference information, you could potentially leave that employer vulnerable to hiring someone whom you know isn't qualified or, worse yet, is dangerous.

Don't immediately decide to adopt the bare bones approach. Although no law requires you to say more than "name, rank and serial number," you must realize that this response sends an unspoken message to the listener that you're choosing silence because you have nothing good to say—and may have something bad that you don't want to share. If your reticence results in your ex-employee not getting work, he may be inspired to sue you—over anything he can think of related to his employment or termination. To avoid that unfortunate turn of events, it may be wiser to respond more fully, as explained below.

2. Follow Safe Reference Procedures

You can respond to reference requests without risking a lawsuit from the terminated employee if you stick to provable documented facts, if you remain mindful of the defamation and blacklisting laws described above and if you follow the safe reference procedures described in this section.

Pick a reference policy and stick with it. Apply the policy to all your employees, not just the ones whom you fire. Otherwise, you leave yourself vulnerable to claims of discrimination or unfair treatment.

a. Make One Person Responsible

If it is feasible, make one person at your business responsible for handling references for former employees. That person should be familiar with all of the legal pitfalls involved in giving references, and she should know all the guidelines that we discuss in this section.

Whom should you pick? Ideally, someone who has been trained in human resource issues. For a small business, however, that's usually not an option. In that case, the person should be in management, and she should be discreet.

b. Keep A Record

As you will see below, we recommend that you require all reference requests to be made in writing, and we also recommend that all of your responses be written. Keep a copy of every request you receive and every response you send out. You should also keep notes of any phone calls you receive, even if your response to the phone call is simply to demand that the request be made in writing.

Keep copies of all correspondence with the employee about references, including any letters you send to the employee informing him about reference requests and any releases that the employee signs. In addition, keep notes of all conversations you have with the employee and anyone else about this issue.

If you are never sued, these files will simply take up space in your filing cabinet until you decide to throw them out (keep them for at least four years, however). If you are sued, they will come in very handy:

- You can prove what you said and to whom.
- With your file cabinet full of similar requests and responses, which you can show the judge or jury, you can argue that your normal business practice is to respond in writing to reference requests. This makes it harder for an employee to claim that you made oral statements.

c. Consult The Terminated Employee

The most common reason employees consult lawyers about references happens when a reference contains unexpected information. To avoid surprising the employee, you should discuss with the employee what you plan to tell prospective employers. A good time to do this is either at the termination meeting or at the exit interview (see Chapter 9). Make sure the employee understands exactly what you will reveal when called for a reference. Don't use vague words such as "positive" or "negative." Be precise and be concrete.

Ordinarily, former employers will tell prospective employers dates of employment, job title(s), responsibilities and salary. They also give factual information—both positive and negative—about the terminated employee's performance and productivity. They might even disclose the number and nature of customer complaints that they have received.

In addition to discussing with the employee the information that you will give in a reference, explain to the employee your reference policy. Tell the employee that you will notify her each time someone requests a reference (see subsection g, below), and tell her that you will only give out information to prospective employers who send you a release signed by her (see subsection e, below).

d.   Only Respond To Written Requests

Precision is important when giving references. The best way to give a precise reference is to demand that all requests be made in writing. That way, you can determine exactly what information is being requested and by whom.

e.   Insist On A Release

A release is a document that the employee signs giving you and others permission to give information to a prospective employer. The prospective employer, and not you, has the responsibility for getting the terminated employee to sign a release. If you get a written request for a reference that does not contain a release, write to the prospective employer and say that you won't respond until you receive a release signed by the employee.

f.   Respond In Writing Only

To keep out of legal hot water, you will need to carefully craft your reference using the guidelines that we discuss in this section. For that reason, you should only respond in writing to reference requests. Otherwise, you might find that you slip up in a casual conversation and say things that you shouldn't have. And once you say something, you can't take it back.

In addition, having your response in writing means that a former employee cannot later claim that you said things about her that you didn't—or in a way that you didn't. The proof, as they say, will be in the pudding.

g.   Give The Former Employee Notice Of The Request

Even when you have a signed release, write a letter to the former employee notifying her that the reference has been requested and by whom.

h.   Review The Former Employee's Personnel File

If you follow the guidelines in this book, you will discuss references with the employee either at the termination meeting or the exit interview. You will also include notes of that discussion in the employee's personnel file.

When you receive a reference request, don't rely on your memory—either of the employee's tenure with you or of the conversation regarding references. Instead, review the employee's personnel file prior to sending out a reference letter. Make sure that everything in the letter is grounded in factual and verifiable information in the employee's file.

Also, if you want to include something in the letter that you didn't discuss with the employee, inform the employee. You don't want anything in the letter to come as a surprise to the employee.

i.   If You Speak, Speak Fully

As we explained above, the law does not require you to give a reference for a former employee. If you do choose to say something more than the minimalist approach, however, you must include any information that you might have about the employee's history of violence, dangerousness or sexual deviance. If you give a lot of information in a reference but don't include this information, and if the employee turns around and injures someone in his new job after you've been mute, you could be liable for damages.

It is important to understand that this rule does not affect you if you choose not to say anything about the employee other than the bare minimum (for example, verifying salary and dates of employment). This rule only applies when you choose to say something substantive in response to a reference request.

Although not all states have supported this rule, more and more states are joining the ranks, including California, Texas, New Mexico and Pennsylvania.

If Only They Had Told the Complete Story

Randi was a female student at a California middle school when she was called into the vice principal's office one day in 1992. Later, she claimed that the vice principal, named Robert Gadams, sexually molested her while she was in his office.

As it turned out, the middle school had hired Gadams after receiving positive recommendations from a school district where Gadams had worked. Even though the former school district knew that Gadams had been accused of sexual misconduct and impropriety with students, it failed to mention these claims when the new middle school asked for a reference. In fact, the former district gave letters of recommendation for Gadams that contained unreserved and unconditional praise. One letter recommended Gadams "for an assistant principalship or equivalent position without reservation."

When Randi sued the school district where Gadams had previously worked, the district claimed that she had no legal grounds for suit. After all, it argued, it didn't have any sort of obligation to her, a student in a different district. The California Supreme Court disagreed. They said that Randi could sue because the school district had a duty to not misrepresent the facts when describing the character and qualifications of an employee to a prospective employer—in this case, the middle school that Randi attended.

If you want to read the case, you can find it by going to your local law library or by logging onto Nolo's Legal Research Center at www.nolo.com. The case citation is *Randi W. v. Muroc Joint Unified School District, et al*, 14 Cal. 4th 1066, 60 Cal.Rptr.2d 263 (1997).

j.   Tell The Truth and State Facts, Not Conclusions

Only include in a reference letter information that is true and that you can verify in some way. (If you've followed the advice in this book, you'll have a lot of documentation about the employee through your performance evaluation system and your progressive discipline system. See Chapters 3 and 4, respectively, for information about these systems.) Don't include gossip or conjecture. Don't include your opinions or your theories. Avoid stating what you believe might be true; only say what you know is true and what you can back up with documentation.

> **EXAMPLE:** Stephanie owns a café in a trendy part of town. She has a lot of competition, but she manages to keep ahead by offering superior customer service. She has one of the busiest cafés in town, and the waitresses must work at a breakneck pace to keep up with the customers. Stephanie recently fired Jan because numerous customers complained that Jan was too slow and kept mixing up their orders. Even though the customers seemed to like Jan, the mistakes became a problem. Although Stephanie gave Jan a number of chances, Jan never improved. A few days after firing Jan, Stephanie received a call from another café looking for a reference for Jan. Stephanie asked that the café owner make the request in writing. When she received the request and a release signed by Jan, she sat down to write the reference. The request specifically asked that Stephanie address how Jane related to customers.
>
> **Wrong:** "Jan had poor relations with our customers. Her mind was always somewhere else, and she never paid much attention to her work. She didn't try very hard and didn't care if she made a lot of mistakes. She was lazy and a bit of an airhead. I don't think that she is very smart. She isn't cut out for the café world. I wouldn't hire her again."
>
> **Right:** "Numerous customers commented that they liked Jan's personality. To my knowledge, she never yelled at a customer or was rude to a customer. However, I received an average of

five customer complaints per week about Jan. About half of the complaints that I received were from customers who felt that Jan was too slow in filling their orders. The other half of the complaints were from customers who indicated that Jan had mixed up their orders and given them the wrong drink."

EXAMPLE: Lewis is the senior partner in a law firm. He recently fired Mark after receiving complaints from two female secretaries and one female attorney that Mark made lewd and sexually suggestive comments and gestures in their presence. Another law firm has now asked for a reference for Mark. In the reference letter, Lewis indicates that Mark's legal work is excellent and that he has never received a complaint from any client about Mark. He also notes Mark's win/loss record in the courtroom. Because he has decided to give some information about Mark, he must also address the sexual harassment issue.

Wrong: "I think Mark is some sort of sexual deviant. He has a demeaning attitude toward women, and he thinks they are nothing more than sexual objects for his amusement. He doesn't have any respect for them at all, and he shouldn't be left alone with any female employee. He made lewd gestures and disgusting comments to female members of my firm. When I asked him about this, he just laughed it off and didn't have the decency to look embarrassed."

Right: "I received complaints from two female secretaries and one female attorney that Mark had made lewd and sexually suggestive comments and gestures in their presence. I received the complaints—five in all—during the same one-month period. As part of my investigation into the complaints, I asked Mark for his side of the story. He verified what the secretaries and the attorney said."

k.   Include Both Positive And Negative Information

It is a rare employee who lacks even one redeeming feature. When giving a reference, don't forget to include any positive facts about the employee. Remember, just because an employee was a bad fit at your business, that doesn't mean she won't fit in somewhere else.

Saying something positive, however, doesn't mean you have to perfectly balance the reference by saying one positive thing for every negative thing. After all, if you fired the employee, there's probably a lot more negative to say about her than positive. That's fine. Just be sure you include whatever positive facts you know.

l.   Don't Answer Every Question

Some references will specifically ask questions that require you to break the rules we've set out in this section. You don't have to answer all of the questions in a reference—especially those that ask you to give your opinion or to give conclusions. Stick with the verifiable and relevant facts.

m.   Avoid the Possibility of Blacklisting

As we explained in Section A2, above, blacklisting is a deliberate effort by a former employer to prevent an ex-employee from finding a job. You are always within the law when you respond truthfully to reference requests from prospective employers. The mere fact that a former employee has to work hard at finding a new job usually is not sufficient evidence to suggest blacklisting.

But you may stray dangerously close to legal trouble if you talk about your former employee in contexts other than a formal request for a reference, such as social gatherings where colleagues may be present. While you may have no intention of preventing employment, your loose lips may be all that a lawyer needs to begin a lawsuit.

To avoid problems, be especially careful not to talk about former employees at informal gatherings, when your guard may be down. If a colleague tells you at a cocktail party that she is looking forward to interviewing a former employee of yours—and that person was a particular thorn in your side—it may be best to simply nod and smile and shift the conversation to another topic. Never call prospective employers and volunteer information when you haven't been asked for it.

D. Continuing Health Insurance

Given the astronomical increases in the costs of medical care, health insurance has become a coveted employee benefit. The importance of healthcare coverage means that this will be one of the first questions a newly terminated employee will ask you. Know before you go into the termination meeting how you will deal with the healthcare issue.

Many employers offer to foot the bill to continue insurance coverage—at least for a time—as part of the severance package for a former employee. Often, this benefit helps give former workers peace of mind and makes them feel more kindly disposed toward a former employer. (See Chapter 8 for more about severance packages.)

Warm sentiments aside, there are also federal and state laws that may require you to make continued coverage available for former employees, even if you aren't required to pay for it.

1. Federal Law

A federal workplace law, the Consolidated Omnibus Budget Reconciliation Act or COBRA (29 U.S.C. §1162), applies to your business if you have 20 or more employees and if you offer a group healthcare plan. Among other things, it requires you to offer former employees the option of continuing their healthcare coverage for 18 months if you fire them for any reason other than gross misconduct. You must also give this opportunity to the employee's spouse and dependents.

The employee must pay for continuing coverage under COBRA, including both your share and the employee's share. You can charge 102% of the premium cost—using the extra 2% to cover your administrative costs. COBRA applies to HMO and PPO plans in addition to more traditional group insurance plans. COBRA also covers all other types of medical benefits, including dental and vision care and plans under which you reimburse employees for medical expenses.

For more about the Consolidated Omnibus Budget Reconciliation Act. You can find a comprehensive discussion of COBRA and other federal employment laws in *Federal Employment Laws: A Desk Reference,* by attorneys Amy DelPo & Lisa Guerin (Nolo).

2. State Laws

Most states also have laws that give former employees the right to continue group health insurance after they leave a job. You need to know about these state protections because you have to comply with both state and federal law. In many instances, simply complying with COBRA will not get you off the hook. State protections are generally more detailed and more generous to workers than COBRA. In addition, even small businesses, which escape the purview of COBRA, may have to comply with state laws.

While the basic coverage of the state health insurance laws is usually easy to understand, your role in complying with them and the state's practice in enforcing them can get rather complicated. For more specific information, contact your state's insurance department. (See the Appendix for contact details.) You can read the controlling law at a local law library or through the research section of Nolo's website at www.nolo.com.

State Health Insurance Continuation Laws

Note: The states of Alaska, Delaware and Idaho are not included in this chart because they do not have laws specifically controlling health insurance continuation. Check your state department of labor if you need more information (see the Appendix for contact list).

Alabama

Ala. Code § 27-55-3 (4)

No general continuation laws, but subjects of domestic abuse, who have lost coverage under abuser's plan and who do not qualify for COBRA, may have 18 months' coverage (applies to all employers).

Arizona

Ariz. Rev. Stat. Ann. §§ 20-1377, 20-1408

Employers affected: All employers who offer group health and disability insurance.

Qualifying event: Death of employee; change in marital status.

Length of coverage for dependents: May convert to individual policy upon death of covered employee or divorce or legal separation. Coverage must be the same unless the insured chooses a lesser plan. (Insurer may offer group insurance as long as there is no change in coverage.)

Time employer has to notify employee of continuation rights: No provisions for employer. Insurance policy must include notice of conversion privilege. Clerk of court must provide notice to anyone filing for divorce that dependent spouse is entitled to convert health insurance coverage.

Time employee has to apply: 31 days after termination of existing coverage.

Special benefits: Applies to blanket accident and sickness insurance policies and to all disability insurance issued by hospital, medical, dental and optometric service corporations, healthcare services organizations and fraternal benefit societies.

Arkansas

Ark. Code Ann. §§ 23-86-114 to 23-86-116

Employers affected: All employers who offer group health insurance.

Eligible employees: Employees continuously insured for previous 3 months.

Qualifying event: Termination of employment; death of employee; change in marital status.

Length of coverage for employee: 120 days.

Length of coverage for dependents: 120 days.

Time employee has to apply: 10 days.

Special benefits: Excludes dental care; prescription drugs; vision services.

State Health Insurance Continuation Laws (continued)

California

Cal. Health & Safety Code §§ 1373.6, 1373.621; Cal. Ins. Code §§ 10128.50 to 10128.59

Employers affected: Employers with 2 to 19 employees.

Eligible employees: Employees continuously insured for previous 3 months.

Qualifying event: Termination of employment; reduction in hours.

Length of coverage for employee: 18 months; 29 months if disabled at termination or during first 60 days of continuation coverage. (Employee also has choice of converting to an individual insurance plan.)

Length of coverage for dependents: 18 months; 29 months if disabled at termination or during first 60 days of continuation coverage; 36 months upon death of employee, divorce or legal separation, loss of dependent status, employee's eligibility for Medicare. (Dependents also have choice of converting to an individual insurance plan.)

Time employer has to notify employee of continuation rights: 15 days.

Time employee has to apply: 31 days after group plan ends; 30 days after COBRA or Cal-COBRA ends (63 days if converting to an individual plan).

Special benefits: Includes vision and dental benefits (if the employer offers them).

Special situations: Employee who is 60 or older and has worked for employer for previous 5 years may continue benefits for self and spouse beyond CO-BRA or Cal-COBRA limits (also applies to COBRA employers). Beginning 9/1/03, any employee who began receiving COBRA coverage on or after 1/1/03 and whose coverage is for less than 36 months, is entitled to additional continuation coverage to total 36 months.

Colorado

Colo. Rev. Stat. § 10-16-108

Employers affected: All employers who offer group health insurance.

Eligible employees: Employees continuously insured for previous 3 months. (If eligible due to reduction in hours, must have been continuously insured for previous 6 months.)

Qualifying event: Termination of employment; reduction in hours; death of employee; change in marital status.

Length of coverage for employee: 18 months.

Length of coverage for dependents: 18 months.

Time employer has to notify employee of continuation rights: Within 10 days of termination of coverage.

Time employee has to apply: 31 days after termination of coverage.

Special benefits: Excludes specific diseases; accidental injuries.

State Health Insurance Continuation Laws (continued)

Connecticut

Conn. Gen. Stat. Ann. §§ 38a-538, 38a-554; § 31-51o

Employers affected: All employers who offer group health insurance.

Eligible employees: Employees continuously insured for previous 3 months.

Qualifying event: Layoff; reduction in hours; termination of employment; death of employee; change in marital status.

Length of coverage for employee: 18 months.

Length of coverage for dependents: 18 months; 36 months in case of employee's death or divorce.

Time employer has to notify employee of continuation rights: 14 days.

Time employee has to apply: 60 days.

Special benefits: Excludes specific diseases; accidental injuries.

Special situations: When facility closes or relocates, employer must pay for insurance for employee and dependents for 120 days or until employee is eligible for other group coverage, whichever comes first. (Does not affect employee's right to regular continuation coverage which begins when 120-day period ends.)

District of Columbia

D.C. Code Ann. §§ 32-731 to 32-732

Employers affected: Employers with fewer than 20 employees.

Eligible employees: All insured employees are eligible.

Qualifying event: Any reason employee or dependent becomes ineligible for coverage.

Length of coverage for employee: 3 months.

Length of coverage for dependents: 3 months.

Time employer has to notify employee of continuation rights: Within 15 days of termination of coverage.

Time employee has to apply: 45 days after termination of coverage.

Special benefits: Excludes dental or vision only insurance.

Florida

Fla. Stat. Ann. § 627.6692

Employers affected: Employers with fewer than 20 employees.

Eligible employees: Full-time (25 or more hours per week) employees covered by employer's health insurance plan.

Qualifying event: Layoff; reduction in hours; termination of employment; death of employee; change in marital status.

Length of coverage for employee: 18 months.

State Health Insurance Continuation Laws (continued)

Length of coverage for dependents: 18 months.

Time employer has to notify employee of continuation rights: Carrier notifies employee within 14 days of learning of qualifying event (employer is responsible for notifying carrier).

Time employee has to apply: 30 days from receipt of carrier's notice.

Georgia

Ga. Code Ann. §§ 33-24-21.1 to 33-24-21.2

Employers affected: All employers who offer group health insurance.

Eligible employees: Employees continuously insured for previous 6 months.

Qualifying event: Termination of employment (except for cause).

Length of coverage for employee: 3 months plus any part of the month remaining at termination.

Length of coverage for dependents: 3 months plus any part of the month remaining at termination.

Special situations: Employee, spouse or former spouse, who is 60 or older and who has been covered for previous 6 months may continue coverage until eligible for Medicare. (Applies to companies with more than 20 employees; does not apply when employee quits for reasons other than health.)

Hawaii

Haw. Rev. Stat. § 393-15

Employers affected: All employers required to offer health insurance (those paying a regular employee a monthly wage at least 86.67 times the state hourly minimum wage—about $542).

Qualifying event: Employee is hospitalized or prevented by sickness from working.

Length of coverage for employee: Employer must pay insurance premiums for 3 months or for as long employer continues to pay employee's wages, whichever is longer.

Illinois

215 Ill. Comp. Stat. §§ 5/367e, 5/367.2

Employers affected: All employers who offer group health insurance.

Eligible employees: Employees continuously insured for previous 3 months.

Qualifying event: Termination of employment.

Length of coverage for employee: 9 months.

Length of coverage for dependents: 9 months.

Time employee has to apply: 10 days after termination or receiving notice from employer, whichever is later, but not more than 60 days from termination.

State Health Insurance Continuation Laws (continued)

Special benefits: Excludes dental care; prescription drugs; vision services; disability income; specified diseases.

Special situations: Upon death or divorce, 2 years' coverage for spouse under 55; until eligible for Medicare or other group coverage for spouse over 55.

Indiana

Ind. Code Ann. § 27-8-15-31.1

Employers affected: Employers with 2 to 50 employees.

Eligible employees: Employed by same employer for at least one year and continuously insured for previous 90 days.

Qualifying event: Termination of employment; reduction in hours; dissolution of marriage; loss of dependent status.

Length of coverage for employee: 12 months.

Length of coverage for dependents: 12 months.

Time employer has to notify employee of continuation rights: 10 days after employee becomes eligible for continuation coverage.

Time employee has to apply: Must apply directly to insurer within 30 days after becoming eligible for continuation coverage.

Iowa

Iowa Code §§ 509B.3 to 509B.5

Employers affected: All employers who offer group health insurance.

Eligible employees: Employees continuously insured for previous 3 months.

Qualifying event: Any reason employee or dependent becomes ineligible for coverage.

Length of coverage for employee: 9 months.

Length of coverage for dependents: 9 months.

Time employer has to notify employee of continuation rights: 10 days after termination of coverage.

Time employee has to apply: 10 days after termination of coverage or receiving notice of continuation rights from employer, whichever is later, but no more than 31 days from termination of coverage.

Special benefits: Excludes dental care; prescription drugs; vision services.

Kansas

Kan. Stat. Ann. § 40-2209(i)

Employers affected: All employers who offer group health insurance.

Eligible employees: Employees continuously insured for previous 3 months.

Qualifying event: Any reason employee or dependent becomes ineligible for coverage.

Length of coverage for employee: 6 months.

State Health Insurance Continuation Laws (continued)

Length of coverage for dependents: 6 months.

Time employee has to apply: 31 days from termination of coverage.

Kentucky

Ky. Rev. Stat. Ann. § 304.18-110

Employers affected: All employers who offer group health insurance.

Eligible employees: Employees continuously insured for previous 3 months.

Qualifying event: Any reason employee or dependent becomes ineligible for coverage.

Length of coverage for employee: 18 months.

Length of coverage for dependents: 18 months.

Time employer has to notify employee of continuation rights: Employer must notify insurer as soon as employee's coverage ends; insurer then notifies employee.

Time employee has to apply: 31 days from receipt of insurer's notice.

Special benefits: Excludes specific diseases; accidental injury.

Louisiana

La. Rev. Stat. Ann. §§ 22:215.7, 22:215.13

Employers affected: All employers who offer group health insurance.

Eligible employees: Employees continuously insured for previous 3 months.

Qualifying event: Termination of employment.

Length of coverage for employee: 12 months.

Length of coverage for dependents: 12 months.

Time employee has to apply: Must apply and submit payment before group coverage ends.

Special benefits: Excludes dental care; vision care; specific diseases; accidental injury.

Special situations: Surviving spouse who is 50 or older may have coverage until remarriage or eligibility for Medicare or other insurance.

Maine

Me. Rev. Stat. Ann. tit. 24-A, § 2809-A

Employers affected: All employers who offer group health insurance.

Eligible employees: Employees continuously insured for previous 3 months.

Qualifying event: Termination of employment.

Length of coverage for employee: One year (either group or individual coverage at discretion of insurer).

Length of coverage for dependents: One year (either group or individual coverage at discretion of insurer). Upon

State Health Insurance Continuation Laws (continued)

death of insured, continuation only if original plan provided for coverage.

Time employee has to apply: 90 days from termination of group coverage.

Special situations: Temporary layoff or work-related injury or disease: Employee and dependents entitled to one year group or individual continuation coverage. (Must have been continuously insured for previous 6 months; must apply within 31 days.)

Maryland

Md. Code Ann., [Ins.] §§ 15-407 to 15-410

Employers affected: All employers who offer group health insurance.

Eligible employees: Employees continuously insured for previous 3 months.

Qualifying event: Involuntary termination of employment; death of employee; change in marital status.

Length of coverage for employee: 18 months.

Length of coverage for dependents: 18 months upon death of employee; upon change in marital status, 18 months or until spouse remarries or becomes eligible for other coverage.

Time employer has to notify employee of continuation rights: Must notify insurer within 14 days of receiving employee's request.

Time employee has to apply: 45 days from termination of coverage. Em-ployee begins application process by requesting an election of continuation notification form from employer.

Massachusetts

Mass. Gen. Laws ch. 175, §§ 110G, 110I; ch. 176J, § 9

Employers affected: All employers who offer group health insurance; special rules for employers with Small Group Health Insurance (2 to 19 employees).

Eligible employees: All insured employees are eligible.

Qualifying event: Involuntary layoff; death of insured employee. For Small Group Health Insurance employer add: reduction in hours; divorce or legal separation; loss of dependent status; employee's eligibility for Medicare; employer's bankruptcy.

Length of coverage for employee: 39 weeks (but may not exceed time covered under original coverage).

Small Group Health Insurance employer: 18 months. (29 months if disabled.)

Length of coverage for dependents: 39 weeks. (Divorced or separated spouse entitled to benefits only if included in judgment decree.)

Small Group Health Insurance employer: 18 months upon termination or reduction in hours; 29 months if disabled; 36 months on divorce, death of employee, employee's eligibility for Medicare, employer's bankruptcy.

State Health Insurance Continuation Laws (continued)

Time employer has to notify employee of continuation rights: When employee becomes eligible for continuation benefits.

Time employee has to apply: 30 days. Small Group Health Insurance employer, 60 days.

Special situations: Termination due to plant closing: 90 days coverage for employee and dependents, at the same payment terms as before closing.

Michigan

Mich. Comp. Laws § 500.3612

Employers affected: All employers offering group health and disability insurance.

Eligible employees: Employees continuously insured for 3 months.

Qualifying event: Termination of group coverage for any reason except discharge for gross misconduct.

Length of coverage for employee: Eligible employee and dependents may convert to an individual policy without evidence of insurability or regard for pre-existing condition.

Time employer has to notify employee of continuation rights: Within 14 days of termination of coverage.

Time employee has to apply: No later than 30 days from termination of coverage.

Minnesota

Minn. Stat. Ann. § 62A.17

Employers affected: All employers who offer group health insurance.

Eligible employees: All insured employees are eligible.

Qualifying event: Termination of employment; reduction in hours.

Length of coverage for employee: 18 months.

Length of coverage for dependents: 18 months.

Time employer has to notify employee of continuation rights: Within 10 days of termination of coverage.

Time employee has to apply: 60 days from termination of coverage or receipt of employer's notice, whichever is later.

Mississippi

Miss. Code Ann. § 83-9-51

Employers affected: All employers who offer group health insurance.

Eligible employees: Employees continuously insured for previous 3 months.

Qualifying event: Termination of employment; divorce; employee's death; employee's eligibility for Medicare; loss of dependent status.

Length of coverage for employee: 12 months.

Length of coverage for dependents: 12 months.

Time employer has to notify employee of continuation rights: Insurer must notify former or deceased employee's dependent child or divorced spouse of

State Health Insurance Continuation Laws (continued)

option to continue insurance within 14 days of their becoming ineligible for coverage on employee's policy.

Time employee has to apply: Employee must apply and submit payment before group coverage ends; dependents or former spouse must elect continuation coverage within 30 days of receiving insurer's notice.

Special benefits: Excludes dental and vision care; any benefits other than hospital, surgical or major medical.

Missouri

Mo. Rev. Stat. § 376.428

Employers affected: All employers who offer group health insurance.

Eligible employees: Employees continuously insured for previous 3 months.

Qualifying event: Termination of employment.

Length of coverage for employee: 9 months.

Length of coverage for dependents: 9 months.

Time employer has to notify employee of continuation rights: No later than date group coverage would end.

Time employee has to apply: 31 days from date group coverage would end.

Special benefits: Excludes dental and vision care; any benefits other than hospital, surgical or major medical. Must include: maternity benefits if they were provided under group policy.

Montana

Mont. Code Ann. §§ 33-22-506 to 33-22-510

Employers affected: All employers who offer group health insurance.

Eligible employees: Employees continuously insured for previous 3 months.

Qualifying event: Reduction in hours.

Length of coverage for employee: One year. Upon reduction in hours (with employer's consent).

Length of coverage for dependents: One year. Upon reduction in hours (with employer's consent).

Time employee has to apply: 31 days from date group coverage would end.

Special situations: Insurer may not discontinue benefits to child with disabilities after child exceeds age limit for dependent status.

Nebraska

Neb. Rev. Stat. §§ 44-1640 and following, 44-7406

Employers affected: Employers not subject to federal COBRA laws.

Eligible employees: All insured employees are eligible.

Qualifying event: Involuntary termination of employment (layoff due to labor dispute not considered involuntary).

Length of coverage for employee: 6 months.

State Health Insurance Continuation Laws (continued)

Length of coverage for dependents: One year upon death of insured employee.

Time employer has to notify employee of continuation rights: Within 10 days of termination of employment must send notice by certified mail.

Time employee has to apply: 10 days from receipt of employer's notice.

Special situations: Subjects of domestic abuse, who have lost coverage under abuser's plan and who do not qualify for COBRA, may have 18 months' coverage (applies to all employers).

Nevada

Nev. Rev. Stat. Ann. §§ 689B.245 and following; 689B.0345

Employers affected: Employers with fewer than 20 employees.

Eligible employees: Employees continuously insured for previous 12 months.

Qualifying event: Involuntary termination of employment; involuntary reduction in hours; death of employee; divorce or legal separation; loss of dependent status; employee's eligibility for Medicare.

Length of coverage for employee: 18 months.

Length of coverage for dependents: 36 months.

Time employer has to notify employee of continuation rights: 14 days after receiving notice of employee's eligibility.

Time employee has to apply: Must notify employer within 60 days of becoming eligible for continuation coverage; must apply within 60 days after receiving employer's notice.

Special situations: Leave without pay due to disability: 12 months for employee and dependents (applies to all employers).

New Hampshire

N.H. Rev. Stat. Ann. § 415:18(VIIg), (VII-a)

Employers affected: Employers with 2 to 19 employees.

Eligible employees: All insured employees are eligible.

Qualifying event: Any reason employee or dependent becomes ineligible for coverage.

Length of coverage for employee: 18 months; 29 months if disabled at termination or during first 60 days of continuation coverage.

Length of coverage for dependents: 18 months; 29 months if disabled at termination or during first 60 days of continuation coverage; 36 months upon death of employee, divorce or legal separation, loss of dependent status, employee's eligibility for Medicare.

Time employer has to notify employee of continuation rights: Within 15 days of termination of coverage.

Time employee has to apply: Within 31 days of termination of coverage.

State Health Insurance Continuation Laws (continued)

Special benefits: Includes dental insurance.

Special situations: Layoff or termination due to strike: 6 months' coverage with option to extend for an additional 12 months. Surviving, divorced or legally separated spouse who is 55 or older may continue benefits until eligible for Medicare or other employer-based group insurance.

New Jersey

N.J. Stat. Ann. §§ 17B:27-30, 17B:27-51.12, 17B:27A-27

Employers affected: Employers with 2 to 50 employees.

Eligible employees: Employed full-time (25 or more hours).

Qualifying event: Termination of employment; reduction in hours.

Length of coverage for employee: 12 months.

Length of coverage for dependents: 180 days upon death of employee (applies to all employers).

Time employer has to notify employee of continuation rights: At time of qualifying event employer or carrier notifies employee.

Time employee has to apply: Within 30 days of qualifying event.

Special benefits: Coverage must be identical to that offered to current employees.

Special situations: Total disability— Employee who has been insured for

previous 3 months and employee's dependents entitled to continuation coverage that includes all benefits offered by group policy (applies to all employers).

New Mexico

N.M. Stat. Ann. § 59A-18-16

Employers affected: All employers who offer group health insurance.

Eligible employees: All insured employees are eligible.

Qualifying event: Termination of employment.

Length of coverage for employee: 6 months.

Length of coverage for dependents: May continue group coverage or convert to individual policy upon death of employee, divorce or legal separation

Time employer has to notify employee of continuation rights: Must give written notice at time of termination.

Time employee has to apply: 30 days after receiving employer's or insurer's notice.

New York

N.Y. Ins. Law §§ 3221(f), 3221(m)

Employers affected: All employers who offer group health insurance.

Eligible employees: All insured employees are eligible.

Qualifying event: Termination of employment; death of employee; divorce or legal separation; loss of dependent

State Health Insurance Continuation Laws (continued)

status; employee's eligibility for Medicare.

Length of coverage for employee: 18 months; 29 months if disabled at termination or during first 60 days of continuation coverage.

Length of coverage for dependents: 18 months; 29 months if disabled at termination or during first 60 days of continuation coverage; 36 months upon death of employee, divorce or legal separation, loss of dependent status, employee's eligibility for Medicare.

Time employee has to apply: 60 days after termination or receipt of notice, whichever is later.

Special situations: Employee who has been insured for previous 3 months and dependents may convert to an individual plan instead of group continuation (must apply within 45 days of termination).

Employee who is 60 or older and has been continuously insured for at least 2 years is entitled to a converted policy with set maximum premium limits.

North Carolina

N.C. Gen. Stat. §§ 58-53-5 to 58-53-40

Employers affected: All employers who offer group health insurance.

Eligible employees: Employees continuously insured for previous 3 months.

Qualifying event: Termination of employment.

Length of coverage for employee: 18 months.

Length of coverage for dependents: 18 months.

Time employer has to notify employee of continuation rights: Employer has option of notifying employee as part of the exit process.

Time employee has to apply: 60 days.

Special benefits: Excludes dental care; prescription drugs; vision care; any benefits other than hospital, surgical or major medical.

North Dakota

N.D. Cent. Code §§ 26.1-36-23, 26.1-36-23.1

Employers affected: All employers who offer group health insurance.

Eligible employees: Employees continuously insured for previous 3 months.

Qualifying event: Termination of employment.

Length of coverage for employee: 39 weeks

Length of coverage for dependents: 39 weeks. 36 months if required by divorce or annulment decree.

Time employee has to apply: Within 10 days of termination or of receiving notice of continuation rights, whichever is later, but no more than 31 days from termination.

State Health Insurance Continuation Laws (continued)

Special benefits: Excludes dental care; prescription drugs; vision care; any benefits other than hospital, surgical or major medical.

Ohio

Ohio Rev. Code Ann. §§ 3923.38; 1751.53

Employers affected: All employers who offer group health insurance.

Eligible employees: Employees continuously insured for previous 3 months who are entitled to unemployment benefits.

Qualifying event: Involuntary termination of employment.

Length of coverage for employee: 6 months.

Length of coverage for dependents: 6 months.

Time employer has to notify employee of continuation rights: At termination of employment.

Time employee has to apply: Whichever is earlier: 31 days after coverage terminates; 10 days after coverage terminates if employer notified employee of continuation rights prior to termination; 10 days after employer notified employee of continuation rights, if notice was given after coverage terminated.

Special benefits: Excludes dental care; prescription drugs; vision care; any benefits other than hospital, surgical or major medical.

Oklahoma

Okla. Stat. Ann. tit. 36, § 4509

Employers affected: All employers who offer group health insurance.

Eligible employees: Insured for at least 6 months. (All other employees and their dependents entitled to 30 days' continuation coverage.)

Qualifying event: Any reason coverage terminates.

Length of coverage for employee: 3 months for basic coverage, 6 months for major medical at the same premium rate prior to termination of coverage.

Length of coverage for dependents: 3 months for basic coverage, 6 months for major medical at the same premium rate prior to termination of coverage.

Special benefits: Includes maternity care.

Oregon

Or. Rev. Stat. §§ 743.600 to 743.610

Employers affected: Employers not subject to federal COBRA laws.

Eligible employees: Employees continuously insured for previous 3 months.

Qualifying event: Termination of employment.

Length of coverage for employee: 6 months.

Length of coverage for dependents: 6 months.

Time employee has to apply: 10 days after termination or receiving notice of

State Health Insurance Continuation Laws (continued)

continuation rights, whichever is later, but not more than 31 days.

Special benefits: Excludes dental care; prescription drugs; vision care; any benefits other than hospital, surgical or major medical.

Special situations: Surviving, divorced or legally separated spouse who is 55 or older and dependent children entitled to continuation benefits until spouse remarries or is eligible for other coverage. Must include dental, vision or prescription drug benefits if they were offered in original plan (applies to employers with 20 or more employees).

Pennsylvania

40 Pa. Cons. Stat. Ann. § 756.2(d)

No laws for continuation insurance. Employees who have been continuously insured for the previous 3 months may convert to an individual policy.

Rhode Island

R.I. Gen. Laws §§ 27-19.1-1, 27-20.4-1 to 27.20.4-2

Employers affected: All employers who offer group health insurance.

Eligible employees: All insured employees are eligible.

Qualifying event: Involuntary termination of employment; death of employee; change in marital status; permanent reduction in workforce; employer's going out of business.

Length of coverage for employee: 18 months (but not longer than continuous employment).

Length of coverage for dependents: 18 months (but not longer than continuous employment).

Time employer has to notify employee of continuation rights: Employers must post a conspicuous notice of employee continuation rights.

Time employee has to apply: 30 days from termination of coverage.

Special situations: If right to receive continuing health insurance is stated in the divorce judgment, divorced spouse has right to continue coverage as long as employee remains covered or until divorced spouse remarries or becomes eligible for other group insurance. If covered employee remarries, divorced spouse must be given right to purchase an individual policy from same insurer.

South Carolina

S.C. Code Ann. § 38-71-770

Employers affected: All employers who offer group health insurance.

Eligible employees: Employees continuously insured for previous 6 months.

Qualifying event: Any reason employee or dependent becomes ineligible for coverage.

Length of coverage for employee: 6 months (in addition to part of month remaining at termination).

State Health Insurance Continuation Laws (continued)

Length of coverage for dependents: 6 months (in addition to part of month remaining at termination).

Time employer has to notify employee of continuation rights: At time of termination must clearly and meaningfully advise employee of continuation rights.

Special benefits: Excludes accidental injury; specific diseases.

South Dakota

S.D. Codified Laws Ann. §§ 58-18-7.5, 58-18-7.12; 58-18C-1

Employers affected: All employers who offer group health insurance.

Eligible employees: Employees continuously insured for previous 6 months.

Qualifying event: Termination of employment; death of employee; divorce or legal separation; loss of dependent status; employee's eligibility for Medicare.

Length of coverage for employee: 18 months; 29 months if disabled at termination or during first 60 days of continuation coverage.

Length of coverage for dependents: 18 months; 29 months if disabled at termination or during first 60 days of continuation coverage; 36 months upon death of employee, divorce or legal separation, loss of dependent status, employee's eligibility for Medicare.

Special situations: When employer goes out of business: 12 months continuation coverage available to all employees. Employer must notify employees within 10 days of termination of benefits; employees must apply within 60 days of receipt of employer's notice or within 90 days of termination of benefits if no notice given.

Tennessee

Tenn. Code Ann. § 56-7-2312

Employers affected: All employers who offer group health insurance.

Eligible employees: Employees continuously insured for previous 3 months.

Qualifying event: Termination of employment; death of employee; change in marital status.

Length of coverage for employee: 3 months (in addition to part of month remaining at termination).

Length of coverage for dependents: 3 months (in addition to part of month remaining at termination); 15 months upon death of employee or divorce.

Special situations: Employee or dependent who is pregnant at time of termination entitled to continuation benefits for 6 months following the end of pregnancy.

Texas

Tex. Ins. Code Ann. §§ 3.51-6(d3), 3.51-8

Employers affected: All employers who offer group health insurance.

State Health Insurance Continuation Laws (continued)

Eligible employees: Employees continuously insured for previous 3 months.

Qualifying event: Termination of employment (except for cause); employee leaves for health reasons.

Length of coverage for employee: 6 months.

Length of coverage for dependents: 6 months.

Time employee has to apply: 31 days from termination of coverage or receiving notice of continuation rights from employer or insurer, whichever is later.

Special situations: Layoff due to a labor dispute—employee entitled to continuation benefits for duration of dispute, but no longer than 6 months.

Utah

Utah Code Ann. §§ 31A-22-703, 31A-22-714

Employers affected: All employers who offer group health insurance.

Eligible employees: Employees continuously insured for previous 6 months.

Qualifying event: Termination of employment.

Length of coverage for employee: 6 months.

Length of coverage for dependents: 6 months.

Time employer has to notify employee of continuation rights: In writing within 30 days of termination of coverage.

Time employee has to apply: Within 30 days of receiving employer's notice of continuation rights.

Special benefits: Excludes accidental injury; catastrophic benefits; dental care; specific diseases.

Vermont

Vt. Stat. Ann. tit. 8, §§ 4090a to 4090c

Employers affected: All employers who offer group health insurance.

Eligible employees: Employees continuously insured for previous 3 months.

Qualifying event: Termination of employment; death of employee; change of marital status; loss of dependent status.

Length of coverage for employee: 6 months.

Length of coverage for dependents: 6 months.

Time employee has to apply: Within 60 days (upon death of employee or group member), or within 30 days (upon termination of employment, change of marital status or loss of dependent status) of the date that group coverage terminates, or the date of being notified of continuation rights, whichever is sooner.

Virginia

Va. Code Ann. §§ 38.2-3541 to 38.2-3542; 38.2-3416

Employers affected: All employers who offer group health insurance.

State Health Insurance Continuation Laws (continued)

Eligible employees: Employees continuously insured for previous 3 months.

Qualifying event: Any reason employee or dependent becomes ineligible for coverage.

Length of coverage for employee: 90 days.

Length of coverage for dependents: 90 days.

Time employer has to notify employee of continuation rights: 15 days from termination of coverage.

Time employee has to apply: Must apply for continuation and pay entire 90-day premium before termination of coverage.

Special situations: Employee may convert to an individual policy instead of group continuation coverage (must apply within 31 days of termination of coverage).

Washington

Wash. Rev. Code Ann. §§ 48.21.250, 48.21.075

Employers affected: Optional for all employers who offer group health insurance (except during strike).

Eligible employees: All insured employees are eligible.

Qualifying event: Any reason employee or dependent becomes ineligible for coverage.

Length of coverage for employee: Term and rate of coverage agreed upon by employer and employee.

Length of coverage for dependents: Term and rate of coverage agreed upon by employer and employee.

Special situations: Layoff or termination due to strike—6 months' coverage with employee paying premiums (mandatory for all employers). In other situations: If optional continuation benefits are not offered, employee may convert to an individual policy (must apply within 31 days of termination of group coverage).

West Virginia

W.Va. Code §§ 33-16-2, 33-16-3(e)

Employers affected: Employers providing insurance for at least 10 employees.

Eligible employees: All insured employees are eligible.

Qualifying event: Involuntary layoff.

Length of coverage for employee: 18 months.

Wisconsin

Wis. Stat. Ann. § 632.897

Employers affected: All employers who offer group health insurance.

Eligible employees: Employees continuously insured for previous 3 months.

Qualifying event: Any reason employee or dependent becomes ineligible for coverage.

Length of coverage for employee: 18 months (or longer at insurer's option).

State Health Insurance Continuation Laws (continued)

Length of coverage for dependents: 18 months (or longer at insurer's option).

Time employer has to notify employee of continuation rights: 5 days from termination of coverage.

Time employee has to apply: 30 days after receiving employer's notice.

Wyoming

Wyo. Stat. § 26-19-113

Employers affected: Employers not subject to federal COBRA laws.

Eligible employees: Employees continuously insured for previous 3 months.

Qualifying event: Termination of employment.

Length of coverage for employee: 12 months.

Length of coverage for dependents: 12 months.

Time employee has to apply: 31 days from termination of coverage.

Special benefits: If dental, vision care or any benefits other than hospital, surgical or major medical were included in the group policy, they may be continued at employee or dependent's request.

Current as of February 2003

E.   Unemployment Compensation

When you tell the employee that he has been terminated, he will likely ask you for information about unemployment compensation. This is understandable, as life—and bills—won't stop just because he has lost his job. As with the other issues discussed in this chapter, you must prepare now, prior to the termination, so that you can answer the employee's questions during the termination. Common questions include whether the termination will make the employee ineligible for benefits and whether you will contest the employee's claim for benefits.

1.   Will the Employee Be Eligible?

Fired employees can claim unemployment benefits if they were terminated because of financial cutbacks or because they were not a good fit for the job for which they were hired. They can also receive benefits if their actions that led to the termination were relatively minor, unintentional or isolated.

In most states, a fired employee will not be able to receive unemployment benefits if he was fired for "misconduct." Although you may think that any action that leads to termination should constitute misconduct, the unemployment laws don't look at it that way. Some actions that result in termination simply aren't serious enough to be viewed as misconduct and to justify denying benefits to the terminated worker.

So how serious does an action have to be to rise to the level of misconduct? Generally speaking, an employee engages in misconduct if he willfully does something that substantially injures your business interests. Thus, revealing trade secrets or sexually harassing coworkers is misconduct, while mere inefficiency or an unpleasant personality is not. Other common types of actions that constitute misconduct include extreme insubordination, chronic tardiness, numerous unexcused absences, intoxication on the job and dishonesty.

Common types of actions that do *not* constitute misconduct are poor performance because of lack of skills, good faith errors in judgment, off-work conduct that does not have an impact on the employer's interests and poor relations with coworkers.

> **EXAMPLE:** Miller works in the warehouse of a shipping company that belongs to Juanita. One night, Miller is arrested for public drunkenness and fined $500. Although Miller has never appeared at work drunk, and although he is an exemplary employee, Juanita fires Miller because she does not want lawbreakers working for her company. When Miller applies for unemployment benefits, the unemployment office grants his application, because the action that led to Miller's termination was off-work conduct that did not damage the shipping company's interests.

It is important to remember that the issue of what is or is not misconduct is a matter of interpretation and degree. Annoying one co-worker might not be misconduct, but intentionally engaging in actions that anger an entire department even after repeated warnings might.

2.   Should You Contest the Claim?

Your state's unemployment office—and not you—will ultimately decide whether the terminated employee can receive unemployment benefits. You do, however, have the option of contesting the employee's application, and that option gives you a great deal of power as far as the employee is concerned. In California, for example, the unemployment board presumes that a terminated employee did not engage in misconduct unless the employer contests the claim. The effect of this presumption is that all terminated employees receive unemployment benefits unless the former employer intervenes.

a.   When Not to Contest the Claim

There will be no reason—and no grounds—for you to contest an unemployment claim if the reason for the employee's firing was sloppy work, carelessness or poor judgment. Similarly, if the worker simply failed to meet your performance expectations or was unable to learn new skills, you would have no basis for challenging the claim.

Even in cases where an employee does engage in misconduct, you might want to waive your right to contest as part of a severance package that you give to the employee. (See Chapter 8, Section D for more about severance packages and unemployment insurance.)

b.   When to Contest a Claim

You should contest a claim only if you truly believe that you have grounds to do so—that is, that the employee engaged in serious misconduct. And even then, you should contest a claim only if you have a good and pragmatic reason for doing it. Employers will typically fight for one of two reasons:

- They are concerned that their unemployment insurance rates may increase. After all, the employer—and not the employee—pays for unemployment insurance. The amount the employer pays is often based in part on the number of claims made against the employer by former employees.

- They are concerned that the employee plans to file a wrongful termination action. The unemployment application process can be a valuable time for discovering the employee's side of the story, and it can also provide an excellent opportunity for gathering evidence—both from the employee and from witness.

If you are leaning towards fighting an unemployment compensation claim, proceed with extreme caution. Such battles not only cost time and money, they also ensure that the fired employee will become an enemy. You might even inspire the employee to file a wrongful termination action when he otherwise might not have. If the fired worker has friends who remain on the job, they too may doubt and distrust your tactics.

Before making any decisions, you might want to do some research by contacting your state's unemployment office for specific information about what constitutes misconduct in your state. This office can tell you what effect a successful claim will have on your rates. If it's relatively small, you might be wise to back off.

If you still want to fight the claim, however, consider paying for a consultation with a lawyer. (Getting legal advice is covered in Chapter 11.) In addition to advising you about the claim, the lawyer can advise you on whether it's wise to tell this particular employee face to face that you will contest his claim. Generally speaking, we suggest that you answer the employee's questions in a truthful and straightforward manner. If, after doing your research and consulting with an attorney, you know that you will contest the employee's claim, you gain nothing by evading the employee's questions.

The Anatomy of an Unemployment Compensation Claim

Although the details of unemployment compensation vary in each state, some general principles apply in most cases. An unemployment claim will typically proceed through the steps described below.

The claim is filed. The process starts when the former employee files a claim with the state unemployment program. You receive written notice of the claim and can file a written objection—usually within seven to ten days.

Eligibility is determined. The state agency makes an initial determination of whether the former employee is eligible to get unemployment benefits. Usually there's no hearing at this stage.

The referee conducts a hearing. You or the former employee can appeal the initial eligibility decision and have a hearing before a referee —a hearing officer who is on the staff of the state agency. Normally conducted in a private room at the unemployment office, this airing of the situation is the most important step in the process. At the hearing, you and the former employee each have your say. In addition, you are entitled to have a lawyer there and to present witnesses and any relevant written records, such as employee evaluations or warning letters.

Administrative appeal. Either you or the employee can appeal the referee's decision to an administrative agency, such as a board of review. This appeal usually is based solely on the testimony and documents recorded at the referee's hearing, although in some states the review board can take additional evidence. While the review board is free to draw its own conclusions from the evidence and overrule the referee, more often than not it goes along with the referee's ruling.

Judicial appeal. Either side can appeal to the state court system, but this is rare. Typically, a court will overturn the agency's decision only if the decision is contrary to law or isn't supported by substantial evidence.

Adapted from *The Employer's Legal Handbook,* by Fred S. Steingold (Nolo)

F.   Written Explanations of the Termination

When you conduct the termination meeting, we suggest that you give the employee a brief but truthful explanation for the termination. Sometimes, an employee will ask that you put the reasons in writing. If this makes you nervous, it should. Unfortunately, about half the states have laws requiring you to do as the employee asks. Although you don't have to present this document at the time you fire the employee, it's a good idea to begin preparing it now.

Laws that require employers to give former employees letters describing their work histories are known as service letter laws. These laws vary widely from state to state. In Minnesota, for example, an employer must provide a written statement of the reasons for an employee's dismissal within five days after the employee requests it in writing. Kansas also has a service letter law, but it does not require employers to provide a reason for the firing; they need only state length of employment, job classification and wage rate.

When a former employee asks you to provide a service letter, he or she is usually asking for the truth—meaning the whole truth about the firing. Chances are, many of them will not like the letters they receive. Fortunately, a number of states specifically prevent employers from being sued for defamation because of what they write in a service letter, as long as the employer's statement is "truthful" or "in good faith." Keep in mind, however, there is usually nothing to be gained from being painfully blunt. Even though the law protects you in telling the truth, a modicum of politeness is always better than unbridled boorishness.

State Laws on Information from Former Employers

Alaska

Alaska Stat. § 09.65.160

Information that may be disclosed

- job performance

Who may request or receive information

- prospective employer
- former or current employee

Employer immune from liability unless

- employer knowingly or intentionally discloses information that is false or misleading or that violates employee's civil rights

Arizona

Ariz. Rev. Stat. Ann. § 23-1361

Information that may be disclosed

- job performance
- reasons for termination or separation
- performance evaluation or opinion
- knowledge, qualifications, skills or abilities
- education, training or experience
- professional conduct

Who may request or receive information:

- prospective employer
- former or current employee

Copy to employee required

- copy of disclosures must be sent to employee's last known address

Employer immune from liability

- employer with fewer than 100 employees who provides only the information listed above, or
- employer with at least 100 employees who has a regular practice of providing information requested by a prospective employer

No employer immunity if:

- information is intentionally misleading, or
- employer provided information knowing it was false or not caring if it was true or false

Arkansas

Ark. Code Ann. § 11-3-204

Information that may be disclosed

- reasons for termination or separation
- length of employment, pay level and history
- performance evaluation or opinion
- job description and duties
- eligibility for rehire
- attendance
- drug and alcohol test results from the past year
- threats of violence, harassing acts or threatening behavior

Who may request or receive information

- prospective employer (employee must provide written consent)
- former or current employee

State Laws on Information from Former Employers (continued)

Employer immune from liability unless

- employer disclosed information knowing it was false or not caring if it was true or false

Other provisions

- employee consent required before employer can release information
- consent must follow required format and must be signed and dated
- consent is valid only while employment application is still active, but no longer than 6 months

California

Cal. Civ. Code § 47(c); Cal. Lab. Code §§ 1053, 1055

Information that may be disclosed

- job performance
- reasons for termination or separation
- knowledge, qualifications, skills or abilities (based upon credible evidence)
- eligibility for rehire

Who may request or receive information

- prospective employer

Employer required to write letter

- public utility companies only

Colorado

Colo. Rev. Stat. § 8-2-114

Information that may be disclosed

- job performance
- reasons for termination or separation

- knowledge, qualifications, skills or abilities
- eligibility for rehire
- work-related habits

Who may request or receive information

- prospective employer
- former or current employee

Copy to employee required

- upon request, a copy must be sent to employee's last known address
- employee may obtain a copy in person at the employer's place of business during normal business hours
- employer may charge reproduction costs if multiple copies are requested

Employer immune from liability unless

- information disclosed was false and employer knew or reasonably should have known it was false

Connecticut

Conn. Gen. Stat. Ann. § 31-51

Information that may be disclosed

- "truthful statement of any facts"

Who may request or receive information

- prospective employer
- former or current employee

State Laws on Information from Former Employers (continued)

Delaware

Del. Code Ann. tit. 19, §§ 708 to 709

Information that may be disclosed

all employers

- job performance

- performance evaluation or opinion

- work-related characteristics

- violations of law

health or child care employers

- reasons for termination or separation

- length of employment, pay level and history

- job description and duties

- substantiated incidents of abuse, neglect, violence or threats of violence

- disciplinary actions

Who may request or receive information

- prospective employer (health or child care employers must provide signed statement from prospective applicant authorizing former employer to release information)

Employer immune from liability unless

- information was known to be false, was deliberately misleading or was disclosed without caring whether it was true, or

- information was confidential or disclosed in violation of a nondisclosure agreement

Employer required to write letter

- letter required for employment in healthcare and child care facilities

- letter must follow required format

- employer must have written consent from employee

- employer must send letter within 10 days of receiving request

Florida

Fla. Stat. Ann. §§ 768.095; 435.10; 655.51

Information that may be disclosed

- reasons for termination or separation (employers that require background checks)

- disciplinary matters (employers that require background checks)

- violation of an industry-related law or regulation, that has been reported to appropriate enforcing authority (banks and financial institutions)

Who may request or receive information

- prospective employer

- former or current employee

Employer immune from liability unless

- information is known to be false or is disclosed without caring whether it is true, or

- disclosure violates employee's civil rights

Employer required to write letter

- only employers that require background checks

State Laws on Information from Former Employers (continued)

Georgia

Ga. Code Ann. § 34-1-4

Information that may be disclosed

- job performance
- qualifications, skills or abilities
- violations of state law

Who may request or receive information

- prospective employer
- former or current employee

Employer immune from liability unless

- information was disclosed in violation of a nondisclosure agreement, or
- information was confidential according to federal, state or local law or regulations

Hawaii

Haw. Rev. Stat. § 663-1.95

Information that may be disclosed

- job performance

Who may request or receive information

- prospective employer

Employer immune from liability unless

- information disclosed was knowingly false or misleading

Idaho

Idaho Code § 44-201(2)

Information that may be disclosed

- job performance
- performance evaluation or opinion
- professional conduct

Employer immune from liability unless

- information is deliberately misleading or known to be false

Illinois

745 Ill. Comp. Stat. § 46/10

Information that may be disclosed

- job performance

Who may request or receive information

- prospective employer

Employer immune from liability

- if information is truthful
- no employer immunity if information is knowingly false or in violation of a civil right

Indiana

Ind. Code Ann. §§ 22-5-3-1(b),(c); 22-6-3-1

Information that may be disclosed

- reasons for termination or separation
- length of employment, pay level and history
- job description and duties

State Laws on Information from Former Employers (continued)

Who may request or receive information

- former or current employee (must be in writing)

Copy to employee required

- prospective employer must provide copy of any written communications from current or former employers that may affect hiring decision
- prospective employee must make request in writing within 30 days of applying for employment

Employer immune from liability unless

- information was known to be false

Employer required to write letter

- only upon written request from employee
- letter must state nature and length of employment and reason, if any, for separation
- employers that don't require written recommendations do not have to provide them

Iowa

Iowa Code § 91B.2

Information that may be disclosed

- "work-related information"

Who may request or receive information

- prospective employer
- former or current employee

Employer immune from liability unless

- information violates employee's civil rights
- information is not relevant to the inquiry being made
- information is disclosed without checking its truthfulness, or
- information is given to a person who has no legitimate interest in receiving it

Kansas

Kan. Stat. Ann. §§ 44-808(3); 44-199a

Information that may be disclosed

does not have to be in writing

- length of employment, pay level and history
- job description and duties

must be in writing

- performance evaluation or opinion (written evaluation conducted prior to employee's separation)
- reasons for termination or separation

Who may request or receive information

- prospective employer (written request required for performance evaluation and reasons for termination or separation)
- former or current employee (request must be in writing)

Copy to employee required

- employee must have access to reasons for termination or separation and performance evaluations

State Laws on Information from Former Employers (continued)

- employee must be given copy of written evaluation upon request

Employer immune from liability

- employer who provides information as it is specified in the law

Employer required to write letter

- upon written request, must give former employee a service letter stating the length of employment, job classification and rate of pay

Louisiana

La. Rev. Stat. Ann. § 23:291

Information that may be disclosed

- job performance
- performance evaluation or opinion
- knowledge, qualifications, skills or abilities
- job description and duties
- attendance, attitude and effort
- awards, demotions and promotions
- disciplinary actions

Who may request or receive information

- prospective employer
- former or current employee

Employer immune from liability unless

- information is knowingly false or deliberately misleading

Maine

Me. Rev. Stat. Ann. tit. 26, §§ 598, 630

Information that may be disclosed

- job performance
- work record

Who may request or receive information

- prospective employer

Employer immune from liability unless

- employer knowingly discloses false or deliberately misleading information, or
- employer discloses information without caring whether or not it is true

Employer required to write letter

- employer must provide a discharged employee with a written statement of the reasons for termination within 15 days of receiving employee's written request

Maryland

Md. Code Ann. [Cts. & Jud. Proc.] § 5-423

Information that may be disclosed

- job performance
- reasons for termination or separation
- information disclosed in a report or other document required by law or regulation

Who may request or receive information

- prospective employer
- former or current employee
- federal, state or industry regulatory authority

Employer immune from liability unless

- employer intended to harm or defame employee, or
- employer intentionally disclosed false information or disclosed without caring if it was false

State Laws on Information from Former Employers (continued)

Massachusetts

Mass. Gen. Laws ch. 111, § 72L 1/2

Information that may be disclosed (applies only to hospitals, convalescent or nursing homes, home health agencies and hospice programs)

- reasons for termination or separation
- length of employment, pay level and history

Employer immune from liability unless

- information disclosed was false and employer knew it was false

Michigan

Mich. Comp. Laws §§ 423.452; 423.506 to 423.507

Information that may be disclosed

- job performance (only information that is documented in personnel file)

Who may request or receive information

- prospective employer
- former or current employee

Employer immune from liability unless

- employer knew that information was false or misleading
- employer disclosed information without caring if it was true or false, or
- disclosure was specifically prohibited by a state or federal statute

Other provisions

- employer may not disclose any disciplinary action or letter of reprimand

that is more than 4 years old to a third party

- employer must notify employee by first class mail on or before the day of disclosure (does not apply if employee waived notification in a signed job application with another employer)

Minnesota

Minn. Stat. Ann. § 181.933

Employer immune from liability

- employer can't be sued for libel, slander or defamation for sending employee written statement of reasons for termination

Employer required to write letter

- employer must provide a written statement of the reasons for termination within 10 working days of receiving employee's request
- employee must make request in writing within 15 working days of being discharged

Missouri

Mo. Rev. Stat. §§ 290.140, 290.152

Information that may be disclosed

- reasons for termination or separation
- length of employment, pay level and history
- job description and duties

State Laws on Information from Former Employers (continued)

Who may request or receive information

- prospective employer (request must be in writing)

Copy to employee required

- employer sends copy to employee's last known address
- employee may request copy of letter up to one year after it was sent to prospective employer

Employer required to write letter

- applies only to employers with 7 or more employees, and to employees with at least 90 days' service
- letter must state the nature and length of employment and reason, if any, for separation
- employee must make request by certified mail within one year after separation
- employer must reply within 45 days of receiving request

Other provisions

- all information disclosed must be in writing and must be consistent with service letter

Montana

Mont. Code Ann. §§ 39-2-801, 39-2-802

Information that may be disclosed

- reasons for termination or separation

Who may request or receive information

- prospective employer

Employer required to write letter

- upon request, employer must give discharged employee a written statement of reasons for discharge
- if employer doesn't respond to request within a reasonable time, may not disclose reasons to another person

Nebraska

Neb. Rev. Stat. §§ 48-209 to 48-211

Employer required to write letter

- applies only to public utilities, transportation companies and contractors doing business with the state
- upon request from employee, must provide service letter that states length of employment, nature of work and reasons employee quit or was discharged
- letter must follow prescribed format for paper and signature

Nevada

Nev. Rev. Stat. Ann. § 613.210(4)

Employer required to write letter

- upon request of an employee who leaves or is discharged, employer must provide a written statement listing reasons for separation and any meritorious service employee may have performed
- statement not required unless employee has worked for at least 60 days
- employee entitled to only one statement

State Laws on Information from Former Employers
(continued)

New Mexico

N.M. Stat. Ann. § 50-12-1

Information that may be disclosed

- job performance

Who may request or receive information

no person specified ("when requested to provide a reference. . .")

Employer immune from liability unless

- information disclosed was known to be false or was deliberately misleading, or
- disclosure was careless or violated former employee's civil rights

North Carolina

N.C. Gen. Stat. § 1-539.12

Information that may be disclosed

- job performance
- reasons for termination or separation
- knowledge, qualifications, skills or abilities
- eligibility for rehire

Who may request or receive information

- prospective employer
- former or current employee

Employer immune from liability unless

- information disclosed was false and employer knew or reasonably should have known it was false

North Dakota

N.D. Cent. Code § 34-02-18

Information that may be disclosed

- job performance
- length of employment, pay level and history
- job description and duties

Who may request or receive information

- prospective employer

Employer immune from liability unless

- information was known to be false or was disclosed without caring whether it was true, or
- information was deliberately misleading

Ohio

Ohio Rev. Code Ann. § 4113.71

Information that may be disclosed

- job performance

Who may request or receive information

- prospective employer
- former or current employee

Employer immune from liability unless

- employer disclosed information knowing that it was false or with the deliberate intent to mislead the prospective employer or another person, or
- disclosure constitutes an unlawful discriminatory practice

State Laws on Information from Former Employers (continued)

Oklahoma

Okla. Stat. Ann. tit. 40, §§ 61, 171

Information that may be disclosed

- job performance

Who may request or receive information

- prospective employer (must have consent of employee)
- former or current employee

Employer immune from liability unless

- information was false and employer knew it was false or didn't care whether or not it was true

Employer required to write letter

- applies only to public utilities, transportation companies and contractors doing business with the state
- upon request from employee, must provide letter that states length of employment, nature of work and reasons employee quit or was discharged
- letter must follow prescribed format for paper and signature

Oregon

Or. Rev. Stat. § 30.178

Information that may be disclosed

- job performance

Who may request or receive information

- prospective employer
- former or current employee

Employer immune from liability unless

- information was knowingly false or deliberately misleading

- information was disclosed without caring whether or not it was true, or
- disclosure violated a civil right of the former employee

Rhode Island

R.I. Gen. Laws § 28-6.4-1(c)

Information that may be disclosed

- job performance

Who may request or receive information

- prospective employer
- former or current employee

Employer immune from liability unless

- information was knowingly false or deliberately misleading
- information was in violation of current or former employee's civil rights under the employment discrimination laws in effect at time of disclosure

South Carolina

S.C. Code Ann. § 41-1-65

Information that may be disclosed

- length of employment, pay level and history
- reasons for termination or separation
- job performance
- performance evaluation or opinion (evaluation must be signed by employee before separation)
- knowledge, qualifications, skills or abilities
- job description and duties
- attendance, attitude and effort

State Laws on Information from Former Employers (continued)

- awards, demotions and promotions
- disciplinary actions

Who may request or receive information

- prospective employer (written request required for all information except dates of employment and wage history)
- former or current employee

Copy to employee required

- employee must be allowed access to any written information sent to prospective employer

Employer immune from liability unless

- employer knowingly or thoughtlessly releases or discloses false information

Other provisions

- all disclosures other than length of employment, pay level and history must be in writing for employer to be entitled to immunity

South Dakota

S.D. Codified Laws Ann. § 60-4-12

Information that may be disclosed

- job performance (must be in writing)

Who may request or receive information

- prospective employer (request must be in writing)
- former or current employee (request must be in writing)

Copy to employee required

- upon employee's written request

Employer immune from liability unless

- employer knowingly, intentionally or carelessly disclosed false or deliberately misleading information, or
- information is subject to a nondisclosure agreement or is confidential according to federal or state law

Tennessee

Tenn. Code Ann. § 50-1-105

Information that may be disclosed

- job performance

Who may request or receive information

- prospective employer
- former or current employee

Employer immune from liability unless

- information is knowingly false or deliberately misleading
- employer disclosed information regardless of whether it was false or defamatory, or
- disclosure is in violation of employee's civil rights according to current employment discrimination laws

Texas

Tex. Lab. Code Ann. §§ 52.031(d); 103.001 to 103.003; Tex. Civ. Stat. Ann. Art. 5196

Information that may be disclosed

- reasons for termination or separation (must be in writing)
- job performance

State Laws on Information from Former Employers (continued)

- attendance, attitudes and effort

Who may request or receive information

- prospective employer
- former or current employee

Copy to employee required

- within 10 days of receiving employee's request, must send copy of written disclosure or true statement of verbal disclosure, along with names of people to whom information was given
- employer may not disclose reasons for employee's discharge to any other person without sending employee a copy, unless employee specifically requests disclosure

Employer immune from liability

- employer who makes disclosure based on information any employer would reasonably believe to be true

Employer required to write letter

- employee must make request in writing and employer must respond within 10 days of receiving it
- discharged employee must be given a written statement of reasons for termination
- employee who quits must be given a written statement, including all job titles and dates, that states that separation was voluntary and whether employee's performance was satisfactory

- any employee entitled to another copy of statement if original is lost or unavailable

Utah
Utah Code Ann. § 34-42-1

Information that may be disclosed

- job performance

Who may request or receive information

- prospective employer
- former or current employee

Employer immune from liability unless

- there is clear and convincing evidence that employer disclosed information with the intent to mislead, knowing it was false or not caring if it was true or false

Virginia
Va. Code Ann. § 8.01-46.1

Information that may be disclosed

- job performance
- reasons for termination or separation
- performance evaluation or opinion
- knowledge, qualifications, skills or abilities
- job description and duties
- attendance, effort and productivity
- awards, promotions or demotions
- disciplinary actions
- professional conduct

State Laws on Information from Former Employers (continued)

Who may request or receive information

- prospective employer

Employer immune from liability unless

- employer disclosed information deliberately intending to mislead, knowing it was false or not caring if it was true or false

Washington

Wash. Admin. Code § 296-126-050

Employer required to write letter

- within 10 working days of receiving written request, employer must give discharged employee a signed statement of reasons for termination

West Virginia

W.Va. Code § 31A-4-44

Information that may be disclosed

- violation of an industry-related law or regulation, that has been reported to appropriate enforcing authority (applies only to banks and financial institutions)

Wisconsin

Wis. Stat. Ann. §§ 134.02(2)(a); 895.487

Information that may be disclosed

- job performance
- reasons for termination or separation

- knowledge, qualifications, skills or abilities

Who may request or receive information

- prospective employer
- former or current employee
- bondsman or surety

Employer immune from liability unless

- employer knowingly provided false information in the reference
- employer made the reference without caring whether it was true or permitted by law, or
- reference was in violation of employee's civil rights

Wyoming

Wyo. Stat. § 27-1-113

Information that may be disclosed

- job performance

Who may request or receive information

- prospective employer

Employer immune from liability unless

- information was knowingly false or deliberately misleading, or
- disclosure was made with no concern for whether it was true or permitted by law

Current as of June 2003

Chapter 8

Severance and Releases

*I*f you've decided to fire a problem employee, you're probably not eager to offer that employee a severance package, particularly if that employee has caused you nothing but trouble. However, there are several reasons why you might need or want to pay severance:

- **To fulfill a legal obligation.** If, by word or by deed, you've led the employee to believe that he would receive severance, you must follow through. Section A explains how to figure out whether you are legally required to pay severance, based on the policies or agreements that may be in effect in your company.

- **To help the worker out.** You may want to give a severance package to an employee whom you've had to fire, especially if the employee tried (but failed) to improve. Section B covers this situation.

- **To avoid lawsuits.** A severance package can help a fired worker find a new job, ease the transition and demonstrate that you care about the worker's well-being. A worker who receives these benefits will have an easier time moving on and letting go of any bad feelings towards your company—and will be less inclined to sue. If you are really concerned about lawsuits, you might want to ask the employee to sign a release, which is an agreement not to sue you (see Section C, below).

- **To get something you want in exchange.** You can offer a severance package (or an enhanced package, if you are already legally obligated to pay severance) in exchange for the employee's agreement not to sue you. These agreements, called releases, are covered in Sections C and E. Or, you can offer severance contingent on the employee's signing a noncompete, nondisclosure or nonsolicitation agreement, contracts covered in Section F.

This chapter covers severance packages and releases—two related, yet distinct concepts. A severance package refers to the combination of items—often including money, insurance continuation, outplacement services or other benefits—that you might give to a departing worker. A release is a legal agreement between you and the worker, in which the worker agrees not to sue you in exchange for some benefit you provide—often, a severance package. You can give a severance package without a release, or you can condition your severance package on the worker signing the release. Both options are explained below.

A. Are You Obligated to Pay Severance?

Although many employers assume they must offer a severance package to fired workers, no state or federal statute requires it. However, you might still be legally obligated to pay severance if you led your employees to believe they would be paid. In short, you can obligate *yourself* to pay severance.

There are several ways in which you might legally commit yourself to paying severance. We explain them in subsection 1, below. If you decide that you have an obligation to offer severance, subsection 2 will help you analyze and implement your current policy.

If your workplace is unionized, you might be required to pay severance or other benefits to fired workers. Check the terms of your collective bargaining agreement to find out.

1. When Severance is Required

You will have to pay severance if you have promised to do so, either in a contract with the fired worker or in your written policies. You may also have to pay severance if you have regularly done so in the past.

a. Written Contracts

If you and the employee have a written employment contract in which you promise to pay severance, you must honor that promise. Some employment contracts promise severance if the worker is fired before the end of the contract term, if the worker meets certain performance goals or if the worker stays at the company for a certain period of time (Chapter 2, Section B gives more information on employment contracts). The contract might also include restrictions on the payment of severance, most notably that it will not be paid if you fire the worker for willful misconduct. Whatever the language of the contract, however, you must honor its terms.

b. Oral Promises

An oral promise to pay severance is as binding as any written contract or written policy. If you've promised to pay severance, you're legally bound to follow through. Although it can be tough for an employee to prove that an oral promise was made, there is always the possibility that a judge or jury might believe the worker—and order you to pay up.

c. Written Policies

If you have a written policy that states that you will pay severance, you must follow that policy. Often, the policy will be announced in your employee handbook or documented in another communication from management, such as an email or memo to all employees. A policy of paying one week's salary for every year worked at the company is common. Like employment contracts, written policies often carry their own conditions or limitations. For example, your handbook might specify that severance will be given only to employees who make above a certain amount or who have been with the company for a minimum number of years. Subsection 2 offers information on understanding your written policy.

d.   Employment Practices

Your conduct as an employer can be every bit as important as your written words. If you have an unwritten company practice of paying severance to employees in a certain position or to workers fired for certain reasons, you may be obligated to keep it up—even if you don't want to pay severance to this particular employee.

> **EXAMPLE:** Manolo owns a clothing store. He fires Josh, a salesperson, for persistent absences. Manolo has fired four other employees—two were laid off during tough financial times and two were fired for performance problems. He paid severance to all. Because Manolo has always paid severance to fired employees, he may be obligated to pay Josh.

> **EXAMPLE:** Same as above, but Manolo only paid severance to the two employees he had to lay off. Manolo has a good argument that his practice is not to pay severance to every fired employee, but only to those fired for economic reasons that aren't related to their performance or productivity. Because Josh was fired for cause, he is not entitled to severance.

Special Rules for Mass Layoffs

Some states require an employer to pay a small severance amount to workers who are laid off in a plant closing or mass layoff (usually when more than 50 to 100 workers are laid off at the same time). Because these laws do not apply when you fire an individual employee, we do not cover them here.

⚠ This book covers only severance payments to problem employees who are fired. It does not explain the full gamut of possible severance policies you might adopt to cover your whole workforce. You may wish to adopt a different policy for workers who are fired for reasons unrelated to their conduct or performance, such as those who are laid off or downsized.

2. Assess Your Current Severance Practices

Having read subsection 1, above, you should be able to decide whether you have, even unwittingly, instituted a severance policy at your company. (Readers who are satisfied that they have no obligation to pay severance can skip ahead to Section B.) If the conclusion is yes, consider what you have promised. Does your policy or practice obligate you to pay severance to the problem employee whom you plan to fire?

The answer depends on the scope of your policy. Most employers adopt one of four basic severance arrangements, sometimes with slight variations.

a. Severance for All Employees

Some employers adopt a policy or practice of paying a set severance amount to all fired employees. This amount might be fixed or vary depending on the employee's salary and tenure at the company. A common formula is one or two weeks of severance pay, at the employee's current salary, for each year of service.

If your policy is a blanket approach like this, you don't have too much leeway now, even if the employee whom you're terminating is one whom you feel does not deserve the benefit. If you decide to depart from your established practice, do so at your own risk. Your ex-employee may argue (through his lawyer) that your policy is like a contract, which binds you to its terms. Employers who get into legal fights over severance benefits often discover that their lawyer bills quickly outstrip the amount of pay involved.

b.   Severance for Some Employees

Your company might have a policy that limits severance to only certain employees. For example, you may give severance only to employees who have been with the company for a certain period of time. Or you may give no severance to employees fired for serious misconduct. If the employee whom you intend to terminate fits within the exception in your policy, you do not have to give severance to that worker.

Deciding whether an employee fits within your stated exceptions—particularly if you have a serious misconduct exception—can be tricky. Even if your policy is clear and the reasons for termination well documented, you may have a hard time deciding whether the employee's problem qualifies as serious misconduct. Some cases will be easy—an employee who threatens violence, steals or engages in another crime or engages in egregious harassment won't be entitled to severance. For those employees whose acts or intent are not so clearly bad, the safest approach is probably to err on the side of paying severance.

c.   Severance at the Discretion of the Employer

Some companies reserve the right to make decisions about whether to pay severance (and how much to give) on a case-by-case basis. Unlike the approach explained in subsections a and b, above, this approach starts with the assumption that no employees will receive benefits unless the employer decides otherwise. The factors the employer might consider are generally not announced. These written policies might include language like "severance will be paid at the sole discretion of the employer" or "the company will decide whether to pay severance on a case-by-case basis."

Although this type of policy gives you the most leeway, it also exposes employers to possible legal trouble from employees claiming that the policy was applied in a discriminatory fashion. Even if you have sound, decent reasons for your decisions, your employees won't know what factors you considered—and might suspect that you had improper motives when picking and choosing among your workers. Section B, below, includes advice on whether to grant severance in situations where you have the choice.

> **EXAMPLE:** Betty has fired six workers in the last two years. Her severance policy allows her to pay severance at her sole discretion. Betty has paid severance to only two of the workers fired, both of them women. She decided to pay these workers severance because both had worked for the company since its inception ten years before—Betty felt bad about firing them and wanted to reward their loyalty. Betty did not pay severance to the other four workers because all were fired within a couple of years of starting with the company. However, these four other workers are all men. Even though Betty's decisions have not been based on the sex of the fired worker, one of these fired men might believe differently—and might find a lawyer willing to argue about it.

d.   No Severance Policy

You may have run your company without ever giving a thought to severance benefits. Perhaps you're just starting out, or you've been fortunate in not having to terminate many employees. Or, you may have subconsciously decided that no one will receive benefits, but you just haven't made that decision a known policy. Can you decide to give severance now?

Yes, you can. There's no legal requirement that you announce a policy before giving severance. However, an employer who suddenly decides to bestow benefits puts himself legally "at risk" in the same way as the employer who gives them according to his sole discretion, explained in subsection c above. That is, since you haven't shared your criteria for giving severance, you make it possible for someone to impute illegal motives to your decision. Section B will help you figure out whether the risk is worth it.

Legal Requirements for Severance Policies

Under a federal law known as ERISA (the Employee Retirement Income Security Act of 1974), employers are required to follow strict requirements in administering severance plans. If you have a regular policy or practice of paying severance to fired employees under all circumstances, even if the policy is unwritten, chances are good that this law applies to you. ERISA does not apply to payments that are individually negotiated with a fired worker, such as payments made in exchange for the employee's agreement not to sue (called releases—see Section C, below, for more about these agreements).

ERISA is a notoriously confusing and very technical law. Its purpose is clear enough—to ensure that employers provide workers with information about their retirement and severance plans and treat them fairly when administering the plans. ERISA requires employers to use a plan adminis-trator, provide workers with a written summary of the plan, file a copy of the plan with the U.S. Department of Labor, establish a written procedure for employees to file and appeal claims under the plan and follow a host of other rules. If you believe your plan might be covered under ERISA, consult a lawyer to make sure you are in compliance with the law. You can find more information about ERISA and a plain-English explanation of its requirements in *Federal Employment Laws: A Desk Reference,* by Amy DelPo & Lisa Guerin (Nolo).

B. If You Have a Choice, Should You Pay Severance?

If your policies, written or oral, obligate you to pay severance to all or some fired employees, or if you have made a practice of doing so in the past, you must pay fired problem workers according to your usual formula. However, if your policy allows you to give severance at your discretion—or if you have no policy at all—you have two choices to make. This section addresses the first: Should you offer severance? Section C addresses the second: Should you condition your offer on the worker signing a release?

1.   Reasons to Offer Severance

The problem employee whom you intend to let go may be completely responsible for his predicament, particularly if it's the result of willful misconduct, calculated and serious dishonesty or premeditated violence. If you were unlucky enough to have hired and worked with a truly bad egg, you probably feel that you've already paid enough, and you certainly don't want to reward egregiously bad behavior. In such cases, you won't find yourself losing sleep over his departure or wishing there was something you could do to ease his pain. But as counterintuitive as it may seem, don't automatically conclude that this undeserving employee is not a candidate for a severance offer, as explained below.

On the other hand, you may be terminating a problem worker for whom you feel some sympathy, even though his behavior or performance proved to be ultimately unacceptable. For instance, the worker who couldn't learn new skills required for the job, the employee whose divorce so distracted him that he failed to produce and even the worker who couldn't control his drinking or his temper might still have to go, but you'd like to soften the blow. In these situations, offering severance might feel like the fair and humane thing to do.

Giving a worker something to live on until he finds his next job can also provide a little insurance against future lawsuits. A severance package may help defuse the anger a worker feels about being fired. And a happier former employee is a less litigious former employee. If you believe that severance benefits will head off a potential lawsuit— and particularly if some responsibility for the employee's problems rests with you or other members of your company—it may make good business sense to pay now rather than later, in the form of legal fees and jury awards. Remember, however, that paying severance is no guarantee that you will avoid a lawsuit—you can do that only with a release, discussed in Sections C and E, below.

2. Risks of Offering Severance

Even when you can make a good case for granting severance, you must think twice. Sadly, even if you have good reasons for handing out benefits, whether you're trying to do the right thing or trying to avoid a lawsuit, there's a risk involved. The risk lies not in what the fired worker might do (after all, she will probably be pleased to receive a package), but in what remaining employees—some of whom you might have to fire later—will expect.

For example, suppose you're firing a single mother and you know that she'll have a tough time financially until she's reemployed. If the reasons that led to her firing were not extreme, she may be a candidate for severance. But what happens if the next person you terminate is a single father? If you don't extend the same severance to him, he may charge you with sex discrimination. Even if his sex had nothing to do with your decision not to offer a severance—perhaps his income level was higher or he had another job lined up, for example—a lawyer might still take the man's case if she thinks there is a chance of prevailing.

And if you decide to buy off employees who threaten to sue or act as if they might, you may be encouraging others to make the same threats. Most employees will not be surprised when they are fired, and some may begin to think about what they can get out of you before the axe falls. Knowing that a threat to sue has been met with quiet money, the next employee may make hollow threats just to see what you'll cough up.

C. Should You Ask For a Release?

If you're lucky, the employee whom you've decided to fire may pose little threat to you in terms of future lawsuits over the termination. Perhaps the employee has acknowledged his failings or has simply accepted the inevitable and wants to move on.

Unfortunately, there are other employees who will walk out your door and head straight to a lawyer's office. Workers with persistent problems may have seen the writing on the wall and talked to a lawyer even before you fire them. Sometimes you'll be tipped off, by references to his lawyer or even by the employee's use of legal terms that you can assume were picked up during conversations with his counsel. Other times, the employee's level of anger and general disposition may lead you to reasonably conclude that there's trouble ahead. And if your own conduct has been less than stellar—if you've been harsher with this employee than others, for example—the chances of legal trouble are greatly increased.

This is the time to consider whether to ask the problem employee to sign a release, which is an agreement between you and a fired worker. It's a contract in which you give the worker something of value (usually the same things you might consider in a voluntary severance package, like compensation, continued insurance coverage and/or other benefits) in exchange for her agreement not to sue you. The employee "releases" or gives up any potential legal claims against you. A release buys you protection against the unpredictable (but assuredly high) costs of defending a lawsuit in the future.

1. Getting a Release When You Have a Severance Policy

You may be obligated to give severance to a fired employee because your written or oral policies, or your established practices, have reasonably led the employee to expect that benefits would be offered. (Section A, above, explains these situations in detail.) Legally speaking, you and the employee have a contractual understanding: The employee agrees to continue working for you, and you agree to give the announced severance benefits if there's a termination.

If you want to extract a further promise not to sue, you need to give something more than the severance to which the employee is already entitled. After all, you're asking for something extra from the employee, so you have to give something extra in exchange to make the agreement enforceable. In short, you need to sweeten the deal.

You can add to your usual severance package by throwing in money, extended COBRA coverage or any of the benefits explained in Section D. The important point is to make sure that you're giving the employee something extra, something that he would not ordinarily get under your severance policies, in exchange for signing the release.

2.   Getting a Release When You Do Not Have a Severance Policy

If your policies and practices don't require you to offer severance, you may still choose to do so, as explained in Section B. If you want the employee to sign a release, you can simply condition the severance on the employee's promise not to sue. Without a release, a voluntary severance package is a gift from you to the employee. Once the employee signs a release, that gift becomes a contract: In exchange for your severance package, the employee gives up his right to sue you.

A Release By Any Other Name

Lawyers have come up with a lot of different terms for a release. It might be called a release of claims, a waiver of rights, a covenant not to sue or a non-suit agreement. All of these terms refer to the same thing, however: a contract in which the employee agrees to give up the right to sue you in exchange for something of value.

3.   Asking for a Release: Pros and Cons

Releases can be invaluable to employers. A release buys you peace of mind—once a worker signs away his rights, he cannot being a lawsuit against you. If he tries to sue, a court will throw out the claim—as long as the release is valid. (See Section E.) For the price of an enhanced severance payment now, you can buy protection against the possibility of lawsuits in the future. For this reason, many companies routinely request a release from every fired worker. However, there are some real drawbacks to asking for a release. In making your decision, you will have to weigh what you might gain from a release against what it might cost you.

How Broad Can a Release Be?

The scope of a release—the types of claims that the worker agrees to give up—can be quite broad. As explained below, employers routinely ask their workers to give up any and all claims arising from the employment relationship—not just claims of wrongful termination. And these broad clauses are just as routinely enforced by courts.

There are a few exceptions to this expansive rule, however. Some states have passed laws putting certain claims off limits, including claims for unemployment compensation or other benefits provided, at least in part, by state funds. Even if a worker agrees to release these claims, courts in these states will allow the worker to sue anyway. And some states impose special rules if an employer wants the employee to release "unknown claims"—claims based on facts that the employee does not know at the time he signs the release. These claims are discussed in Section E1, below.

a.   When a Release Makes Sense

When deciding whether to ask for a release, your first consideration should be the strength of the worker's legal claims—whether he has anything solid to sue you about. We have explained some of the practices and policies you should follow to stay out of legal trouble when dealing with problem employees. Make a frank assessment of how well you've done. Have you documented the employee's problems? Have you fulfilled your legal obligations? Have you followed your own policies? Remember, too, that this book is not an exhaustive manual on how to legally run your business or deal with employees on all issues. If there are skeletons in your closet that do not pertain to our discussions of problem employees, they might also surface in a lawsuit—and be squelched by a release.

Next, consider the context of the employee's firing. Might the employee have reason to suspect—or argue—that he has been mistreated, regardless of your motivation? For example, did the employee recently make a complaint of discrimination, harassment or illegal activity? Is the employee the only member of a particular demographic group in your workplace or the work group from which he was fired (for example, the only woman or Japanese-American)? Even if you had a good reason to fire the worker, completely unrelated to these factors, you might consider offering an enhanced severance package in return for the employee's agreement to release these claims, which tend to be difficult and expensive to fight.

Finally, think about the worker's attitude about litigation. Has she threatened to sue you, hired a lawyer or talked generally about taking you to the cleaners? Has she been involved in other lawsuits, either on her own behalf or assisting a friend or family member? Is she related to any lawyers? If you have any indication that the worker is thinking about a lawsuit, a release is probably a good idea.

b.   Risks of Asking for a Release

Although there are substantial benefits to getting a release, there are also some potential drawbacks to consider. Offering a release might convince some workers that they have legitimate legal claims against you—why else would you offer to pay them to give up those claims? Other employees might feel so resentful at being asked to give up their rights that they will take legal action they might never have considered otherwise. A worker asked to release claims often decides to talk to a lawyer before signing away her rights, which could result in a protracted round of negotiations and, ultimately, a higher severance payment. And if you ask for a release from an employee who never would have brought a lawsuit against you, you will end up paying severance money you otherwise could have saved.

D.   What Should You Offer?

Whether you decide to offer severance voluntarily or only as a condition of signing a release, you must decide what to offer. Your goal will be to offer enough to ease the worker's transition, forestall a lawsuit, and/or convince your worker to sign a release, without giving away the store. Here are some ideas to consider.

1.   Money

Realistically, this is what most fired workers want. Giving money allows the worker to use it as she pleases, to help with basic living expenses, to support a career change or to take some time off to think about the next step. How much is enough? That will depend on how you answer the following questions.

How much can you afford to pay? Consult the bottom line before making any decisions. If you're paying a worker out of a sense of generosity, that figure should be well within the bounds of what you can afford. If the severance is offered in hopes that it will forestall a lawsuit or convince a worker to sign a release, you may be willing to pay a bit more, knowing that the alternative—litigation—will be more expensive.

How long will it be until the employee finds her next job? Take a look at the job market for this particular worker, with her skills and work history. If it will be tough to find a comparable job, you might want to pay as much as possible to help support her during the weeks of job searching. On the other hand, if the employee can walk across the street and land a similar position, she'll have less need of a severance cushion.

Can you cash out the employee's unused vacation time? You might also consider cashing out a worker's unused vacation time, if your policies and state law do not already require you to pay the worker for these days. Many states require employers to pay a terminated worker for all accrued vacation days that have not been used. If your state is one of them, this vacation pay is money to which your employee is already entitled, apart from any severance arrangement. Contact your state labor department for details (see Appendix for contact information).

2. Insurance Benefits

Some employers offer to pay for continued insurance coverage for a period of time after an employee is fired. Although a federal law called the Consolidated Omnibus Benefits Restoration Act (COBRA) and similar state laws require most employers to offer their fired employees the opportunity to continue their health insurance, it does not require employers to foot the bill. (See Chapter 7, Section D for more information on COBRA.) You might also consider continuing to pay for other insurance benefits, such as life or disability insurance.

3. Uncontested Unemployment Compensation

Fired employees can claim unemployment benefits if they were terminated for reasons other than deliberate and repeated misconduct. As you probably know, the former employer pays a portion of these benefits. For this reason, after a worker applies for benefits the employer has an opportunity to fight the worker's claim.

If you are terminating an employee for unintentional but poor performance, you will have no grounds for disputing that employee's application for unemployment benefits. In this situation, agreeing in a severance package not to contest any unemployment application will be meaningless. But if you are firing someone for reasons that are arguably within the ban on getting compensation, your promise not to contest the application has real value. By agreeing not to fight the claim, you make it more likely that the employee will be found not to have engaged in serious misconduct and will receive benefits. (See Chapter 7 for a discussion of unemployment compensation issues.)

4. Outplacement Services

An outplacement program helps an employee find a new job. It may offer counseling on career goals and job skills, tips on resume writing, help in finding job leads, use of computers, telephones and fax machines for the job search, practice interview sessions and assistance in negotiating with potential employers. Some programs also offer therapeutic counseling to help the employee deal with losing a job and move on.

The cost of outplacement services varies depending on the kinds of services included. However, most firms charge a flat fee of $500 to $1,500 for individual counseling, plus a percentage—commonly 15%—of the employee's total yearly compensation. Many firms will give you a discount if you are offering outplacement to a number of workers or if you contract for services repeatedly within the space of a year or so. Because competition in outplacement services is fairly stiff, you will likely have leeway in negotiating the cost you pay and the services you receive.

For most employers, the cost is worth it. Former employees whose time and minds are taken up by a new job are far less likely to sue you for wrongful termination or to file claims for unemployment or workers' compensation insurance. In a study conducted by Cornell University in September 2000, researchers found that offering outplacement services decreased the chances that a terminated employee will file a lawsuit over the termination.

Should You Let a Fired Worker Use Your Office Resources?

If you own a small business, you might balk at the cost of hiring a consulting firm to provide outplacement services to your employees. Some employers avoid these costs by allowing the fired employee to use company resources to search for another job. For example, you might offer to let a former employee use office equipment, such as the copy machine, fax machine, computer, laser printer and telephone.

There are pros and cons to opening your doors to a fired employee. Of course, if you have any reason to fear that the fired employee poses a threat of sabotage, violence or theft, you should not allow him back on site once he has been fired. Letting a fired employee use your office space can also lead to the "guest who wouldn't leave" problem: Some of these former workers are still there, using the copier, months after termination. And you might not want a particular fired worker hanging around with the rest of your workforce.

However, if you believe that a worker could benefit from using your office resources, you can set some reasonable limits while still offering him valuable help. For example, you might allow the worker to use your equipment only for a set amount of time—one or two months, say. Or you could arrange to have the worker come in only at certain times and on certain days—Tuesdays and Fridays from 2 p.m. to 5 p.m., for example.

5. Other Benefits

You might want to consider offering other benefits, such as allowing the fired worker to keep advances or money paid for moving expenses, letting an employee keep company equipment (like a computer, cell phone or car) or releasing an employee from contractual obligations, like a covenant not to compete (explained below in Section F).

6. Designing a Severance Package

Now that you have some idea of the range of benefits you can choose from, you need to make up your benefits package. A good way to figure out exactly what combination of benefits to offer is to talk to your employee. Certain items—like continued health insurance coverage or outplacement assistance—might be particularly important to a fired worker. If possible, have an honest discussion to find out what your worker would like in a severance package. You may find that you can save money—and provide the most helpful package—by offering some combination of benefits.

A fired worker might approach you with a list of benefits she'd like to see in a severance offer. Be prepared to negotiate—and create a ready list of items you might be willing to offer in a counter-proposal. As always, don't forget your motivation for offering severance—are you leading with your heart or with your head? If you're mollifying an employee whom you suspect may sue you, be ready to offer a bit more, knowing that it will be money well spent if it helps you avoid litigation.

Proceed cautiously if there's a lawyer in the picture. If an employee who asks for severance has consulted an attorney, you will probably want to tie your benefits to a release, which will remove the possibility that you will be sued over the termination. (Releases are explained below in Section E.) You should also contact your own attorney for advice.

E.   Writing a Release

Because a release is a legal contract, you must follow certain rules to make it valid. You may also want to take a few additional steps to make sure that a court will enforce the agreement, should the worker later change her mind and try to sue you anyway.

⚠ Some states have specific requirements about the form and content of releases. You may have to use particular words and phrases, type the agreement in a specified font size or provide certain information about the worker's rights. If you don't follow these rules to the letter, a court may later decide that the release is invalid—and let the worker sue you anyway.

Because of these technical requirements, we recommend that you consult a lawyer about your release. You needn't ask the lawyer to draft the whole document for you, however. Using the guidelines provided here, you can put together the basic release, then ask the lawyer to fine tune the language to make sure it follows your state's rules.

1.   Release Basics

Your release must meet a few basic legal requirements. If your release is lacking in any one respect, your former employee may be able to disregard it and sue you. A valid release, on the other hand, will be upheld by a judge, who will use it to dismiss any lawsuits that the employee may file against you concerning the termination or other aspects of the employment relationship.

a.   Giving Something Valuable

Every legal contract involves the exchange of value—for example, in exchange for your money, which is valuable, Nolo will send you a book, which is also valuable. In legal terms, the promise or valuable things—like money, goods, services or benefits—that each party to the contract agrees to give the other is called "consideration."

Because a release is a legal contract, you must give the employee something of value—benefits, money or services—in exchange for his agreement to give up legal claims against you (claims which are valuable because he could otherwise sue you and perhaps win money). As explained in Section C, above, if you already have a severance policy, you must offer additional benefits that aren't already in the package. And if the worker is already entitled to cash out accrued vacation time, receive reimbursement for work-related expenses or exercise stock options, those won't qualify as "consideration" for a release—the worker would get those even if he refused to sign.

Any of the items discussed in Section D could qualify as consideration, as long as the employee is not already entitled to receive them. Once you have decided what you want to offer, specify each item in the release and state that you are giving it in exchange for the worker's release of claims.

> **EXAMPLE:** "As consideration for his release of claims, Lloyd Astin agrees to accept a lump sum cash payment of $20,000 and continued payment of his health and disability insurance premiums for three months. Mr. Astin will also be allowed to keep the computer he has used while employed at Techno.com, after all company-related materials are removed from the computer by a technical support person."

> **EXAMPLE:** "In exchange for his agreement to release all claims relating to his employment, the company agrees to reimburse Greg Borden for costs he incurs for outplacement services up to a maximum of $3,000."

b.   Release of Claims

In exchange for your consideration, the worker should agree to give up the right to sue you for all employment-related claims. Legally, a release can cover almost any claim the worker might have against you that relates in any way to his employment. You do not have to limit the release to claims relating only to the worker's termination, for example. However, a release can only cover claims arising up to the date the release is signed. If you and the worker have problems later—for example, if the worker claims that you have blacklisted her or defamed her by giving a false and harmful reference (see Chapter 7)—those disputes will not be included, which means that the worker can still sue you over them.

The key to drafting a solid release—one that will give you the most protection against legal trouble—is to be all-inclusive. Don't limit the release to only those claims you are most concerned about. For example, if you have fired someone with whom you had an employment agreement, don't ask the worker to give up only the right to sue you for breach of contract. As you have probably gathered from previous chapters, a worker can bring myriad claims for wrongful termination. Although the worker had a contract, he may believe he was fired for discriminatory reasons or in violation of public policy. If you limit your release to only contract-related claims, you leave yourself open to lawsuits based on other legal theories.

At the same time, however, the release must be specific enough to inform the worker of the rights she is giving up. Some courts even require employers to list the specific anti-discrimination laws—like Title VII, the ADA or the ADEA (see Chapter 2 for more about these laws)— that provide the rights the worker is waiving. If the employee can later argue successfully that she didn't know what the release covered, your contract will not provide you with much protection. A typical release states that the worker is giving up any right to sue you for claims arising out of his or her employment or the termination of that employment, then lists the specific types of claims that might include. The release should also explain what a release entails—that is, that the worker is giving up the right to sue you.

EXAMPLE: "In exchange for the consideration provided in paragraph A, Sean Dennis agrees to unconditionally release the company from liability for any and all claims or liabilities arising out of his employment or the termination of his employment. This release expressly includes, but is not limited to, claims of discrimination under federal or state law (including Title VII, the Americans with Disabilities Act, the Age Discrimination in Employment Act and California's Fair Employment and Housing Act), claims for breach of contract and breach of the covenant of good faith and fair dealing, claims of wrongful termination in violation of public policy, tort claims (including claims of fraud, intentional and negligent infliction of emotional distress and intentional interference with contractual relations), wage and hour claims under the Fair Labor Standards Act and California labor law, claims under the Occupational Health and Safety Act and similar California law, claims under the Family and Medical Leave Act and California's Family Rights Act and any and all other claims related to his employment.

By signing this release, Mr. Dennis understands that he is giving up his right to sue the company for any of the claims that he has released."

Special Rules for Unknown Claims

Even if you use very inclusive language in your release—like that in the example above—it might not cover every claim an employee could bring. Some courts have held that a release generally does not prevent an employee from suing over issues that she did not know about when she signed the release. If the worker later learns of facts that would support a legal claim—for example, if she finds out that her employer illegally withheld money from her paycheck or discovers that she was exposed improperly to toxic chemicals—she may still be able to sue over those claims.

To forestall future lawsuits based on these types of unknown claims, an employer might have to include specific language in the release. The employer must state that the release includes claims that are not known to the worker at the time the release is signed. Some states require the employer to use particular words in this portion of the release and/or require particular typeface and font size. Consult a lawyer if you wish to include unknown claims in your release.

c.   Written and Signed

A release should be in writing, signed and dated both by the worker and by someone authorized to sign on the company's behalf. You and the worker should each sign and date two copies, so you will each have a document with original signatures for your files.

d.   Knowing and Voluntary Waiver

A release is valid only if the worker enters into it freely, knowing that he is signing away his right to sue. The release will not be enforceable if the employee is coerced or threatened into signing, or if the employee's agreement is not voluntary for any other reason. Also, if the language of the release is too vague, the employee might argue that she didn't understand that she was giving up her legal rights.

Avoid any hint of coercion in asking an employee to sign a release. Don't threaten or talk tough with your employees to convince them to sign. And don't withhold any benefits to which the worker is entitled—such as a final paycheck or payment for accrued vacation time—until the worker signs. These tactics will only create ill will with your employees—and you won't gain anything for your actions if the release gets thrown out of court.

To ensure that your release will be enforced, include language stating that the agreement was knowing and voluntary. You can further protect yourself from claims of coercion by giving the worker ample time to consider the release and suggesting that the worker consult a lawyer.

> **EXAMPLE:** "This release has been negotiated between Ms. Hernandez and the company. Ms. Hernandez has agreed to this release knowingly and voluntarily. Her signature on this release acknowledges that she has not been coerced in any way and that she has been advised to consult with a lawyer about the legal rights she is giving up and the terms of this release."

> **EXAMPLE:** "I have had the opportunity to read and carefully consider this release. I have also been advised to consult with a lawyer about the release. I am signing this agreement voluntarily" (followed by signature line).

Special Rules for Older Workers

If you are firing a worker who is 40 years of age or older, a federal law—the Older Workers' Benefits Protection Act, or OWBPA—requires you to include additional terms in a release. Among other things, you must

- specifically refer to the Age Discrimination in Employment Act (ADEA) in the release
- advise the worker, in writing, to consult with a lawyer before signing the release
- give the worker at least 21 days to consider the release before signing, and
- allow the worker to revoke the agreement (in other words, to change her mind) for seven days after she signs.

For more information on the OWBPA, check out the Equal Employment Opportunity Commission (EEOC) website at www.eeoc.gov.

2. Tips on Making Your Release Stronger

In addition to the foregoing release requirements, there are additional steps you can take to protect yourself. Anything you can do to show that the worker knew his rights and signed them away voluntarily will improve your chances in court. Here are some tips that will make your release more likely to be enforced.

a. Use Clear Language

Write your release as clearly as possible, using language the employee can understand. If your release uses a lot of legalisms and technical terms, a worker who is not familiar with that language might legitimately argue that he did not understand what he was signing. And if the employee challenges your release in a lawsuit, the court will be required to interpret any ambiguities in the worker's favor. Gear the release towards the employee—if you are dealing with a well-educated and savvy businessperson, you don't need to worry as much about sticking to basic terms.

b.   Make Sure the Employee Knows Her Rights

A court will be more likely to enforce a release if the employee knew the rights she was giving up by signing. If the worker threatened to sue or talked to an attorney before signing the release, a judge will likely presume that the worker was aware of her rights. The best way you can prove that the worker knew her rights is to include a list of rights in the release, as illustrated in the example in subsection 1, above.

c.   Encourage the Worker to Talk to a Lawyer

When you are discussing the release with the worker, suggest that the worker consult a lawyer to review the release and decide whether to sign. If the worker decides to talk to a lawyer first, add language to the release stating that the worker consulted with a lawyer before signing the

release. If the worker doesn't take your suggestion, put in a sentence stating that you advised her to consult a lawyer about the release before signing.

d.   Negotiate the Release

A court is more likely to find that a release was made voluntarily if you negotiate its terms—particularly the consideration offered—with the employee. You don't have to negotiate every term, but you should have a serious discussion with the worker about what he would like in the release. There may be any number of possible compromises that offer the worker a better deal without necessarily costing you more money. For example, a worker who can get insurance through his spouse might ask you to fund outplacement services instead of continuing to pay his health insurance. Or a worker might ask to receive half the severance payment immediately and half in the following year, to save on taxes.

e.   Give the Worker Time to Decide

It is reasonable for an employee to take a few weeks to decide whether to give up the right to sue you. The shorter the time you allow for reflection, the more likely it is that a court find that the worker was coerced. For example, if you hand a worker a release agreement and insist that he sign by the end of the day, you might be in trouble. State in the release how many weeks you allowed the worker to decide.

If the employee asks you for more time to consider the release, you should strongly consider granting the request. If the worker wants a lawyer's opinion before signing the release, he will have to find an attorney, make an appointment and get in to the lawyer's office for a consultation before he can make a decision. Your best course of action is to give the employee as much time as he needs—within reason—to make an informed decision now, rather than face the possibility of a lawsuit later from a worker who claims that you forced him to make a hasty decision.

f.   Consider a Revocation Period

You might want to give the employee an opportunity to change her mind—to revoke the release—for a few days after signing. There are pros and cons to allowing revocation. The biggest drawbacks are that the agreement is not final when the employee signs and that the employee might change her mind. The main benefit is that the worker will have a very hard time proving she was coerced into signing if you gave her a chance to undo the agreement. If you are dealing with a particularly slippery character or a worker who just doesn't seem to be able to decide, offering a revocation period might make sense.

3.   Additional Release Terms

You can include other terms in the release as well. Many employers include a provision requiring the worker to keep confidential the amount of money paid (or other consideration). Indeed, some employers require the worker to keep the whole agreement—even the fact that an agreement was made—confidential. The purpose of these provisions is to prevent other employees from finding out about the arrangement and arguing for similar terms if and when they get fired.

Some employers also include a statement denying any wrongdoing. These provisions typically state that the employer does not admit any liability for the claims being released.

You may also wish to include information on the employee's rights and obligations in the release. For example, you might indicate the date on which the employee was fired, a listing of any benefits or payments to which the employee is entitled and a statement of the employee's duties, such as returning company property, paying back loans from the company and maintaining the confidentiality of the company's trade secrets.

Employees Who Change Their Minds

If a worker tries to sue you after signing a release, traditional legal principles require that worker to first return to you whatever she got in exchange for the release. This requirement, referred to as the "tender back" rule, prevents the worker from having his cake and eating it too. After all, if the worker is arguing that the release is invalid—which he has to do in order to bring a lawsuit—then he shouldn't be able to keep what he received under the contract.

Most courts require the worker to return the consideration as soon as the worker learns that the release is invalid; otherwise, the worker has "ratified" the agreement by acting as if it was valid. However, workers who file a lawsuit based on the Age Discrimination in Employment Act (the ADEA) are not required to tender back—older workers may keep their release money *and* file an ADEA claim. The employer is entitled to reimbursement of the money paid for the release if the worker wins the lawsuit. The employer can recover either the full amount paid for the release or the full amount of the award, whichever is lower. The EEOC's Website has more information on this rule at www.eeoc.gov.

F.   Agreements to Protect Your Business

When a worker leaves your company, either voluntarily or because she was fired, you face the risk that the worker will take your confidential information to a competitor. You may also worry that she'll hire away your remaining employees. Of course, if the worker you fired was a real incompetent, you might secretly hope that the worker gets hired by a business rival—and lowers productivity over there. Even so, you probably don't want that worker to raid your workforce and reveal your company's secrets. You can protect your business by asking the worker to sign a noncompete, nondisclosure and/or nonsolicitation agreement.

Each of these agreements is a contract between you and the worker. This means that, like a release, you must give the worker something of value in exchange for his promise not to compete, disclose or solicit. To exact this promise, you might choose to pay voluntary severance or pay additional severance over and above the package to which the employee is already entitled.

1.   Noncompete Agreements

By entering into a noncompete agreement, an employee agrees not to compete directly with your company, by working for a competitor in the same capacity or by starting a competing business of her own—at least for a certain period of time after she leaves your company. Some courts are reluctant to enforce noncompete agreements, particularly if they unduly restrict the worker's right to earn a living in his chosen profession. An agreement is more likely to be enforced if it:

- lasts for a relatively short time after the worker is fired (a period of months or a year, for example)
- is limited to the geographic area where you do business, and
- prohibits the employee from engaging in only specific types of business activities (such as opening a vitamin factory or working in a gardening supply store).

Some states do not enforce noncompete agreements. In California, for example, noncompete provisions for employees are invalid. Montana, North Dakota and Oklahoma also do not enforce these agreements. And in Alabama, Colorado, Florida, Louisiana, Oregon, South Dakota and Texas, courts limit whether, how and when you can use noncompete provisions. (See the source listed below for more details.)

For detailed information on noncompete agreements and forms you can use to create your own agreements, see *How to Create a Noncompete Agreement,* by attorney Shannon Miehe (Nolo).

Think hard before you ask a fired worker to sign a noncompete agreement. You are asking that worker to give up the right to work for a competitor, at least for a certain period of time, at the very moment when that worker needs a job, badly. Anything you do to restrict the worker's ability to find her next job is likely to fuel her anger and resentment towards you—emotions that sometimes lead to the courthouse steps.

Of course, you may feel strongly that you need a noncompete agreement, despite this risk. If so, be prepared to negotiate. It is unlikely that a fired employee will sign a noncompete agreement that severely restricts his ability to find work unless you offer a significant financial incentive.

2.   Nondisclosure Agreements

At some point, you may have to fire a worker who has access to your company's most confidential information. You may be concerned that the worker will take your trade secrets to a competitor or use them for his own purposes. To prevent this from happening, you can ask the employee to sign a nondisclosure agreement. This type of contract restricts the employee's ability to use or disclose to others the employer's confidential information.

Courts are most likely to enforce a nondisclosure agreement if the fired employee had access to your company's trade secrets. A trade secret is information that gives your company a competitive advantage because it is not generally known, you have taken steps to keep it private and others cannot readily figure it out. Examples include chemical formulas, customer lists, recipes, software programs and manufacturing processes. If you can demonstrate in court that the employee had access to your company's most sensitive confidential material, the court will be more likely to restrict the employee's use of that information.

For more information and step-by-step instructions on drafting a nondisclosure agreement, see *How to Create a Noncompete Agreement,* by attorney Shannon Miehe (Nolo) and *Nondisclosure Agreements:*

Protect Your Trade Secrets & More, by attorneys Richard Stim & Stephen Fishman (Nolo).

3. Nonsolicitation Agreements

If you are concerned about your fired worker stealing your employees or customers, you might consider asking the worker to sign a nonsolicitation agreement. This type of contract prohibits the worker from poaching your valued employees or soliciting your customers and clients for her new business or employer.

A court is more likely to enforce a limited nonsolicitation agreement —one that prohibits the fired employee from soliciting only a specific list of customers or only the customers with whom that employee had a professional relationship while working for you. If you try to keep the employee away from every one of your customers, a court might decide that you are asking for too much. Also, a nonsolicitation agreement limits only the former employee's actions. If your customers or other employees decide, on their own, to join or patronize the fired employee's new business, they are free to do so—and you cannot require your former employee to turn them away at the door.

For more information on these agreements and step-by-step instructions on drafting a nonsolicitation contract, see *How to Create a Noncompete Agreement,* by attorney Shannon Miehe (Nolo) ■

Chapter 9

How to Fire

7he only thing more difficult than deciding whether to fire an employee is actually breaking the bad news to the poor soul.

Indeed, facing an employee and telling him that you've decided to terminate his employment is one of the saddest and most difficult tasks you will encounter as an employer.

Unfortunately, there is little we can tell you to make you feel better about firing, and truth be told we would be doing you a disservice if we made your comfort the focus of this chapter. This is because how you fire an employee—what you say, where you say it, how you say it and so on—could determine whether the employee decides to sue you for wrongful termination. In addition, there are practical risks involved in terminating an employee—risks such as theft and sabotage and violence—that you need to keep in mind when choosing the way that you will fire the employee.

Your feelings, then, must take a back seat to these legal and practical considerations. Over and over in this chapter, we will ask you to do things that might make the process harder on you personally. There is a method to our madness: Our goal is for your business to survive the termination unscathed.

Of course, the advice we give you in this chapter is just that— advice. With few exceptions, there are no rock solid rules. As always, you may need to tailor this information to meet the needs of your particular situation. You know your workplace and your employees best. Often, this means you might do things differently from the way we suggest. In the end, common sense should be your guide. If you treat the employee with care and respect, you should do just fine.

We recommend a two-step firing process. The first step is the actual termination itself, and the second step is an optional exit interview with the employee that takes place several days after the termination meeting. The benefit of this process is that it allows you to break the news quickly to the employee while leaving most of the details of the termination— for example, explaining when the employee's health insurance will end—to a later date when emotions have cooled. In addition, the exit interview provides a less emotionally charged forum where the employee can vent his feelings about your company in general and about the termination in particular.

Pick a termination process and stick with it for all of your employees. This will minimize the chances that an employee will feel that you discriminated against him in the way that you terminated him. If you ever do vary from your standard procedures, have a good reason for doing so, such as fearing violence or criminal conduct from the employee.

What Goes Around Comes Around

A September 2000 study by Cornell University concludes that the primary reason people decide to sue their former employers is the treatment they received during the termination itself and not the desire for money. The study concluded that, all else being equal, employees who receive unfair and insensitive treatment are more likely to sue than employees who receive fair, honest and dignified treatment. The study advised that fair and sensitive treatment includes the following things:

- giving employees honest and straightforward reasons for the termination
- giving employees advance notice of the termination
- treating the employees with dignity and respect
- reducing the financial burden of the termination (through things such as a severance package and continued benefits)
- allowing the employees to voice their opinions about the termination
- offering counseling to ease the psychological shock of termination, and
- offering outplacement services.

Source: Cornell University, Graduate School of Business and Public Administration (2000)

A. The Termination Meeting

The 15 or so minutes it takes you to break the bad news to the employee may be the most important of the employment relationship. Those 15 minutes may help determine whether the employee sues you, poisons coworkers against you, targets your business for criminal conduct such as theft or sabotage or resorts to violence.

Therefore, it pays to carefully plan the termination meeting ahead of time. Don't act on instinct or assume that the right words will come to you during the meeting. Nail down every detail before the meeting—from who is going to conduct it to what that person will say to the employee. Don't leave anything to the last minute.

The Termination Letter: Should You Or Shouldn't You?

Many experts advise employers to give to the newly terminated employee a letter detailing the reasons for the termination and the status of the employee's benefits. The theory is that the definite and final nature of the letter will dissuade employees from bringing lawsuits and will document the termination.

Although termination letters can be beneficial, they can also be very dangerous. Unless they are crafted carefully with an eye toward the legal implications of what they say, they can get you into a lot of legal hot water. Indeed, they look like "Exhibit 1" to trial lawyers. The first thing an attorney for the terminated employee will ask to see is the termination letter. And that's the first thing she'll introduce at trial, having spent the better part of two years finding ways to hang you on your own words.

As a result, we advise against using termination letters. You can get the same benefits through conducting a direct and professional termination meeting and through documenting the termination in internal company memos.

1. Who Should Break the Bad News?

The person who tells the employee that he is fired should be someone in management or human resources with whom the employee has a positive, or at least neutral, relationship. Don't give this assignment to someone who has an antagonistic relationship with the employee or who is emotionally involved in the decision to terminate.

For these reasons, the employee's supervisor is often the wrong choice for the job. Often, that individual is the one who had to deal with the employee's problems and misconduct on a daily basis, and he or she is usually emotionally invested in the termination decision. The supervisor's supervisor or someone from human resources might be a better choice.

⚠️ **The person who breaks the news should not be a stranger to the employee.** Choose someone whom the employee knows and who has a position of authority in the eyes of the employee. A manager from another store would not be a good choice, nor would a mid-level manager from corporate headquarters whom the employee has never heard of or met.

Make sure you choose someone who is discreet—don't pick a gossip. If you can, use a person who has some training or background in employee relations. If you have to pick someone who doesn't have this training, take the time to counsel her beforehand on how to conduct the meeting and on what to say (and what not to say).

For the balance of this chapter, we direct our advice to you, the reader. Obviously, if someone else conducts the termination meeting, make sure that he or she knows the information. Even though you yourself won't be at the meeting, you will be the one to pay the price if the meeting or the interview doesn't go well.

2. Who Should Attend the Meeting?

The two essential participants are you and the problem employee. Depending on circumstances and choices, however, you may end up with a larger group.

a.   Representing the Employer

The conventional wisdom is that two people should attend the meeting on behalf of the employer: the person who will break the news to the employee and a witness. If the employee files a lawsuit, the wisdom goes, the witness will be there to verify what happened in the meeting.

Recent studies suggest, however, that having more than one employer-side person at the meeting humiliates the employee by making the termination feel more public than private. This humiliation increases the likelihood that an employee will feel hostile or violent, which could lead to a lawsuit or something worse. So what should you do now that conventional wisdom has clashed with newly minted research results?

As always, our advice is to let common sense—and common courtesy—be your guide. If you have an employee whom you feel is fairly trustworthy and not a likely candidate for suing, we suggest you send only one person to the meeting. To do otherwise is to risk antagonizing an employee who might not otherwise sue. If you don't send a witness, make sure that whoever conducts the interview takes detailed notes of everything that he says and everything that the employee says during the meeting.

On the other hand, if you have an employee who has already made loud noises about contacting his lawyer, you don't have a lot to lose by sending in a witness, and you might even have something to gain.

If you do send in a witness, he should be a neutral person in management or human resources. The witness should not be the employee's coworker. The less connection the witness has to the employee and to anyone involved in the decision to terminate the employee, the better. A manager from another department or another plant or another store is ideal.

The debate over witnesses notwithstanding, it's never wise to have more than two employer representatives at a termination meeting. More than two begins to feel more like an ambush than a conversation.

b.   The Role of the Employer Witness

If you decide to bring an employer-side witness to the meeting, that person's job will be to record what happens. If you and the employee ever disagree over what was said at the meeting, the witness will be there to give her recollection.

The witness should not talk at the meeting, except in cases where the witness is a human resources representative who explains the employee's benefits to him. (Explaining benefits is covered in Section 5, below.) Immediately after the meeting, the witness should write a detailed memo recounting everything she saw and heard at the meeting.

c.   Representing the Employee

You are required by law to allow the employee to have a coworker or friend or representative with him at the meeting if he wishes. The law is unclear about whether you are obligated to inform the employee of this right, however. To be on the safe side, we suggest that you tell the employee that you want to meet with him regarding disciplinary matters and that he can have someone by his side at the meeting if he wishes. He can also choose to go it alone, however.

⚠ **If the employee is in a union, the collective bargaining agreement may require that a union representative be at the meeting.** It may also require that you inform the union of the meeting before it takes place. Check your collective bargaining agreement.

3. When Should the Meeting Take Place?

There are as many theories about which day to fire employees as there are days in the week. One theory holds that early in the week is best. Firing first thing Monday morning allows the fired worker to get on with life and connect up quickly with outplacement services that may help in searching for a new job. It eliminates the weekend downtime the former worker will have to fester over the decision and plot revenge.

Under another theory, it is best to deliver the news last thing on Friday. This approach allows workers to gather their personal possessions at the end of the week, when coworkers are most likely to be gone— or to come in the next day to finish the task in private. Echoing this advice, one recent study indicates that an employee's hostility is greater when the employee is terminated earlier in the week rather than later. Presumably, an employee is more likely to feel humiliated if he is sitting at home during the workweek rather than on a weekend.

So what day should you choose? Intuition must be your guide. You know the doomed employee and your workplace best. Whichever day you choose, we recommend scheduling the meeting for sometime in the morning which will give the employee a chance to clean out his desk, tie up loose ends and say his good-byes—all at his own pace.

In cases where you are not offering the employee a severance package, consider paying the employee in full for the day (or—if you can afford it—the remainder of the week) in which you break the news to the employee. Although this might seem pricey at first blush, this goodwill gesture will pay for itself by reducing the chances that the employee will sue. Explain to the employee that you will pay him even though you don't expect him to do any work.

If you fear violence or sabotage from the employee, the best time to break the news is at the end of the last day of the workweek. You will want to get this employee out the door as soon as possible. And the fewer people around when that happens, the better.

4. Where Should the Meeting Take Place?

Unless you fear violence, sabotage or theft from the employee, your choice of where to hold the meeting will depend primarily on where you can make the employee feel most comfortable. Remember—the employee's comfort is paramount in avoiding a wrongful termination lawsuit. Choose a private place that ensures confidentiality. A noisy cubicle, for example, is not a good place.

If the employee has his own private office, that's the ideal place to hold the termination meeting for several reasons:

- The employee's own office is his home turf and will be the most comfortable environment for him.
- You want to be able to control the duration of the meeting and end it quickly when you're done. If you're in the employee's office, you can simply walk out of the office when you feel the meeting is over, closing the door behind you.
- Breaking the news in the employee's office spares him the embarrassment and discomfort of having to walk through the building and face his coworkers immediately after being terminated. He can sit in private and collect his thoughts before facing his colleagues and coworkers.

If the employee does not have his own private office, a conference room or other private area is your next best choice. If possible, the place should be one where you can leave the employee alone to regain his composure and collect his thoughts after the meeting.

Usually, your office is the least desirable place to hold the meeting, for two reasons:

- Your office is your base of power and authority. Terminating the employee in such a place only increases the employee's sense of powerlessness and humiliation.

- When you are in your office, you cannot easily control when the meeting ends. If the employee does not gracefully exit on your cue, you'll have to tell the employee to leave or ask someone to escort him out. Either scenario makes the situation more difficult for both of you.

Don't escort the employee out the door unless you have to. If you don't fear violence, theft or sabotage from the employee (and you won't with the vast majority of employees), it's usually best to avoid the strong-arm tactic of having the fired employee escorted through the building with a guard—or even with a supervisor escort. Not only is it unnecessary, but it is likely to embarrass the fired worker. Many an employee has complained to her lawyer—and to a jury: "After working hard for them all those years, they treated me like a common criminal." In addition, the tactic is likely to unsettle coworkers who may conclude they are one misstep from receiving the same harsh treatment.

If you fear violence from the employee, choose an area that is as isolated as possible from other employees. It should be private and close to a building exit, so that you can escort the employee out of the building as quickly as possible. You might also arrange to have a mental health professional or security personnel stationed near your meeting place. In all but the most extreme cases, however, it's probably unnecessary—and even counterproductive—to have these outsiders at the meeting. Indeed, their presence might further anger or disrupt a potentially volatile employee.

5.   What to Say and How to Say It

No matter how carefully you plan the other aspects of the termination meeting, the words you say and how you say them will stand out. More than any other aspect of termination, you words and demeanor will determine whether the employee leaves on a positive or a negative note.

In choosing your words, always keep your goal at the front of your mind: You want to terminate the employee, but not hurt him or anger him to such an extent that he takes action against your company—either through a lawsuit or some other means. Be firm, yet kind.

> **Avoid any attempt at humor or glibness.** This isn't a funny event—for you or the employee. Unless you are an unusually skilled individual, your attempts will fall flat, at best, or be insulting at worst.

Prior to the meeting, you should have reviewed the employee's personnel file and learned the details of the employee's misconduct or poor performance that led to the discharge. You should also know what your company has done to help the employee improve and to give the employee second chances. It's also a good idea to familiarize yourself with the employee's entire history with your company. Although you won't discuss all of these things during the meeting, you should know about them in case the employee refers to them or wants to ask questions.

a.   Announce the Termination Decision

Start the meeting by informing the employee that he is being terminated and as of what date. Do not ask about his day or about his family. Such pleasantries will only ring hollow and make the employee feel foolish once he learns the real reason behind the meeting.

When you break the news, be direct and focused. A large part of your job is to convey a sense of serious purpose so that the employee realizes that this is the final word on the situation, not a decision that can be negotiated. For this reason, don't use ambiguous language. For example, avoid "this isn't a good fit" or "things just aren't working out" or "we've decided to let you go." Be clear and straightforward. Actually using the word "termination" is often the best approach.

b. Give Your Reasons

The next step is to concisely explain to the employee why you are terminating him. This step requires a difficult balance between being direct and clear and being kind and sympathetic. You must do both, but you must never allow yourself to stray too far to either side. Don't be so direct that you seem coldhearted; don't be so sympathetic that you appear to be apologizing or backtracking from the decision. The best tone to strike is objective and professional.

Some employers fall into the trap of thinking they have to justify their decisions during this step. This isn't a wise move. Simply state the reasons and leave it at that. To do any more is to risk hurting the employee's feelings unnecessarily or—worse yet—to risk drawing the employee into an argument. In addition, you will gain nothing by making excuses or by offering defensive or wordy justifications. Indeed, once you have delivered the bad news, the worker is not likely to be in the state of mind to indulge your attempts to ease your own conscience.

Resist minimizing the problem that resulted in the termination. Employers sometimes try to spare the employee's feelings by minimizing the misconduct. If the employee sues for wrongful termination, however, these soothing, disingenuous words will come back to haunt you when you attempt to tell the jury about the severity of the misconduct that resulted in the termination.

It is also usually a mistake to try to paint a positive gloss on the job loss by sayings things such as:

- "Good jobs are easy to come by these days; it should take you no time at all to find a new one."
- "Now you will be able to pursue a career that fits better with your interests."
- "This will free you up to spend more time with the kids."

This also isn't the time or the place to tell the employee what a lout he has been. You simply want to end the relationship as quickly and as cleanly as possible. Dwelling on the employee's problems will only make him feel worse—and could lead him right to a lawyer's doorstep.

c.   Don't Debate or Undermine the Decision

You can allow the employee time to air his feelings—to express confusion or anger or disagreement—without being drawn into an argument or debate over the merits of the decision. Tell the employee, "I understand that you feel that way, but the decision is final." If the employee starts to argue with you or defend himself, end the meeting.

If you are going to conduct an exit interview as described in Section B, below, mention this to an employee who wants to argue and debate. Tell him that the exit interview is the place where he can air his grievances and his opinions, both about his termination in particular and about his employment in general.

It's fine to be sympathetic, but don't offer hope where there isn't any. If the employee starts to plead for his job, don't flee from the situation by promising to "think it over one more time" or some such thing. You won't be doing yourself or the employee any favors by prolonging the inevitable.

If you are the person delivering the bad news but don't support the decision, resist the temptation to tell the employee that you are really an ally in a wolfskin coat. Firing a worker is not the time to seek personal exoneration or to attempt to foster an us-against-them mindset by saying, for example: "Off the record, I don't think this is a good decision. I have always enjoyed working with you." Like it or not, you are a messenger with bad news. Deliver it without hesitation and without a hint that you aren't fully behind it. To do otherwise will encourage the employee to file a wrongful termination lawsuit—and encourage a jury to side with the employee if your comments are ever aired in a courtroom.

What Not To Say

In this book, we assume that you are only firing the employee because that employee has been a problem—either through continual misconduct (including poor performance) or because of one very severe incident. In such situations, you have what lawyers call "just cause" to fire the employee. (See Chapter 2 for an explanation of just cause.) And when you've got just cause to fire, you can truthfully tell the employee the reasons for the termination with little fear of brushing up against wrongful termination laws.

Still, every once in a while employers will say and do things that make it look like they are violating the law, even when they aren't. Sometimes, knowing what *not* to say is as important as knowing what to say.

Cutting Back

It is fine to tell a fired worker that he or she is being fired as part of a plan to shed workers. But never use this reason unless it is absolutely true. Even though it may appear to be more humane, less judgmental or less accusatory to tell an employee that a position has been eliminated rather than point to his or her poor performance, it is a mistake.

If you later get caught in this type of fib by a former employee who claims the real reason for the firing was discriminatory or in some other way illegal, you would be caught unable to document your bogus claim. This will look bad to a jury. You could easily find yourself on the losing end of an employee's charge that the firing was based on discrimination or some other illegal motive.

Changing the Company Image

When firing a worker, do not refer to your desire to change the composition or culture of the workplace. Similarly, avoid either talking of your plans to recast the workforce or implying that the employee somehow does not fit your intended new image. Any of these pronouncements could leave the impression that the employee is truly being fired for any number of illegal discriminatory reasons, such as being the wrong race, the wrong gender or the wrong age. (See Chapter 2, Section E for more information about anti-discrimination laws.)

What Not To Say (continued)

Personal Characteristics

The best way to steer clear of discrimination laws in the termination interview is to never say anything that touches on a person's race, gender, national origin, age, religion or any other characteristic that might be protected in your state. Obviously, this means no slurs or insults. But more subtly, it means no well-meaning comments designed to give the employee an insight into why he or she didn't do well—insight that is based on that person's protected characteristic(s). Avoid comments like:

- "I know it's hard for a woman to be assertive, but you should not have let the fact that you were the only woman on staff keep you from speaking up at meetings."
- "You always seemed to have a chip on your shoulder about your race. It got in the way of your performance."
- "You talked about your faith in God too much. It made people uncomfortable."

Mentioning Physical Limitations

It's a mistake to mention an employee's injury or physical condition. This can be a particularly damaging if the employee is disabled and legally protected by the Americans With Disabilities Act. (See Chapter 2, Section E.)

Mentioning someone's physical condition also holds potential danger if the worker has been injured on the job and has filed a workers' compensation claim. This person is strongly protected under the laws that prohibit retaliating against such filers. While you can fire an employee for excessive absences or for violating clear-cut safety rules, you cannot do so because he or she has filed an injury claim—even if it causes your insurance costs to skyrocket.

Quieting the Troublemaker

Never imply that you are firing someone because he or she is "not a team player"—usually code for being a troublemaker. This is especially true if the person truly is someone with a penchant for filing workplace complaints. When up against such a soul, be prepared to state your independent business reason for the firing.

d.   Explain the Final Paycheck

If you can, have the employee's final paycheck with you at the termination meeting. When you give it to the employee, tell him whether it includes accrued vacation and any extra days (for example, if you have paid him through the end of the week even though you expect him to stop work immediately). If you have a policy of paying departing employees for their accrued sick leave, you should explain that as well.

If it's not possible to have the employee's final paycheck at the meeting, be prepared to tell the employee the amount of the check, everything it will include and the exact date on which he will receive it. Many states have laws specifying when employers must issue final paychecks. Some states give employers one week; others give you to the end of the pay period. The following chart gives a state-by-state rundown of the laws governing final paychecks.

State Laws That Control Final Paychecks

Note: The states of Alabama, Florida, Georgia, Mississippi and Ohio are not included in this chart because they do not have laws specifically controlling final paychecks. Contact your state department of labor for more information (see the Appendix for contact list).

State	Paycheck due when employee is fired	Paycheck due when employee quits	Unused vacation pay included	Special employment situations
Alaska Alaska Stat. § 23.05.140(b)	Within 3 working days	Next regular payday at least 3 days after employee gives notice	Yes	
Arizona Ariz. Rev. Stat. § 23-353	Next payday or within 3 working days, whichever is sooner	Next payday	Yes	
Arkansas Ark. Code Ann. § 11-4-405(b)	Within 7 days from discharge date	No provision	No	Railroad or railroad construction: Day of discharge
California Cal. Lab. Code §§ 201 to 202, 227.3	Immediately	Immediately if employee has given 72 hours' notice; otherwise, within 72 hours	Yes	Motion picture business: If fired, within 24 hours (excluding weekends and holidays); if laid off, next payday Oil drilling industry: Within 24 hours (excluding weekends and holidays) of termination Seasonal agricultural workers: Within 72 hours of termination
Colorado Colo. Rev. Stat. § 8-4-104	Immediately. (Within 6 hours of start of next workday, if payroll unit is closed; 24 hours if unit is offsite.) Employer decides check delivery.	Next payday	Yes	
Connecticut Conn. Gen. Stat. Ann. § 31-71c	Next business day after discharge	Next payday	No	

State Laws That Control Final Paychecks (continued)

State	Paycheck due when employee is fired	Paycheck due when employee quits	Unused vacation pay included	Special employment situations
Delaware Del. Code Ann. tit. 19, § 1103	Next payday	Next payday	No	
District of Columbia D.C. Code Ann. § 32-1303	Next business day.	Next payday or 7 days after quitting, whichever is sooner	Yes, unless there is express contrary policy	
Hawaii Haw. Rev. Stat. § 388-3	Immediately	Next payday or immediately, if employee gives one pay period's notice	No	
Idaho Idaho Code §§ 45-606; 45-617	Next payday or within 10 days (excluding weekends and holidays), whichever is sooner; if employee makes written request for earlier payment, within 48 hours of receipt of request (excluding weekends and holidays)	Next payday or within 10 days (excluding weekends and holidays), whichever is sooner. If employee makes written request for earlier payment, within 48 hours of receipt of request (excluding weekends & holidays)	Yes	
Illinois 820 Ill. Comp. Stat. § 115/5	At time of separation if possible, but no later than next payday	At time of separation if possible, but no later than next payday	Yes	
Indiana Ind. Code Ann. §§ 22-2-5-1, 22-2-9-2	Next payday	Next payday (if employee has not left address, 10 days after employee demands wages or provides address where check may be mailed)	No	
Iowa Iowa Code §§ 91A.4, 91A.2(7.b.)	Next payday	Next payday	Only if required by employer's policies	If employee is owed commission, employer has 30 days to pay.

State Laws That Control Final Paychecks (continued)

State	Paycheck due when employee is fired	Paycheck due when employee quits	Unused vacation pay included	Special employment situations
Kansas Kan. Stat. Ann. § 44-315	Next payday	Next payday	No	
Kentucky Ky. Rev. Stat. Ann. §§ 337.010(c), 337.055	Next payday or 14 days, whichever is later	Next payday or 14 days, whichever is later	Yes	
Louisiana La. Rev. Stat. Ann. § 23:631	Next payday or within 15 days, whichever is earlier	Next payday or within 15 days, whichever is earlier	Yes	
Maine Me. Rev. Stat. Ann. tit. 26, § 626	Next payday or within 2 weeks of requesting final pay, whichever is sooner	Next payday or within 2 weeks of requesting final pay, whichever is sooner	Yes	
Maryland Md. Code Ann., [Lab. & Empl.] § 3-505	Next scheduled payday	Next scheduled payday	No	
Massachusetts Mass. Gen. Laws ch. 149, § 148	Day of discharge	Next payday; if no scheduled payday, then following Saturday	Yes	
Michigan Mich. Comp. Laws §§ 408.474 to 408.475; Mich. Admin. Code R. § 408.9007	Next payday	Next payday	Yes	Hand-harvesters of crops: Within one working day of termination
Minnesota Minn. Stat. Ann. §§ 181.13 to 181.14	Immediately, but no later than 24 hours after employee demands wages	Next payday; if payday is less than 5 days from last day of work, then following payday or 20 days from last day of work, whichever is earlier	Yes	Migrant agricultural workers who resign: Within 5 days

State Laws That Control Final Paychecks (continued)

State	Paycheck due when employee is fired	Paycheck due when employee quits	Unused vacation pay included	Special employment situations
Missouri Mo. Rev. Stat. § 290.110	Day of discharge	No provision	No	
Montana Mont. Code Ann. § 39-3-205	Immediately if fired for cause or laid off, (unless there is a written policy extending time to earlier of next payday or 15 days)	Next payday or within 15 days, whichever comes first	No	
Nebraska Neb. Rev. Stat. §§ 48-1229 to 48-1230	Next payday or within 2 weeks, whichever is sooner	No provision	Yes	
Nevada Nev. Rev. Stat. Ann. §§ 608.020 to 608.030	Immediately	Next payday or 7 days, whichever is earlier	No	
New Hampshire N.H. Rev. Stat. Ann. §§ 275: 43(III), 275:44	Within 72 hours; if laid off, next payday	Next payday, or within 72 hours if employee gives one pay period's notice	Yes	
New Jersey N.J. Stat. Ann. § 34:11-4.3	Next payday	Next payday	No	
New Mexico N.M. Stat. Ann. §§ 50-4-4 to 50-4-5	Within 5 days	Next payday	No	If paid by task or commission, 10 days after discharge
New York N.Y. Lab. Law §§ 191(3), 198-c(2)	Next payday	Next payday	Yes	
North Carolina N.C. Gen. Stat. §§ 95-25.7, 95-25.12	Next payday	Next payday	Yes	If paid by commission or bonus, on next payday after amount calculated

State Laws That Control Final Paychecks (continued)

State	Paycheck due when employee is fired	Paycheck due when employee quits	Unused vacation pay included	Special employment situations
North Dakota N.D. Cent. Code § 34-14-03; N.D. Admin. Code R. 46-02-07-02(12)	Next payday; must pay by certified mail or as agreed upon by both parties	Next payday	No	
Oklahoma Okla. Stat. Ann. tit. 40, §§ 165.1(4), 165.3	Next payday	Next payday	Yes	
Oregon Or. Rev. Stat. §§ 652.140, 652.145	End of first business day after termination	Immediately, with 48 hours' notice (excluding weekends and holidays); without notice, within 5 days (excluding weekends and holidays) or next payday, whichever comes first	No	Seasonal farm workers: Fired or quitting with 48 hours' notice, immediately; quitting without notice, within 48 hours or next payday, whichever comes first
Pennsylvania 43 Pa. Cons. Stat. Ann. § 260.5	Next payday	Next payday	No	
Rhode Island R.I. Gen. Laws § 28-14-4	Next payday	Next payday	Yes, if employee has worked for one full year	
South Carolina S.C. Code Ann. §§ 41-10-10(2), 41-10-50	Within 48 hours or next payday, but not more than 30 days	Within 48 hours or next payday, but not more than 30 days	No	
South Dakota S.D. Codified Laws Ann. §§ 60-11-10 to 60-11-14	Next payday (or until employee returns employer's property)	Next payday (or until employee returns employer's property)	No	

State Laws That Control Final Paychecks (continued)

State	Paycheck due when employee is fired	Paycheck due when employee quits	Unused vacation pay included	Special employment situations
Tennessee Tenn. Code Ann. § 50-2-103	Next payday or 21 days, whichever is later	Next payday or 21 days, whichever is later	Yes	Applies to employers with 5 or more employees
Texas Tex. Lab. Code Ann. § 61.014	Within 6 days	Next payday	No	
Utah Utah Code Ann. §§ 34-28-2, 34-28-5	Within 24 hours	Next payday	No	
Vermont Vt. Stat. Ann. tit. 21, § 342(c)(1)	Within 72 hours	Next regular payday or next Friday, if there is no regular payday	No	
Virginia Va. Code Ann. § 40.1-29(A.1)	Next payday	Next payday	No	
Washington Wash. Rev. Code Ann. § 49.48.010	Next payday	Next payday	No	
West Virginia W.Va. Code §§ 21-5-1, 21-5-4	Within 72 hours	Immediately if employee has given one pay period's notice; otherwise, next payday	Yes	
Wisconsin Wis. Stat. Ann. §§ 109.01(3), 109.03	Next payday; if termination is due to merger, relocation or liquidation of business, within 24 hours	Next payday	No	Does not apply to sales agents working on commission basis
Wyoming Wyo. Stat. Ann. § 27-4-104	5 working days	5 working days	No	

Current as of February 2003

e. Explain the Severance Package, If There Is One

If you plan to offer the employee a severance package, explain it now rather than at the exit interview. The employee may be worried about how he will survive financially while looking for a new job; telling him now about a generous severance package will go a long way toward easing that strain. (See Chapter 8 for more about severance packages.)

If the severance package comes with a catch—such as the employee signing a document called a release, which waives his right to sue—take care not to pressure the employee into making a decision about severance at the termination meeting. Simply lay out the terms of the severance and give the employee a specific amount of time to decide. (See Chapter 8, Section E for a discussion of how much time to give the employee.)

f. Review Any Noncompete and/or Confidentiality Documents

If the employee signed any noncompete or confidentiality agreements when he was hired, review those with the employee at some point before he leaves the company.

If you plan to have an exit interview with the employee, that is a better time to review those documents. After all, a noncompete document means that the employee will not be able to seek employment from your competitors. This isn't the sort of news you want to deliver right on the heels of terminating an employee if you can avoid it. Better to wait and give him time to calm down and digest the termination.

If the employee has never signed a noncompete or confidentiality agreement, you might consider having him do so. If you do decide to have him sign new agreements, the exit interview is probably the better time to introduce the idea. If you will not have an exit interview, however, discuss this issue with the employee during the termination meeting. This issue is explained more full in Chapter 8.

g. Explain the Status of Benefits

Now that you've broken the bad news, you must help the employee deal with the practicalities of losing his job by explaining to him what will happen to his benefits.

This discussion will be longer or shorter depending on whether you plan to have an exit interview with the employee. If the employee will receive this information in detail in an exit interview, you can gloss over it a bit during the termination meeting. Don't ignore it entirely, however. The employee will want some information immediately—and will not feel comfortable waiting a few days for answers to questions about important issues, such as when his health insurance will end. If a human resources representative is acting as your witness for this meeting, she can take over at this point and explain the benefits.

h. Explain Your Position on References

Many employees will want to know whether you will provide a reference for prospective employers. In Chapter 7, we explained the issues to think about when deciding whether you will give information beyond the dates, job responsibilities and salary of your former employee. Hopefully, you have come to the termination meeting prepared to explain your position.

Sharing your intentions with the employee may head off legal trouble in the future. When employees go to lawyers with complaints about references, the most common reason is that the employee was surprised by the information given and not that the reference was unflattering or negative.

To avoid surprising the employee, discuss what you plan to tell prospective employers. Make sure the employee understands exactly what you will reveal when called for a reference. Don't use vague words such as "positive" or "negative." Employers who choose to tell a well-rounded story should tell the employee that that's what the prospective boss will hear. Be precise and concrete. When you disclose exactly what facts you will reveal in a reference, the employee is free not to list you as a source if he doesn't like what he hears.

In addition to discussing the information that you will give in a reference, explain your reference policy. Tell the employee that you will notify her each time someone requests a reference and that you will only give out information to prospective employers who send you a release signed by the employee. (See Chapter 7, Section B for more about developing a safe reference policy.)

i.   Tie Up Loose Ends

After learning that he's been fired, the employee will most likely feel confused and disoriented. Be prepared to lead him through his confusion and answer questions such as:

- "Do I work the rest of the day or leave immediately?"
- "Do other people know this is happening?"
- "When can I collect my belongings?"
- "Can I go home now and come back tomorrow to deal with this?"
- "What do I tell my clients?"
- "I have appointments scheduled for the rest of the week. What do I do about those?"

We don't presume to be able to give answers to these questions that will be appropriate for every situation. Here are some suggestions that have proved workable in many cases.

Work in progress. Prior to the meeting, find out what the employee is working on and have a plan for passing that work to a coworker or a supervisor. Explain whether you want the employee to complete the work he is doing at the moment. It's best not to leave this up to the employee. Doing so is unfair and unkind, and it's not in the best interest of your business.

Telling coworkers. Before the meeting, you should have thought about what you'll tell the rest of the company about the termination.

(See Chapter 7, Section B for guidance on what to tell coworkers about a termination.) Discuss your intentions with the employee and ask if the employee has any thoughts. You should not, however, allow the employee to convince you to say anything at the meeting that is untrue. Nor should you stray from the advice contained in Chapter 7 just to please the employee.

Outplacement help. If you are going to provide the employee with any outplacement services, explain them during the termination meeting. (See Chapter 8, Section D for information about outplacement services.)

Set up the exit interview. If you are going to conduct an exit interview with the employee, explain what the exit interview will entail. Schedule the interview for a date and time that is convenient for the employee. (Section B, below, gives details on how to run an exit interview.)

j.   End the Meeting on a Congenial Note

End the meeting on the most positive note possible. Shake the employee's hand and wish him good luck. If you can say something positive about him and his tenure at your company, do it. But don't say anything that is untrue or that undercuts the termination decision.

6.   Give the Employee a Contact

To facilitate the employee's transition out of your company, give him the name of someone within the company who can answer his questions. Ideally, this would be someone from human resources, but anyone in management who has a positive relationship with the employee will do. This person's job will be to hold the employee's hand through the termination and beyond. The employee may come to this person with questions about any number of things, including the following:

- handing off remaining work to coworkers
- turning in company materials such as keys, computers and cell phones
- understanding the termination's impact on his benefits
- understanding any noncompete, nonsolicitation and non-disclosure contracts he may have signed, and
- understanding the severance package, if there is one.

7. Document the Meeting

As soon as the meeting is over, write down what was said and by whom. Use the guidelines for documenting an event as explained in Chapter 4, Section B.

8. Collect Company Property and Cancel Passwords

Knowing when and how to collect company property and block the employee's access to the building and computer system is a matter of judgment and tact. If you trust the employee and don't fear that he will become violent or destructive, there is no reason to treat him like a criminal, especially at a time when he is apt to be feeling pretty low. Be casual and patient, giving him time to digest the termination before you swoop in for the company credit card and cell phone.

If you do fear violence, theft or sabotage—or if the employee held a highly sensitive position in your company (such as managing your computer system)—act quickly to block the employee's access to the computer system, confidential files and documents, trade secrets and the building. If you can arrange it, the best time to have access blocked is while you are in the termination meeting with the employee. There's no sense in leaving your entire computer system open for the crashing.

Company Property

Make sure you collect all company property and turn off all passwords before the employee walks out the door for the last time. Among the things you might need to gather are the following:

- the company car
- keys to the building
- corporate credit card (and call the credit card company to cancel the account)
- computer password
- corporate long distance card (call the phone company and cancel the number)
- confidential files
- client lists
- manuals
- laptop computer, and
- cell phone.

9. Keep It Confidential

As with every other aspect of the employment relationship, keep the termination meeting as confidential as possible. Only tell people about it on a need-to-know basis.

Checklist of Things to Do Before the Termination Meeting

- ☐ Cut a final paycheck for the employee that includes all unused accrued vacation time. Also include earned commissions.
- ☐ Issue any outstanding expense reimbursements.
- ☐ If you have a payroll or accounting department or clerk, tell them to drop the employee from payroll.
- ☐ Determine who in management needs to know about the termination decision. Notify them.
- ☐ Choose someone to conduct the termination meeting.
- ☐ Choose someone who will be the employee's contact after the termination meeting.
- ☐ Make sure that the individual who conducts the termination meeting is familiar with the employee's personnel file.
- ☐ Make sure that the individual who conducts the termination meeting is familiar with the status of the employee's benefits.
- ☐ Decide if you will have an exit interview with the employee.
- ☐ If you will have an exit interview, choose someone to conduct the exit interview.
- ☐ Determine whether the employee had access to confidential information. Take steps to ensure that the employee does not disclose that information.
- ☐ Determine whether you will offer a severance package to the employee.
- ☐ Create an action plan for handing off the employee's current projects to coworkers and supervisors.
- ☐ Decide how you will handle calls from prospective employers seeking a reference for the employee.
- ☐ Decide what you will tell the employee's coworkers about the termination.

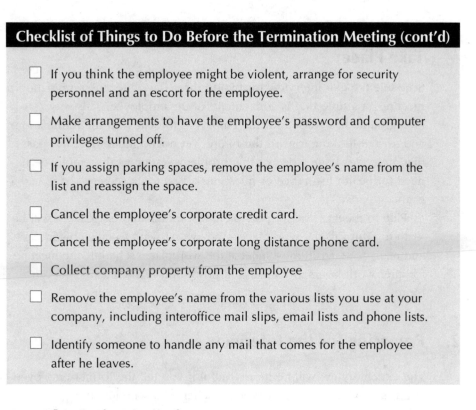

Checklist of Things to Do Before the Termination Meeting (cont'd)

☐ If you think the employee might be violent, arrange for security personnel and an escort for the employee.

☐ Make arrangements to have the employee's password and computer privileges turned off.

☐ If you assign parking spaces, remove the employee's name from the list and reassign the space.

☐ Cancel the employee's corporate credit card.

☐ Cancel the employee's corporate long distance phone card.

☐ Collect company property from the employee

☐ Remove the employee's name from the various lists you use at your company, including interoffice mail slips, email lists and phone lists.

☐ Identify someone to handle any mail that comes for the employee after he leaves.

B. The Exit Interview

Imagine the exit interview as the calm *after* the storm. The firing was tough—both deciding to do it and breaking the news to the employee —but now everyone has had time to let their emotions cool and get used to the fact that the employment relationship is over. All that remains is to pick up the pieces and to move on.

Picking up the pieces is what the exit interview is all about. It gives both employer and employee a chance to reflect on the employment relationship—both the good and the bad of it—and to finish any business remaining between them. If handled with care and tact, the exit interview can be a healing process as well—for both you and the employee.

1.   When and Where Should the Exit Interview Take Place?

Schedule the exit interview for two to three days after the termination meeting, at a time that is convenient for the employee. This way, enough time has passed for the employee to deal with the termination and to start looking toward the future; yet not so much time has passed that memories have faded or that problems—such as the employee's need for health insurance or questions about trade secrets—have had a chance to arise.

Plan to meet off site, if possible. Most terminated employees will be loath to return to the workplace—they won't want to face coworkers and managers. If you must meet at the workplace, schedule the meeting for after work hours and meet in a private place such as a conference room.

2.   Preparing for the Interview

The exit interview will be more fruitful if you tell the former employee in advance what you'll be covering. When you schedule the meeting, suggest that the employee give you questions in advance so that you can find the answers before the interview.

You, too, should do some homework before holding the interview. In addition to answering the employee's questions and explaining the issues listed below in subsection 3, such as healthcare continuation and benefits, you might want to think about what you can learn from this employee about your company. A terminated employee may feel he has nothing to lose when asked about problems or issues at the company, especially if they had nothing to do with his termination, and he may give you frank information on his supervisor or manager that current employees may hesitate to divulge. The exit interview is a rare chance to get a worker's eye view on what goes on in your business. Subsection 4, below, suggests some general questions you might consider.

3. Who Should Conduct the Exit Interview?

Someone who is neutral and unconnected to the termination decision should conduct the exit interview. Usually, the employee's immediate supervisor is not the best choice. The ideal person would be someone from human resources or an office manager.

If you operate a small business, you probably don't have much choice in who conducts the interview. Anyone can do in a pinch. Just make sure that whoever conducts the interview takes care to keep the tone neutral and friendly—especially if there has been any animosity between that person and the employee.

Immediately after the interview, document what was said according to the guidelines explained in Chapter 4, Section B. As ever, keep the details of your conversation to yourself, sharing them only with people who must know.

4. What Should You Cover During the Interview?

The exit interview is the place where you finalize all of the details of the termination and allow the employee to vent his feelings about the company and his termination. We suggest covering the details first, leaving time for the more emotional part at the end. With any luck, this will be the last official contact that you or anyone from your company has with the employee.

a. Benefits

At the termination meeting, you gave the employee a brief explanation of the status of his benefits post-employment. Now is the time to go into more depth. Include any information necessary to continue benefits after employment and inform him of any vested interests that he has, such as stock options and retirement contributions that he can take with him.

Among the benefits you should explain are:

- health insurance, including dental and vision (see Chapter 7, Section D for more about health insurance issues)
- life insurance
- unemployment eligibility (see Chapter 7, Section E for more about unemployment issues)
- retirement, and
- stock options.

b.   Confidentiality Agreements

If the employee has signed a confidentiality agreement, give him a copy of the agreement and review it with him. To be sure that he understands it, review the employee's workload and give him examples of things he has handled that are confidential. Be careful to explain, however, that these are merely examples and that there may be other information that falls within the confidentiality agreement.

Without appearing threatening or condescending, explain what types of conduct will violate the agreement and what the repercussions of violating the agreement will be.

If the employee has any confidential documents or items still in his possession, retrieve them from him at the meeting. If he doesn't have them with him, set a specific date when he will turn those things over to you.

c.   Noncompete Agreements

If the employee has signed an agreement not to compete with you after he leaves your employ, give the employee a copy of the agreement, review it with him and make sure he understands it. Provide him with names of companies and businesses that he can't work for (but make sure he understands that these are just examples and not an exhaustive list). Explain to him what will happen if he violates the agreement—but make sure not to sound like you are threatening him.

d. Outplacement Services

If you plan to offer the employee any assistance in finding another job, explain this at the exit interview. (See Chapter 8, Section D for more about outplacement services.)

e. Company Property

Retrieve from the employee any company property that he has in his possession. (See Section A, above, for a list of property that an employee might have in his possession.)

f. Severance Agreement

If you are offering the employee a severance package in exchange for a release, now is the time to finalize the agreement. (See Chapter 8 for more about severance agreements.) Explain the agreement and, if the employee is signing a release as part of the agreement, review the release with him as well.

Before finalizing the severance agreement by signing it, make sure that the employee has turned over to you all confidential documents and all pieces of company property that he has in his possession. The severance package is the final bit of leverage that you have to hold over the employee. Don't use it until you've gotten everything you want back from the employee.

g. Final Paycheck

If you did not give the employee his final paycheck at the termination meeting, give it to him at the exit interview—even if the law of your state allows you more time. (See Section A, above, for a list of state laws regulating final paychecks.) In addition to the final paycheck, pay the employee any money you owe him for expenses.

h.   References

Discuss with the employee how you will handle any request you receive for a reference. You may have already covered this point at the termination meeting, but it is a good idea to review it again in this calmer context. (See Chapter 7, Section C for a discussion of giving references for terminated employees.)

i.   Listen to the Employee

When we discussed the termination interview above, we cautioned you to not allow the employee to argue with you or engage in a time-consuming diatribe about the termination. Keep it short, we said; keep it focused.

In contrast, the exit interview is the ideal time to allow the employee to vent and to tell you exactly what he thinks of you and of the termination. His emotions have leveled out, and he's had time to organize his thoughts and feelings. Encourage the employee to talk about the company, his supervisors and managers, his job and his termination. Of course, listen with a critical ear and beware of people with axes to grind or grudges to satisfy. And under no circumstances should you allow the employee to go overboard and start abusing you or yelling at you. If the employee can't act professionally, end the interview.

This is also your opportunity to learn a thing or two that will enable you to make your company better. You may have prepared a list of questions to ask about the worker's experience with your company and supervisors; or you may want to refer to "Learn More About Your Company," below, for some suggestions.

Learn More About Your Company

Here is a list of issues you could raise with the ex-employee at the exit interview. It will be a rare termination interview, however, where you would feel it appropriate to ask most of them.

- Describe why you decided to work for this company.
- In what ways did the company meet your expectations?
- In what ways did the company fail to meet your expectations?
- Describe what you liked most about working for this company.
- Describe what you liked least about working for this company.
- Explain why you think you were terminated.
- Do you think that you were treated fairly by the company? Why? Why not?
- Describe any instances where you think that the company treated other employees unfairly.
- What did you think about your job?
- Do you believe that you were paid fairly?
- How did you feel about the amount of work expected of you? Did you ever feel too much pressure?
- Did you ever want additional training? Did you ask for it? Did you receive it? What did you think about it?
- How would you rate your own job performance?
- Did you get along with your supervisor? How would you rate her job performance?
- Did you feel free to talk to your supervisor or manager about problems in your job? Did you feel like your input was appreciated and respected?
- Did your supervisor give you sufficient feedback about your work? Did she describe to you areas where you could improve? Did she recognize your efforts and achievements?
- Did you get along with your coworkers?
- Do you think the company's policies are sensible? If not, please explain.
- What would you do to improve your department?
- What would you change about this company if you were in charge?

Chapter 10

Looking Forward

Congratulations! You've solved your employee problem of the moment—either by using evaluations, discipline and other management techniques to turn a struggling worker around; or by making a careful decision to fire a problem employee and following through. So now you can just rest on your laurels and look forward to smooth sailing ahead, right?

Well, not necessarily. To make sure you don't run into similar problems in the future, you'll have to figure out what went wrong this time around—and how you can avoid making the same mistake twice. Take a few minutes now to think back on your dealings with this employee. Were there warning signs—offhand remarks or actions that didn't add up to much at the time, but developed newfound resonance as the employment relationship soured? Were you less than enthusiastic when you hired the worker? Were there problems that you could have dealt with earlier? Were your hands tied by your policies—or lack of them? Were you stymied by a supervisor's failure to manage the worker effectively or document the worker's problems?

Most honest employers would have to answer "yes" to at least one of these questions, much as it might pain them to do so. In fact, no matter what kind of business, management structure, company culture and individual employees you have, your preventable employee problems can probably be traced back to one or more of the following three basic sources:

- poor hiring
- flawed (or nonexistent) workplace policies, and/or
- failing to follow commonsense procedures.

The strategies we've given you in this book—for conducting performance evaluations, using progressive discipline, investigating workplace problems and firing, if necessary—focus primarily on the third reason listed. Using these techniques can help you deal with employee problems as they crop up. And as we've pointed out, these same tools can help you prevent employee problems in the first place, by letting your workers know what you expect of them, showing employees that there are consequences for poor performance or misconduct and giving struggling workers the chance to turn things around.

But to really protect yourself from the problem employees yet to come, you'll want to think about revamping your hiring and personnel practices so that you can avoid employee problems in the future (or at least give yourself the leeway to deal with them immediately, before you're facing a crisis). In this chapter, we explain how to do just that. Section A gives you the information you need to hire right—from figuring out if you really need to bring in someone new, to interviewing, checking references and making job offers. Section B covers personnel policies that will give you the tools you need to deal with trouble as soon as it crops up—and let your employees know exactly what you expect of them.

Unfortunately, there's no way to guarantee, with absolute certainty, that you'll never face another difficult employee issue. But, by following the tips and strategies covered here, you can inoculate your workplace against future trouble and give yourself every advantage in dealing with the problem employees that slip through your defenses.

A.   Improve Your Hiring Process

The best way to deal with problem employees is to avoid hiring them in the first place. After all, if you managed to hire only the right people, then you would have a workplace virtually free of employee trouble. What a dream that would be. No unpleasant realizations that the person you hired doesn't really have the right qualifications and skills for the job. No time spent away from your job as you write memo after memo about a problem employee's performance and productivity woes. No lying awake at night wondering whether the termination you just handled will turn into an expensive lawsuit.

Does such a utopian workplace exist? Probably not. But you can go a long way toward minimizing the number of employee problems you have to deal with each year by hiring the right people. Of course, we think that the first step in hiring top-notch employees is to provide a great place to work. Assuming you already do that, however, you can probably still use some help in your hiring process. For many managers and employers, hiring employees is a rushed and poorly thought out process. In such a world, is it any wonder that problem employees get hired every day, often at the expense of better qualified and more suitable candidates?

In this section, we take a look at some trouble spots in the hiring process. This is not a primer on how to hire. Rather, it is a discussion of dos and don'ts intended to protect your hiring process from some of the most common mistakes that result in hiring problem employees.

Many worthwhile books focus exclusively on hiring and delve deeply into important topics such as advertising, interviewing and pre-employment testing. If you are serious about whipping your hiring process into shape, consider taking a look at some of them. In particular, we recommend *The Costs of Bad Hiring Decisions and How to Avoid Them,* by Carol A. Hacker (St. Lucie Press, 1998) and *Hiring Great People,* by Kevin C. Klinvex, Matthew S. O'Connel and Christopher P. Klinvex (McGraw-Hill, 1999).

1.   Understand the Position

Before spending the time and expense to advertise, interview and hire, take a moment to make sure you understand what the job entails. Assuming you decide to go ahead and hire for it, you're going to have a tough time hiring the right person if you don't really know what the job requires. This is an absolutely crucial step, because no one benefits when you hire someone who lacks the proper skills or qualifications for a job. Eventually, the new hire will be miserable because he can't meet your expectations; coworkers will have to take on the burden of doing the new hire's work; the supervisor will have to take time out from her job to train or discipline; and you will eventually have to endure a termination and all the unpleasantness and legal risk that comes along with it.

a. Consult the Performance Evaluation Sheets

This process of analyzing the job is similar to the process of identifying job standards for a performance evaluation system. (See Chapter 3 for more about job standards and performance evaluations.) In fact, if you are filling a vacant position (instead of creating a new one), a good place to start analyzing the job is to look at the job standards that you identified in the former employee's performance evaluations. If you're satisfied that the standards are still relevant, fine, but take this opportunity to tweak them, particularly if your recent experience with a former employee has taught you something about the usefulness of the standards.

b. Talk to Individuals Who Used to Hold the Position

You're likely to learn valuable practical information about this job by talking to people who used to hold the position. What skills did they feel were most important for doing the job? What were their day-to-day tasks? How did their job fit within the overall business of the company? What qualifications do they think a person needs to perform the job well? What skills would have helped them perform better?

If you conducted exit interviews with former employees who once held the position you are filling, take a look at the notes from those interviews. (See Chapter 9 for more about exit interviews.) Perhaps they left because they felt ill equipped to handle the position, or perhaps they felt overqualified for the position.

c. Think Back on What Went Wrong Last Time

If you're filling a position vacated by an employee whom you fired, think back and ask yourself if there is anything this experience has taught you about the position. For example, did fuzzy reporting lines contribute to that employee's inability to keep the job? Was too much (or too little) expected of one person, or did you assume a level of training or experience that your fired employee was not explicitly expected to have at the time of hiring? It's a rare employer who, in her heart of hearts, can say, even of a justly fired employee, "I did everything right from the start." If improving the job description might have helped, take this opportunity to fix it.

d.   Talk to Colleagues and Customers

You're likely to learn valuable information by talking to the people at your company who interact and work with the person holding the position you are seeking to fill. For example, the person who will supervise the new hire may be able to tell you how the job has evolved since you last considered it. Or the folks who will report to the new person may have some thoughts on how that employee could better supervise them. If appropriate, consult customers or clients who may have insights on aspects of the job that you are unaware of.

e.   Write a Job Description

Once you have analyzed the job, writing a job description should be a cinch. Not only will it help you choose a person who is a good fit for the job, but it will also help job candidates decide whether they are qualified and whether they even want the job in the first place. Your job description should include:

- **Job title.** Use the same title that people at your company will use once the employee is hired.
- **Placement within the organization.** Describe how the position fits within the company.
- **A task summary.** Write a paragraph of what this person will do in your company, including specific responsibilities.
- **Required qualifications.** Include the required education level, years of experience, necessary licenses and the like.
- **Reporting lines.** Explain to whom the job holder would report, and whether others would report to the job holder.

2.   Is This Job Necessary?

Having figured out what this job entails, you're now in a position to decide whether you really need to fill it. There are all sorts of reasons why a job might not be necessary, even if it seems indispensable at first blush. Ask yourself the following questions:

- Have your business needs changed such that you don't need this position anymore?
- Will changing business needs make this job obsolete in the near future?
- Can you transfer the duties and responsibilities of this position to other people?
- Can you collapse two positions into one?
- Can you purchase new technology that eliminates the need for the position?
- Would it be more economical to use independent contractors for the work?

There are both pros and cons to using independent contractors. On the plus side, you can save money by avoiding costly payroll taxes and benefits. In addition, you can hire someone for a short, specific project without incurring the costs and long-term responsibilities of an employee. On the con side, you lose continuity and control when you have non-employees coming in and out of your organization. Also, you risk misclassifying the individual, which could result in a government audit and fines. For more about using independent contractors in your workforce, see *Hiring Independent Contractors,* by Stephen Fishman (Nolo).

3.   Screen Out Poor Candidates

Careful screening will filter out many potential problem employees. You also spare yourself the time and disruption of interviewing people who are not suited for the job.

a.   Cover Letters, Resumes and Applications

Your first clues about a candidate come from the cover letter and resume that you receive either in the mail or, these days, via email. Happily, this is also an ideal way to separate the problematic candidates from the attractive ones—if you read these documents with a critical eye.

Start by reading the cover letter for more than just content. Look at the candidate's style, spelling and grammar. Even if you're not hiring a proofreader or an editor, you'll want to see a letter that is done right. Sloppiness at this stage may well presage a sloppy attitude towards work, too.

Next, look for evidence that this letter was tailored to your company and is not a form letter sent to multiple employers. An applicant who has taken the time and trouble to learn about your company and pitch her letter accordingly is one who understands the importance of evaluating a situation individually. This quality is valuable in every employee.

You'll want to use a similar critical eye when evaluating resumes. Look for the following red flags:

- gaps in information (for example, are there years that are unaccounted for?)
- poor appearance and layout
- poor grammar, misspellings and typographical errors
- vague phrases that really give you no information (such as "helped," "familiar with" and "have knowledge of")
- possible evasions, such as "attended" a school rather than "graduated from," and
- incomplete information (for example, listing the state of a former employer but not providing an address).

A good resume will include concrete details about job duties and responsibilities. It should have specific language and details that give you a vivid picture of what the candidate did—and, more importantly, what he accomplished—at his last job. If it has those qualities, consider putting that candidate's resume in the to-be-interviewed stack.

b.   Evaluating Work Histories

Look for candidates with careers that look like logical steps up a ladder. You don't want someone who has been jumping around—or worse, down—in ways that seem puzzling. Look for candidates who have accomplished things in their careers and not just performed their jobs adequately.

As you review a candidate's job history, it's important that you not be too rigid. People who take time off to travel, raise children or explore different career options aren't necessarily the stuff of problem employees. Is a particular nontraditional job history evidence of a rational yet unusual series of decisions that spell stability for this position, or indicative of someone who won't stick very long at any job? You'll have to make the call.

Try not to let stereotypes and biases enter into your thinking. Don't assume someone is smart or will make an ideal employee just because she graduated from an Ivy League school. (And, similarly, avoid rejecting someone out of hand just because he received his education at a state college.) It's a mistake to automatically assume that an applicant is a leader because he was the president of an organization. And beware of the person who has a laundry list of personal interests—this may spell hyperbole rather than genuine energy.

c.   Applications

Cover letters and resumes can be quite valuable, but since they vary so much from candidate to candidate, they can make it difficult for you to compare people using the same criteria. In addition, they may not contain the information that you really want, or they may include irrelevant information that will distract you or cloud your judgment. A way to solve these problems is to have all viable candidates complete the same application, which forces applicants to give you just the information you need.

If you are going to take the extra step of sending out applications, don't cut corners by using a generic application from a book or stationery store. The whole point of the application is to get information that is tailored to the job you are trying to fill, and few generic applications will do that for you. They can be helpful in one regard, though—look at them to get ideas for creating your own application. Use the following tips when drafting your applications.

Draft your application while looking at your job analysis (see subsection 1, above). Ask questions designed to elicit information about the skills and qualifications that the position requires. For example, if you are hiring a legal secretary, you might ask:

- How many words per minute can you type?
- Please list the word processing programs (for example, Word or WordPerfect) in which you are proficient.
- Imagine you must file a pleading in an unfamiliar jurisdiction. How would you find out about that court's filing requirements?

Use closed questions. A closed question requests specific information on issues that are important to you. (See subsection 5, below, for more about closed questions.) Ideally, it calls for a short answer that will quickly tell you whether this candidate is worth pursuing. For example:

- When are you available to begin work?
- When and where did you attend college?
- Did you graduate? With what major and degree?

Avoid questions that would require the applicant to write at length about the topic. Anything that requires more than a sentence or two is probably best reserved for the pre-interview and interview.

Ask questions about absolute job criteria—things that will immediately knock candidates out of the running if they don't have them. For example, if you are hiring for a position that requires driving, ask "Do you have a valid state driver's license?" Or, if you are hiring for a position that requires travel, ask "Are you willing to travel out of state for work?"

Don't ask any questions that violate the law. Of course, you wouldn't intentionally ask such questions, but remember that even seemingly innocuous queries can violate the law. For example, in an effort to learn about the applicant, a question about the applicant's date of birth could land you in legal hot water if that candidate isn't hired and complains to an attorney or state employment department about age discrimination. (For more on this issue, see "Interview Questions," below.)

d. Assembling Your Application

Take some care in assembling and mailing your job application. Don't forget that it represents your company, just as a resume and cover letter represent an applicant. Make it neat, clean and professional. Include a cover letter thanking the applicant for his interest, congratulating him on making the first cut and asking him to return the application to you prior to the interview. Enclose a release to be signed by the applicant, which gives you permission to talk to references and former employers and to conduct a background check. As a courtesy, provide a self-addressed stamped envelope and give the applicant a date by which you must receive a completed application.

e. Evaluate the Returned Applications

You'll find that it's easier to review the completed applications than it was to read through cover letters and resumes. You'll be able to quickly discard applicants whose answers to your closed, "job breaker" questions put them out of the running. As for the rest, adopt a set of guidelines that you can apply to each question, and evaluate every application consistently. But don't be too rigid—you don't want to ignore overall impressions, which can be as important as the answer to one question.

4. Conduct an Initial Interview on the Phone

Having sifted through the returned applications, your pile of possible candidates for the job should now be manageable. But don't issue invitations for an interview just yet. Doing an initial interview on the phone can help screen out candidates that the paper screening process doesn't catch, leaving you fairly sure that the people you bring in for on-site interviews are top-notch candidates.

The employer isn't the only one who can benefit from a phone interview. Just as you are in a constant process of evaluating candidates, applicants, too, want to evaluate you and your organization. The phone interview may result in some "self-screening" if the applicant decides that, after all, the job isn't a good fit. When you call the candidate, let him know immediately that you are calling to conduct an initial interview over the phone. Ask if this is a good time, or if you can arrange a time to call back. Have the candidate's resume, cover letter and application in front of you. Know what you are going to ask before you call. Prepare some open-ended questions about the applicant's experience, skills and qualifications. Ask about anything in the applicant's paperwork that you find puzzling or that you'd simply like more information on. Be prepared to answer the applicant's questions about your hiring process, the position and your company.

5.   Interview Effectively

Once you have screened out unacceptable applicants by reviewing their paperwork and conducting a phone interview, the time has come to bring people in for face-to-face interviews. Most employers say that the interview is the most significant part of the hiring process, the event that determines whether they will hire or reject a hopeful applicant. Yet, few take the time to choose the best environment for the interview, prepare questions in advance, create an interview schedule or plan what they will say to the candidate.

Failing to prepare for an interview is a shame, because the interview is your best chance to find a good person for the job—but only if you do it right. If you have ever prepared to interview a candidate by reading her resume five minutes before she arrives—or, worse yet, while she is cooling her heels at your receptionist's desk—you've turned your hiring process into a game of chance, one in which you've created ideal conditions for bringing a problem employee into your workplace.

There are a number of theories popular today about the best way to interview job candidates. Some are quite complex and require a certain amount of manipulation and deviousness on the part of the interviewer. Others ask you to orchestrate the interview like a chess match, planning all of your moves beforehand. The one thing all of these theories have in common is that they require you to prepare and think in advance. If you just do that, you will have gone a long way toward improving your hiring process.

a.   Prepare Your Interview Questions

Walking in the door thinking that you'll get all of the information you need from a candidate simply by saying whatever occurs to you in the moment is a mistake. An interview is not a conversation. You need specific information from the candidate, which you'll get only if you ask for it. You are doing yourself and the candidate a disservice if you walk in without a plan.

If you have analyzed the job as we suggested in this chapter, then you know what qualifications, skills and traits you want in your new hire. Start here as you prepare questions. For each quality you want, list questions that you think will elicit information from the candidate about whether he possesses that quality. Use both closed and open questions, but avoid leading questions.

- **Closed questions invite a short factual answer:** "How many people do you supervise?" "Which states are in your sales territory?" "Have you ever written something for publication?"
- **Open questions, in contrast, invite the candidate to speak at length.** "Tell me about a work experience you've had that demonstrates your leadership abilities." "What drew you to the plastics industry?" "Tell me about the accomplishment at your previous job that you are most proud of."
- **Leading questions suggest the answer:** "You have written for child audiences before, haven't you?" "You have a lot of leadership experience, right?" "You must enjoy sales a lot."

Some information—such as number of years of experience, level of education achieved and licenses held—is fairly easy to elicit through simple closed questioning.

Other information is more difficult to learn. Do you have problem solving skills? Are you a motivated worker? Can you work as part of a team? If you ask these questions directly, of course, you're going to get the obvious answers. Can you problem solve? Yes! Do you work well as part of a team? Of course! Not very helpful.

Asking ordinary, open-ended questions may not get you much farther. For example, asking, "Describe for me your ability to problem solve" is almost too vague a question to answer. Who knows what sort of response you will get and whether it will give you any real information?

The ideal way to deal with these difficult areas is to ask open-ended questions that are rooted in real-world examples. This way, the question is specific enough for the candidate to answer and for you to learn the information you need. As a bonus, these answers are often of the sort that can be verified when you talk to the candidate's references. For example, to learn about a candidate's problem-solving skills, you might ask, "Describe for me a workplace problem that you've faced in the past year and tell me how you resolved it."

Questions that are tied to specific problems or issues are known as behavioral questions. Some common examples of behavioral questions include the following:

- To elicit information about management ability, ask: "Tell me about a time when you have had to coach a difficult employee."
- To elicit information about sales ability, ask: "Describe an important sale from your last job. How did you accomplish it? Why are you particularly proud of it?"
- To elicit information about problem-solving skills, ask: "Tell me about a recent problem that you faced in your current position. What did you do to resolve it?"
- To elicit information about adaptability, ask: "Tell me about a time when your current employer changed your job duties. What happened? How did you handle it?"

In most instances, behavioral questions will elicit the most valuable information. When responding to your questions, candidates should be able to give specific examples of having performed the tasks or used the skills you are looking for in the current position. In other words, it's not good enough for a candidate to say he is capable of doing something; you want him to give a specific example of having done it and to describe how he did it.

Similarly, candidates should be able to give specific, real-world examples of qualities and personality traits that you want in the position.

b.   Avoid Illegal Questions

The spontaneous and unpredictable nature of any interview makes it rife with traps even for employers with the best of intentions. Well-meaning, innocent comments could be construed by an applicant as prejudicial or could be used later by an unhappy applicant as the basis of a discrimination lawsuit. For example, a casual discussion about a female applicant's home life could lead you to ask if the applicant plans to have children soon. If you don't hire her, she might claim you discriminated against her based on her gender.

Don't let fear of breaking the law render you speechless. If you follow two simple rules, you'll avoid trouble during the interview process:

Rule One: Do not ask about any characteristic that the law prohibits you from considering in making your decision. (To learn about these characteristics, see Chapter 2.) For example, don't ask an applicant what her race or religion is, because you are not allowed to consider these factors in making your decision. And don't panic if an applicant raises a delicate subject—such as disability or national origin—without any prompting from you. You can't raise such subjects, but the applicant can. If the applicant does broach the subject, however, tread lightly. Unless the applicant raises an issue that directly relates to the job (for example, she needs you to accommodate her disability so that she can do the job—see "Applicants With Disabilities," below), politely steer the conversation in another direction.

Rule Two: Respect the applicant's privacy. Although federal law does not require you to do so, many state laws and rules of etiquette do. For example, asking applicants in California about their sexual fantasies (yes, that has happened in real life) violates their state-protected right to privacy.

So, what can you ask? If you've followed the advice in this chapter, you should have analyzed the job and determined all the tasks the applicant will have to perform as part of the job and all the skills and experience the position requires. These lists will help you confine the interview to what you really need to know—whether the applicant can do the job. You can ask the applicant whether she will be able to perform each essential task, and you can also ask her if she has the requisite skills and experience. Remember, the law absolutely allows you to ask questions that directly relate to the job you are trying to fill. "Interview Questions," below, gives examples of acceptable and unacceptable questions.

In a very rare and narrow exception to antidiscrimination law, you can discriminate against people on the basis of gender, religion, national origin or age (but never race) if the very nature of the job requires you to do so. And because you can discriminate in this situation, you can ask about the trait.

This exception—called the bona fide occupational qualification (BFOQ) exception—arises from the fact that some jobs require people who have certain characteristics that the law usually protects, such as people of a certain national origin or people of a certain religion. For example, if you are a movie director searching for someone to play the role of Hamlet's mother, you can discriminate against men in filling the part. Or if you are an official in the Catholic Church, you can discriminate against non-Catholics when hiring priests.

In order to use this exception, you must prove that no member of the group that you want to discriminate against can perform the job. This is a very tough thing to prove, and courts often reject arguments that most employers find perfectly legitimate. For example, the airlines can't discriminate against older applicants when hiring flight attendants

Interview Questions

Topic	Acceptable Question(s)	Unacceptable Question(s)
Marital status	If you are married, does your spouse work for this company?	Are you married?
Gender	None	All questions that touch on this topic
Age	Are you 18 years of age or older?	How old are you? What is your birth date?
Religion	None	All questions that touch on this topic
Race or national origin	None	All questions that touch on this topic
Citizenship	Are you legally authorized to work in the United States on a full-time basis?	What country are you from? Are you a citizen of the United States? Are your parents citizens of the United States?
Disability	Please review the attached list of job requirements and duties. Are you able to perform all of them?	Do you have any physical or mental problems that would prevent you from performing this job? Do you have any medical problems that this company should be aware of? Have you ever requested an accommodation from an employer pursuant to the Americans With Disabilities Act?

simply because they think that passengers prefer young faces. If you look at the actual job duties—maintaining order in the plane's cabin, serving meals and beverages—a 45-year-old is just as able to perform the job of flight attendant as a 25-year-old.

Applicants With Disabilities

Of all the antidiscrimination laws, the Americans With Disabilities Act or ADA (42 U.S.C. §§ 12101-12213) is often the hardest for employers to understand and comply with, especially when it comes to hiring. Employers want to find out if the person they hire can actually perform the job, but often aren't sure how to explore this issue without running afoul of the law.

If you remember one simple rule, you'll be in good shape: You can ask people about their abilities, not their disabilities. For instance, you can ask an applicant how she plans to perform each function of the job, but you can't ask her whether she has any disabilities that will prevent her from performing each function of the job.

One way to stay within the rules is to attach a job description with specific information about the job duties to the job application. Or describe these things to the applicant during the job interview. Then ask the applicant how she plans to perform the job. This way, the applicant can tell you about her qualifications and strengths. It also gives her the opportunity to raise with you any needs she might have for reasonable accommodations. A reasonable accommodation is either something you do for the applicant or equipment you provide to the applicant that makes it possible for her to do the job despite her disability.

Some other rules to keep in mind:

- If you have no reason to believe that the applicant has a disability, you cannot ask her if she will need an accommodation from you to perform the job.
- If you know the applicant has a disability (for example, the disability is obvious or the applicant has told you about the disability), you can ask her if she will need an accommodation from you to perform the job.

c.   Orchestrate the Event

Too often, companies lose out on top-notch hires because they have made the hiring process uncomfortable and confusing. Just as you are evaluating whether you want to hire the candidate, the candidate is evaluating whether he wants to come work for you. He's not going to if you present the process—and, by extension, your company—as inconsiderate and disorganized. If you lose out on a good employee, you're more likely to hire a problem employee.

Choose a comfortable setting for the interview. A conference room is a good choice, but an office with you sitting behind a desk is not. Most likely, you expect the candidate to be on time, so you should be prepared to meet the candidate promptly. Notify the receptionist or whoever greets nonemployees at the door so that the candidate can feel welcome right from the start. You don't want candidates showing up only to find that no one knows who they are, why they are there or where to find you.

Know in advance which people from your department are going to interview the candidate. They should prepare for the interview by reading through the candidate's paperwork, the application and your notes from the pre-interview. You should also meet with them beforehand to discuss what information you want to elicit from the candidate and what information you want to convey. Pick someone to run the interview. That person is in charge of essentially befriending the candidate during the process. He will greet the candidate at the door, usher the candidate to the interview location, make sure the conversation flows during the interview, keep the interview on schedule and make sure that all of the relevant information gets covered.

Choose the right social butterfly for the job. Although we assume in this chapter that the person running the interview is the same person who is in charge of the hiring process (the "you" we are addressing), it doesn't have to be that way. Interviewing candidates takes a certain amount of social skill. It's not up to the candidate to move the conversation along and make everyone feel comfortable. It's up to the interviewers. If you are painfully shy or have a great deal of trouble talking to people whom you don't know, you may not be the best person to run the interview, even if you are the most senior person in the room—and the one who will ultimately make the hiring decision. You can sit in and participate, certainly, but put a more socially adept person in charge.

Decide how much time you want to spend interviewing the candidate. Prepare an agenda. If the interview is going to last more than an hour, plan a break or two. Know whether you want potential coworkers to take the candidate to lunch. This can be a nice way for your employees to get a personal feel for the candidate and for the candidate to learn more about the personal interactions within your company.

When you call the candidate to arrange the interview, tell her whom she will be meeting with, the agenda for the interview and any special circumstances that might exist (for example, mention whether you will be requiring the candidate to take a skills test, whether the candidate should wear any special attire or if you expect the candidate to bring anything with her).

Send the candidate a confirming letter with the time and the place for the interview, the name of the person whom the candidate should ask for when she arrives at your company, a copy of the agenda and the names and job descriptions of the people whom she will be meeting.

d.   Relate to the Candidate

As the interviewer, your chief job is to put the candidate at ease. When the candidate arrives, shake her hand warmly and offer her a beverage.

Make pleasant conversation before the official interview starts. Was she able to find the office easily? Has the day warmed up yet? Did she have a pleasant weekend? Point out different areas of the office as you walk with the candidate to the interview location. If appropriate, introduce the candidate to people whom you meet along the way.

e. Conduct the Interview

Start the interview by reviewing the candidate's qualifications and skills. As a courtesy, ask the candidate if you can take notes during the interview, and offer the candidate a notepad and pen so she can do the same.

> ⚠️ **When taking notes during an inteview, write down only job-related comments.** If the candidate ever decides to sue you for discriminatory hiring practices, your notes could become evidence. The last thing you want are notes of a nonprofessional kind, such as "pretty" or "too manly" or "seems too religious." Write down only those comments that you'd feel comfortable having a judge review. The same warning goes for doodles.

Listen actively. When appropriate, make comments to encourage the candidate to continue speaking. Make eye contact and ask follow-up questions to show you have been listening.

Before you end the interview, give the candidate the opportunity to ask questions. What she chooses to ask can be as revealing as the answers she has given you. When you respond, be honest and professional. Be positive about the job and the workplace, but don't lie or embellish the truth. (Otherwise, you may find yourself on the hook in a breach of contract lawsuit for making promises you didn't keep. See Chapter 2 for more about unintentionally creating employment contracts.) Tell the candidate what happens next: How much longer you will be conducting interviews; when, or under what circumstances, you will call her references; and when you expect to make a decision. Thank the candidate for coming and walk her to the door.

6.   Investigate the Candidate

Once you have settled on the handful of candidates whom you want to consider for the position, the next big step in your process is to do a little digging into the candidates' pasts. We urge you to take this step even if you're convinced that one person shines out among the rest and is the one for you—there are important legal reasons to do your homework here. There are two primary ways of obtaining information about candidates—contacting references and conducting background checks.

a.   Legal Reasons to Investigate

From a legal standpoint, it is critical that you investigate a potential hire. If you're among the convinced, great—skip ahead to subsection b to read about how to conduct your investigations. But if you need convincing, bear with us while we give you a short course on what can happen to an employer who unwittingly hires someone who causes major trouble—and whose background would have revealed that potential had the employer taken the time to check it out.

A person who is injured by your employee can sue you for failing to take reasonable care in selecting your workers, using one of two legal theories, negligent hiring or negligent retention (or both). Negligent hiring occurs when an employer fails to use ordinary caution, under the circumstances, in selecting employees; negligent retention happens when an employer carelessly retains an employer whom a reasonable person would know is likely to cause a problem. These legal theories can be used against you even when your worker's misdeeds have nothing to do with the job the worker was hired to do—in fact, these theories often are used to hold an employer responsible for a worker's violent criminal acts on the job, such as rape, murder or robbery.

You are responsible under these theories only if you acted carelessly—that is, if you knew or should have known that an applicant or employee was unfit for the job, yet you did nothing about it. The following are a few situations in which employers have had to pay up:

- A pizza company hired a delivery driver without looking into his criminal past—which included a sexual assault conviction and an arrest for stalking a woman he met while delivering pizza for another company. After he raped a customer, he was sent to jail for 25 years—and the pizza franchise was successfully sued by his victim for many thousands of dollars.
- A car rental company hired a man who later raped a coworker. Had the company verified his resume claims, it would have discovered that he was in prison for robbery during the years he claimed to be in high school and college. The company was liable to the coworker.
- A furniture company hired a deliveryman without requiring him to fill out an application or performing a background check. The employee assaulted a female customer in her home with a knife. The company was liable to the customer for negligent hiring.

Thorough Checking Protects You Even if a Bad Apple Slips By

The main reason to check out a prospective hire is to give you information that will eliminate an unsuitable candidate. But what if you routinely and dutifully perform the checks, yet inexplicably have a serious problem with a new hire? As we say in the law, every dog has a first bite, and you may be the unfortunate employer who has hired that dog.

Having performed a reasonable check will help shield you from liability if this happens to you. Remember, you are liable only if you have acted carelessly. If your background investigation or your new employee gave no hint of probable misbehavior, you could not reasonably have anticipated it—and chances are that a judge or jury won't hold you responsible. In short, you must be careful, not clairvoyant, but this protection will apply only if you have, indeed, done a reasonable job of learning about your new hire's past.

Many states have allowed claims for negligent hiring and retention. Although these lawsuits have not yet appeared in every state, the clear legal trend is to allow injured third parties to sue employers for hiring or keeping on a dangerous worker. What can you do to stay out of trouble? Here are a few tips:

- **Gather information.** Verify information on resumes; look for criminal convictions and check driving records when appropriate, based on the requirements of the job. These simple steps will weed out many dangerous workers—and help you show that you were not careless in your hiring practices. (For more about gathering information, see subsection c, below.)

- **Use special care in hiring workers who will have a lot of public contact**. You are more likely to be found responsible for a worker's actions if the job involves working with the public. Workers who go to a customer's home (those who make deliveries, perform home repairs or manage apartment buildings, for example), workers who deal with children, vulnerable adults or the elderly and workers whose jobs give them access to weapons (for example, security guards) all require more careful screening.

- **Root out problem employees immediately.** Under the theory of negligent retention, you can be responsible for keeping a worker on after you learn (or should have been aware) that the worker posed a potential danger. If an employee has made violent threats against customers, brought an unauthorized weapon to work or racked up a few moving violations, you have to take immediate action.

b.   Contact References

In some ways, interviewing references is not unlike interviewing candidates: Know what you want to ask in advance; ask closed questions to obtain factual information and ask behavioral questions to elicit softer information. In one very key way, however, interviewing references is entirely unlike interviewing candidates: Candidates want to talk to you, references often do not.

Many companies now have a strict policy of verifying only factual information when contacted about a former employee (typically, they'll give you only dates of employment and positions held). They are afraid of being sued by the candidate for defamation, and it's simpler to have a bright-line policy than to follow the law on a case-by-case basis. (For more about references and the legal risks involved, see Chapter 7.)

A wise employer will anticipate a "name and serial number" response from most references and will prepare in advance to get around it. The way to do so is to require candidates to provide you with references and tell them that they won't be hired if their former employers refuse to speak to you. Have your candidates sign a release, which gives former employers permission to talk freely to you (if you used an employment application as suggested above in subsection A3, you already have a release).

Although you should contact the people that the candidate placed on his resume list, don't limit your checking to those people. Contact former employers even if they aren't listed as references. If you can, avoid talking to the human resources manager at the candidate's former company. Instead, talk to people who had direct, one-on-one experience working with, working for or supervising the candidate.

When you talk to a reference, explain that you have a release signed by the candidate. Offer to mail or fax the release to the reference. Be courteous and professional. Don't get gossipy about the candidate—you have no idea what sort of relationship the reference has with the candidate, and you can't be sure your words won't get back to the candidate. Don't ask any questions that violate the law. If you can't ask a candidate something, then you can't ask it of a reference, either. Don't say anything to the reference that you wouldn't want a judge and jury to hear.

In addition to verifying factual information and learning about the reference's opinion of the candidate, try to verify some of what the candidate said about himself during the interview. You can even quote the candidate: "Albert told me that he solved a computer networking problem last year. Do you remember that event? Can you explain to me what happened?"

Document carefully everything the reference says. Too often, people jot down notes of a reference check in the margins of a resume. Take legible notes that you, and others, will be able to read later.

c. Conduct a Background Check

Depending on what sort of position you are hiring for, you may want to check into various aspects of the applicant's history. A background check can be as extensive or as minimal as you need. Sometimes, all you will want to do is verify educational information. Other times, you'll want to check credit reports and criminal records.

Understand that you do not have the right to dig into all of an applicant's or employee's personal affairs. Workers have a right to privacy in certain personal matters, a right they can enforce by suing you if you pry too deeply. How can you avoid crossing this line? Here are a few tips to keep in mind:

- **Make sure your inquiries are related to the job.** If you decide to do a background check, stick to researching information that is relevant to the position. For example, if you are hiring a security guard who will carry a weapon and be responsible for large amounts of cash, you might reasonably check for past criminal convictions. If you are hiring a seasonal farm worker, however, a criminal background check is probably unnecessary.

- **Ask for consent.** You are on safest legal ground if you ask the applicant, in writing, to consent to your background check. Explain clearly what you plan to check and how you will gather information. This gives the worker the opportunity to take herself out of the running if there is something in her past she wants to keep private. It also prevents the worker from later claiming that her privacy was unfairly invaded. If an applicant refuses to consent to a reasonable request for information, you may legally decide not to hire her on that basis.

- **Be reasonable.** Employers can get in legal trouble if they engage in background check overkill. You do not need to perform an extensive background check on every applicant. Even if you check, you probably won't need to get into excessive detail. If you find yourself questioning neighbors, ordering credit checks and performing exhaustive searches of public records every time you hire a clerk or counterperson, you need to scale it back.

In addition to these general considerations, specific rules apply to certain types of information, such as:

- **School records.** Under federal law and the law of some states, educational records—including transcripts, recommendations and financial information—are confidential. Because of these laws, most schools will not release records without the consent of the student. And some schools will only release records directly to the student.

- **Credit reports.** Under the Fair Credit Reporting Act or FCRA (15 U.S.C. § 1681), employers must get an applicant's written consent before reviewing that person's credit report. Many employers routinely request this consent in their employment applications. However, if you decide not to hire someone based on information in the credit report, you must give the person a copy of the report and tell him of his right to challenge the report under the FCRA. Some states have even more stringent rules limiting the use of credit reports.

- **Bankruptcies.** Federal law prohibits employers from discriminating against persons who file for bankruptcy. This means you cannot refuse to hire or take a negative job action (like demote or transfer) a worker who declares bankruptcy. Courts currently disagree over whether this law applies to job applicants as well as current employees. In situations such as this, when the law is in flux, it's best to play it safe. Don't discriminate against applicants based on their bankruptcy declaration.

- **Criminal records.** The law varies from state to state on whether, and to what extent, a private employer may ask about or consider an applicant's criminal history in making hiring decisions. Some states prohibit employers from asking about arrests, convictions that occurred well in the past, juvenile crimes or sealed records. Some states allow employers to consider convictions only if the crimes are relevant to the job. And some states allow employers to consider criminal history only for certain positions: nurses, childcare workers, private detectives and other jobs requiring licenses, for example. You should consult with a lawyer or do further legal research on the law of your state before digging into an applicant's criminal past. At the end of this chapter, you can find a chart summarizing state laws regarding criminal history and employment.

- **Workers' compensation records.** An employer may consider the information contained in the public record from a workers' compensation appeal as a basis for rejecting an applicant only if the injury in question might interfere with the applicant's or worker's ability to perform required duties. However, if the worker's injury amounts to a disability under the Americans with Disabilities Act or ADA (42 U.S.C. § 12101 and following), you must make sure not to discriminate in hiring

- **Other medical records.** Under the ADA, employers may ask about an applicant's ability to perform specific job duties—but they may not request an employee's medical records.

- **Records of military service.** Members and former members of the armed forces have a right to privacy in their service records. These records may be released only under limited circumstances, and consent is generally required. However, the military may disclose name, rank, salary, duty assignments, awards and duty status without the member's consent.

- **Driving records.** An employer should check the driving record of an applicant whose job will require large amounts of driving (delivery persons, bus drivers and childcare providers, for example). Although these records are usually not confidential, some states restrict the information that will be released or require the driver's consent. Check with your state's department of motor vehicles for information on your state's law.

If you hire a third party to do any aspect of a background check for you (for example, you pay a private investigator to check into someone's criminal past), then you must comply with the FCRA, because these third-party reports also fall under the law. Essentially, the FCRA requires that you obtain permission from the applicant before seeking the report. If, however, you conduct the background check in-house, the FCRA's notification rule won't apply and you'll need to comply with the FCRA only if you obtain information about an applicant's credit history.

To learn more about your duties under the FCRA, see *Federal Employment Laws: A Desk Reference,* by Amy DelPo & Lisa Guerin (Nolo).

7. Pick the Best Candidate

Now that you have carefully screened, interviewed and investigated applicants for your open position, picking the best candidate should be a cakewalk, right? Well, not quite. There are still a few pitfalls out there as you make this final decision:

- **Beware of your gut instincts.** We're not saying ignore them entirely, but do be careful. Too often, these feelings are based on biases that are more troublesome than helpful. For example, if you find yourself drawn toward someone because they are like you, remind you of your daughter or are attractive, you may not be choosing the right applicant. If your instincts include illegal biases (for example, disliking someone because he is black), you'll be risking a discrimination lawsuit.
- **Don't be sidetracked.** Too often, employers get stars in their eyes about a candidate's one or two exceptional skills and ignore everything the person can't do. Refer to your job analysis from the

beginning of the hiring process and use it to find someone with as many of those skills and qualifications as possible.

Don't abandon your criteria just because you like someone. You're engaged in this process to find a new employee, not to make a new friend. Too often, however, the hiring process comes down to whom the employer likes the most. Unfortunately, liking someone isn't going to help very much a few months down the line when that person can't perform the job. Of course, liking someone can be one of the qualities that you consider—it just can't be the only quality. And disliking some-one—if it is for nondiscriminatory reasons—is a legitimate reason not to hire someone.

Evaluate In-House Candidates Like the Others

Hiring a candidate from within your company can be a winning situation for everyone involved. The candidate gets rewarded for his service to your company—and gets a fresh challenge to motivate him. You get a known quantity with no worries about whether the candidate will fit in or whether he's got hidden problems just waiting to come out. And cowork-ers get the satisfaction of knowing that hard work is rewarded in the com-pany. What could be better?

This rosy picture will quickly become grim if you don't put this candi-date through the same screening process that you would use for outside candidate. If you let your affection for the candidate cloud your judgment as to whether he really has the qualifications and skills necessary for the job, you are running the real risk of hiring someone who isn't qualified for the job. Such a mistake can turn a valued employee into a problem employee as that person finds himself in a job that he can't do, unable to meet your expectations.

So, in the end, how should you make your hiring decision? Hire based on job-related criteria—that is, only hire someone who has the needed skills and qualifications. Keep in mind that job-related criteria include more than just those two things, however. Whether someone will be easy or difficult to work with is a job-related factor, as is whether you think the person will fit into your company culture. Just take care that you don't let illegal biases enter into these considerations.

B. Workplace Policies

Many employers create employee problems inadvertently, by failing to think through their employment practices and workplace rules. If you haven't given some careful consideration to what you expect from your employees and what you will give them in return, you can't communicate that information to your workers and managers—and you can't expect them to follow your rules.

Throughout this book, we've suggested personnel policies and forms that will help you handle current problems and avoid future trouble, including:

- a hiring letter that clearly explains the at-will nature of the job, to protect you from claims that you offered the applicant an employment contract (Chapter 2)
- an evaluation form that gives you a structured way to track—and give feedback about—an employee's performance (Chapter 3)
- a progressive discipline policy that you can use to give employees notice of what's going wrong and the chance to improve (Chapter 4), and
- a complaint policy that allows you to take action before problems fester (Chapter 5).

These policies will be valuable allies in your efforts to stay out of trouble. However, many businesses will want (and need) more than a handful of written policies. They'll want a handbook that explains the rules of the workplace.

Smaller businesses often get along fine without any written employment policies. But at some point, especially as your company grows, a handbook that clearly sets out your policies makes good business sense. Although compiling the policies will take some effort, you will save on time, headaches and possibly legal fees in the long run.

Create an employee handbok—with a little help from Nolo. *Create Your Own Employee Handbook,* by attorneys Lisa Guerin & Amy DelPo (Nolo) provides all the help you'll need to make an employee handbook that works for your company. Packed with forms, sample policies and modifications you can use to tailor the policies to your business, this resource allows you to cut and paste policies drafted by legal experts into an employee handbook. The book comes with a CD-ROM, so you can make your employee handbook right on your own computer.

1. What an Employee Handbook Can Do For You

Some problem employees are just bad to the bone. The best personnel policies in the world aren't going to turn the serial sexual harasser, the thief or the utter incompetent into employee of the month (although they will help you avoid hiring that employee in the first place or, if he slips through your screening process, identify the problem quickly and get him out the door without legal trouble).

However, most problem employees are made, not born—you create them by following sloppy personnel habits. Lack of planning, poor communication (or none at all), treating workers inconsistently and failing to document important decisions can lead even well-meaning employers straight into employee disasters.

The strategies we've described in this book will help you avoid these traps. And an employee handbook can serve as your roadmap to stay on the right path, by helping you to:

- crystallize and evaluate your employment practices
- communicate with your employees
- manage your workforce (and your managers), and
- protect your business from lawsuits.

a.   Evaluate Your Personnel Practices

Many employers create personnel practices haphazardly, deciding each issue as it comes up rather than taking the time to think through their workplace rules. This is a very dangerous habit. Without a clear set of rules to apply to each situation, you run the risk of acting inconsistently—treating one employee differently than another. Because your supervisors won't have clear guidelines to follow, they will manage employee problems according to their own rules or whims. What's more, you have virtually guaranteed a communication breakdown. If you don't have a clear sense of your rules, you won't be able to communicate them to your workers, and your workers certainly won't be able to follow them.

The process of creating your handbook will force you to think about every aspect of your relationship with your employees. And after you've laid those policies and habits on the table, you'll have an opportunity to evaluate their legality and value. Perhaps some changes are in order. If you've been inconsistent in your dealings with employees, you can decide on a single set of rules to guide your actions in the future.

b.   Communicate With Your Employees

An employee handbook is a great communication tool that can help you avoid turning potentially good employees into bad ones. Your handbook tells workers what your company expects from them and what they can expect from the company. "What time do I have to be at work?" "Does my employer provide health insurance?" "How do I complain about my supervisor's sexual advances?" A well-drafted handbook will answer all of these questions and many more.

In addition to relaying basic information about benefits, hours and pay, your employee handbook imparts your company's culture, values and history. When was your company founded? Why do you think it is successful? What attitude do you want your employees to take towards their jobs and customers? This information helps your employees feel like part of a team, one that takes pride in its work and its history.

You can also include important performance and conduct rules in your handbook—such as policies on appropriate workplace behavior, a performance evaluation policy and a progressive discipline policy (see Chapter 4). This information lets employees know that they will be held accountable, rewarded for good performance and disciplined for bad.

c. Let Everyone Know the Rules

Workers are not mind readers. Although you may know what your practices and policies are, without a handbook, employees, managers and supervisors have no place to turn for this information. This creates an environment ripe for trouble, both legal and practical. Employee morale will drop if some employees are treated differently from others, and you might find yourself involved in a discrimination lawsuit if employees think that this inconsistent treatment is based on race, gender or some other protected characteristic.

An employee handbook promotes positive employee relations by ensuring that all of your employees get treated consistently and fairly. It will also save you time—you won't have to explain all of your workplace policies and procedures to every new employee. And it prevents misunderstandings, confusion and complaints by giving everyone in your workplace the same resource for learning your personnel practices. If there is ever any doubt or dispute about a particular policy, you can simply open the book and take a look. You don't need to have long, agonizing discussions or try to reinvent the wheel.

d. Protect Your Company from Lawsuits

Just having a handbook on your shelf can help you comply with the law and cut your risk of lawsuits:

- Some laws require that employers communicate certain information to their employees. The handbook gives you a convenient place to put this material.
- Even when you aren't required to give information to your employees, there are times when you can protect yourself by providing it. For example, no law requires you to tell your employees how to complain about sexual harassment, but if you do, you can use the complaint policy as a defense should someone ever sue you. (See Chapter 5 for more information on this defense.)
- Your policies can affirm your commitment to equal employment opportunity laws. This is one step toward creating a tolerant and discrimination-free workplace—something that most employers are legally obligated to do.
- In certain situations, your company will be responsible for the actions of its employees and supervisors who violate the law, even if the company did not condone or even know about the illegal conduct. You can cut down the risk of unlawful behavior by providing guidance and prohibitions in your handbook.

e. Preserve Your At-Will Employment Policy

Perhaps the most important reason to have an employee handbook is to protect your legal right to terminate employees at will. As explained in detail in Chapter 2, unless you have entered into a contract with an employee promising something else, your relationship with that employee is automatically at will—meaning you can terminate the employment relationship at any time for any reason that is not illegal, and the employee can quit at any time, too.

Even when you haven't given your employee a written contract, you can inadvertently destroy your right to terminate at will by creating an *implied* contract with your employees, promising not to fire them unless you have a legitimate business reason. Including an at-will provision in your employee handbook—and making sure that none of your policies promise continued employment—can help you fight off implied contract claims.

2.   Policy Topics

Effective employee handbooks vary widely in size, style and content. Some large corporations produce handbooks that come in multiple volumes and cover every conceivable aspect of the business. Smaller companies might have a more limited handbook that covers only the basics (and might more properly be called an "employee pamphlet").

No matter how extensive your handbook, it should incorporate the style and values of your company. Your goal is to communicate your policies to your workers, in language they will understand. Through your written policies, you are talking to your employees. Make sure you are saying what you want to say, in the way you want to say it.

A handbook is a legal document. Although an employee handbook can help you avoid problems, it can also land you in legal hot water if you're not careful. Before you distribute a handbook to your workers, double-check it with an attorney (or a self-help resource) to make sure that your proposed policies don't violate the law, you've included all legally required information and you haven't made any promises that a clever employee's lawyer might interpret as a contract.

a.   Information About Your Company

A welcoming statement is a nice way to start your handbook. It gives new employees a positive feeling about the company and explains why you think your business is special. In this opening section of the handbook, you can also include a mission statement, a company history, biographies of the company's founders and an organizational chart.

This information will help assimilate your new employees into your company culture and lets workers share in the company's goals and spirit. A handbook that makes new employees feel that they belong to a hard-working team really helps get the employment relationship off

on the right foot, and fosters positive attitudes about your company—
the best inoculation against employee problems.

b.   Your At-Will Policy Statement and Employee Acknowledgment

These are must-have policies—an airtight at-will provision and a form
for employees to sign, acknowledging their at-will status. In your at-will
provision, explain that employment is at will, that employees are free
to quit at any time, for any reason, and that the company is free to terminate employment, at any time and for any reason. Make clear that
nothing in the handbook constitutes an employment contract or a
promise of continued employment.

You should also state that no one has the authority to alter an
employee's at-will status or make an agreement to the contrary, except
a person you name in the policy (such as the company president or
CEO). The purpose of this part of the policy is to fend off implied contract claims, while leaving your options open to enter into a contract
that limits your right to fire if you choose to do so. (See Chapter 2 for
more information on employment at will, and on the circumstances in
which you might want to create an employment contract.)

The savviest employers also ask their employees to sign a Handbook Acknowledgment—a form indicating that the employee has received a copy of the handbook and understands and agrees to the
at-will provision.

c.   Hiring and New Employee Information

Here's where you can explain any rules or policies you follow when
hiring workers, including job posting, affirmative action or anti-
discrimination practices, referral bonuses, employment of relatives
(nepotism), hiring from within and any testing requirements you impose on applicants. As explained above, careful hiring practices are
your first defense against problem employees.

You can also explain the rules for new employees. For example, if you impose an orientation or probationary period or provide orientation meetings or programs to bring new workers into the company fold, you can describe them here.

d.   Wages and Hours

Pay and hours form the basic exchange of the employment relationship: You pay for your workers' time. Realistically, pay is what your workers care most about—and hours are probably among your primary concerns. You can avoid a lot of problems by making your expectations (and what your employees can expect) very clear.

Explain your pay policies—including your rules on overtime, compensatory time, show up or on-call time, payroll deductions and wage garnishments. If you have policies on expense reimbursements and pay advances, you can include those here as well. And you can let your workers know when they will be paid and according to what formula—for example, if you pay commissions or a piece rate.

You can also describe your work hours here—your usual hours of operation, meal and rest breaks, shift schedules, attendance policies, flextime or other flexible scheduling arrangements and rules on time cards or other ways of keeping track of hours. Laying out these rules clearly will help you avoid absenteeism and attendance problems (or give you the tools you need to handle them when they crop up).

e.   Benefits

Explain the benefits you offer your employees, such as health insurance, dental and vision coverage, life insurance, disability insurance, pensions or other retirement plans, profit-sharing plans and so on. You probably won't want to go into all of the details about every plan, but you can explain who's eligible for coverage, what each plan offers in a nutshell and whether employees will be expected to pick up part of the cost. These policies should refer your employees to someone who can give them written materials on your benefits programs and explain them in detail. This information shows your employees that you are concerned about their well-being beyond the workplace—and can help you retain high-quality employees.

f.   Company Property

What property do you make available to employees—company cars? Telephones? Computers? In this section, you can explain your rules for use of this equipment. Tell employees whether they can use company equipment for personal reasons, and under what circumstances. This will avoid misunderstandings in the future—and pave the way for you to discipline employees who take advantage.

All employers need cyber-policies. Many employers have faced the very unpleasant prospect of having to read employee email looking for evidence of wrongdoing, such as harassment or theft of trade secrets. These forays are necessary to protect your company, but run the risk of violating your employees' privacy rights. To protect themselves, prudent employers adopt a policy explaining that the computer and email system is company property, and that the company reserves the right to read employee emails at any time. To be on the safe side, consider this a must-have policy.

g.   Time Off

If you offer your employees vacation days, sick leave, personal days or paid time off, you can explain your policies here. You can also describe any parental leave, pregnancy leave, disability leave or bereavement leave you offer. And if you have policies on leave for military service, jury duty and voting (all of which might be required under federal law and the laws of your state), you can explain them here. Setting these policies down in writing helps prevent employee abuse—and ensures that your managers won't play favorites when employees request time off.

If you are covered by the Family and Medical Leave Act or FMLA (see Chapter 2 for more information) and you provide your employees with a handbook or other written materials explaining your benefits, you are legally required to include information on the FMLA, including an explanation of employee rights and responsibilities under the law.

h.   Workplace Conduct and Behavior

Here, you can describe your standards of conduct—such as rules on employee dress, prohibitions on horseplay, conflicts of interest and un-professional behavior, and policies about bringing children (or pets) to work. You can also explain your performance evaluation system—how often you will evaluate and how evaluations will be used. If you've de-cided to adopt our progressive discipline policy (see Chapter 4), you can describe it in this section of your handbook, too. As explained in Chapters 3 and 4, these policies will help you turn problem employees around—or document your reasons for firing, if necessary.

i.   Health, Safety and Security

Most employers benefit from adopting a clear policy explaining the safety rules for the workplace (for example, that hardhats or hairnets are required, or that open-toed shoes or jewelry are prohibited). Your safety policy should also tell workers what to do in case of an accident. You can also include policies on workplace security (for example, rules on visitors in the workplace, setting the building alarm, working after hours or dealing with workplace security guards), violence, emergency preparedness, drug and alcohol use and smoking. These policies will lay the groundwork for disciplining employees who endanger them-selves or others.

j.   Discrimination and Harassment

Your company should have a policy prohibiting discrimination and ha-rassment (you can put this information all in one policy or adopt separate policies). Explain the types of discrimination and harassment that are prohibited, what employees should do if they have been harassed or discriminated against and what the company will do in response. Explain that managers are responsible for reporting discrimination or harassment, and that retaliation is prohibited. (For more information on discrimination and harassment—and why you must have a harassment policy—see Chapter 2.)

You should also have a separate complaint policy—see Chapter 5 for details and sample policy language.

k.   Confidential Company Information

In this section, you can describe company policies on trade secrets, proprietary information and conflicts of interest. Almost every company has some confidential information—a customer list, a recipe or formula, a process for doing a task or other company know-how. To make sure that your employees don't reveal this information unnecessarily, you can adopt a policy explaining what types of information are confidential and how you expect employees to treat that information. You can also explain what you consider a conflict of interest—such as working for a competitor, using the company's resources for a personal business or owning an interest in a competitor.

l.   Termination

In this section, explain your procedures for handling departing employees. You might include policies on exit interviews, final paychecks, continuing benefits and insurance coverage, returning company property and references. These policies will tell employees what they can expect when they leave the company, to avoid the types of misunderstandings and unrealistic expectations that can lead to bad feelings (and fuel revenge-inspired lawsuits).

State Laws on Employee Arrest & Conviction Records

The following chart summarizes state laws and regulations concerning access to an employee's or prospective employee's criminal record. It also lists websites for state fair employment guidelines on interview questions about arrests and convictions. Some states have both statutes and agency guidelines; others have only one source of rules, and a handful are silent on the subject. It is always a good idea to consult agency guidelines; they are easy to understand and are designed to help employers comply with state and federal law as interpreted by court decisions enforcing fair employment and civil rights legislation. If your state is not listed, or you need further information, check with your state agency that enforces laws prohibiting discrimination in employment. (See contact list in the Appendix.)

Alaska

Agency guidelines for pre-employment inquiries: Alaska Department of Labor and Workforce Development, Alaska Employer Handbook, "Pre-Employment Questioning," at www.labor.state.ak.us/handbook/legal7.htm.

Arizona

Ariz. Rev. Stat. § 13-904(E)

Rights of employees and applicants: Unless the offense has a reasonable relationship to the occupation, an occupational license may not be denied solely on the basis of a felony or misdemeanor conviction.

California

Cal. Lab. Code § 432.7

Rules for employers:
- **Arrest records.** May not ask about an arrest that did not lead to conviction; may not ask about pretrial or post-trial diversion program. May ask about arrest if prospective employee is awaiting trial.
- **Convictions.** May ask about conviction even if no sentence is imposed.

Agency guidelines for pre-employment inquiries: Department of Fair Employment and Housing, "Pre-Employment Inquiry Guidelines" DFEH-161. (Not currently available to download or view. Ordering information at www.dfeh.ca.gov/posters/postersEmp.asp.)

Colorado

Colo. Rev. Stat. §§ 24-72-308 (IIfI); 8-3-108(m)

Rules for employers: May not inquire about arrest for civil or military disobedience unless it resulted in conviction.

Rights of employees and applicants: May not be required to disclose any information in a sealed record; may answer questions about arrests or convictions as though they had not occurred.

Agency guidelines for pre-employment inquiries: Colorado Civil Rights Division, Publications, "Preventing Job Discrimination," at www.dora.state.co.us/civil-rights/Publications.htm.

Connecticut

Conn. Gen. Stat. Ann. §§ 46a-79 to 79-80; 31-51i

Rules for employers: State policy encourages hiring qualified applicants with criminal records. If an employment application form

State Laws on Employee Arrest & Conviction Records (continued)

contains any question concerning criminal history, it must include the following notice in clear and conspicuous language: "The applicant is not required to disclose the existence of any arrest, criminal charge or conviction, the records of which have been erased." Employer may not disclose information about a job applicant's criminal history to anyone except members of the personnel department. (If there is no personnel department, then only to person[s] in charge of hiring or conducting the interview.)

Rights of employees and applicants: May not be asked to disclose information about a criminal record that has been erased; may answer any question as though arrest or conviction never took place. May not be discriminated against in hiring or continued employment on the basis of an erased criminal record.

Delaware
Del. Code Ann. tit. 11, § 4374(e)

Rights of employees and applicants: Do not have to disclose an arrest record that has been expunged.

District of Columbia
D.C. Code Ann. § 2-1402.66

Rules for employers:
- **Arrest records.** May not obtain or inquire into arrest record.
- **Convictions.** May obtain record of convictions occurring within the last 10 years.

Florida
Fla. Stat. Ann. § 112.011

Rights of employees and applicants: May not be disqualified to practice or pursue any occupation or profession that requires a license, permit or certificate because of a prior conviction, unless it was for a felony or first degree misdemeanor and is directly related to the specific line of work.

Georgia
Ga. Code Ann. §§ 35-3-34; 42-8-62 to 42-8-63

Rules for employers: In order to obtain a criminal record from the state Crime Information Center, employer must supply the individual's fingerprints or signed consent. If an adverse employment decision is made on the basis of the record, must disclose all information in the record to the employee or applicant and tell how it affected the decision.

Rights of employees and applicants: Probation for a first offense is not a conviction; may not be disqualified for employment once probation is completed.

Hawaii
Haw. Rev. Stat. §§ 378-2.to 378-2.5; 831-3.2

Rules for employers:
- **Arrest records.** It is a violation of law for any employer to refuse to hire, to discharge or to discriminate in terms of compensation, conditions or privileges of employment because of a person's arrest or court record.
- **Convictions.** May inquire into a conviction only after making a conditional offer of employment, provided it has a rational relation to job. May not examine any convictions over 10 years old.

State Laws on Employee Arrest & Conviction Records (continued)

Rights of employees and applicants: If an arrest or conviction has been expunged, may state that no record exists and may respond to questions as a person with no record would respond.

Agency guidelines for pre-employment inquiries: Hawaii Civil Rights Commission, "Guide to Pre-Employment Inquiries," at www.state.hi.us/hcrc/brochures.html.

Idaho

Agency guidelines for pre-employment inquiries: Idaho Human Rights Commission, "Pre-Employment Inquiries," at www2.state.id.us/ihrc/preemp21.htm.

Illinois

775 Ill. Comp. Stat. § 5/2-103

Rules for employers: It is a civil rights violation to ask about an arrest or criminal history record that has been expunged or sealed, or to use the fact of an arrest or criminal history record as a basis for refusing to hire or to renew employment. Law does not prohibit employer from using other means to find out if person actually engaged in conduct for which they were arrested.

Iowa

Agency guidelines for pre-employment inquiries: Iowa Civil Rights Commission, "Successfully Interviewing Job Applicants," at www.state.ia.us/government/crc/successfullyinterviewingtitle.html.

Kansas

Kan. Stat. Ann. §§ 12-4516(g); 21-4619(h); 22-4710

Rules for employers: Cannot inspect or inquire into criminal record unless employee or applicant signs a release.

Rights of employees and applicants: If arrest, conviction or diversion record is expunged, do not have to disclose any information about it.

Special situations: Employers are entitled to obtain complete criminal record information for brokers or investment advisors, commercial drivers and sensitive positions in the state lottery, state gaming agency or parimutuel racing.

Agency guidelines for pre-employment inquiries: Kansas Human Rights Commission, "Guidelines on Equal Employment Practices: Preventing Discrimination in Hiring," at www.khrc.net/hiring.html.

Louisiana

La. Rev. Stat. Ann. § 37:2950

Rights of employees and applicants: Prior conviction cannot be used as a basis to deny employment or an occupational or professional license, unless conviction is for a felony and directly relates to the job or license being sought.

Special situations: Protection does not apply to medical, engineering and architecture or funeral and embalming licenses.

Maine

Me. Rev. Stat. Ann. tit. 5, § 5301; tit. 28-A, § 703-A; Code Me. R. 94-348 Ch. 3, § 3.06(B7)

Rights of employees and applicants: No one can be denied employment because of refusing to answer a pre-employment inquiry that is unlawful under the Maine Human Rights Act or Maine Human Rights Commission

State Laws on Employee Arrest & Conviction Records (continued)

Rules. A conviction is not an automatic bar to obtaining an occupational or professional license; only convictions that directly relate to the profession or occupation; that include dishonesty or false statements; that are subject to imprisonment for more than one year; or involve sexual misconduct on the part of a licensee may be considered.

Special situations: Liquor retailers may not employ anyone convicted of selling liquor to minors or selling liquor without a license within the past two years (for a first offense), or within the past five years (for a second offense).

Agency guidelines for pre-employment inquiries: Maine Human Rights Commission, Publications, "Pre-Employment Inquiry Guidelines" at www.state.me.us/mhrc/publish.htm.

Maryland

Md. Code Ann. [Crim. Proc.], § 10-109; Md. Regs. Code 09.01.10.02

Rules for employers: May not enquire about any criminal charges that have been expunged. May not use a refusal to disclose information as basis for not hiring an applicant.

Rights of employees and applicants: Need not refer to nor give any information about an expunged charge. A professional or occupational license may not be refused or revoked simply because of a conviction; agency must consider the nature of the crime and its relation to the occupation or profession; the conviction's relevance to the applicant's fitness and qualifications; when conviction occurred and other convictions, if any; and the applicant's behavior before and after conviction.

Massachusetts

Mass. Gen. Laws ch. 151B, § 4; ch. 276, § 100A; Mass. Regs. Code tit. 804, § 3.02

Rules for employers: If job application has a question about prior arrests or convictions, it must state that an applicant with a sealed record is entitled to answer, "No record."

- **Arrest records.** May not ask about arrests that did not result in conviction.
- **Convictions.** May obtain record of convictions occurring within the last 10 years. May not ask about first-time convictions for drunken-ness, simple assault, speeding, minor traffic violations or disturbing the peace; may not ask about misdemeanor convictions 5 or more years old.

Rights of employees and applicants: If criminal record is sealed, may answer, "No record," to any inquiry about past arrests or convictions.

Michigan

Mich. Comp. Laws § 37.2205a

Rules for employers: May not request information on any arrests or misdemeanor charges that did not result in conviction.

Rights of employees and applicants: Employees or applicants are not making a false statement if they fail to disclose information they have a civil right to withhold.

Agency guidelines for pre-employment inquiries: Michigan Civil Rights Commission, "Pre-Employment Inquiry Guide," at www.michigan.gov/documents/pre-employment_inquery_guide_13019_7.pdf.

State Laws on Employee Arrest & Conviction Records (continued)

Minnesota

Minn. Stat. Ann. §§ 364.01 to 364.03

Rules for employers: State policy encourages the rehabilitation of criminal offenders; employment opportunity is considered essential to rehabilitation.

Rights of employees and applicants: No one can be disqualified from pursuing or practicing an occupation that requires a license, unless the crime directly relates to the occupation. Agency may consider the nature and seriousness of the crime and its relation to the applicant's fitness for the occupation. Even if the crime does relate to the occupation, a person who provides evidence of rehabilitation and present fitness cannot be disqualified.

Agency guidelines for pre-employment inquiries: Minnesota Department of Human Rights, "Hiring, Job Interviews and the Minnesota Human Rights Act," at www.humanrights.state.mn.us /employer_hiring.html.

Missouri

Agency guidelines for pre-employment inquiries: Commission on Human Rights, Missouri Department of Labor and Industrial Relations, "Pre-Employment Inquiries," at www.dolir.state .mo.us/hr/interview.htm.

Nebraska

Neb. Rev. Stat. § 29-3523

Rules for employers: May not obtain access to information regarding arrests that do not lead to conviction.

Nevada

Nev. Rev. Stat. Ann. § 179A.100(3)

Rules for employers: May obtain a prospective employee's criminal history record only if it includes convictions or a pending charge, including parole or probation.

Agency guidelines for pre-employment inquiries: Nevada Equal Rights Commission, "Pre-Employment Inquiry Guide," at http:// detr.state.nv.us/nerc/nerc_preemp.htm.

New Hampshire

N.H. Rev. Stat. Ann. § 651:5 (Xc); N.H. Code Admin. R. Hum 405.03

Rules for employers: May ask about a previous criminal record only if question substantially follows this wording, "Have you ever been arrested for or convicted of a crime that has not been annulled by a court?"

- **Arrest records.** It is unlawful discrimination for an employer to ask about an arrest record, to have a job requirement that applicant have no arrest record or to use information about arrest record to make a hiring decision, unless it is a business necessity. It is unlawful discrimination to ask about arrest record if it has the purpose or effect of discouraging applicants of a particular racial or national origin group.

New Jersey

N.J. Admin. Code tit. 13, §§ 59-1.2, 59-1.6

Rules for employers: In order to determine work qualifications, employer may obtain criminal record information about convictions and about any pending arrests or charges. When requesting record, employer must certify in writing that he will notify applicant; will

State Laws on Employee Arrest & Conviction Records (continued)

provide sufficient time for applicant to challenge, correct or complete record; and will not presume guilt for any pending charges or court actions.

Rights of employees and applicants: Applicant who is disqualified for employment based on criminal record must be given adequate notice and reasonable time to confirm or deny accuracy of information.

New York

N.Y. Correct. Law §§ 750 to 754; N.Y. Exec. Law § 296(16)

Rules for employers:

- **Arrest records.** It is unlawful discrimination to ask about any arrests or charges that did not result in conviction, unless they are currently pending.
- **Convictions.** Employers with 10 or more employees may not deny employment based on a conviction unless it relates directly to the job or would be an "unreasonable" risk to property or to public or individual safety.

Rights of employees and applicants: Upon request, applicant must be given, within 30 days, a written statement of the reasons why employment was denied.

Agency guidelines for pre-employment inquiries: New York State Division of Human Rights, "Rulings on Inquiries (Pre-employment)," at www.nysdhr.com/employment.html.

North Dakota

N.D. Cent. Code § 12-60-16.6

Rules for employers: May obtain records of convictions or of criminal charges (adults only) occurring in the past year.

Agency guidelines for pre-employment inquiries: North Dakota Department of Labor, Human Rights Division, "Employment Applications and Interviews" www.state.nd.us/labor/publications/brochures.html.

Ohio

Ohio Rev. Code Ann. §§ 2151.358 (I); 2953.33

Rules for employers: May not inquire into any juvenile records that have been sealed. May not ask about any other sealed conviction or unsealed bail forfeitures unless question has a direct and substantial relation to job.

Rights of employees and applicants: May not be asked about arrest records that are expunged; may respond to inquiry as though arrest did not occur.

Oklahoma

Okla. Stat. Ann. tit. 22, § 19(F)

Rules for employers: May not inquire into any criminal record that has been expunged.

Rights of employees and applicants: If record is expunged, may state that no criminal action ever occurred. May not be denied employment for refusing to disclose sealed criminal record information.

Oregon

Or. Rev. Stat. §§ 181.555 to 181.560; 659A.030

Rules for employers: Before requesting information, employer must notify employee or applicant; when submitting request, must tell State Police Department when and how person was notified. May not discriminate against

State Laws on Employee Arrest & Conviction Records (continued)

an applicant or current employee on the basis of an expunged juvenile record unless there is a "bona fide occupational qualification."

- **Arrest records.** May request information about arrest records less than one year old that have not resulted in acquittal or have not been dismissed.
- **Convictions.** May request information about conviction records.

Rights of employees and applicants: Before State Police Department releases any criminal record information, it must notify employee or applicant and provide a copy of all information that will be sent to employer. Notice must include protections under federal civil rights law and the procedure for challenging information in the record. Record may not be released until 14 days after notice is sent.

Agency guidelines for pre-employment inquiries: Oregon Bureau of Labor and Industries, Civil Rights Division, Fact Sheets, "Pre-Employment Inquiries," at www.boli.state.or.us/civil/tarpreemp.html.

Pennsylvania

18 Pa. Cons. Stat. Ann. § 9125

Rules for employers: May consider felony and misdemeanor convictions only if they directly relate to person's suitability for the job.

Rights of employees and applicants: Must be informed in writing if refusal to hire is based on criminal record information.

Agency guidelines for pre-employment inquiries: Pennsylvania Human Relations Commission, Publications, "Pre-Employment Inquiries," at http://sites.state.pa.us/PA_Exec/PHRC/publications/other_publications.html.

Rhode Island

R.I. Gen. Laws §§ 12-1.3-4; 28-5-7 (7)

Rules for employers:

- **Arrest records.** It is unlawful to include on an application form or to ask as part of an interview if the applicant has ever been arrested or charged with any crime.
- **Convictions.** May ask if applicant has been convicted of a crime.

Rights of employees and applicants: Do not have to disclose any conviction that has been expunged.

South Dakota

Agency guidelines for pre-employment inquiries: South Dakota Division of Human Rights, "Pre-employment Inquiry Guide," at www.state.sd.us/dcr/hr/preemplo.htm.

Texas

Tex. Health & Safety Code Ann. § 765.001 and following; Tex. Gov't. Code Ann. § 411.118

Special situations: A criminal background check is permitted upon a conditional offer of employment in a private "residential dwelling project," which includes a condominium, apartment building, hotel, motel or bed and breakfast, where the employee may be reasonably required to have access to residential units. Ap-

State Laws on Employee Arrest & Conviction Records (continued)

plicant must give written consent to release of criminal record information.

Utah

Utah Admin. R. 606-2

Rules for employers: Utah Labor Division Anti-Discrimination Rules, Rule R606-2.

"Pre-Employment Inquiry Guide," at www.rules.utah.gov/publicat/code/r606/r606-002.htm.

- **Arrest records**. It is not permissible to ask about arrests.
- **Convictions.** Asking about felony convictions is permitted, but is not advisable unless related to job.

Vermont

Vt. Stat. Ann. tit. 20, § 2056c

Rules for employers: Only employers who provide care for children, the elderly and the disabled or who run postsecondary schools with residential facilities may obtain criminal record information from the state Criminal Information Center. May obtain record only after a conditional offer of employment is made and applicant has given written authorization on a signed, notarized release form.

Rights of employees and applicants: Release form must advise applicant of right to appeal any of the findings in the record.

Virginia

Va. Code Ann. § 19.2-392.4

Rules for employers: May not require an applicant to disclose information about any criminal charge that has been expunged.

Rights of employees and applicants: Need not refer to any expunged charges if asked about criminal record.

Washington

Wash. Rev. Code Ann. §§ 43.43.815; 9.94A.640(3), 9.96.060(3), 9.96A.020; Wash. Admin. Code 162-12-140

Rules for employers:

- **Arrest records.** Employer who asks about arrests must ask whether the charges are still pending, have been dismissed or led to conviction.
- **Convictions.** Employer who obtains a conviction record must notify employee within 30 days of receiving it, and must allow the employee to examine it. May make an employment decision based on a conviction only if it is less than 10 years old and the crime involves behavior that would adversely affect job performance.

Rights of employees and applicants: If a conviction record is cleared or vacated, may answer questions as though the conviction never occurred. A person convicted of a felony cannot be refused an occupational license unless the conviction is less than 10 years old and the felony relates specifically to the occupation or business.

Special situations: Employers are entitled to obtain complete criminal record information for positions that require bonding, or that have access to trade secrets, confidential or proprietary business information, money or items of value.

State Laws on Employee Arrest & Conviction Records (continued)

West Virginia

Agency guidelines for pre-employment inquiries:
Bureau of Employment Programs, "Pre-Employment Inquiry Guide," at
www.state.wv.us/BEP/Bepeeo/empinqu.htm.

Wisconsin

Wis. Stat. Ann. §§ 111.31 to 111.35

Rules for employers: It is a violation of state civil rights law to discriminate against an employee on the basis of a prior arrest or conviction record.

- **Arrest records.** May not ask about arrests unless there are pending charges.

- **Convictions.** May not ask about convictions unless charges substantially relate to job.

Special situations: Employers are entitled to obtain complete criminal record information for positions that require bonding and for burglar alarm installers.

Agency guidelines for pre-employment inquiries:
Wisconsin Department of Workforce Development, Civil Rights Division Publications, "Fair Hiring & Avoiding Loaded Interview Questions," at www.dwd.state.wi.us/er/
discrimination_civil_rights/publications.htm.

Current as of March 2003

Chapter 11

Hiring a Lawyer

*E*ven the most conscientious employer occasionally needs help from a lawyer. Although you can handle many employment problems on your own, some issues are particularly tricky and will require some legal expertise. Certain employment laws are highly technical, rapidly changing or difficult to figure out. Courts and government agencies issue new opinions interpreting these laws every day, sometimes completely overturning what everyone thought the law meant.

Consider also that some lawsuits by former employees—especially by workers who claim that they suffered discrimination, harassment or retaliation—end in huge damages awards against the employer. In these cases, an employer can save money by seeking legal advice at the first sign of trouble, rather than waiting to be served with a lawsuit.

This chapter describes how and when to seek help from a lawyer. We explain the trickier employment issues that might require legal assistance— and tasks you can perform on your own to lower the legal bills. We explain how to find and work with a good lawyer, and how lawyers charge for their services. And if you get stuck with a dud despite these tips, we tell you how to fire your lawyer.

Other Sources of Help

Lawyers are not the only source of legal information for enterprising employers. Federal agencies—including the U.S. Equal Employment Opportunity Commission, the U.S. Department of Labor, the U.S. Department of Justice and the U.S. Internal Revenue Service—offer many publications at little or no cost explaining federal laws and regulations that affect employers. You can find these materials on the agencies' websites (listed in the Appendix).

Similarly, many state agencies have helpful printed materials available. State departments of labor and state fair employment offices can assist you in understanding a variety of state labor laws and anti-discrimination laws. You can find those agencies listed in the Appendix.

Some professional and trade organizations or local business groups occasionally hold seminars, educational programs or trainings that explain employment laws and regulations. Check with your local professional group, Chamber of Commerce, Small Business Administration, community college schedule or trade newsletter to find out if these programs are available in your area.

Keep in mind, too, that other professionals can help you with specific workplace issues—for less than you would have to pay a lawyer. Consider whether an accountant, workplace consultant or professional trainer might meet your needs.

A. When to Hire a Lawyer

You don't need to talk to a lawyer every time you evaluate, discipline or even fire a worker. After all, lawyers don't come cheap—if you run to a lawyer every time you face an employment decision, you will quickly go broke. In certain situations, however, money spent on legal advice is a sound investment. A lawyer can review your policies, contracts and other documents you use with your workers to make sure that they will stand up in court. And you can protect yourself from future lawsuits—and save time and money—by getting legal advice before you take any risky action against a problem employee. Finally, you should definitely get legal help if you are faced with a lawsuit or other adversarial proceeding.

1.   Reviewing Documents

A lawyer can review and troubleshoot any employment-related agreements you routinely use with your workers, like employment contracts, severance agreements or releases. A lawyer can check your contracts to make sure they contain all the necessary legal terms and will be enforced by a court. If you have included any language that might cause problems later, or if you have gone beyond what the law requires of you, a lawyer can also draw these issues to your attention. And a lawyer can give you advice about when to use these contracts—for example, you may not want to give severance to every departing employee or enter into an employment contract with every new worker. A lawyer can help you figure out what makes sense for your business and your employees.

You can also ask a lawyer to give your employee handbook or personnel policies a thorough legal review. First and foremost, a lawyer can make sure your policies don't violate laws regarding overtime pay, family leave, final paychecks or occupational safety and health, to name a few. A lawyer can also check for any language that might create an implied employment contract. (See Chapter 2, Section B for more about implied employment contracts.) And a lawyer might advise you about additional policies to consider. (See Chapter 10 for more on workplace policies.)

2. Advice on Employment Decisions

A lawyer can also help you make difficult employment decisions about your problem employees. Particularly if you are worried that the employee might sue, you should consider getting legal advice before firing an employee for misconduct, performance problems or other bad behavior. A lawyer can tell you not only whether terminating the worker will be legal, but also what steps you can take to minimize the risk of a lawsuit.

Consider asking a lawyer to review your decision to fire in these situations:

- the worker has a written or oral employment contract restricting your right to fire (see Chapter 2, Sections A and B for more about written and oral contracts)
- your policies and statements may create an implied contract (see Chapter 2, Section B for more about implied contracts)
- the employee is due to vest benefits, stock options or retirement money shortly (which means that firing the employee could lead to a bad faith claim, covered in Chapter 2, Section C)
- the worker recently filed a complaint or claim with a government agency or complained to you of illegal or unethical activity (see Chapter 2, Section D)
- the employee recently filed a complaint of discrimination or harassment (see Chapter 2, Section E)
- firing the employee would dramatically change your workplace demographics (see Chapter 2, Section E)
- the worker recently revealed that she is in a protected class—for example, is pregnant, has a disability or practices a particular religion (see Chapter 2, Section E)
- you are concerned about the worker's potential for violence, vandalism or sabotage
- the worker has access to your company's high-level trade secrets or competitive information

- you are firing the worker for excessive absenteeism or leave, if you are concerned that the absences or leave may be covered by the Family and Medical Leave Act or the Americans with Disabilities Act (see Chapter 2, Sections D and E)
- the employee denies committing the acts for which you are firing him, even after an investigation (see Chapter 5), or
- the employee has hired a lawyer to represent her in her dealings with you.

You may also want to seek legal advice before taking employment actions short of termination. For example, a lawyer can help you plan a thorough and legal investigation, decide on appropriate disciplinary action or accommodate a worker's disability. If money is tight, however, spend your legal budget getting advice on those issues that could cause the most trouble. You don't need a lawyer's help with every workplace investigation, for example, but you should consider getting legal advice if a number of workers are accused of serious misconduct, such as harassing female employees.

3. Representation in Legal or Administrative Proceedings

If a current or former employee sues you, hire a lawyer right away. Employment lawsuits can be very complex. You have to take certain actions immediately to make sure that your rights are protected—and to preserve evidence that might be used in court. The time limits for taking action are very short—many courts require you to file a formal, legal response to a lawsuit within just a few weeks. As soon as you receive notice of a lawsuit against you, begin looking for a lawyer.

For more information on lawsuits, see *The Lawsuit Survival Guide: A Client's Litigation Companion,* **by attorney Joseph Matthews (Nolo).** This book covers every aspect of a civil lawsuit, from choosing a lawyer through deciding whether to appeal.

Your Insurance Company Might Foot the Bill

Your insurance company might pay for a lawyer to defend you in a lawsuit—and pay for any damages you have to pay as a result of a lawsuit. One of three types of policies might apply:

- **Commercial general liability (CGL) insurance:** This policy protects you when others sue you. However, many CGL policies exclude employment-related claims by employees, either expressly or by denying coverage for intentional acts—defined by the insurance industry to include many discrimination, harassment and other wrongful termination claims.

- **Directors and officers (D&O) insurance:** D & O insurance covers a company's directors and officers for lawsuits by third parties, including employees. Many of these policies also fall short because they provide personal coverage only for the individuals named in the policy, not the company itself. This exclusion leaves employers uninsured for most employment claims.

- **Employment practices liability insurance (EPLI):** These policies are fairly new and are intended to fill in the gaps left by the more traditional policies by covering most employment-related litigation. The terms and definitions of these policies can vary widely. Some of these policies will pay for "risk management" assistance as well, such as the cost of having an attorney review employment policies, applications, handbooks and procedures for dealing with complaints.

Sometimes, a current or former worker initiates some kind of adversarial process short of a lawsuit. For example, an employee might file an administrative complaint of discrimination, retaliation or harassment with the U.S. Equal Employment Opportunity Commission or a similar state agency. Or, a former employee might appeal the denial of unemployment benefits, which in many states allows the employee to ask for a hearing.

In these situations, you should at least consult a lawyer, if not hire one. It's also wise to contact your insurance broker and ask if your policies cover administrative proceedings. Although some employers can and do handle these administrative matters on their own, most could probably benefit from some legal advice on the strength of the employee's claim, preparing a response for the agency or administrative board, dealing with agency investigations or requests for information and presenting evidence at a hearing. A lawyer can advise you of your rights and what to expect as the process continues.

If you have the money and the claim seems serious, you can also hire a lawyer to represent you in these proceedings. It might be worth paying for legal representation if:

- The employee raises serious claims that could result in a significant monetary award. If the worker alleges that severe harassment, discrimination or retaliation took place, for example, you may not want to risk fighting the claim on your own.
- Other employees or former employees have made similar allegations, either to the agency or within the workplace. An agency will be more likely to investigate closely—and more likely to find in the employee's favor—if other workers have come forward.
- The worker has indicated that he intends to file a lawsuit. In this situation, the employee may simply be using the administrative proceeding to gather evidence to support his legal claims.
- The employee has hired a lawyer.

An Accused Employee May Need a Separate Lawyer

Believe it or not, you may actually have to pay for two lawyers to handle a single employment problem. This might happen if both the company and an individual employee or manager are accused of wrongdoing. For example, if a former employee claims that a manager sexually harassed her or that a coworker assaulted her in the workplace, you and your accused employee might need separate lawyers.

The reason? A lawyer cannot represent more than one client if the joint representation creates a conflict of interest—that is, if the interests of the company and the interests of the individual employee are at odds. In the examples given above, the company might want to blame the accused employee—for example, by arguing that even though the employee engaged in this misconduct, it was not something for which the company should be held responsible. Obviously, if the accused employee wants to argue that he didn't do it, the two defenses will conflict.

In these situations, you might have to not only get a separate lawyer for your employee, but pay the lawyer's bill as well. Some states handle this issue by requiring employers to indemnify—pay back—their workers for any employment-related expenses, including the cost of defending against a lawsuit. Ask your lawyer about your state's rules.

B. How to Find a Good Lawyer

We can't overestimate the importance of choosing the right lawyer to help you with employment-related legal issues. An experienced, skilled lawyer can help you make careful employment decisions, defend you in legal disputes with your employees and even prevent legal problems before they start by advising you about your company's employment policies and practices. A lousy lawyer might do none of this—and charge you exorbitantly nonetheless. The sad truth is, legal advice is expensive regardless of its quality. Get your money's worth by hiring the right lawyer for your company.

1. Getting Leads

Your first step in finding the right lawyer is to get some recommendations —called "referrals"—from other people and organizations. Remember to ask for referrals to *employment* lawyers. Because most lawyers specialize in one or two areas of law, a lawyer who skillfully handles divorces, bankruptcies or trademark disputes won't do you much good in dealing with your employees. Consider also why you need help from a lawyer. If you are facing a lawsuit, you will need help from a litigator—a lawyer who regularly handles lawsuits all the way through trial and knows his or her way around a courtroom. If you need someone to review your personnel policies or a severance agreement, litigation experience isn't necessary.

Questions to Ask Your Sources

If you get a lead from a person who has actually worked with the recommended lawyer, find out what the person liked about the lawyer and why. Ask how the legal problem turned out—was the lawyer successful? Ask about the lawyer's legal abilities, communication skills and billing practices. Here are some questions to consider:

- Did the lawyer respond promptly to your telephone calls and other communications?
- Did the lawyer keep you informed of developments in your lawsuit or other legal dispute?
- Were your legal bills properly itemized and in line with the costs the lawyer projected at the outset?
- Did the lawyer handle your case personally or hand it off to a less experienced lawyer in the same firm?
- Did the lawyer respect your feelings about how your legal dispute should be handled?
- Did the lawyer deliver what she promised?

You can get leads from many sources, including:

- **Business associates.** Other employers are perhaps your best source of leads. Talk to the people in your community who own or operate excellent businesses. Find out who their lawyers are and whether they like their lawyers' work.

- **Friends and relatives.** You may know someone who was recently involved in an employment dispute. Even if your acquaintance was suing an employer, find out whether he or she had a good lawyer. Even a lawyer who represents only employees (as many do) can probably refer you to some lawyers who work with employers.

- **Lawyers.** If you have a regular lawyer you use for estate planning, tax advice or other legal issues, find out whether your lawyer knows any employment lawyers. Chances are good that your lawyer is acquainted with lawyers who practice employment law, through law school, professional meetings or other lawyerly pursuits.

- **Trade and business organizations.** If you belong to a professional group, ask other members for legal recommendations. Local groups that support the rights of business owners, such as the chamber of commerce, might also know of some employment lawyers.

- **Professionals outside your field.** People who provide services to the business community—such as bankers, accountants, insurance agents or real estate brokers—might also give you some leads.

- **Articles and newsletters.** Some employment lawyers write articles for trade magazines or newspapers. Track down these authors and find out whether they are taking on new clients—or can refer you to other employment lawyers.

Where Not to Look for a Lawyer

The best way to get a referral to a good lawyer is to talk to other people who have actually used a particular lawyer's services. The worst is to comb through advertisements or unscreened lists of lawyers provided by a bar association, lawyers' professional group or the phone company.

Bar associations and other lawyer groups often maintain and advertise lawyer referral services. However, a lawyer can usually get on this list simply by volunteering. Very little (if any) screening is done to find out whether the lawyers are any good. Similarly, advertisements in the yellow pages, in newspapers, on television or online say nothing meaningful about a lawyer's skills or manner—just that he could afford to pay for the ad. In many states, lawyers can advertise any specialization they choose—even if they have never handled a case in that area of law.

While there is always a possibility that you will find a good lawyer through one of these methods, your chances are hit and miss. And you will waste a lot of time interviewing lawyers who are neither qualified nor competent to handle your legal problems while searching for your needle in the haystack.

2.   Comparison Shopping

Once you have some leads, do a little research. A good source of information about lawyers is the Martindale-Hubbell Law Directory, available at most law libraries and some local public libraries. This resource contains biographical sketches of most practicing lawyers and information about their experience, specialties, education, the professional organizations to which they belong and cases they have handled. Many firms also list their major clients in the directory—a good indication of the types of problems these lawyers have tackled. Lawyers purchase the space for these biographical sketches, so don't be overly impressed by their length.

You can find Martindale-Hubbell online at www.martindale.com. You can find additional information about lawyers in West's Legal Directory at www.wld.com.

Next, call the lawyers on your list. Some lawyers take these calls directly; others have staff who screen calls from potential clients to weed out problems that are clearly outside the lawyer's area of expertise. The lawyer or screening person will usually ask some basic questions about why you need legal advice to determine whether a more detailed discussion is in order. If so, the lawyer will schedule a meeting with you.

Don't Hire a Lawyer Sight Unseen

No matter how positive your initial conversation with a lawyer or how glowing the referral, it is never a good idea to hire a lawyer without meeting face to face. You have to assess the lawyer's demeanor and professionalism, how the lawyer interacts with you and the many other intangibles that go into a solid working relationship. And few lawyers will take on a case—particularly one that might turn into a lawsuit—without meeting the client.

3. Prepare to Meet the Lawyer

Before your first meeting, organize your thoughts. Prepare to give the lawyer all the key facts necessary to evaluate your problem. One good way to make sure no important details get left out of the conversation is to make an outline. Write down, in chronological order, the main events and conversations leading to the dispute. There is no need to go overboard; a page or two of notes should suffice. Also jot down the names and telephone numbers of any important witnesses the lawyer might need to interview.

Gather any documents the lawyer should review—an employment contract, employee handbook, offer letter, severance agreement, sexual harassment policy or investigation notes, for example—and make copies to bring with you. Some lawyers will ask you to send the documents to them ahead of time, so they can do any necessary legal research before the meeting.

You May Have to Pay for the Privilege

Some lawyers require potential clients to pay a consultation fee—a fee for meeting with the lawyer to discuss your legal concerns and the possibility of working together. If a lawyer charges such a fee, you should ask what you will get for your money. Generally, you can expect a consultation fee to cover time the lawyer spends reviewing documents important to your case, doing research and meeting with you. A consultation fee is usually a flat rate—sometimes up to several hundred dollars. If you find the right lawyer and can afford the charge, this will be money well spent.

---

4.   Speaking With the Lawyer

When you meet with a lawyer, explain your legal problem and ask for the lawyer's advice about what to do next. Ask any questions you might have about your situation. Also, ask about the lawyer's background, experience and billing practices (paying lawyers is covered below in Section C). As you talk, consider not only the legal advice you receive, but also your impression of the lawyer's communication skills and style. Does the lawyer listen well? Are you getting answers to your questions? Do you feel comfortable talking honestly to the lawyer? Can you understand what the lawyer is talking about? Particularly if you are facing a lawsuit, these issues will only become more important as you move forward.

Whenever you talk privately to a lawyer about your legal matters, that conversation is privileged—meaning no one can force you or the lawyer to disclose what either of you said. This is true even before you actually hire the lawyer and even if you decide, ultimately, not to hire the lawyer at all.

This means that when you interview lawyers to decide whether you want them to represent you, you can freely discuss the facts of your situation, warts and all. The lawyer's advice will only be as good as the information you reveal. If you hold back important facts because you think they make you look bad or weaken your claims, you won't receive a candid assessment of your situation—or sound advice about how to avoid further trouble.

C. Legal Fees

Many disputes between lawyers and their clients are about fees. This shouldn't be surprising—lawyers charge a lot of money for their time, no matter what results they achieve. Your best protection against problems over attorney fees is to work out a fee agreement with your lawyer before any legal work is started.

Before you make a final decision to hire a lawyer, have a frank discussion about fees and costs. Ask the lawyer how she charges (by the hour or in some other manner), what her hourly rate is and what she thinks your total legal bill will be. Tell the lawyer how much you are willing to spend. Although it is rare, a lawyer may sometimes agree to charge a lower fee for some or all of her hours, change her fee structure (for example, accept some payment in free services or products your company makes, or in stock options) or otherwise accommodate your needs.

1.   How Lawyers Charge for Their Time

There are four basic ways that lawyers charge for their services, depending on the type and amount of legal help you need.

- **Hourly.** Most employers will pay their lawyer an hourly fee, a set rate of anywhere from $150 to $300 or more per hour of legal work.
- **Flat fee.** For discrete tasks that are fairly straightforward, a lawyer might charge a set amount for the whole job. For example, a lawyer might draft a severance agreement or employment contract for $500.
- **Retainer.** Larger companies may be able to hire a lawyer for a flat annual fee, called a retainer, which covers any and all routine legal business during the year. If you run into extraordinary legal problems (a lawsuit, for example), you will usually have to pay more for the lawyer's additional time.
- **Contingency fee.** A lawyer who charges a percentage of the amount she wins for you in settlement or trial is charging a contingency fee. This is usually not an option for employers, who do not stand to collect any money in most lawsuits with former employees. However, if you are suing a former employee for money—for misappropriating trade secrets, for example—and the employee is rich enough to pony up if you win, a lawyer might consider taking on at least that part of the work for a contingency fee.

2.   Paying for Costs

In many cases, you'll be paying for more than just the lawyer's time. You might also have to pay legal costs—the expenses the lawyer must pay to handle your legal work. If you are seeking legal advice to review contracts or help you make an employment decision, you will probably be facing minimal costs—perhaps just the price of copying documents and postage. However, if you are involved in a lawsuit, your costs will be substantial. You will have to pay for depositions, expert witnesses, private investigators, court fees and exhibits. Ask your lawyer ahead of time for a description and estimate of the costs you might have to pay.

Lawyers charge their clients for costs in several different ways. Some require clients to deposit a sum of money with the lawyer, to be used to pay costs as they accrue. Others bill clients monthly for costs, or bill clients when their legal work is finished. Find out which of these methods your lawyer plans to use.

Some lawyers engage in the deceptive practice of billing their clients for costs that are really part of the lawyer's own operating expenses or overhead. If you get billed for something for which the lawyer didn't have to pay (using the law firm's conference room, for example) or something that the lawyer must have in order to stay in business (local phone service or fax charges, for example), question the charge.

3.   Get It in Writing

Once you have hammered out a fee agreement, get it in writing. Make sure the written agreement includes every important detail—including the per-hour billing rate or other charges, how often you will be billed, whether you will be required to deposit money in advance, how costs are billed and when the lawyer will be paid. If the lawyer will be delegating some of your legal work to a less experienced lawyer, paralegal or secretary in his office, that work should be billed at a lower hourly rate—and that rate should be included in the written fee agreement.

D.   Working With Your Lawyer

Your lawyer's job is to protect and enforce your legal rights. For an employer, this might include reviewing important documents, providing legal representation in court, helping with difficult employment decisions or keeping you out of lawsuits. Remember, although your lawyer has the legal expertise, it is your business and your reputation that are on the line. To get the best representation possible, you must work well with your lawyer—and make sure your interests are being safeguarded. Start by following these tips:

- **Be honest.** Tell your lawyer all the facts that relate to your legal problem. Armed with this information, your lawyer can figure out how best to prevent legal trouble and meet your needs.
- **Keep in touch.** Stay in regular contact with your lawyer to find out what's going on in your dispute. Keep your lawyer apprised of any planned vacations or other lengthy absences, in case your presence will be required at upcoming legal proceedings.
- **Keep track of important documents and deadlines.** Keep a file that includes all the important documents relating to your legal dispute. This will allow you to discuss your case with your lawyer intelligently and efficiently—even over the phone. Make a note of any important deadlines.

- **Do your own research.** By learning as much as you can about the laws and court decisions that apply to your dispute, you will be able to monitor your lawyer's work, make informed decisions about settlement offers and—perhaps—keep yourself out of legal trouble the next time around.
- **Check billing statements.** Every bill you receive from your lawyer should list the costs and fees incurred that month. If you have questions about your bill or don't agree with all the charges, talk to your lawyer about it. Most states require a certain amount of detail in a lawyer's billing statements, so ask for more information if you need it.

Time Is Money

If you are getting billed by the hour, remember that the lawyer's time is your money. Most lawyers bill in increments as small as 1/10th of an hour (six minutes). Even if you use less than that time, you will get billed for the full six. And any time the lawyer spends on you—talking on the phone, reviewing documents or doing research—is billable.

With this in mind, you can take a few steps to minimize your legal bills. Before you pick up the phone to talk to your lawyer, think about the purpose of your call. Do you need documents, scheduling information or other routine assistance? Maybe the lawyer's secretary can take care of it (for free.) Do you have questions you need to ask? Write them down ahead of time, so you don't have to call back and get billed for a second conversation. If you have to give your lawyer information, consider writing a letter—that way, you will have the opportunity to collect your thoughts and will have your lawyer's undivided attention. Finally, remember that the meter is running when you are on the phone with your lawyer. You needn't dispense with all pleasantries, but try to keep the small talk to a minimum (especially if your lawyer is doing the talking).

E.   Firing a Lawyer

You have the right to change lawyers for any reason, at any time (although you may have to get a judge's permission to switch if you are in the midst of trial—see subsection 2). Here we explain when and how to do it.

1.   When to Make the Change

Changing lawyers—especially if you are in the middle of a lawsuit—will take time and money. Your new lawyer will have to get up to speed on your legal affairs, and you will have to spend time meeting with the lawyer to explain your situation and develop a working relationship. Given these drawbacks, it doesn't make sense to fire a lawyer at the drop of a hat. But do give serious consideration to switching lawyers in these circumstances:

- When your dispute becomes a lawsuit, if your lawyer doesn't have litigation experience.
- When you and your lawyer cannot agree on important strategic decisions. You may not agree on everything, but if you find yourself butting heads with your lawyer frequently over significant legal matters, you might think about finding a lawyer who is more attuned to your wishes.
- When you and your lawyer consistently disagree about fee and cost issues. Because lawyers charge so much for their services, some discomfort over fees is inevitable. But if you keep getting billed for expenses that you think are unfair and your lawyer cannot or will not explain the logic behind the tab, consider going elsewhere.
- When your lawyer fails to stay in touch. Sometimes a lawyer will be unable to take your phone call right away or need to postpone a meeting. But if your lawyer drops out of sight or stops returning your calls, it might be time for a change.

- When you cannot get along with your lawyer. Sometimes, lawyers and clients just have a personality clash. Some friction is probably inevitable (particularly if you are involved in a lawsuit), but you shouldn't reach a point where you can't stand each other.
- When you lose confidence in your lawyer. Perhaps your lawyer has done something truly upsetting—lied to you, missed an important court deadline or misplaced crucial documents—that has ruined your working relationship. Or you may be unimpressed with your lawyer's skills or advice. Any time you have lost confidence in your lawyer's abilities, competence or ethics, you should find another lawyer.

2. How to Fire Your Lawyer

The first thing to do is tell your lawyer—in writing—that you are taking your business elsewhere. You should ask your former lawyer to send all of your files and related materials to your new lawyer. Your new lawyer should also send your former lawyer a letter saying that the new lawyer is taking over the case.

If a lawsuit has already been filed, you will have to file a court document called a Substitution of Attorneys. This document officially informs the court, the other parties and their lawyers that you have changed lawyers. Your new lawyer can prepare this form. If you are in or about to start a trial, the judge will have to approve the change. In deciding whether to allow it, the judge will consider, among other things, whether your opponent will be unfairly affected by any delay necessitated by the change in lawyers.

If you are changing lawyers because of deceptive, unethical or otherwise illegal behavior by your attorney, consider taking action. Call the local or state bar association, listed in the telephone book under Attorneys, for guidance on what types of lawyer misconduct are prohibited and how to file a complaint. ■

Appendix

Federal Agencies Enforcing Workplace Laws

U.S. Equal Employment Opportunity Commission
1801 L Street, N.W.
Washington, D.C. 20507
Phone: 202-663-4900
To be connected with the field office closest to you: 800-669-4000
www.eeoc.gov

U.S. Department of Labor
Office of Public Affairs
200 Constitution Avenue, N.W.
Room S-1032
Washington, D.C. 20210
Phone: 202-693-4650
www.dol.gov

U.S. Department of Justice
950 Pennsylvania Avenue
Washington, D.C. 20530
Phone: 202-514-2007
www.usdoj.gov

Internal Revenue Service
U.S. Department of Treasury
1500 Pennsylvania Avenue, N.W.
Washington, D.C. 20220
Phone: 202-622-2000
www.irs.gov
www.ustreas.gov

Federal Fair Employment Laws

Title VII of the Civil Rights Act of 1964 (commonly referred to as "Title VII")

Legal citation:

42 U.S.C. §§ 2000e and following

Covered employers:

- private employers with 15 or more employees
- state governments and their agencies
- local governments and their agencies
- the federal government and its agencies
- employment agencies
- labor unions

Prohibited conduct:

Title VII prohibits employers from discriminating against applicants and employees on the basis of race or color, religion, sex, pregnancy, childbirth and national origin (including membership in a Native American tribe).

Title VII also prohibits harassment based on any of the protected characteristics listed above.

Title VII also prohibits an employer from retaliating against someone who asserts his or her rights under Title VII.

Title VII's prohibition against discrimination applies to all terms, conditions and privileges of employment.

Enforcing agency:

The U.S. Equal Employment Opportunity Commission

The Age Discrimination in Employment Act (commonly referred to as the "ADEA")

Legal citation:

29 U.S.C. §§ 621-634

Covered employers:

- private employers with 20 or more employees
- the federal government and its agencies (note that the ADEA does not apply to the state government and its agencies)
- local governments and their agencies
- employment agencies
- labor unions

Prohibited conduct:

The ADEA prohibits discrimination against employees who are age 40 or older. The ADEA also prohibits harassment against those employees based on their age. The ADEA also prohibits employers from retaliating against employees who assert their rights under the ADEA.

The ADEA's prohibition against discrimination applies to all terms, conditions and privileges of employment.

Enforcing agency:

The U.S. Equal Employment Opportunity Commission

The Equal Pay Act

Legal citation:

29 U.S.C. § 206(d)

Covered employers:

- virtually all private employers (regardless of the number of employees)
- the federal government and its agencies

- state governments and their agencies
- local governments and their agencies
- employment agencies
- labor unions

Prohibited conduct:

Employers cannot pay different wages to men and women who do substantially equal work.

Enforcing agency:

The U.S. Equal Employment Opportunity Commission

The Immigration Reform and Control Act of 1986 (commonly referred to as the "IRCA")

Legal citation:

8 U.S.C. § 1324

Covered employers:

- private employers with four or more employees
- the federal government
- state governments and their agencies
- local governments and their agencies
- employment agencies
- labor unions

Prohibited conduct:

The IRCA prohibits employers from discriminating against applicants or employees on the basis of their citizenship or national origin. The IRCA's prohibition against discrimination applies to all terms, conditions and privileges of employment.

The IRCA also makes it illegal for employers to knowingly hire or retain in employment people who are not authorized to work in the United States.

It also requires employers to keep records that verify that their employees are authorized to work in the United States.

The Americans with Disabilities Act (commonly referred to as the "ADA")

Legal citation:

42 U.S.C. §§ 12101-12213

Covered employers:

- private employers with 15 or more employees
- the federal government and its agencies (but not the state governments and their agencies)
- local governments and their agencies
- employment agencies
- labor unions

Prohibited conduct:

The ADA prohibits employers from discriminating against a person who has a disability or who is perceived to have a disability in any aspect of employment.

The ADA also prohibits employers from refusing to hire someone or discriminating against someone because that person is related to or associates with someone with a disability.

The ADA also prohibits harassment against the people described above.

The ADA prohibits retaliation against people who assert their rights under the ADA.

Enforcing agencies:

The U.S. Equal Employment Opportunity Commission and the U.S. Department of Justice

State Laws Prohibiting Discrimination in Private Employment

This is a state-by-state synopsis of factors that private employers may not use as the basis for any employment decisions. In legal parlance, the groups that have these factors are called "protected classes."

Keep in mind that this is only a synopsis and that each state has its own way of interpreting who is or is not a member of a protected class. For example, one state may have a different way of determining who is disabled under its laws than other states do. In addition, many of the laws in this chart apply only to employers with a minimum number of employees, such as five or more.

For details about your state laws, contact your state fair employment agency. Where no special agency has been designated to enforce anti-discrimination laws, your state's labor department or the closest office of the federal Equal Employment Opportunity Office should direct you to the right agency or person who can give you information about fair employment laws in your state. All of these agencies are listed in this Appendix.

This list only describes state laws. Your city or county may have its own set of fair employment ordinances. To learn more about those, contact someone within your local government, such as your county clerk's office. Also, local offices of the Small Business Administration or the Chamber of Commerce can be good sources for information about local laws.

The following chart was last revised in March 2003.

	Laws Prohibiting Discrimination in Employment				
		Private employers may not make employment decisions based on			
State	Law applies to employers with	Age	Ancestry or national origin	Disability	AIDS/HIV
Alabama Ala. Code §§ 21-7-1; 25-1-20	20 or more employees	40 and older			
Alaska Alaska Stat. §§ 18.80.220; 47.30.865	One or more employees	40 and older	✓	Physical and mental	✓
Arizona Ariz. Rev. Stat. § 41-1461	15 or more employees	40 and older	✓	Physical	✓
Arkansas Ark. Code Ann. §§ 16-123-101; 11-4-601; 11-5-403	9 or more employees		✓	Physical, mental and sensory	
California Cal. Gov't. Code §§ 12920,12941; Cal. Lab. Code § 1101	5 or more employees	40 and older	✓	Physical and mental	✓
Colorado Colo. Rev. Stat. §§ 24-34-301, 24-34-401; 27-10-115	Law applies to all employers.	40 to 70	✓	Physical, mental and learning	✓
Connecticut Conn. Gen. Stat. Ann. §§ 46a-51, 46a-60	3 or more employees	40 and older	✓	Present or past physical, mental or learning	✓
Delaware Del. Code Ann. tit. 19, § 710	4 or more employees	40 to 70	✓	Physical or mental	✓
District of Columbia D.C. Code Ann. §§ 2-1401.01; 7-1703.03	Law applies to all employers.	18 and older	✓	Physical or mental	✓

[1] Employees covered by FLSA

Gender	Marital status	Pregnancy, childbirth and related medical conditions	Race or color	Religion or creed	Sexual orientation	Genetic testing information	Additional protected categories
✓	✓ (Includes changes in status)	✓ Parenthood	✓	✓			Mental illness
✓			✓	✓		✓	
✓		✓	✓	✓		✓[1]	
✓	✓	✓	✓	✓	✓	✓	• Medical condition • Political activities or affiliations
✓		✓	✓	✓			• Lawful conduct outside of work • Mental illness
✓	✓	✓	✓	✓		✓	Mental retardation
✓	✓	✓	✓	✓		✓	
✓	✓	✓ Parenthood	✓	✓	✓		• Enrollment in vocational or professional or college education • Family duties • Perceived race • Personal appearance • Political affiliation • Smoker

Laws Prohibiting Discrimination in Employment (continued)						
		Private employers may not make employment decisions based on				
State	Law applies to employers with	Age	Ancestry or national origin	Disability	AIDS/HIV	
Florida Fla. Stat. Ann. §§ 760.01, 760.50; 448.075	15 or more employees	No age limit	✓	"Handicap"	✓	
Georgia Ga. Code Ann. §§ 34-6A-1; 34-1-23; 34-5-1	15 or more employees (disability) 10 or more employees (gender)	40 to 70		Physical or mental		
Hawaii Haw. Rev. Stat. § 378-1	One or more employees	No age limit	✓	Physical or mental	✓	
Idaho Idaho Code § 67-5909	5 or more employees	40 and older	✓	Physical or mental		
Illinois 775 Ill. Comp. Stat. §§ 5/ 1-101, 5/2-101; Ill. Admin. Code tit. 56, § 5210.110	15 or more employees	40 and older	✓	Physical or mental	✓	
Indiana Ind. Code Ann. §§ 22-9-1-1, 22-9-2-1	6 or more employees	40 to 70	✓	Physical or mental		
Iowa Iowa Code § 216.1	4 or more employees	18 or older	✓	Physical or mental	✓	
Kansas Kan. Stat. Ann. §§ 44-1001, 44-1111, 44-1125; 65-6002(e)	4 or more employees	18 or older	✓	Physical or mental	✓	
Kentucky Ky. Rev. Stat. Ann. §§ 344.040; 207.130; 342.197	8 or more employees	40 or older	✓	Physical (Includes black lung disease)	✓	

[2] Wage discrimination only

Gender	Marital status	Pregnancy, childbirth and related medical conditions	Race or color	Religion or creed	Sexual orientation	Genetic testing information	Additional protected categories
✓	✓		✓	✓			Sickle cell trait
✓[2]							
✓	✓	✓ Breastfeeding	✓	✓	✓	✓	Arrest and court record (unless there is a conviction directly related to job)
✓		✓	✓	✓			
✓	✓	✓	✓	✓			• Arrest record • Citizen status • Military status • Unfavorable military discharge
✓			✓	✓			
✓		✓	✓	✓			
✓			✓	✓		✓	Military status
✓			✓	✓			Smoker or nonsmoker

Laws Prohibiting Discrimination in Employment (continued)						
		Private employers may not make employment decisions based on				
State	Law applies to employers with	Age	Ancestry or national origin	Disability	AIDS/HIV	
Louisiana La. Rev. Stat. Ann. §§ 23: 301 to 23:352	20 or more employees	40 or older	✓	Physical or mental		
Maine Me. Rev. Stat. Ann. tit. 5, §§ 4551, 4571	Law applies to all employers.	No age limit	✓	Physical or mental		
Maryland Md. Code 1957 Art. 49B, § 15	15 or more employees	No age limit	✓	Physical or mental		
Massachusetts Mass. Gen. Laws ch. 151B, § 4	6 or more employees	40 or older	✓	Physical or mental	✓	
Michigan Mich. Comp. Laws §§ 37.1201, 37.2201, 37.1103	One or more employees	No age limit	✓	Physical or mental	✓	
Minnesota Minn. Stat. Ann. §§ 363.01; 181.974	One or more employees	18 or older	✓	Physical or mental	✓	
Mississippi No state law						
Missouri Mo. Rev. Stat. §§ 213.010; 191.665; 375.1306	6 or more employees	40 to 70	✓	Physical or mental	✓	
Montana Mont. Code Ann. §§ 49-2-101, 49-2-303	One or more employees	No age limit	✓	Physical or mental		
Nebraska Neb. Rev. Stat. §§ 48-1101; 48-1001; 20-168	15 or more employees	40 to 70 [3]	✓	Physical or mental	✓	

[3] Employers with 25 or more employees

Gender	Marital status	Pregnancy, childbirth and related medical conditions	Race or color	Religion or creed	Sexual orientation	Genetic testing information	Additional protected categories
✓		✓ (Applies to employers with 25 or more employees)	✓	✓		✓	Sickle cell trait
✓		✓	✓	✓	✓	✓	
✓	✓	✓	✓	✓	✓	✓	
✓			✓	✓	✓	✓	
✓	✓	✓	✓	✓		✓	• Height or weight • Arrest record
✓	✓	✓	✓	✓	✓	✓	• Member of local commission • Perceived sexual orientation • Receiving public assistance
✓		✓	✓	✓		✓	
✓		✓	✓	✓			
✓	✓	✓	✓	✓		✓	

	Laws Prohibiting Discrimination in Employment (continued)					
		Private employers may not make employment decisions based on				
State	Law applies to employers with	Age	Ancestry or national origin	Disability	AIDS/HIV	
Nevada Nev. Rev. Stat. Ann. § 613.310 and following	15 or more employees	40 or older	✓	Physical or mental		
New Hampshire N.H. Rev. Stat. Ann. §§ 354-A:2 and following; 141-H:3	6 or more employees	No age limit	✓	Physical or mental		
New Jersey N.J. Stat. Ann. §§ 10:5-1; 34:6B-1	Law applies to all employers.	18 to 70	✓	Past or present physical or mental	✓	
New Mexico N.M. Stat. Ann. § 28-1-1	4 or more employees	40 or older	✓	Physical or mental		
New York N.Y. Exec. Law § 296; N.Y. Lab. Law § 201-d	4 or more employees	18 and over	✓	Physical or mental	✓	
North Carolina N.C. Gen. Stat. §§ 143-422.2; 168A-1; 95-28.1; 130A-148	15 or more employees	No age limit	✓	Physical or mental	✓	
North Dakota N.D. Cent. Code §§ 14-02.4-01; 34-01-17	One or more employees	40 or older	✓	Physical or mental		
Ohio Ohio Rev. Code Ann. §§ 4111.17; 4112.01	4 or more employees	40 or older	✓	Physical, mental or learning		
Oklahoma Okla. Stat. Ann. tit. 25, § 1301; tit. 36, § 3614.2; tit. 40, § 500; tit. 44, § 208	15 or more employees	40 or older	✓	Physical or mental		

Gender	Marital status	Pregnancy, childbirth and related medical conditions	Race or color	Religion or creed	Sexual orientation	Genetic testing information	Additional protected categories
✓		✓	✓	✓	✓	✓	Lawful use of any product when not at work
✓	✓	✓	✓	✓	✓	✓	
✓	✓	✓	✓	✓	✓	✓	• Hereditary cellular or blood trait • Military service or status • Smoker or nonsmoker
✓	✓ (Applies to employers with 50 or more employees)	✓	✓	✓			Serious medical condition
✓	✓	✓	✓	✓	✓	✓	• Lawful use of any product when not at work • Observance of Sabbath • Political activities
✓			✓	✓		✓	• Lawful use of any product when not at work • Sickle cell trait
✓	✓	✓	✓	✓			• Lawful conduct outside of work • Receiving public assistance
✓		✓	✓	✓			
✓			✓	✓		✓	• Military service • Smoker or nonsmoker

Laws Prohibiting Discrimination in Employment (continued)

			Private employers may not make employment decisions based on			
State	Law applies to employers with	Age	Ancestry or national origin	Disability	AIDS/HIV	
Oregon Or. Rev. Stat. §§ 659A.100 and foll.; 659A.303	One or more employees	18 or older	✓	Physical or mental[4]		
Pennsylvania 43 Pa. Cons. Stat. Ann. § 953, 336.3	4 or more employees	40 to 70	✓	Physical or mental		
Rhode Island R.I. Gen. Laws §§ 28-6-17; 28-5-11; 2-28-10; 23-6-22; 23-20.7.1-1	4 or more employees	40 or older	✓	Physical or mental	✓	
South Carolina S.C. Code Ann. § 1-13-20 and following	15 or more employees	40 or older	✓	Physical or mental		
South Dakota S.D. Codified Laws Ann. §§ 20-13-1; 60-12-15; 60-2-20; 62-1-17	Law applies to all employers.		✓	Physical, mental and learning		
Tennessee Tenn. Code Ann. §§ 4-21-102; 4-21-401 and following; 8-50-103; 50-2-202	8 or more employees	40 or older	✓	Physical or mental		
Texas Tex. Lab. Code Ann. §§ 21.002, 21.101, 21.401	15 or more employees	40 or older	✓	Physical or mental		

[4] Employer
[5] Employers with 100 or more employees

Gender	Marital status	Pregnancy, childbirth and related medical conditions	Race or color	Religion or creed	Sexual orientation	Genetic testing information	Additional protected categories
✓		✓	✓	✓		✓	
✓		✓ (Pregnancy not treated as a disability in terms of benefits)	✓	✓			• Familial status • GED rather than high school diploma
✓		✓	✓	✓	✓	✓	• Domestic abuse victim • Gender identity or expression • Smoker or nonsmoker
✓		✓	✓	✓			
✓			✓	✓		✓	Preexisting injury
✓		✓ (Full-time employee who worked the previous 12 months is entitled to 4 months' maternity leave. Pay at discretion of employer.)[5]	✓	✓			
✓		✓	✓	✓		✓	

Laws Prohibiting Discrimination in Employment (continued)

State	Law applies to employers with	Age	Ancestry or national origin	Disability		
		Private employers may not make employment decisions based on				
Utah Utah Code Ann. § 34A-5-102	15 or more employees	40 or older	✓	Follows federal law	✓[6]	
Vermont Vt. Stat. Ann. tit. 21, § 495; tit. 18, § 9333	One or more employees	18 or older	✓	Physical, mental or learning	✓	
Virginia Va. Code Ann. §§ 2.2-3900; 40.1-28.6; 51.5-3	Law applies to all employers.	No age limit	✓	Physical or mental		
Washington Wash. Rev. Code Ann. §§ 49.60.040, 49.60.172 and foll.; 49.12.175; 49.44.090; Wash. Admin. Code § 162-30-020	8 or more employees	40 or older	✓	Physical, mental or sensory	✓	
West Virginia W.Va. Code §§ 5-11-3, 5-11-9; 21-5B-1	12 or more employees	40 or older	✓	Physical or mental	✓	
Wisconsin Wis. Stat. Ann. § 111.32	One or more employees	40 or older	✓	Physical or mental	✓	
Wyoming Wyo. Stat. §§ 27-9-105; 19-11-104	2 or more employees	40 to 69	✓			

[6] Follows federal ADA statutes

[7] Employers with one or more employees

Gender	Marital status	Pregnancy, childbirth and related medical conditions	Race or color	Religion or creed	Sexual orientation	Genetic testing information	Additional protected categories
✓		✓	✓	✓			
✓			✓	✓	✓	✓	Place of birth
✓	✓	✓	✓	✓			
✓	✓	✓	✓	✓			Member of state militia
✓[7]			✓	✓			Smoker or nonsmoker
✓	✓	✓	✓	✓	✓	✓	• Arrest or conviction • Lawful use of any product when not at work • Military service or status
✓			✓	✓			• Military service or status • Smoker or nonsmoker

Agencies That Enforce Laws Prohibiting Discrimination in Employment

United States Agencies

Equal Employment Opportunity
  Commission (EEOC)
Washington, D.C.
202-663-4900
800-669-4000
www.eeoc.gov
Field Office Locations and phone
  numbers
www.eeoc.gov/teledir.html

State Agencies

Alabama

EEOC Distrist Office
Birmingham, AL
205-731-0082/0083

Alaska

Commission for Human Rights
Anchorage, AK
907-274-4692
800-478-4692
www.gov.state.ak.us/aschr/
  aschr.htm

Arizona

Civil Rights Division
Phoenix, AZ
602-542-5263
www.attorneygeneral.state.az.us/
  civil_rights/index.html

Arkansas

Equal Employment Opportunity
  Commission
Little Rock, AR
501-324-5060
www.eeoc.gov/index.html

California

Department of Fair Employment
  and Housing
Sacramento District Office
Sacramento, CA
916-445-5523
800-884-1684
www.dfeh.ca.gov

Colorado

Civil Rights Division
Denver, CO
303-894-2997
800-262-4845
www.dora.state.co.us/Civil-Rights

Connecticut

Commission on Human Rights &
  Opportunities
Hartford, CT
860-541-3400
800-477-5737
www.state.ct.us/chro

Agencies That Enforce Laws Prohibiting
Discrimination in Employment (continued)

Delaware
Office of Labor Law Enforcement
Division of Industrial Affairs
Wilmington, DE
302-761-8200
www.delawareworks.com/
    divisions/industaffairs/
    law.enforcement.htm

District of Columbia
Office of Human Rights
Washington, DC
202-727-4559
www.ohr.dc.gov/main.shtm

Florida
Commission on Human Relations
Tallahassee, FL
850-488-7082
800-342-8170
http://fchr.state.fl.us

Georgia
Atlanta District Office
U.S. Equal Employment
    Opportunity Commission
Atlanta, GA
404-562-6800
www.eeoc.gov

Hawaii
Hawai'i Civil Rights Commission
Honolulu, HI
808-586-8640 (Oahu only)
800-468-4644 x68640 (other islands)
www.state.hi.us/hcrc

Idaho
Idaho Human Rights Commission
Boise, ID
208-334-2873
www2.state.id.us/ihrc

Illinois
Department of Human Rights
Chicago, IL
312-814-6200
www.state.il.us/dhr

Indiana
Civil Rights Commission
Indianapolis, IN
317-232-2600
800-628-2909
www.in.gov/icrc

Iowa
Iowa Civil Rights Commission
Des Moines, IA 50309
515-281-4121
800-457-4416
www.state.ia.us/government/crc

Agencies That Enforce Laws Prohibiting Discrimination in Employment (continued)

Kansas

Human Rights Commission
Topeka, KS
785-296-3206
www.ink.org/public/khrc

Kentucky

Human Rights Commission
Louisville, KY
502-595-4024
800-292-5566
www.state.ky.us/agencies2/kchr

Louisiana

Commission on Human Rights
Baton Rouge, LA
225-342-6969
www.gov.state.la.us/depts/
   lchr.htm

Maine

Human Rights Commission
Augusta, ME 04333
207-624-6050
www.state.me.us/mhrc/
   index.shtml

Maryland

Commission on Human Relations
Baltimore, MD 21202
410-767-8600
800-637-6247
www.mchr.state.md.us

Massachusetts

Commission Against
   Discrimination
Boston, MA 02108
617-994-6000
www.state.ma.us/mcad

Michigan

Department of Civil Rights
Detroit, MI 48226
313-456-3700
800-482-3604
www.michigan.gov/mdcr

Minnesota

Department of Human Rights
St. Paul, MN 55101
651-296-5663
800-657-3704
www.humanrights.state.mn.us

Missisippi

Equal Opportunity Department
Employment Security Commission
Jackson, MS
601-961-7420
www.mesc.state.ms.us

Missouri

Commission on Human Rights
Jefferson City, MO 65102
573-751-3325
www.dolir.state.mo.us/hr

Agencies That Enforce Laws Prohibiting Discrimination in Employment (continued)

Montana
Human Rights Bureau
Employment Relations Division
Department of Labor & Industry
Helena, MT 59624
406-444-2884
http://erd.dli.state.mt.us/
    HumanRights/HRhome.htm

Nebraska
Equal Opportunity Commission
Lincoln, NE 68509
402-471-2024
800-642-6112
www.nol.org/home/NEOC

Nevada
Equal Rights Commission
Reno, NV 89509
775-688-1288
http://detr.state.nv.us/nerc

New Hampshire
Commission for Human Rights
Concord, NH 03301
603-271-2767
http://webster.state.nh.us/hrc

New Jersey
Division on Civil Rights
Newark, NJ 07102
973-648-2700
www.state.nj.us/lps/dcr

New Mexico
Human Rights Division
Santa Fe, NM 87505
505-827-6838
800-566-9471
www.dol.state.nm.us/dol_hrd.html

New York
Division of Human Rights
Bronx, NY 10458
718-741-8400
www.nysdhr.com

North Carolina
Employment Discrimination
    Bureau
Department of Labor
Raleigh, NC 27601
919-807-2823
www.dol.state.nc.us/edb/edb.htm

North Dakota
Human Rights Division
Department of Labor
Bismarck, ND 58505
701-328-2660
800-582-8032
www.state.nd.us/labor/services/
    human-rights

Agencies That Enforce Laws Prohibiting Discrimination in Employment (continued)

Ohio
Civil Rights Commission
Columbus, OH 43205
614-466-2785
888-278-7101
www.state.oh.us/crc

Oklahoma
Human Rights Commission
Oklahoma City, OK 73105
405-521-2360
www.onenet.net/~ohrc2

Oregon
Civil Rights Division
Bureau of Labor and Industries
Portland, OR 97232
503-731-4200
www.boli.state.or.us/civil/
    index.html

Pennsylvania
Human Relations Commission
Philadelphia, PA 19130
215-560-2496
www.phrc.state.pa.us

Rhode Island
Commission for Human Rights
Providence, RI 02903
401-222-2661
www.state.ri.us/manual/data/
    queries/stdept_.idc?id=16

South Carolina
Human Affairs Commission
Columbia, SC 29204
803-737-7800
800-521-0725
www.state.sc.us/schac

South Dakota
Division of Human Rights
Pierre, SD 57501
605-773-4493
www.state.sd.us/dcr/hr/
    HR_HOM.htm

Tennessee
Human Rights Commission
Knoxville, TN 37902
865-594-6500
800-251-3589
www.state.tn.us/humanrights

Texas
Commission on Human Rights
Austin, TX 78711
512-437-3450
888-452-4778
http://tchr.state.tx.us

Agencies That Enforce Laws Prohibiting Discrimination in Employment (continued)

Utah

Anti-Discrimination & Labor
  Division
Labor Commission
Salt Lake City, UT 84111
801-530-6801
800-222-1238
http://laborcommission.utah.gov/
  Utah_Antidiscrimination___Labo/
  utah_antidiscrimination___labo.htm

Vermont

Attorney General's Office
Civil Rights Division
Montpelier, VT 05609
802-828-3657
888-745-9195
www.state.vt.us/atg/civil rights.htm

Virginia

Council on Human Rights
Richmond, VA 23219
804-225-2292
www.chr.state.va.us

Washington

Human Rights Commission
Seattle, WA 98101
206-464-6500
www.wa.gov/hrc

West Virginia

Human Rights Commission
Charleston, WV 25301
304-558-2616
888-676-5546
www.state.wv.us/wvhrc

Wisconsin

Department of Workforce
  Development
Madison, WI
608-266-6860
www.dwd.state.wi.us/er

Wyoming

Department of Employment
Cheyenne, WY
307-777-7261
http://wydoe.state.wy.us/
  doe.asp?ID=3

Current as of February 2003

Departments of Labor

U.S. Department of Labor

Washington, DC 20210
202-693-4650
www.dol.gov

You can find a list of regional offices of the Wage and Hour Division at the Department of Labor's website at:
www.dol.gov/esa/contacts/whd/america2.htm
and a comprehensive list of state labor resources at:
www.dol.gov/dol/location.htm

State Labor Departments

Note: Phone numbers are for department headquarters. Check websites for regional office locations and numbers.

Alabama

Department of Industrial Relations
Montgomery, AL
334-242-8990
www.dir.state.al.us

Alaska

Department of Labor and
Workforce Development
Juneau, AK
907-465-2700
www.labor.state.ak.us

Arizona

Industrial Commission
Phoenix, AZ
602-542-4411
www.ica.state.az.us

Arkansas

Department of Labor
Little Rock, AR
501-682-4500
www.state.ar.us/labor

California

Department of Industrial Relations
San Francisco, CA
415-703-5070
www.dir.ca.gov

Colorado

Department of Labor and
Employment
Denver, CO
303-318-8000
http://cdle.state.co.us

Connecticut

Department of Labor
Wethersfield, CT
860-263-6000
www.ctdol.state.ct.us

Departments of Labor (continued)

Delaware
Department of Labor
Wilmington, DE
302-761-8000
www.delawareworks.com/
DeptLabor

District of Columbia
Department of Employment
Services
Washington, DC
202-724-7000
http://does.dc.gov

Florida
Agency for Workforce Innovation
Tallahassee, FL
850-245-7105
www.floridajobs.org

Georgia
Department of Labor
Atlanta, GA
404-656-3045
877-709-8185
www.dol.state.ga.us

Hawaii
Department of Labor and
Industrial Relations
Honolulu, HI
808-586-8865
http://dlir.state.hi.us

Idaho
Department of Labor
Boise, ID
208-332-3570
www.labor.state.id.us

Illinois
Department of Labor
Chicago, IL
312-793-2800
www.state.il.us/agency/idol

Indiana
Department of Labor
Indianapolis, IN
317-232-2655
www.in.gov/labor

Iowa
Iowa Workforce Development
Des Moines, IA
515-281-5387
800-JOB-IOWA
www.state.ia.us/government/wd/
index.htm

Kansas
Department of Human Resources
Office of Employment Standards
Topeka, KS
785-296-4062
www.hr.state.ks.us

Departments of Labor (continued)

Kentucky
Labor Cabinet
Frankfort, KY
502-564-3070
www.labor.ky.gov

Louisiana
Department of Labor
Baton Rouge, LA
225-342-3111
www.ldol.state.la.us

Maine
Department of Labor
Augusta, ME
207-624-6400
www.state.me.us/labor

Maryland
Department of Labor, Licensing
   and Regulation
Division of Labor and Industry
Baltimore, MD
410-767-2236
www.dllr.state.md.us/labor

Massachusetts
Department of Labor and
   Workforce Development
Boston, MA
617-727-6573
www.state.ma.us/dlwd

Michigan
Michigan Consumer and Industry
   Services
Lansing, MI
517-373-1820
www.cis.state.mi.us

Minnesota
Department of Labor and Industry
St. Paul, MN
651-284-5005
800-342-5354
www.doli.state.mn.us

Mississippi
Employment Security Commission
Jackson, MS
601-354-8711
www.mesc.state.ms.us

Missouri
Department of Labor and
   Industrial Relations
Jefferson City, MO
573-751-4091
573-751-9691
www.dolir.state.mo.us

Montana
Department of Labor and Industry
Helena, MT
406-444-2840
http://dli.state.mt.us

Departments of Labor (continued)

Nebraska
Department of Labor
Labor and Safety Standards
Lincoln, NE
402-471-2239
Omaha, NE
402-595-3095
www.dol.state.ne.us

Nevada
Division of Industrial Relations
Carson City, NV
775-684-7260
http://dirweb.state.nv.us

New Hampshire
Department of Labor
Concord, NH
603-271-3176
www.state.nh.us/dol

New Jersey
Department of Labor
Labor Standards and Safety
   Enforcement
Trenton, NJ
609-292-2313
www.state.nj.us/labor

New Mexico
Labor and Industrial Division
Department of Labor
Albuquerque, NM
505-827-6875
www.dol.state.nm.us

New York
Department of Labor
Albany, NY
518-457-9000
www.labor.state.ny.us

North Carolina
Department of Labor
Raleigh, NC
919-807-2796
800-625-2267
www.dol.state.nc.us/DOL

North Dakota
Department of Labor
Bismarck, ND
701-328-2660
800-582-8032
www.state.nd.us/labor

Ohio
Labor and Worker Safety Division
Department of Commerce
Columbus, OH
614-644-2239
www.com.state.oh.us/ODOC/
   laws/default.htm

Departments of Labor (continued)

Oklahoma
Department of Labor
Oklahoma City, OK
405-528-1500
888-269-5353
www.oklaosf.state.ok.us/~okdol

Oregon
Bureau of Labor and Industries
Portland, OR
503-731-4200
www.boli.state.or.us

Pennsylvania
Department of Labor and Industry
Harrisburg, PA
717-787-5279
www.dli.state.pa.us

Rhode Island
Department of Labor and Training
Cranston, RI
401-462-8000
www.dlt.state.ri.us

South Carolina
Department of Labor, Licensing
    and Regulation
Columbia, SC
803-896-4300
www.llr.state.sc.us

South Dakota
Division of Labor and
    Management
Pierre, SD
605-773-3681
www.state.sd.us/dol/dlm/dlm-
    home.htm

Tennessee
Department of Labor and
    Workforce Development
Nashville, TN
615-741-6642
www.state.tn.us/labor-wfd

Texas
Texas Workforce Commission
Austin, TX
512-463-2222
www.twc.state.tx.us

Utah
Labor Commission
Salt Lake City, UT
801-530-6801
800-222-1238
www.labor.state.ut.us

Vermont
Department of Labor and Industry
Montpelier, VT
808-828-2288
www.state.vt.us/labind

Departments of Labor (continued)

Virginia
Department of Labor and Industry
Richmond, VA
804-371-2327
www.dli.state.va.us

Washington
Department of Labor and
Industries
Tumwater, WA
360-902-5799
800-547-8367
www.lni.wa.gov

West Virginia
Division of Labor
Charleston, WV
877-558-5134
304-558-7890
www.state.wv.us/labor

Wisconsin
Workforce Development
Department
Madison, WI
608-266-1784
www.dwd.state.wi.us

Wyoming
Department of Employment
Cheyenne, WY
307-777-6763
http://wydoe.state.wy.us

Current as of February 2003

State Departments of Insurance

Alabama

Alabama Department of Insurance
Montgomery, AL 36130
334-269-3550
www.aidoi.gov

Alaska

Alaska Division of Insurance
Anchorage, AK 99501
907-269-7900
Juneau, AK 99811
907-465-2515
www.dced.state.ak.us/insurance

Arizona

Arizona Department of Insurance
Phoenix, AZ 85018
602-912-8444
www.id.state.az.us

Arkansas

Arkansas Department of Insurance
Little Rock, AR 72201
501-371-2600
www.state.ar.us/insurance

California

California Department of
  Insurance
Sacramento, CA 95814
916-322-3555
www.insurance.ca.gov

Colorado

Colorado Division of Insurance
Denver, CO 80202
303-894-7499
800-930-3745
www.dora.state.co.us/insurance/
  index.htm

Connecticut

State of Connecticut Insurance
  Department
Hartford, CT 06142
860-297-3800
www.state.ct.us/cid

Delaware

Delaware Insurance Department
Dover, DE 19904
302-739-4251
www.state.de.us/inscom

District of Columbia

Department of Insurance and
  Securities Regulation
Washington, DC 20002
202-727-8000
www.disr.dc.gov

State Departments of Insurance (continued)

Florida
Florida Department of Financial
  Services
Division of Consumer Services
Tallahassee, FL 32399
800-342-2762
850-413-3132
www.fldfs.com/Consumers

Georgia
Office of the Commissioner of
  Insurance and Safety
Atlanta, GA 30334
404-656-2070
www.inscomm.state.ga.us

Hawaii
Hawaii Department of Commerce
  & Consumer Affairs
Division of Insurance
Honolulu, HI 96811
808-586-2790
www.state.hi.us/dcca/ins

Idaho
Idaho Department of Insurance
Boise, ID 83720
208-334-4250
www.doi.state.id.us

Illinois
Illinois Department of Insurance
Springfield, IL 62767
217-782-4515
www.ins.state.il.us

Indiana
Indiana Department of Insurance
Indianapolis, IN 46204-2787
317-232-2385
www.state.in.us/idoi

Iowa
Iowa Insurance Division
Des Moines, IA 50319
515-281-5705
877-955-1212
www.iid.state.ia.us

Kansas
Kansas Insurance Department
Topeka, KS 66612
785-296-3071
www.ksinsurance.org

Kentucky
Kentucky Department of Insurance
Frankfort, KY 40601
800-595-6053
http://doi.ppr.ky.gov/kentucky

State Departments of Insurance (continued)

Louisiana
Louisiana Department of Insurance
Baton Rouge, LA 70804
252-342-0895
www.ldi.state.la.us

Maine
Maine Bureau of Insurance
Augusta, ME 04333
207-624-8475
800-300-5000
www.state.me.us/pfr/pfrhome.htm

Maryland
Maryland Insurance
  Administration
Baltimore, MD 21202
410-468-2005
www.mdinsurance.state.md.us

Massachusetts
Massachusetts Division of
  Insurance
Boston, MA 02110
617-521-7794
www.state.ma.us/doi

Michigan
Michigan Consumer and Industry
  Services
Office of Financial and Insurance
  Services
Lansing, MI 48909
517 373-0220
877 999-6442
www.michigan.gov/cis

Minnesota
Minnesota Department of
  Commerce
Consumer Info and Services
St. Paul, MN 55101
651-297-7161
www.state.mn.us

Mississippi
Mississippi Department of
  Insurance
Jackson, MS 39205
601-359-2453
www.doi.state.ms.us

Missouri
Missouri Department of Insurance
Jefferson City, MO 65102
573-751-4126
www.insurance.state.mo.us

State Departments of Insurance (continued)

Montana

Montana State Auditor
Insurance Division
Helena, MT 59601
406-444-2040
800-332-6148
http://sao.state.mt.us/sao/
    insurance/index.html

Nebraska

Nebraska Department of Insurance
Lincoln, NE 68508
402-471-2201
www.nol.org/home/NDOI

Nevada

Nevada Division of Insurance
Carson City, NV 89701
702-687-4270
Las Vegas, NV 89104
702-486-4009
http://doi.state.nv.us

New Hampshire

New Hampshire Insurance
    Department
Concord, NH 03301
603-271-2261
800-852-3416
www.state.nh.us/insurance

New Jersey

New Jersey Department of
    Banking and Insurance
Trenton, NJ 08625
609-292-5360
www.state.nj.us/dobi

New Mexico

New Mexico Public Regulation
    Commission
Insurance Division
Santa Fe, NM 87504
505-827-4601
www.nmprc.state.nm.us/
    insurance/inshm.htm

New York

New York State Insurance
    Department
Albany, NY 12257
518-474-6600
www.ins.state.ny.us

North Carolina

North Carolina Department of
    Insurance
Raleigh, NC 27611
919-733-7487
www.doi.state.nc.us

State Departments of Insurance (continued)

North Dakota
North Dakota Department of
    Insurance
Bismarck, ND 58505
701-328-2440
www.state.nd.us/ndins

Ohio
Ohio Department of Insurance
Columbus, OH 43266
614-644-2658
www.ins.state.oh.us

Oklahoma
Oklahoma Insurance Department
Oklahoma City, OK 73152
405-521-2828
www.oid.state.ok.us

Oregon
Oregon Department of Consumer
    and Business Services
Insurance Division
Salem, OR 97301
503-947-7980
www.cbs.state.or.us/external/ins

Pennsylvania
Pennsylvania Insurance
    Department
Harrisburg, PA 17120
717-783-3898
www.ins.state.pa.us/ins

Rhode Island
Rhode Island Department of
    Business Regulation
Division of Insurance
Providence, RI 02903
401-222-2223
www.dbr.state.ri.us/insurance.html

South Carolina
South Carolina Department of
    Insurance
Columbia, SC 29202
803-737-6180
www.doi.state.sc.us

South Dakota
South Dakota Department of
    Revenue and Regulation
Division of Insurance
Pierre, SD 57501
605-773-3563
www.state.sd.us/drr/reg/insurance

Tennessee
Tennessee Department of
    Commerce and Insurance
Nashville, TN 37243
800-342-4029
615-741-2218
www.state.tn.us/commerce/

State Departments of Insurance (continued)

Texas

Texas Department of Insurance
Austin, TX 78714
512-463-6169
www.tdi.state.tx.us/

Utah

Utah Insurance Department
Salt Lake City, UT 84114
801-538-3800
www.insurance.state.ut.us

Vermont

Vermont Department of Banking,
   Insurance, Securities &
   Health Care Administration
Montpelier, VT 05620-3101
802-828-3301
www.bishca.state.vt.us

Virginia

Virginia Bureau of Insurance
Richmond, VA 23219
804-371-9741
www.state.va.us/scc/division/boi

Washington

Office of the Insurance
   Commissioner
Tumwater, WA 98501
800-397-4422
800-562-6900
360-725 7000
www.insurance.wa.gov

West Virginia

West Virginia Insurance
   Commission
Charleston, WV 25301
304-558-3354
800-642-9004
www.state.wv.us/insurance

Wisconsin

Office of the Commissioner of
   Insurance
Madison, WI 53702
608-266-3585
800-236-8517
http://oci.wi.gov

Wyoming

Wyoming Insurance Department
Cheyenne, WY 82002
307-777-7401
800-438-5768
http://insurance.state.wy.us

Current as of June 2003

State OSHA Laws

If a state has a health and safety law that meets or exceeds federal OSHA standards, the state can take over enforcement of the standards from federal administrators. This means that all inspections and enforcement actions will be handled by your state OSHA rather than its federal counterpart.

So far, these states have been approved for such enforcement regarding private employers: Alaska, Arizona, California, Hawaii, Indiana, Iowa, Kentucky, Maryland, Michigan, Minnesota, Nevada, New Mexico, North Carolina, Oregon, South Carolina, Tennessee, Utah, Vermont, Virginia, Washington and Wyoming. (See the contact details below.)

New York, New Jersey and Connecticut also have OSHA-type laws, but they only apply to government employees. Other states are considering passing OSHA laws—and some of the above states are considering amending coverage and content of existing laws.

If your business is located in a state that has an OSHA law, contact your state agency for a copy of the safety and health standards that are relevant to your business. State standards may be more strict than federal standards, and the requirements for posting notices may be different.

State OSHA Offices

Alaska
Alaska Department of Labor and
  Workforce Development
Labor Standards and Safety
  Division
Occupational Safety and Health
  Section
Juneau, AK
907-465-4855 (Juneau)
907-269-4955 (Anchorage)
www.labor.state.ak.us/lss/
  oshhome.htm

Arizona
ADOSH
Industrial Commission of Arizona
Phoenix, AZ
602-542-5795 (Phoenix)
602-628-5478 (Tuscon)
www.ica.state.az.us/ADOSH/
  oshatop.htm

California
Cal-OSHA
California Department of Industrial
  Relations
San Francisco, CA
415-703-5100 (information about
  local offices)
www.dir.ca.gov/DOSH

Connecticut
Conn-OSHA *(Public sector only)*
Connecticut Department of Labor
Wethersfield, CT
860-566-4550
www.ctdol.state.ct.us/osha/
  osha.htm

Hawaii
HIOSH
Hawaii Department of Labor and
  Industrial Relations
Honolulu, HI
808-586-9100
www.state.hi.us/dlir/hiosh

Indiana
IOSHA
Indiana Department of Labor
Indianapolis, IN
317-232-2685
www.in.gov/labor/iosha

Iowa
IOSH
Iowa Division of Labor Services
Des Moines, IA
515-281-3606
www.iowaworkforce.org/labor/
  iosh

State OSHA Offices (continued)

Kentucky
KYOSH
Kentucky Labor Cabinet
Frankfort, KY
502-564-3070
www.kylabor.net/kyosh

Maryland
MOSH
Maryland Division of Labor and
    Industry
Department of Labor, Licensing
    and Regulation
Baltimore, MD
410-767-2215
www.dllr.state.md.us/labor/
    mosh.html

Michigan
MIOSHA
Michigan Department of
    Consumer & Industry Services
Bureau of Safety and Regulation
Lansing, MI
517-322-1814
www.michigan.gov/cis

Minnesota
MNOSHA
Minnesota Department of Labor
    and Industry
St. Paul, MN
651-284-5050
800-342-5354
www.doli.state.mn.us/
    mnosha.html

Nevada
OSHES
Nevada Division of Industrial
    Relations
Henderson, NV
702-486-9044 (Henderson)
775-688-1380 (Reno)
http://dirweb.state.nv.us/oshes.htm

New Jersey
PEOSH *(Public sector only)*
New Jersey Department of Labor
Trenton, New Jersey
609-292-7036
www.state.nj.us/labor/lsse/
    lspeosh.html

State OSHA Offices (continued)

New Mexico

Occupational Health and Safety
   Bureau
New Mexico Environment
   Department
Environmental Protection Division
Santa Fe, NM
505-827-4230
www.nmenv.state.nm.us/
   OHSB_Website/ohsb_home.htm

New York

Public Employee Safety and
   Health (PESH) Bureau *(Public
   sector only)*
Division of Safety and Health
New York Department of Labor
Albany, NY
518-457-5508 (Albany)
212-352-6132 (New York City)
www.labor.state.ny.us/
   working_ny/worker_rights/
   safety_health.html

North Carolina

Occupational Safety & Health
   (OSH) Division
North Carolina Department of
   Labor
Raleigh, NC
919-807-2900
www.dol.state.nc.us/osha/osh.htm

Oregon

OR-OSHA
Oregon Occupational Safety and
   Health Division
Department of Consumer &
   Business Services
Salem, OR
503-378-3272
800-922-2689
www.cbs.state.or.us/external/osha

South Carolina

OSHA
South Carolina Department of
   Labor, Licensing and Regulation
Columbia, SC
803-734-9669
www.llr.state.sc.us/osha.asp

Tennessee

TOSHA
Tennessee Department of Labor &
   Workforce Development
Nashville, TN
615-741-2793
800-249-8510
www.state.tn.us/labor-wfd/
   tosha.html

State OSHA Offices (continued)

Utah
UOSH
Utah Labor Commission
Salt Lake City, UT
801-530-6901
www.uosh.utah.gov

Vermont
VOSHA
Vermont Department of Labor &
   Industry
Montpelier, VT
802-828-2765
www.state.vt.us/labind/vosha.htm

Virginia
VOSH
Virginia Department of Labor &
   Industry
Richmond, VA
804-786-0574 (Health
   Compliance)
804-786-2391 (Safety
   Compliance)
www.doli.state.va.us/whatwedo/
   index.html

Washington
WISHA
Washington Department of Labor
   & Industries
Olympia, WA
360-902-5433
800-423-7233
www.lni.wa.gov/wisha

Wyoming
Wyoming Department of
   Employment
Workers' Safety / OSHA
Cheyenne, WY
307-777-7786
http://wydoe.state.wy.us

Current as of March 2003

Index

■